CW00429142

Subordination and Authorship in Early Modern England:

The Case of Elizabeth Cavendish Egerton and Her "Loose Papers"

MEDIEVAL AND RENAISSANCE
TEXTS AND STUDIES

VOLUME 208

*Subordination and Authorship in
Early Modern England:*

*The Case of Elizabeth Cavendish Egerton
and Her "Loose Papers"*

edited with an introductory monograph by

BETTY S. TRAVITSKY

Arizona Center for Medieval and Renaissance Studies
Tempe, Arizona
1999

© Copyright 1999

Arizona Board of Regents for Arizona State University

Library of Congress Cataloging-in-Publication Data

Egerton, Elizabeth Cavendish, 1626–1663.
Subordination and authorship in early modern England : the case of Elizabeth Cavendish Egerton and her "loose papers" / edited with an introductory monograph by Betty S. Travitsky.
p. cm. — (Medieval & Renaissance texts & studies ; v. 208)
Includes bibliographical references (p.) and index.
ISBN 0-86698-250-7 (hardcover : alk. paper)
1. Egerton, Elizabeth Cavendish, 1626–1663. 2. Great Britain—History—Puritan Revolution, 1642–1660—Sources. 3. England—Social life and customs—17th century—Sources. 4. Women—England—History—17th century—Sources. 5. Nobility—Great Britain—Biography. 6. Autobiography—Women authors. 7. Women—England—Biography. 8. Meditations. 9. Prayers. I. Travitsky, Betty, 1942– . II. Series: Medieval & Renaissance Texts & Studies (Series) ; v. 208.
DA407.E34A3 1999
941.06 '092–dc21
[B]   99–34319
                                                                        CIP

This book is made to last.
It is set in Caslon,
smythe-sewn and printed on acid-free paper
to library specifications.

Printed in the United States of America

Table of Contents

Illustrations

Acknowledgements

This study of Elizabeth Egerton and her writings is rooted in my earliest efforts in the 1970s, as a doctoral student, to recover writings by women in early modern England. It was, however, not until 1986, many years after George Ballard's notice of "Elizabeth Countess of Bridgewater" first led me to the mention of BL MS Egerton 607 in the entry in the *Dictionary of National Biography* for John Egerton, the husband of the countess, that I had the opportunity to read that compilation of her "Loose Papers." An afternoon's reading was enough to show me that this was an unusual document. When I reported my gleanings, in 1987, at sessions at the Twenty-Second International Congress on Medieval Studies in Kalamazoo and at the Folger Colloquium on Women and the Renaissance, my auditors seemed to be as moved as I had been by the selections that I presented to them. At the Folger, Jeanne Addison Roberts unintentionally began the long process that has culminated in this volume by asking, "Have you thought of doing an edition of the manuscript?" No, I assured her, I hadn't thought of doing any such thing, but the idea resonated as I completed work on a number of essays about Elizabeth Egerton.

When, in 1988, as a student at the School of Library Service at Columbia University, I learned that I could edit a manuscript as an independent study project, I decided to try my hand at editing Elizabeth Egerton's "Loose Papers." Assigned by Terry Belanger to the gracious tutelage of G. Thomas Tanselle (who "will teach you something"), I soon found myself conducting a blind canvass of repositories to seek additional materials by the countess and made the first of many unanticipated discoveries when, among a good deal of other material by her and by other members of her family, I located facsimiles, housed at the Huntington Library in San Marino, of two radiating scribal copies of BL MS Egerton 607. I learned from Jean Preston, my former instructor in paleography and the former curator of manuscripts at the Huntington, and from Mary

L. Robertson, the current curator, that the Huntington had purchased large parts of the Bridgewater family library early in this century and that these facsimiles were copies of materials retained by the present-day heirs of the Bridgewater family at the time of the purchase. To examine the originals I would have to visit Mertoun, the Scottish seat of Sir John Sutherland Egerton, sixth duke of Sutherland. Since one of these facsimiles incorporates important and distinctive annotations, examining the manuscripts at Mertoun became a priority. Indeed, it became a necessity, since these marks rendered one of the copies of the "Loose Papers" at Mertoun the logical choice for reproduction in a documentary edition. As described in the pages that follow, I have come to believe that these marks open windows into the writings of the countess and of other subordinated early modern persons.

In 1990, the American Council of Learned Societies generously awarded me a grant-in-aid to travel to Great Britain in order to perfect my transcriptions of the three extant manuscripts of the so-called "Loose Papers" of Elizabeth Egerton (BL MS Egerton 607 and the two manuscripts at Mertoun). In the course of that research trip, the Duke of Sutherland very kindly allowed me to examine his copies during a memorable visit to Mertoun, and he has generously permitted me to reproduce the text of one of them in this volume. In 1991 and in 1993, the Huntington Library awarded me short-term fellowships and the National Endowment for the Humanities a travel-to-collections grant, all allowing me to immerse myself in the riches of the Huntington's Ellesmere Collection of Bridgewater family papers. (The Ellesmere Collection, named for the progenitor of the Bridgewater family, Sir Thomas Egerton, Baron Ellesmere, is most commonly mined for political information, but as the appendices and references in this volume show, it also contains a treasury of materials for those studying the early modern family.) The Center for Medieval and Early Renaissance Studies, located in Binghamton, N.Y., provided further assurance about the project by awarding me a contract for publication in 1993. Despite this support, a number of outside pressures prevented me from turning full attention to this project until late 1995, when the NEH awarded me a full-time Fellowship for College Teachers and Independent Scholars, thereby enabling me to complete it. Over this long period of germination, my original focus—and certainly my original, tentative conclusions—have shifted, and the study that follows is far different from—and I hope richer than—the earlier, short studies I have published about Elizabeth Egerton and her writings. Among many other shifts, the documentary edition of her "Loose Papers" contained in this volume came to seem the most appropriate format for this text, rather than the eclectic edition I had originally planned to prepare.

As suggested by the foregoing account, this volume could not have been completed without a great deal of assistance and support. Very deep appreciation indeed is due the duke of Sutherland for his kind permission to base this edition on one of his manuscripts of the "Loose Papers" and to reproduce copies of a number of other documents as well. It is also a great pleasure to express my gratitude to Christine Miller, estate administrator at Mertoun, for invaluable support that included pleasant rides in one of the estate vehicles and encouraging notes. In addition to the reproductions from Mertoun, images are reproduced in this volume by kind permission of the Beinecke Library; the Bodleian Library, Oxford; the British Library; the English Heritage Photographic Library; the Folger Shakespeare Library; the Huntington Library; J. M. Dent; Maggs Brothers, Ltd.; the New York Public Library; and the University of Nottingham Library. The support of the ACLS, the Huntington Library, and the NEH provided the opportunity to study and write this volume. The University of Massachusetts Press, *Women's Studies*, and *American Notes & Queries* provided outlets at different times for my evolving thoughts about Elizabeth Egerton and her writings. I also owe deep thanks to many teachers, fellow researchers, and librarians. Carolyn Kent and the late Josephine Roberts provided support and encouragement at crucial times. More thanks than I could ever express go to G. Thomas Tanselle, who patiently taught me to distinguish a lemma from a stemma and who kindly reviewed the edition of the "Loose Papers" contained in this volume. Discussions with Anne Lake Prescott, who read the entire manuscript, have given me the courage to pursue some jumbled, early ideas about subordinated early modern individuals. Patrick Cullen, who read the essay on Elizabeth Cavendish Egerton, made many very helpful suggestions for its improvement. Members of the Society for the Study of Women in the Renaissance (New York City) and participants in the Trinity-Trent Migratory Seminar (U.K.) gave a kindly reception to presentations of portions of this study in 1997 and 1998 and suggested a number of refinements that I have attempted to incorporate into the final draft. Others who provided assistance at many stages include Susan Amussen, Terry Belanger, Nicholas Barker, Victoria Burke, Elizabeth Clarke, Kathryn Coad, Robert Evans, Alison Findlay, Susan Gilchrist, Germaine Greer, Earle Havens, Kimball Higgs, Eric Holzenberger,

Dorothy Johnston, Alan Jutzi, Hilton Kelliher, Karen Lemiski, Lisa Ann Libby, Jeslyn Medoff, Mark Padnos, Ted-Larry Pebworth, Jean Preston, Jeanne Roberts, Mary Robertson, Jay Shuman, George Thomson, Timothy Wales, and Georgianna Ziegler. Of course, the remaining mistakes are my own.

*Subordination and Authorship in
Early Modern England:*

*The Case of Elizabeth Cavendish Egerton
and Her "Loose Papers"*

Introduction

Unlike many manuscript materials by early modern women which have escaped notice altogether, the "Loose Papers" of Elizabeth Egerton, countess of Bridgewater—and therefore the countess herself—have achieved a modicum of historical visibility. Originating, as I will detail below, in the epitaph about the countess composed by her husband John Egerton, the second earl of Bridgewater, this faint historical trace came to be publicized more widely through the scrupulosity of Sir Henry Chauncy, a Hertfordshire antiquarian[1] who was in turn cited by Arthur Collins[2] and by George Ballard. It is Ballard's unusually nebulous entry in his foundational *Memoirs of Severall Ladies of Great Britain* on "Elizabeth, Countess of Bridgewater" (for whom he had "searched very carefully, though ineffectually, for some concurrent testimonies of her merit") that forms the point of entry of the countess into the historical record for the student of early modern women.[3]

---

[1] Chauncy (1632–1719), who actually knew the second earl and has left us a description of him (cited below), included the text of the epitaph in *The Historical Antiquities of Hertfordshire* (London, 1700), 488–89.

[2] Collins (1682?–1760) is perhaps best known for his *Peerage of England*. First published in 1709, the work was continually enlarged both during his lifetime and beyond. The epitaph was included in the edition of 1735 (Vol. I: 480–82). I thank Georgianna Ziegler for checking this edition for me at the Folger Shakespeare Library.

[3] Writing from a conservative perspective, Ballard (d. 1755) was nevertheless original enough a scholar to have created a public display of the learned Englishwoman that was revolutionary in his day and that displeased some of his more reactionary contemporaries. Ballard's entry for Egerton is on 266–67 of *Memoirs*; we will consider his uncertainties

Almost fifty years later, as discussed in greater detail below, she was noticed in Henry John Todd's successive editions of Milton and in his family history of the Bridgewaters.[4] A passing mention of the countess in Francis Espinasse's entry in the *Dictionary of National Biography* (hereafter *DNB*) about her husband, the second earl, added a beginning—very partial—specificity to these earlier accounts by citing "No. 607 of the Egerton MSS., ... a transcript of *his* wife's prayers and meditations, with *his* autograph note, 'Examined by J. Bridgewater.'"[5]

These early notices opened an unusual, if tiny, window into the history and manuscript writings of an extremely privileged, personally venerated— yet (I will show below) paradoxically powerless and ultimately victimized— seventeenth-century noblewoman, Elizabeth Cavendish Egerton (1626– 1663), second daughter of William Cavendish (the "loyal" first duke of Newcastle) and wife of John Egerton, the second earl of Bridgewater. It is my purpose in these pages to widen this window and to illuminate her life further, for unfortunately these early glimpses, however unusual and however welcome to the student of early modern women, are askew: even an afternoon's reading of BL MS Egerton 607 indicates that this manuscript is not adequately described as a compilation of prayers and meditations.[6] Never-

---

about the countess below. Later in the eighteenth century, Ballard's comments on Elizabeth Egerton were discussed in print by Samuel Egerton Brydges. *Memoirs of Severall Ladies of Great Britain* (1752) has been reprinted with supplementary bibliographies and an introduction by Ruth Perry for Wayne State Univ. Press (1985). A number of other early notices of Elizabeth Egerton (*Biographium femineum*; Walpole; Williams) that followed Ballard's are listed in n. 149.

[4] The notices begin in Todd's edition of *Comus, a mask* (1798), and continue in his expanded notices of the Bridgewater family in his successive editons of *The Poetical Works of John Milton* (1801; 1809; 1826; 1842; 1852 [posthumous]), and in his *History of the College of Bonhommes, at Ashridge* (1812; 1823).

[5] Francis Espinasse, "Egerton, John, second Earl of Bridgewater (1622–1686)," *Dictionary of National Biography*, eds. Leslie Stephen and Sidney Lee (Oxford: Oxford Univ. Press, 1917–), 6: 574–75 (emphasis added). Regrettably, Espinasse mentions only this one compilation by the countess.

[6] At least two more typical exemplars, i.e., collections exclusively of biblical passages and of prayers, are extant by women within Elizabeth Egerton's extended family: Elizabeth, countess of Huntington (d. 1632/3) and Lady Bridget Egerton (d. 1648). Elizabeth Hastings, wife of Henry Hastings, earl of Huntington (1586–1643) was the third and youngest daughter of Ferdinando Stanley, fifth earl of Derby and his wife Alice, daughter of Sir John Spencer (later renowned as the formidable dowager countess of Derby), who in 1600 became the third wife of Sir Thomas Egerton, grandfather of the second earl of Bridgewater. In 1602, Alice's daughter (and Elizabeth Hastings's sister) Frances (the second of the Stanley sisters) became the wife of the first earl of Bridgewater to whom she

theless, BL MS Egerton 607 has not yielded easily to reappraisal. In my first study of this manuscript—the only detailed study to date that I am aware of—I argued that BL MS Egerton 607 was best classified as a journal or even a "periodic life record."[7] But I have found that my original evaluation of this posthumously bound manuscript has required refinement and revision. It is inadequate, for example, simply to dismiss Espinasse's ascription of BL MS Egerton 607 to "*his*" (i.e., John Egerton's) wife, for a careful, entry-by-entry examinination of the datable entries in the manuscript in conjunction with the facts that can be retrieved about the countess's life, establishes—among other things—that the order of the contents does not match their chronology and that four of the entries are by John Egerton. Other findings raise still further questions about "final authorial intention."[8] As its title page declares, for example (Plate 1), this (puzzlingly) *bound* manuscript "Examined by JBridgewater" consists literally of "True *Coppies* of certaine *Loose* Papers *left* by yᵉ Right ho.ᵇˡᵉ ELIZABETH Countesse OF BRIDGEWATER *Collected and Transcribed together here since Her Death*, Anno Dni. 1663" (emphasis added). As shown on the following pages, therefore, in terms of the murky authority of its contents, BL MS Egerton 607 *is* legitimately, if not in the sense Espinasse suggested—at least partially

---

bore fifteen children, including John Egerton, later the husband of Elizabeth Cavendish Egerton (and second earl of Bridgewater). Elizabeth Hastings was, in other words, the younger sister of Frances Stanley Egerton, and thus an aunt of John Egerton, the second earl. The Huntington Library houses (as HN MS EL 6871) the manuscript of "Certaine Collections of the Right hon:ᵇˡᵉ Elizabeth late Countesse of Huntingdon for her owne private use 1633." Lady Bridget Egerton (d. 1648) was daughter of Arthur, Lord Grey of Wilton (whom Spenser served as secretary during Lord Grey's tenure as lord deputy of Ireland); in 1609, she became the wife of Sir Rowland Egerton of Egerton and Oulton, a descendant of the elder branch of the Egerton family (Collins, [*Peerage*, 1812], 5: 528–36). The Chetham Society has published Lady Bridget's "A Forme of Confession grounded vpon the ancient catholique and apostolique faith" (1636), with an introduction by Sir Philip de Malpas Grey Egerton, in *Chetham Miscellanies* 4 (1871): 9–31.

[7] " 'His wife's prayers and meditations': MS Egerton 607," in *The Renaissance English-woman in Print: Counterbalancing the Canon*, eds. Anne M. Haselkorn and Betty S. Travitsky (Amherst, Mass.: Univ. of Massachusetts Press, 1987), 241–60.

[8] For the standard discussion of this now contentious issue, see G. Thomas Tanselle, "The Editorial Problem of Final Authorial Intention," in his *Selected Studies in Bibliography* (Charlottesville: Univ. Press of Virginia, 1979), 309–53. (Tanselle has published surveys of the controversy over this editorial question in several essays, including "Textual Criticism and Literary Sociology," *Studies in Bibliography* 44 [1991]: 83–143, and more recently "The Varieties of Scholarly Editing," in *Scholarly Editing: A Guide to Research*, ed. D. C. Greetham [New York: Modern Language Association, 1995], 9–32.)

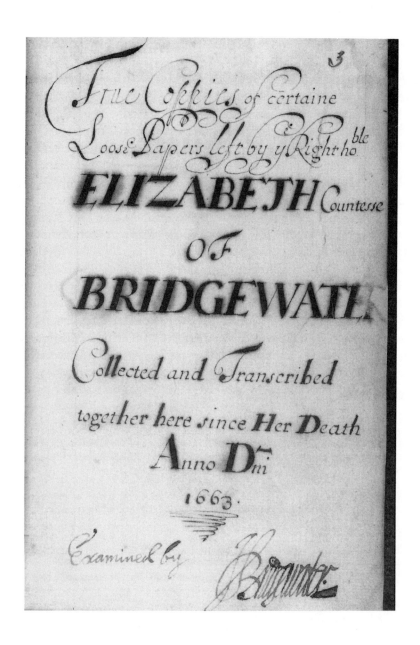

Plate 1: The title page of The British Library copy of "The Loose Papers" (BL MS Egerton 607). Reproduced by permission of The British Library.

described as "*his*" (i.e., John Egerton's). The authority of Elizabeth Egerton's "Loose Papers" (as well as of her other writings) and the reason for the change in tone and content between the writings dating from her teenage years and those she wrote as a married woman are the interrelated puzzles that this study explores.

The difficulty of locating, identifying, and analyzing Elizabeth Egerton's "Loose Papers" is well illustrated by the successive comments about them by Henry John Todd (1763–1845)—first confused, increasingly accurate, but, alas, never altogether illuminating to those who did not trace permutations in his comments carefully or who did not have his opportunities to examine the relatively undispersed holdings of the Bridgewater family library. Todd, the famous nineteenth-century editor of Milton, was a retainee of three successive holders of the Bridgewater titles.[9] As I explain in detail below, Milton's *Comus* is intimately connected to the Bridgewater family, having been first performed before John Egerton, the first earl of Bridgewater, in 1634. Todd published his earliest essay on "John Earl of Bridgewater and His Family" in his edition of *Comus* (1798), an edition prefaced by a letter "To the Reverend Francis Henry Egerton" (from 1823–1829 the eighth earl of Bridgewater, but at that time an unlikely successor to the Bridgewater family estate). In his preface, Todd told Egerton, "The present edition was undertaken by your advice, has been encouraged by your kindness, and derives advantages from your communication." He signed himself Egerton's "much obliged and faithful humble servant" (and this appellation would become literally true in later years when Todd would become domestic chaplain, librarian, and family historian to successive Egertons). This first, relatively brief notice (which would become the sub-section about the Bridgewater family in Todd's "Preliminary Notes to *Comus*" in successive complete editions of the *Works*) cites John Egerton's epitaphs for Elizabeth Egerton and for himself, but does not enlarge about the writings mentioned in them.

In 1801, in the first of his editions of Milton, dedicated "To His Grace, Francis, Duke of Bridgewater ... in Humble but Grateful Acknowledgement of the Assistance Afforded Him by His Grace's Library, and of Other

---

[9] These were Francis Egerton (1736–1803), third and last duke (and sixth earl) of Bridgewater, who was succeeded in 1803 by his cousin, John William Egerton (1753–1823), seventh earl of Bridgewater, and the Reverend Francis Henry Egerton (1756–1829), who in 1823 succeeded his brother John William, and became the eighth earl. At the death of the eighth earl, in 1829, the peerage dignities became extinct.

Favours Conferred,"[10] these remarks are expanded. Todd quotes a letter by Samuel Egerton Brydges, a descendant of the Egertons, that had appeared in 1792 in *Gentleman's Magazine*, and that had repeated family traditions about the countess.[11] As we will see, Brydges's letter had unquestionably referred to the "Loose Papers." Indeed we can be sure that it referred to the copy of the "Loose Papers" now housed at the British Library as BL MS Egerton 607, since in this copy—Brydges's own copy—a prayer by the countess for John Egerton begins on 219. Todd's comments, however, unwittingly confuse Elizabeth Egerton's "Loose Papers" with another manuscript, one devoted totally to religious themes, that is described in John Egerton's epitaph as her "divine Meditations" (Todd's transcription). Citing the earl's epitaph for his wife and his reference to her "divine Meditations" (200) without referring to these meditations as a separate manuscript (or indeed without any further reference to them at all), Todd states that "The Duke of Bridgewater has also an attested copy of these pious and tender Meditations; which I have seen. They answer the character of them, already given" (5: 199). In other words, in 1801 Todd conflates the "Loose Papers" and the "divine Meditations."

In 1802, Todd was appointed domestic chaplain to John William, later seventh earl of Bridgewater. Acting as a family historian during the time of the seventh earl, he wrote his *History of the College of Bonhommmes* (1812 and 1823). Todd, of course, had further access to the Bridgewater Library during this time. Indeed, in Clarke's *Repertorium Bibliographicum* we are told that the library had been "very much neglected during the long life of the last duke ... [and that] [t]he valuable remains of this singularly curious collection ... have been properly classed and arranged in volumes, by the unremitted exertion and care of the Rev. Mr. Todd."[12] Not surprisingly, therefore, in his *second* edition of Milton (1809), having repeated the account of Elizabeth Egerton's prayer for John Egerton, Todd amends his earlier report as follows: "Among the late Duke of Bridgewater's manuscripts are *two attested copies* of these pious and tender Meditations; which I have read.

---

[10] *The Poetical Works of John Milton in Six Volumes* (London, 1801), 1. n.p.n. Francis Egerton (1736–1803) became duke of Bridgewater in 1748.

[11] Samuel Egerton Brydges, "Letter, December 21, 1792, to Mr. Urban," *Gentleman's Magazine* 62 (1792): Second Part (Supplement), 1163.

[12] William Clarke, *Repertorium Bibliographicum; or, some account of the most celebrated British Libraries* (London, 1819), 360.

They answer the character of them, already given" (emphasis added).[13] Significantly, Todd further amplifies his account of the second earl and his wife, citing the epitaph by John Egerton with its reference to the "divine Meditations upon every particular Chapter in the Bible," to which he appends an instructive note: "These Meditations are now in the possession of the Marquis of Stafford. They form a large folio volume, and are beautifully as well as curiously bound, with the unusual appendage of a lock and key. There is also a smaller volume of this Lady's Meditations in Lord Stafford's Library, exhibiting the same proof of modest concealment" (202).[14] In other words, Todd here seems aware of a second composition by Elizabeth Egerton. These copies of the Meditations will be discussed below as an important key to the authority of Elizabeth Cavendish Egerton's writings.

As this example makes clear, my efforts—beginning with the manuscript at the British Library—to recover information about Elizabeth Egerton's life and about her writings have revealed a good deal of unexpected information as well as many uncertainties. They have led me to reassess BL MS Egerton 607 as one of several radiating copies of this manuscript.[15] In addition, recovery of additional extant materials by Elizabeth Cavendish Egerton (and about her) in a number of repositories has documented some disturbing interventions in her writings as well as in those of other members of her family and has connected her with several other outstanding early modern women. In the way that scholarly projects have of developing their own direction, my investigation of BL MS Egerton 607 has therefore led to a consideration of the countess and her writings within the context of her natal

---

[13] *The Poetical Works of John Milton . . . in seven volumes* (London, 1809), 6: 200. This statement establishes the fact that two copies of the "Loose Papers" were in the Bridgewater Library in 1809. These are presumably the same ones that I examined at Mertoun in 1990; the text of one of them is reproduced in the documentary edition of the "Loose Papers" in this volume.

[14] The comment is repeated in the third edition (1826), the fourth (1842), and the posthumous, fifth edition (1852).

[15] I.e., what Fredson Bowers termed "equidistant radiating documents," as discussed in detail below, 169–70. When I conducted a canvass of repositories in anticipation of editing the "Loose Papers," I discovered two other scribal copies, and determined that the British Library exemplar is one of three extant radiating copies of a lost original document. (For a preliminary report on these discoveries, see my "Reconstructing the Still, Small Voice: The Occasional Journal of Elizabeth Egerton," in *Women's Studies* 19 [*Women in the Renaissance: An Interdisciplinary Forum*], eds. Ann Rosalind Jones and Betty S. Travitsky [Summer 1991]: 193–200.) Details of eighteenth- and nineteenth-century reports about other, as yet unrecovered, copies of this manuscript are given below.

family and her family by marriage (families that boasted many writers) and has also suggested a still broader context for studying what turned out to be a number of her writings.

Much of Elizabeth Egerton's personal history has been obscured, and at times we must be satisfied with mere glimpses of her. I have come to believe that it is from the varied familial contexts in which her life was so deeply embedded that an understanding of her writings can be wrested. In the pages that follow, therefore, I have pursued my elusive quarry by analyzing a number of such contexts in a roughly chronological order, examining in turn her birth family, the life and writings of her stepmother, and the ethos of her family by marriage. Each of these contexts is analyzed in an effort to recover an understanding of Elizabeth Egerton, to consider the posthumous collection of her "Loose Papers," and to recover its text—as far as has proved possible.

In turn, study of Elizabeth Egerton's life and writings has led to some unexpected, but suggestive, ancillary hypotheses that shed light on broader issues of subordination and authorship in the early modern period. For familial activities can be shown to have molded not only Elizabeth Egerton's writings but also those of such figures as her sister Jane Cheyne, her son, the third earl, and her famous stepmother, Margaret Cavendish. The pages that follow trace my unexpected findings and indicate the questions they raise, the light they cast, and the directions in which they seem to lead.

§

Despite her elevated status in seventeenth-century British society—she was the daughter of one very prominent and very wealthy nobleman and the wife of another—Elizabeth Egerton's life history is virtually unknown and must be pieced together, almost entirely, from manuscript sources. In this regard she is unlike many men in her family and a number of her female relatives, whose lives, as the apparatus to this study demonstrates, are also recounted in some contemporary printed sources. If not surprising, this undervaluing is inappropriate. True, Elizabeth Egerton's life was outwardly conventional—she was a respectable married woman and the mother of nine children. And, as I show, it was certainly sheltered and privileged—she was descended from and married into wealthy families of peers. Yet much of her life was extraordinary, dramatic, startling, and even raw: she experienced an extended siege of her father's country seat, the political arrest and imprisonment of her husband during the civil war of the mid-seventeenth century, the deaths of three children; she was closely connected both with many famous writers and composers, including some in her own family, and with the principals in the Castlehaven scandal (arguably the most sordid aristocratic scandal in mid-seventeenth-century England); at the very end of her life, she endured the stress of her husband's civil arrest because he responded—quite appropriately—to a challenge by another peer; and though she died, conventionally enough, in childbed, the premature birth that ended her life was probably the result of her visit to him following that arrest.

We have come to recognize that women in general have been submerged ("invisible") historically. Yet the degree of difficulty I experienced in studying this prominent woman and her writings, and particularly in locating, gathering, and consolidating information concerning her, was nevertheless surprising. Elizabeth Egerton's manuscript writings—ranging from single-page letters to extensive documents—are scattered in half a dozen repositories among other papers of the Cavendish and Egerton families (and are listed, therefore, under more than one surname). In the pages that follow, I consider documents that have never before been studied in an effort to recover this woman, identifying as hers one long manuscript that has been misidentified until now, and creating a composite—though, alas, still incomplete—profile. Among the obstacles to consolidating Elizabeth Egerton's writings for study and thus recovering her voice that will be exposed is the fact that no connection has been drawn before among the artifacts from different periods of her life, lived under varied names: Elizabeth Cavendish, Lady Brackley, Elizabeth Egerton, Elizabeth, countess of Bridgewater. Indeed, even some of the most basic facts about Elizabeth Egerton's life have been so obscured that they are subject to debate by those very few scholars who have noticed her at all.[16] The predictable result is a comment

---

[16] Her birthdate and marriage date, for example, although some of the confusion that has developed about them is needless. Jane Cavendish, whose birthdate is known to have been 1621, was older than her sister, and S. P. Cerasano and Marion Wynne-Davies are mistaken in giving Elizabeth's birthdate as 1616, in their *Renaissance Drama by Women: Texts and Documents* (London: Routledge, 1996), 127. Similarly, they confuse Elizabeth's marriage date, giving it incorrectly as 1636, presumably by adding fifteen (her age at the time of her marriage—as given by her stepmother (below, 72, 107)—to 1616. One authoritative witness is her husband's detailed epitaph for her in which he states unequivocally that "her Death was as religious as her Life was vertuous, on the 14th day of *June* in the year of our Lord 1663. of her own age 37. she exchanged her earthly Coronet for an heavenly Crown." Another is her own statement in the "Loose Papers" that her infant son Henry (d. June 1656) "lived dayes as many as my yeares / ... / Twenty & Nine was ye Number."

like the following, in a note to a very recent article on the play she co-authored shortly after her marriage: "Lady Elizabeth Brackley is thus the Elizabeth Egerton, countess of Bridgewater, whose devotional writings have been recently treated. . . ."[17]

§

The state of scholarship on Elizabeth (Cavendish) Egerton can be taken, generally, as a paradigm of the current state of scholarship on the majority of early modern women, a state that results both from past neglect on the part of scholars and from what I would posit as a different sense of subjectivity on the part of early modern women from that which we observe in our own times. In contrast to their counterparts today, few conventionally obedient early modern women have left us records of their thinking because public statements by women—either oral or written (particularly printed)—were frowned on in their time. As a case in point, Elizabeth Egerton—so far as we know—made no effort to preserve the manuscript writings that her husband, John Egerton, second earl of Bridgewater, would claim that she had, during her lifetime, shared with him alone. The entries in the bound volume in the British Library were left behind her merely as "Loose Papers." After her death, these hitherto scattered pages were "Collected and Transcribed together here"—out of the order in which at least some of them had been composed—and were then "Examined" by the second earl (with some changes by him), who was evidently trying to preserve them and to memorialize the countess within their family.[18] The pages of her large volume of meditations on the chapters of the Bible seem, on the other hand, not to have been left scattered about. Of course, since these progress in order of the chapters of the Bible, anyone literate would have been able to organize them properly. This volume of meditations was noted in the very earliest records but not in the entry in the *DNB*; nor are Elizabeth Egerton's contributions to the generally sprightly Bodl. MS Rawl. Poet. 16 (discussed below) mentioned there, this being yet another manuscript that exists at

---

[17] Lisa Hopkins, "Judith Shakespeare's Reading: Teaching *The Concealed Fancies*," *Shakespeare Quarterly* 47: 4 (1996): 396–406 (399 n.10).

[18] It is, of course, possible that her sudden death prevented her from collecting her "Loose Papers" and having them bound together, but we simply cannot know whether this was the case. Certainly her prayers on childbirth in that collection show that she was apprehensive about the possibility of dying in childbearing.

least in part in duplicate. With the exception of some of her contributions to the Bodleian manuscript and of a few snippets from the "Loose Papers," her writings—which include poems on family members, essays on marriage and widowhood, original prayers on both public occasions and occasions of personal stress, and devotional compositions (religious meditations, mourning meditations, and meditations on every chapter of the Bible)—have never been published or studied.

They are, moreover, widely scattered, fortunate, chance survivals, the most important of which are divided among half a dozen private and public places. While the countess maintained contact with her different circles of relatives throughout her life, chronology provides perhaps the most efficient way of distinguishing among the holdings at these locations. Beginning then with her natal family, we note that the Portland Collection at Hallward Library (University of Nottingham) includes a great number of documents relating to the Cavendishes, including a very few connected directly to the young Elizabeth; considering the relative dearth of such early materials, it is rich in records from her younger years. The Bodleian holds an artifact of her teen years: the manuscript miscellany (Bodl. MS Rawl. Poet. 16) mentioned above, the contents of which were apparently composed jointly with her older sister, Jane, in the early 1640s, soon after Elizabeth Cavendish's marriage, but before she took up residence with her husband. As I will detail later, most of the contents of this manuscript are also found in MS Osborn b.233 at the Beinecke Rare Book and Manuscript Library (Yale University). At the British Library, in addition to BL MS Egerton 607, Cavendish family papers are included in the portion of the Portland Deposit there.[19] A particularly useful item that bears on Elizabeth Egerton's younger years is BL MS Add. 70499, a bound miscellany of documents from the Portland Deposit, to which I shall refer further below.[20]

---

[19] On the Portland Deposit, which includes many sixteenth- and seventeenth-century documents connected to the Cavendish family, see R. J. Olney, "The Portland Papers," *Archives* 19. 82 (October 1989): 78–87. No printed index to BL Additional MSS 70001–70523 (the portion of the Portland Collection at the British Library) yet exists. Abstracts of the contents of the relevant holdings at the British Library are contained in Historical Manuscript Commission, *Thirteenth Report, Appendix, Part I, The Manuscripts of His Grace the Duke of Portland* (London, 1891), 2: 110–135 (hereafter *The Portland Papers*). I owe the identification of the items abstracted in these pages with these British Library holdings to the kindness of Dr. Hilton Kelliher, curator of manuscripts at the British Library.

[20] For discussion of Add. MS 70499 (containing Cavendish Papers, 1604–1659), see

For information about Elizabeth Egerton's later life, the most significant and numerous documents were contained in that great collection of manuscripts and printed books, the Bridgewater family library, one of the finest private seventeenth-century libraries amassed in Great Britain,[21] and, as it happens, the library of the family into which Elizabeth Cavendish married. The Bridgewater Library is now located—for the most part—in one of two places. The first of these, by a twist of book history, is in San Marino, California, as a result of the million-dollar purchase in 1917 of the bulk of the Bridgewater Library by Henry E. Huntington, who in 1919 founded the Huntington Library there.[22] In addition to two facsimile (i.e., copyflo) copies of Elizabeth Egerton's "Loose Papers" and dozens of family papers dating from the years of her marriage to John Egerton, the Huntington houses what I identify here for the first time as variant copies of a very lengthy second manuscript by Elizabeth Egerton, one that John Egerton was to describe in his epitaph (as transcribed by Chauncy, *Historical Antiquities*) as her "Divine Meditations upon every particular Chapter in the Bible"; these manuscripts—one an incomplete fair copy and one a facsimile of a holograph bearing her husband's corrections—are valuable for the insights they yield into questions of authority. The site of those items not sold to the Huntington or otherwise dispersed—including the originals of the two copies of the "Loose Papers" mentioned earlier—is Mertoun, in St. Boswell,

---

Hilton Kelliher's article, "Donne, Jonson, Richard Andrews and the Newcastle Manuscript," *English Manuscript Studies, 1100–1700*, 4 (1993): 134–73. This article is, in addition, a valuable source of information on the Cavendish household during the years when Elizabeth Cavendish was growing up.

[21] See, for an early account, "The Marquis of Stafford, Cleveland-House, St. James," 359–73 in Clarke's *Repertorium Bibliographicum*, which begins as follows: "A most invaluable collection of old English literature of the time of Elizabeth, bequeathed by the late Duke of Bridgewater, presents a leading feature in the library of the Marquis of Stafford. A more numerous and choice collection of our early English poets is not known to exist; it was originally formed by the Lord Chancellor Ellesmere and his immediate successors, the first and second Earls of Bridgewater; and by them deposited in their library at Ashridge." (359).

[22] Fairly detailed accounts of the genesis of the Huntington can be found in the August 1969 issue (Volume 32) of the *Huntington Library Quarterly*, in which members of the staff reflect on the institution, then in its fiftieth year: James Thorpe, "The Founder and His Library," 291–308; Ray Allen Billington, "The Genesis of the Research Institution," 351–72. Also useful is an untitled note by William Ingoldsby included in "Intramuralia: Books and People," compiled by Carey S. Bliss, *Huntington Library Quarterly* 37. 1 (1973): 89–92. The research institution, to be directed by an eminent scholar according to the indentures Mr. Huntington signed, was founded in 1927.

Scotland, the seat of the duke of Sutherland to whom the Bridgewater papers have descended. Artifacts by and about the Egertons are also scattered in a number of other repositories, discussed and cited in the pages that follow.[23]

I have come to believe that Elizabeth Egerton's life and writings have a great deal to tell us about early modern social history and about the conditions of early modern authorship. The remarks that follow situate Elizabeth Egerton and her manuscripts in the context of her own life, of her family history, and of her social milieu, as well as within the larger contexts of the experience of women of her time (of varying classes), of the literary traditions of which they are a part, and of the experiences of subordinated early modern persons in general. All her recovered writings will fall within the purview of this survey, which is followed by a documentary edition of her "Loose Papers." This attempt at recovery paradoxically both resurrects the author Elizabeth Egerton—insofar as it is possible to resurrect or truly interpret any person from the past—and raises intricate questions about the authority of this manuscript, some of which cannot be answered definitively in the present state of the evidence. Gaps remain, but even these gaps are silently instructive.

§

Perhaps the most significant of the unexpected insights effected by the gaps and silences in the record is a negative general hypothesis concerning the writings of the countess, of other women in her family, by extension, of other conventional, i.e., law-abiding, women writers in early modern England, and (most unexpectedly to me) of subordinated men: that the subjectivity commonly attributed to these early modern women writers as well as to other subordinated early modern persons should be interrogated, that it may be highly limited, even a fiction, an ahistorical (mis-)reconstruction of early modern consciousness on the model of twentieth-century experi-

---

[23] The Egerton Manuscripts, bequeathed to the British Library in 1829 by Francis Henry Egerton, eighth earl of Bridgewater, along with a fund to augment and keep them, do not bear directly on Elizabeth Egerton. (The provenance of MS Egerton 607 is recounted fully below.) An authoritative and succinct description of the Egerton Manuscripts is provided by Julius P. Gilson, Egerton Librarian in the Department of Manuscripts, in his "Introduction" to the British Museum's *Guide to the Exhibition of Some Part of the Egerton Collection of Manuscripts in the British Museum* (1929).

ence.[24] A number of my findings document the containment and adultera-
tion of writings by the seemingly cherished and highly expressive women in
this family—as well as of some writings by subordinated men—by male relatives who exercised seemingly benign authority over them. The Cavendish
and Egerton families, rich in early modern times in a number of strong
females—including female authors—generally regarded as congenial bases
for women writers who could have served Elizabeth Egerton as role
models,[25] are therefore reassessed here as instances suggesting instead the
general pervasiveness of such interference and containment, to wit:

1) The powerlessness of early modern women was potentially so over-
   whelming, i.e., early modern women could be so unremittantly at the
   mercy of the *individual* male authorities in their *individual* lives, that—

---

[24] The early insights of Catherine Belsey on female subjectivity (*The Subject of
Tragedy: Identity and Difference in Renaissance Drama* [London: Methuen, 1985]) are very
useful, and have been deeply formative of my own efforts to penetrate early modern
subjectivity. While my own interest centers on early modern women, I have come to an
awareness, however, that women are just one of a number of categories of subordinated
early modern persons and that their experiences must eventually be synthesized into a
global framework if we are to be able to attend properly to them. See Elspeth Graham,
"Women's Writing and the Self," *Women and Literature in Britain, 1500–1700*, ed. Helen
Wilcox (Cambridge: Cambridge Univ. Press, 1996), 209–33 (here 209–10), for a recent,
related discussion of some of the difficulties in grappling with women's "subjectivity,"
with "the clear lack of any stable form of self-writing, which related to a wider unfixity
of genres in the period; women's ambiguous status as subjects; and our own incomplete
recovery of early modern women's writings." In another subtle, recent essay, "The Other
Body: Women's Inscription of their Physical Images in 16th- and 17th-Century England," *Women's Studies* 26 (1997): 27–58, Lynette McGrath discusses the ways in "which
a significant number of Englishwomen's texts . . . mediated women's ambiguous position
as at one and the same time both subjects of their bodily and writerly experiences and
objects of powerful ideological constructions" (28).

[25] These women are discussed below, but perhaps it is useful to enumerate them here.
On the Cavendish side, two were Bess of Hardwick, William Cavendish's paternal
grandmother (d. 1608), notorious for her social climbing and for her sensational marital
difficulties with her last husband, the sixth earl of Shrewsbury, and Margaret Lucas Cavendish (1623–1673), William's second wife (and Elizabeth's stepmother), also a notorious
figure in her time and a prolific writer. On the Egerton side were the formidable patron-
ess Alice, dowager countess of Derby (d. 1636), who had been doubly related to John
Egerton, first as a step-grandmother after she became the third wife of his grandfather,
Sir Thomas (who married her in 1600), and also as a maternal grandmother since his
father married her daughter Frances in 1601; Anne Stanley (d. 1647) his sister-in-law
(Alice's daughter and the wife of the felon Mervyn Touchet, executed in part for instigat-
ing a rape of his countess); and Eleanor Davies (1590–1652), Mervyn's sister, the female
prophet (and writer) of the mid-seventeenth century who was popularly dubbed (in an
inversion of an anagram on her chosen name) "Never Soe Mad A Ladie."

paradoxically—these women can be understood only in terms of their particular, *individual* circumstances. The effort, therefore, to formulate generalizations about early modern women's condition—a goal to which scholars of early modern women have long aspired—may be untenable; it is probable—if disappointing—that the only generalizations about these women that can be made are indirect. That is, that we may be able to generalize about the behavior and attitudes of the *individual* male authority figures who influenced these *individual* women since they lived more autonomously, more as subjects, with their actions accordingly more measurable (or at least estimable) as general subject tendencies. Self-awareness (and hence a sort of subjectivity) is a universal characteristic of *homo sapiens* (and apparently of some apes), but subjectivity is apt to shift with culture, and in early modern England a subjectivity that is close to ours today—individualistic, self-conscious, more inclined to guilt than to shame—was more likely to be found in men than in women. Although no one would suggest that we can measure subject tendencies precisely, we may be able to translate our precarious generalizations about early modern men into still more precarious generalizations about early modern women.[26] The same limitation may hold for our efforts concerning subordinated early modern men, although my interest (and this study) remains centered on women.

As an example, the increased number of women writing secular materials in the 1570s and 1580s, previously hypothesized to reflect some sea change in the position of women under a more secure Elizabeth Tudor,[27] in fact may reflect not this hypothetical change in the

---

[26] See, as an extrapolation of the position of subordinated male, Richard Helgerson's discussion of Philip Sidney and his disapproving father in *The Elizabethan Prodigals* (Los Angeles: Univ. of California Press, 1976), 124–55. Helgerson argues that Sidney (and many other writers of his generation) was unable as a poet to "broaden the scope of humanistic values ... to satisfy the expectations of men like Sir Henry Sidney. ... He was too good and too serious a son and pupil to defend successfully values hostile to what he had been taught. As a result his tone is constantly, though engagingly, self-deprecating" (154–55). I thank Anne Lake Prescott for bringing this important and suggestive study to my attention.

[27] This is the hypothesis put forth in two foundational studies, as yet unpublished: Ruth Willard Hughey, "Cultural Interests of Women in England, 1524–1640, Indicated in the Writings of the Women," Ph.D. diss., Cornell University, 1932, and Charlotte Kohler, "The Elizabethan Woman of Letters, the Extent of her Literary Activities," Ph.D. diss., University of Virginia, 1936. (Both these dissertations are expected to be re-

circumstances or world views of women in these decades, but a possible change in those of the *men* of that decade who were associated with these individual writers. For a woman, as noted in *The Lawes Resolutions of Womans Rights*, "glittereth but in the riches of her husband, as the moone hath no light, but it is the sunnes."[28] The prefatory material in the writings by these women often offers us gleanings not only of scant biographical details about these authors but also about the circumstances that enabled them to write. Publication, for example, by Anne Dowriche of her *French History* (1589) was linked to the sufferance of the brother she addresses in her preface, to whom she appealed, "committing the patronage of this my recreation unto your protection."[29] Case by case, conventional, law-abiding woman writers in early modern England can be shown to have expressed awareness of their vulnerability because of what could have been perceived as a lack of conformity not only to the expectations of society as a whole but also to those of the particular male authorities in their lives.

2)   To put it somewhat differently, the materials discussed below suggest that although we have recognized the pervasiveness of patriarchy as a

---

printed with new introductions in Ashgate Press's series, "Women and Gender in Early Modern England.") Despite the intense interest of scholars during the last twenty years, a detailed study of this point remains to be made; for a beginning, see my *Paradise of Women: Writings by Englishwomen of the Renaissance* (1981; reprint, New York: Columbia Univ. Press, 1989); Elaine V. Beilin, *Redeeming Eve: Women Writers of the English Renaissance* (Princeton: Princeton Univ. Press, 1987); and more recently, Kim Walker, *Women Writers of the English Renaissance* (New York: Twayne, 1996).

[28] (London, 1632), 129–30. In her encyclopedic summary of the gender literature, Ruth Kelso notes, "[t]he perfect woman, in general renaissance theory, was the wife, married to a man well born and virtuous, and shining in her restricted realm with her own qualities, but only like the moon, with reflected light" (*Doctrine for the Lady of the Renaissance* [Urbana, 1956], 78). This common observation is used in the title of an article by Robert Williams, "A Moon to Their Sun. . . ." (*Fine Print* 11.2 [April 1985]: 88–98), itself referring to a sentence by Maria Strick, one of the writing mistresses Williams discusses: "I publish this to acknowledge, under the shadow of your benevolence, that I hold you as the sun from which my dim moon draws her light" (98). The metaphor is derived both from the account of creation (Gen 1:16) and from classical culture (e.g., solar–male, lunar–female). Leslie S. B. MacCoull has kindly informed me that it appears in Parmenides frag. B15 D–K.

[29] Anne Dowriche, *The French Historie: that is a lamentable Discourse of three of the chiefe and most famous bloodie broiles that have happened in France for the Gospell of Jesus Christ* (London, 1589), sig. A2v.

general early modern social reality, we have not yet translated this recognition—perhaps because it is so clearly before us—into the deeply felt *individual* reality this patriarchy signified, the personal need the *individual* woman experienced to win the approval of these *individual* male authority figures in her life. And what we have thereby failed to infer is the consequent and inherent frailty of the position of the *individual* woman—the sense of *individual* containment experienced by each of these women. This sense of containment must have been even more insidious than the sense of individual powerlessness of the industrial worker before unionization because early modern women did not live in collective environments and therefore did not have the constant reminder that each *individual* was experiencing a communal disability. Unprovided with many means of meeting and expressing this sense of cohesion, early modern women did not have the opportunity for banding together in collective fashion. Instead, they had to deal *individually* with *individual* variants on personal subordination, often of a very personal kind, while efforts were made to prevent them from meeting and "gossiping," i.e., from disclosing personal details about their lives.[30] Such thinking may be foreign to us in the emancipated twentieth-century West; it also, however, was at least partially true of many early modern men who were in subordinated positions.

We frequently bemoan our failure to apply class analysis to the inequities of gender in the early modern period, but here is the nub of the problem: as many scholars have noted, women were indeed not disenfranchised *as a class*.[31] It is the flip side of this coin that has not, to

---

[30] The suspicion and difficulty associated with meetings of female gossips have been discussed by Diane Wolfthal, "Women's Community and Male Spies: Erhard Schön's *How Seven Women Complain about their Worthless Husbands*," in *Attending to Early Modern Women*, eds. Susan Amussen and Adele F. Seeff (Newark, Del.: Univ. of Delaware Press, 1999), 117–54, and by Catharine Randall in "Telling Tales: Women, Gossip, and the Revision of Institutions in Early Modern France," a paper presented to the Society for the Study of Women in the Renaissance (New York City) in March 1996. Although some historians distinguish between the degree of freedom to band together experienced by early modern women of different classes, these studies suggest a degree of cross-class, gender-specific disability in this connection, a finding analogous to Judith M. Bennett's report of only a minimal effect of social rank on the social relations of the sexes in medieval England (*Women in the Medieval English Countryside* [New York: Oxford Univ. Press, 1987], 177–98).

[31] See, for example, Joan Kelly, "The Social Relations of the Sexes: Methodological Implications of Women's History," *Women, History & Theory: The Essays of Joan Kelly*

my knowledge, been adequately noted: that the solidarity that could have emerged from women's overriding commonality—their gender—was undermined by the presence of *individual* authorities in each of their lives, inhibiting their ability to meet, to speak, and to act in gendered union. Indeed, in a study (in part) of a woman who figures prominently here, the well-known—not to say notorious—Margaret Lucas Cavendish (stepmother of Elizabeth Cavendish Egerton), Sara Mendelson has argued that informal power "confined to the private *milieu* of family and kin" was wielded by *individual* early modern women and "tolerated in certain 'masculine' spheres."[32] One may infer that if early modern women did not attempt to achieve formal power on the basis of gender, their actions might—on an *individual* level—be tolerated, but that the effort to overturn restriction on the basis of gender would have undermined whatever informal, *individual* power *individual* women achieved. Is it any wonder then that (as Mendelson notes), "[w]omen's avidity for class mobility . . . stands in contrast to their indifference, or indeed hostility, to 'gender' mobility. Appeals by English women for the same privileges as men (whether political, legal, educational or sexual) were so unusual at this time that those, like [Margaret Lucas Cavendish] the Duchess of Newcastle, who openly acknowledged such aspirations were liable to be pronounced insane" (*Mental World*, 186). It is precisely as "insane" that two of her contemporaries, Dorothy Osborne and Samuel Pepys, regarded Margaret Cavendish.[33]

(Chicago: Univ. of Chicago Press, 1984), 1–18 and Joan Wallach Scott, *Gender and the Politics of History* (New York: Columbia Univ. Press, 1988).

[32] Sara Heller Mendelson, *The Mental World of Stuart Women: Three Studies* (Amherst, Mass.: Univ. of Massachusetts Press, 1987), 187. In what could be read as an apposite application of this observation to the duchess, Susan Wiseman discusses slippages between representation and reality in the plays of Margaret Cavendish, and specifically in dramatic "scenes of the transformation of power and gender," arguing for the connection of these slippages to the "very circumstances of social change and mobility which contributed to Cavendish's becoming a playwright [and that] simultaneously threatened her position as an aristocrat" ("Gender and Status in Dramatic Discourse: Margaret Cavendish, Duchess of Newcastle," *Women, Writing, History 1640–1740*, eds. Isobel Grundy and Susan Wiseman [Athens, Ga.: Univ. of Georgia Press, 1992], 159–77).

[33] Before seeing Margaret Cavendish's first book, Dorothy Osborne wrote to Temple: "Sure the poore woman is a litle distracted, she could never bee soe rediculous else as to venture at writeing book's and in verse too. If I should not sleep this fortnight I should not come to that" (Letter 17, 75). After seeing the book, she wrote: "You need not send

Such an inference gives a new dimension of meaning to the slogan "divide and conquer." For if women might achieve some power by individual, private action, but would incur ridicule—if not restraint—for an attempt at collective action, only the intrepid (and perhaps the foolish) would attempt collective action. The question posed for every individual would be whether to attempt to succeed within the accepted boundaries, i.e., aggrandizing herself and ignoring the needs of women in general, or whether to fight for other women, thereby incurring general censure and possibly bringing restraints on herself. This understanding connects with the insight of Gerda Lerner that women have been impeded historically because they lacked access to a common tradition teaching them what earlier (and, I would add, contemporary) women had already experienced and discovered; and that their progress was consequently impeded over and over as new pioneers constantly were forced "to reinvent the wheel."[34] It also sheds different light on the vexed issue of studying women's history as the history of *individual*, or great, women. Historians like Natalie Zemon Davis have criticized this approach (although in fairness they actually mean studies that concentrate on figures like queens while ignoring more ordinary women).[35] But in the sense that I am suggesting here, if women could advance the cause of women in general only by striking iconoclastic poses, then the study of the history of women would necessarily be the history of individually exceptional women (though not necessarily queens or duchesses).

---

me lady Newcastles book at all for I have seen it, and am sattisfyed that there are many soberer People in Bedlan, i'le swear her friends are much to blame to let her goe abroad" (Letter 20, 79), in *Letters to Sir William Temple*, ed. Kenneth Parker (Penguin, 1987). Samuel Pepys refers to his attempts to see Cavendish on the streets of London on several occasions in 1667 (11 and 26 April and 11 May), and mentions her visit to the Royal Society on 30 May of that year. In his entry for 18 March 1668, he sharply criticizes her *Life* of her husband as "the ridiculous history of my Lord Newcastle wrote by his wife, which shows her to be a mad, conceited ridiculous woman" (*The Diary of Samuel Pepys*, eds. Robert Latham and William Mathews, et al. 11 vols. [Berkeley: Univ. of California Press, 1971]: 8 (1667): 163–64, 186–87, 243; 9 (1668): 123.

[34] This insight is stated repeatedly in Lerner's *Creation of Feminist Consciousness From the Middle Ages to Eighteen-seventy* (New York: Oxford Univ. Press, 1993).

[35] See her "Women's History in Transition: The European Case," *Feminist Studies* 3 (1976): 83–103.

These observations began in a consideration of Elizabeth Cavendish Egerton as an instance of the law-abiding, conventional (and privileged) early modern woman writer in England—the woman who followed social prescription generally, but who attempted to take what Belsey termed a "subject" position (*Subject of Tragedy*, ix). My thesis is that the efforts of women like Egerton at adopting a subject position were so fraught with the difficulty of negotiating their individual, private arrangements that generalizations about them are virtually impossible to make, beyond, perhaps, the generalization that their difficulties were legion. Margaret Hannay, for example, has familiarized us with a letter in the hand of the young Mary Sidney, arguably the most important woman writer of the sixteenth century in England, that documents her heart-rending difficulty in conceiving of her middle-aged husband as her "lord."[36] In the seventeenth century, to take two examples that are better known, some of Elizabeth Pepys's autobiographical accounts were destroyed by her husband, the famous Samuel,[37] while an explicit issue in the division between Anne Wentworth and her husband was accommodating her freedom to write.[38]

To return to the Cavendish family, one—on the surface—that facilitated a woman's ability to write in public, we might note with Hilda Smith the "profound if inconclusive thoughtfulness" that Margaret Cavendish consistently "brought to her social role of a publicly thinking woman."[39] Yet, as I will show, there is variation in the subject position of Elizabeth Cavendish Egerton at different times in her life—i.e., at times when different men exercised authority over her. When one juxtaposes, on the one hand, variations between Elizabeth Egerton's writings as a young woman and her later *oeuvre* with, on the other hand, the influence exerted by her father, William Cavendish, over the writings of her stepmother, Margaret Cavendish, and then adds to this equation the influence of John Egerton, Elizabeth's husband, over *her* later writings, one begins to perceive the limitations of the early modern woman's subject position.

---

[36] Margaret Hannay, *Philip's Phoenix: Mary Sidney, Countess of Pembroke* (New York: Oxford Univ. Press, 1990), 43.

[37] *Diary*, 9 January 1663 (4: 9–11).

[38] Elaine Hobby, *Virtue of Necessity: English Women's Writing 1649–1688* (Ann Arbor: Univ. of Michigan Press, 1988), 49–53.

[39] Hilda Smith, *Reason's Disciples: Seventeenth-Century English Feminists* (Urbana: Univ. of Illinois Press, 1982), 94.

EARLY YEARS: ELIZABETH CAVENDISH

1. William Cavendish and Elizabeth Basset Howard Cavendish

Because his influence over his daughter Elizabeth's youthful writing looms so large, it seems reasonable to begin with an account of Elizabeth's father, William Cavendish (1593–1676).[40] A grandson of Bess of Hardwick, Cavendish (Plate 2) followed his grandmother's well-known example of social climbing through her marriages, and his father's parallel example of marrying wealthy women; he was created a knight of the Bath (1610), viscount Mansfield (1620), baron of Bolsover (1628), and earl (1628), marquis (1643), and eventually (1664/5) first duke of Newcastle (Cokayne, 4: 519–26). When, "[p]robably in 1618,"[41] he married a widowed heiress, Eliza-

---

[40] Particularly useful for study of Cavendish is the relatively recent biography, *Portrait of a Cavalier: William Cavendish, First Duke of Newcastle* (London: Macmillan, 1979), by Geoffrey Trease. Though Trease disappoints the reader by providing little detailed documentation, he has clearly delved deeply into the primary sources that he refers to globally at the end of each of his chapters. I have caught only one apparent mistake, while Trease supplies some information that I have not found elsewhere in print. Details are noted throughout this chapter, with reference to his book. Information about Cavendish is also culled from the following sources, hereafter cited parenthetically in the text: Francis Bickley, *The Cavendish Family* (Boston: Houghton-Mifflin, 1914); G. E. Cokayne, *Complete Peerage*, 13 vols. in 6 (Gloucester: A. Sutem, 1982); Arthur Collins, *Peerage of England*, 8 vols. (London, 1779); Charles Harding Firth, "Cavendish, William, Duke of Newcastle (1592–1676)," *DNB*, 3: 1273–78; Douglas Grant, *Margaret the First, a Biography of Margaret Cavendish, Duchess of Newcastle 1623–1673* (London: Rupert Hart-Davis, 1957); Henry Ten Eyck Perry, *The First Duchess of Newcastle and her Husband as Figures in Literary History* (Boston: Ginn & Co., 1918); A. S. Turberville, *A History of Welbeck Abbey and Its Owners*, 2 vols. (London: Faber and Faber, 1938/39). Cavendish's poems of courtship to Margaret Lucas and several of her letters have been edited by Douglas Grant as *The Phanseys of William Cavendish, Marquis of Newcastle addressed to Margaret Lucas and her Letters in reply* (London: Nonesuch Press, 1956). Perry corrects the birthdate given in the *DNB* and by Collins. Trease agrees with Perry about this date.

[41] Turberville, *Welbeck Abbey*, 45. The date of her marriage to Cavendish is uncertain. Her first husband, Henry Howard, third son of Thomas, first earl of Suffolk, died suddenly in October 1616 (*Calendar of State Papers Domestic Series of the Reigns of Edward VI, Mary, Elizabeth, and James I*. 12 vols. (1856). She bore him one daughter. Trease (*Cavalier*, 45), citing a report by John Chamberlain, states that William Cavendish had married Elizabeth Basset Howard by 24 October 1618. Chamberlain, however, also reported to Carleton on 25 October 1617 that "Sir William Candish hath a sonne which is no small joy to his father and himself, for yt may be a hundred thousand pound in his way, yf his father kepe his word" (*Letters of John Chamberlain*, ed. Norman Egbert McClure [Philadelphia: American Philosophical Society, 1939], 2: 107). McClure's gloss identifies "Sir William" as "son of Sir Charles Cavendish of Welbeck, Nottinghamshire," and we do not have a record of an earlier marriage by this William Cavendish. A year

Plate 2: William Cavendish, Duke of Newcastle, eng. by Dean
aft Van Dyke. By courtesy of the National Portrait Gallery, London.

beth Basset Howard (1599–1643), daughter of William Basset, Esq., of Blore, Staffordshire, a woman reputed to be exemplary,[42] he began his accumulation and—as detailed below—his expenditures of great wealth. Although, in large part, William and Elizabeth Cavendish (Plate 3) spent their married life in retirement in the country, this quiet state of affairs was punctuated by a number of costly regal visits, by absences on William's part in town on official business, and by the bustle of a number of expensive building projects, including the town house in which his daughter Elizabeth would be married in 1641.[43] There is some evidence that suggests that Elizabeth (Basset) Cavendish was not robust.[44] Yet no aspersions on the quality of the marriage are intended; love poetry addressed by Cavendish to this wife survives,[45] and from surviving letters written to her by Newcastle in 1629 and 1636 (from London and Chatsworth), describing his state of mind concerning his aspirations for preferment, one can reasonably infer that the two shared these aspirations, and that their relationship was

---

later, on 24 October 1618, Chamberlain writes to Carleton "Sir William Candish hath maried Henry Howards widow a great heyre, that was much sought and pursued for Christofer Villers." McClure's gloss identifies this Sir William Candish as our William Cavendish, but does not note the apparent contradiction here.

[42] Little information about Elizabeth Basset seems to be preserved. Richard William Goulding, a twentieth-century family librarian at Welbeck, states that she was "[b]orn 29 April 1599" (*Catalogue of the pictures belonging to His Grace the Duke of Portland* [Cambridge: Cambridge Univ. Press, 1936], 363.) Trease is the only other writer on the Cavendish family to supply her birthdate. Margaret Cavendish, her successor, was later to describe her as "a very kind, loving, and Virtuous lady" (*Life of the Thrice Noble, High and Puissant Prince William Cavendish* [London: A. Maxwell, 1667], 136).

[43] Perry, *First Duchess*, 11; Trease, *Cavalier*, 62–3.

[44] Hilton Kelliher ("Newcastle Manuscript") cites letters to Newcastle from Richard Andrews, a practicing physician who seems to have prescribed medications for the countess (in BL MS Add 70499) during some of her pregnancies. Perry comments, in what we would now think an outmoded—if not unconsciously ironic—fashion, as follows: "This lady, of whom little is known, seems to have led a very troubled life until her death in 1643. We find occasional allusions to her ill health and once an extensive list of remedies to ease her labor in childbirth [Welbeck MSS, II, 120–23]; the fact that she was the mother of ten children, five of whom died in infancy, may explain this, and indeed she seems to have been a poor harmless drudge, destined to be worn out by the highest function of woman" (*First Duchess*, 11). For differing reports on the size of the family, see n. 50.

[45] Newcastle had, according to Douglas Grant, "written many verses to his first wife" (*Phanseys*, xxi), now located at the Nottingham University Library (*Margaret the First*, 76, n. 2).

Plate 3: Elizabeth Bassett, Countess of Newcastle, by William Larkin.
By permission of the English Heritage Photographic Library.

companionable.[46] Well travelled and well initiated into polite accomplish-
ment, Cavendish early developed his lifetime interest in and liberal patronage of the culture—and artists—of his day. Among the writers he assisted
at this time were James Shirley, William Davenant, and Richard Brome, and
he was a major patron of Ben Jonson's. The christening of his son Charles
in 1620, at which the future Charles I stood as godfather, was the occasion
of "An Entertainment at the Blackfriars," Jonson's only entertainment on a
birth, and a composition which, in its fluffy jollity and extravagance, encap-
sulates Newcastle's delight in good living and belles lettres and his lavish
lifestyle.[47] Patron of dramatists and himself a playwright in the years preceding the Civil War, Cavendish was dedicatee in 1635 of an elaborate celebratory poem, "Queene Esters Haliluiahs and Hamans Madrigalls" by
Francis Lenton, commonly dubbed "the Queen's Poet."[48]

The essentially quiet—though exceedingly lavish—country life led by

---

[46] Extracts from several letters, cited by Perry (*First Duchess*, 11) and Turberville
(*Welbeck Abbey*, 57), have been reprinted in *The Portland Papers*, 1: 121, 127. Trease
alludes to liaisons on William's part (56–57), and assumes that given Elizabeth's ill
"health and her husband's passionate nature, there had clearly been infidelities, but nothing approaching open scandal or estrangement" (*Cavalier*, 114). This type of thinking, of
course, is merely an endorsement of the traditional double standard as described in Keith
Thomas's standard essay, "The Double Standard," *Journal of the History of Ideas* 20
(1959): 195–216, an endorsement that will emerge in the accounts of William's son-in-
law, John Egerton, as well.

[47] Charles Cavendish was born on 20 May 1620. The original of the text was copied
into Harley MS 4955, fols. 48–52, a manuscript that also contains the texts of Jonson's
masques for the later entertainments at Welbeck and Bolsover in 1633 and 1634. As
Professor Robert Evans was kind enough to tell me, the masque was first published by
Gifford. In their introduction to the "Entertainment," Percy and Simpson note that "the
scribe was a servant of the [Cavendish] family, probably the Earl's secretary . . . [and] was
also the copyist of . . . MS. Rawlinson Poetry 16" (*Ben Jonson*, eds. C. H. Herford Percy
and Evelyn Simpson. 11 Vols. [Oxford: Clarendon Press, 1941], 7: 767). Bodl. MS Rawl.
Poet. 16 (and the partial duplicate, Beinecke MS Osborn b.233), authored by Elizabeth
and Jane Cavendish, will be discussed at some length below (52–81). Kelliher ("Newcastle
Manuscript") has identified the hand in all three manuscripts as that of John Rolleston,
who long served as Cavendish's secretary.

[48] Lenton (fl. 1630–1640) was firmly affiliated with court poetics, and his presentation of a copy of his poem to Cavendish underlines the (then) earl's significance in
courtly literary circles. A copy of the manuscript that antedates the copy described in the
DNB entry for Lenton was transferred to the Huntington Library in 1917, at the time of
the purchase of the Bridgewater family library. It is now housed at the Huntington as
HN MS EL 6872. Among others who dedicated works to Cavendish in the 1630s were
John Ford (*Perkin Warbeck*), James Shirley (*The Traitor*), Richard Brome (*The Sparagus
Garden*), and William Sampson (*Honour Triumphing over Death*).

William and Elizabeth Cavendish was punctuated from time to time by such events as two visits to Cavendish's Nottinghamshire seat, Welbeck, by James I (in 1619 and 1624), by Cavendish's occasional attendance at court, and by elevations in Cavendish's rank and dignities. He inherited considerable additional wealth on his mother's death in 1629. As surviving documents indicate, during his marriage to Elizabeth Basset (which lasted approximately twenty-five years, till Basset's death in 1643), Cavendish continued to angle for preferment. Probably his most outstanding efforts in that direction are attested to by the extravagant entertainments (including original masques by Ben Jonson) that he provided the court on the occasion of visits by Charles I to two of his residences, Welbeck and Bolsover.[49] Yet another sumptuous display of hospitality—though on not quite as extravagant a scale—was occasioned by a visit by Prince Rupert and the Elector Palatine in 1636 (Turberville, *Welbeck Abbey*, 50; Trease, *Cavalier*, 76). But however much he languished for advancement, Cavendish devoted considerable energy to his growing family,[50] as the following indulgent, affectionate, encouraging and, for our purposes, illuminating verse dialogues between Cavendish and his children suggest (Plates 4–5):

Sweet Charles,

> This letter iff you like It nott then race Itt:
> Butt anser Itt, for Usus promtus facitt.

W.N.

---

[49] The first, produced at Welbeck on the occasion of Charles's journey to Scotland for his coronation in 1633, was entitled *The King's Entertainment at Welbeck in Nottingham-shire . . . 1633*. The second, which took place at Bolsover in the following year when Charles was accompanied by Henrietta Maria, was entitled *Love's Welcome. The King and Queen's Entertainment at Bolsover . . . 1634*. Both were included in *Works of Ben Jonson* (1640) 2: 272–83. The provision of lavish entertainments was continued even during the penurious days of Cavendish's exile, most notably during a visit by the future Charles II to Antwerp in 1658, on which occasion verses composed by Newcastle were recited as a welcome and one of his own songs was sung by Lady Moore to music set by Nicolas Lanier, a royal musician.

[50] Accounts of the size of the family vary: According to Turberville, ten children (six sons and four daughters) were born, five (two sons and three daughters) surviving to adulthood, not an extraordinary number given early modern infant mortality rates (*Welbeck Abbey*, 45). Trease, too, states that "Elizabeth bore in all ten children, of whom five survived" (*Cavalier*, 62). According to Collins, however, the marriage produced four sons and four daughters (*Peerage*, 1: 291).

My Lord,

> I can not tel what to wright

> > > Charles Mansfeild

Sweet Jane

> I knowe you are a rare Inditer.—
> And hath the Pen off a moste redye writer.

> > W.N.

My Lord

> > with
> I know you doo but Jest   mee
> & so in obdence I right this nothing

> > > Jane Cavendysshe

> Bess, you muste write to, write butt what you think.
> Nowe your'e a Girle, disemble when you Linke

> > W.N.

> Franke, prethe write to mee thy runing hande
> Thatt none Can reade, & all Less understande.

> > W.N.

> Sᵣ you muste write to, My beloved Harry,
> Thatt asketh blessinge & will never Tarry.

> > W.N.[51]

---

[51] University of Nottingham MSS Portland Collection Pw V 25: 21–22. Cavendish's exchanges with his children have been cited by Kelliher, "Newcastle Manuscript," 153; Margaret J. M. Ezell, " 'To Be Your Daughter in Your Pen': The Social Functions of Literature in the Writings of Lady Elizabeth Brackley and Lady Jane Cavendish," *Huntington Library Quarterly* 51.4 (1988): 281–96 (here 293–94); Trease, *Cavalier*, 62–63; and Turberville, *Welbeck Abbey*, 45–46.

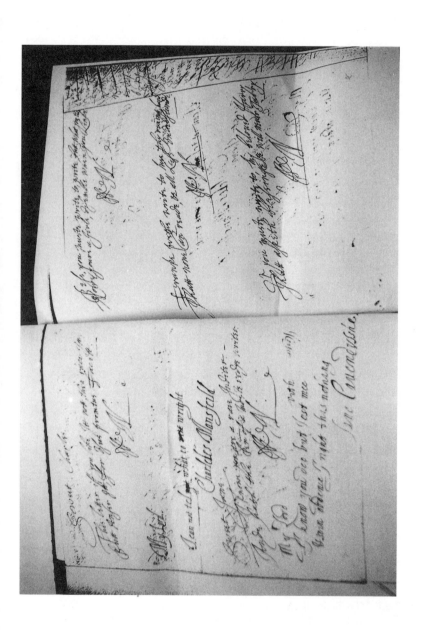

Plates 4–5: Verses addressed to his children by William Cavendish, with some responses.
Portland Collection, Pw V 25 folio 21r-v.
Reproduced by permission of The University of Nottingham Library.

In addition to affection and protectiveness, the lines addressed to "Bess" also suggest some timidity in Elizabeth's makeup.

No one would—or should—equate the exercises Cavendish designed for his young children with the Latin compositions assigned the young More children or suggest that the worldly Cavendish was creator of a humanist academy on the austere model of More's home in Chelsea, but such manuscript witnesses attest to his pride in and nurturing of his very young children, and particularly to his fostering their interest in letters and their efforts at composition.[52] And while it is not surprising, given his daughters' propriety and Margaret Cavendish's notoriety, that Cavendish's influence has been commonly marked in the case of his second wife but less noticed in connection with the far more conventional daughters of his first marriage, yet they too were writers, and Cavendish's influence on them was important. The following extracts from another long verse by Cavendish allude to his own composition of a masque for his family's pleasure, and record his surprise at his daughters' causing it to be copied, further demonstrating the affectionate, kindly, and significant literary exchanges within the family:

To be writt In my Booke, & before the maske booke

> Sweet Daughters
>
>> knowe I was nott nice or coye,
>> Butt made a Countrie Maske, a Christmas toye,
>> Att your desiers; But I did nott Looke
>> You woulde recorde my follies In a Booke
>> You'le loose by thatt, Goe Less, therfore I'de rather,
>> For your sakes, & my one, be helde a Father
>> Off Gravitie, formaletie, precise;
>> An outeside oute off fashion Is held wise.
>
>> . . .

---

[52] I have found no surviving evidence indicating that Elizabeth Basset served as role model to her daughters as a writer, but she served as the model of an affectionate wife and mother; her daughters, raised in a nurturing atmosphere, were drawn into courtly literary activity by their father (of especial interest here, of course, is her daughter Elizabeth).

Butt you will pardon this, Ladies; have pitteye
Forgive the Gate, though much to bigg for'th Cittye.

Your Louinge & In this
Your obediente Father.

W: N.[53]

One should bear in mind, then, the general family atmosphere: the association of Cavendish with the literati of his time meant not only that his
interests would coincide with those developed by his second wife, but also
that the children of his first marriage were exposed to and acquainted with
courtly literary culture even as children. We will see shortly that this expo-
sure bore fruit, yet puzzlingly, that the tone of Elizabeth Cavendish's writings would change profoundly in her later life.

In 1638, Cavendish was appointed a member of the privy council and
governor to the future Charles II. This coveted appointment was by no
means a casual one. On the contrary, it followed a long campaign by many
courtiers for the post (Turberville, *Welbeck Abbey*, 57–58), and the appointment indicates that William Cavendish was not perceived as frivolous by his
peers. While the instructions he drafted for Charles II after his appointment
as his governor do not amount to a humanist plan of studies, both he, in
suing for the post, and Charles I, in granting it, deemed him appropriate to
the role of governor to the prince. That appointment and his instructions
(Chesterfield-like in being heavy on civility, light on study and devotion)
mark him a man of social grace, practicality, and some common sense. They
confirm, and this will be seen to be significant for our purposes, Trease's
evaluation of Cavendish's "indifference" to religion (*Cavalier*, 65):

It is fitt you should have some languages, tho' I confess I woud rather
have you study things then words, matter then language ... I would
not have you too studious, for too much contemplation spoiles action,
and Virtue consists in that ... For the Arts I wou'd have you know
them so far as they are of use, and especially those that are most
proper for war and use. ... Take heed of too much book. Beware of
too much devotion for a King, for one may be a good man but a bad
King ... For Books thus much more, the greatest clerks are not the

---

[53] University of Nottingham MSS Portland Collection Pw V 25: 19–20.

wisest men ... The things that I have discoursed to you most, is to be courteous and civil to every body; sett to, make difference of cabinges, and believe it, the putting off of your hat and making a leg pleases more then reward or preservation ... To women you cannot be too civil ... Certainly Sir you can not loose by curtsey."[54]

What is abundantly clear, then, about Elizabeth Egerton's early life is that intellectually, socially, and emotionally, it was extremely comfortable and even nurturing. She was descended from wealth on both her mother's and her father's side, and was also allied through marriages on both sides with the high peerage. The results of a series of very advantageous marriages in the Cavendish family were a stunning number of alliances with the first families of England,[55] movement in an exalted social circle, and an awesome

---

[54] As quoted by Sir Henry Ellis, *Original Letters Illustrative of English History; including numerous royal letters: from autographs in the British Museum, and one or two other collections*, 3 vols. (London, 1824), 3: 288–90. Ellis names his source as "a Copy preserved with the Royal Letters in the Harleian MS. 6988, art. 62" (288). In Appendix I of *A Catalogue of Letters and Other Historical Documents Exhibited in the Library at Welbeck* (London: John Murray, 1903), S. Arthur Strong, a recent librarian of the descendants of the Cavendish family, at Welbeck, printed a long, untitled document that can be compared most interestingly with these instructions by Cavendish to his young charge. Divided into fifteen heads on such subjects as "The Militia," "The Church," and "Ceremoneye and Order," this book of advice from a much older Cavendish to an older Charles II runs some sixty folio pages. Tinctured by wariness, characterized by expedient thinking, written respectfully but in the tone of an older man giving advice to a less seasoned person, this document is identified by Strong as "Copy in the handwriting of the Duke of Newcastle of a treatise on Government addressed 'for your most sacred Majestie' (Charles II.)." Strong pronounces thus: "This is doubtless the treatise, or letter, to which the Duchess in the life of her husband (p. 186, ed. Firth), alludes: —'And here I cannot forbear to mention, that my noble Lord, when he was in banishment, presumed out of his duty and love to his gracious master, our new Sovereign King, Charles the Second, to write and send him a little book, or rather a letter, wherein he delivered his opinion concerning the government of his dominions, whensoever God should be pleased to restore him to his throne, together with some other notes and observations of foreign states and kingdoms; but it being a private offer to his sacred Majesty, I dare not presume to publish it'" (*Catalogue*, 54).

[55] Her mother's first husband had been the third son of the earl of Suffolk; her paternal great-grandmother, the redoubtable Bess of Hardwick, had maneuvered herself up the matrimonial ladder to land (as fourth husband) the sixth earl of Shrewsbury, and had then engineered the marriages of two of her children from earlier marriages to the earl's children. Hardwick had matched her son Sir Charles Cavendish (Elizabeth's grandfather) to Katherine, the younger daughter of Cuthbert, Lord Ogle, who was created Baroness Ogle in her own right and whose title seems eventually to have descended to her son (although Cokayne notes, "The creation of this Barony is given in *Courthope* and

accumulation of wealth, by the time he was a young man, in the hands of William Cavendish, Elizabeth's father. Throughout his life, even in exile when his finances were in disarray, Cavendish spent his wealth freely on lavish daily living; in his daughter Elizabeth's youngest years, it was perhaps most notoriously spent on the regal entertainments mentioned above. While her mother was noted for her piety, the tone of Elizabeth's daily life as a youngster seems to have been privileged and courtly rather than pious. As we will see, those early writings by her that survive are mainly of a literary nature; none are impious, and they are not as Machiavellian as her father's advice to the young Prince Charles, but they certainly do not betoken a preoccupation with religion.[56]

In 1641, after becoming a focus of Parliamentary dissension, Cavendish withdrew to Welbeck, resigning his post as governor to the prince, but at the king's command he continued to be heavily involved in military operations in support of the increasingly threatened royalists.[57]

In April 1643, during these campaigns, Elizabeth Basset died at Bolsover,[58] leaving two sons (Charles, viscount Mansfield, and Henry, later earl of Ogle and second duke of Newcastle) and three daughters (Jane, later Lady Cheyne; Elizabeth, later countess of Bridgewater; and Frances, later countess of Bolingbroke). According to Bickley, Cavendish "made a secret journey to Welbeck to bury" his wife (*Cavendish Family*, 101, n. 3). Staunchly and substantially supportive of the king, a fealty recognized in his sobriquet "the loyal Duke of Newcastle," Cavendish continued to raise troops and to fight on Charles's behalf after his wife's death.[59] After his forces had suffered a heavy defeat in July 1644 at Marston Moor, however—in large part because of bickering among his fellow commanders—the newly widowed Cavendish left England in the company of his sons and a large

---

almost all other peerage writers, but the Viscountey of Mansfield is given [as the sole creation] in the *Creations*, 1483–1646, in 47th D.K. Pub. Records. Neither is this Barony mentioned in his M.I., where all his titles seem fully set out—*e.g.* 'Baro. Ogle, *jure materno,*' &c" [*Peerage*, 522]).

[56] This assessment also agrees with the tone of Cavendish's letter of advice to Charles just before the Restoration.

[57] His importance in public affairs can be gauged by the numerous references to him in the *Calendar of State Papers Domestic Series of the Reign of Charles I, 1625–1649.* 23 vols. (London, 1848–1897).

[58] The cause of her death does not seem to have been recorded. She died, according to Cokayne, on the 17th and was buried on the 19th of that month.

[59] That Christmas, there was a brief respite and reunion with his family at Welbeck.

number of attendants,[60] eventually attending Henrietta Maria at her court-in-exile in Paris, and leaving his young daughters at Welbeck Abbey. A smashing figure at fifty-one years of age (at least, in the eyes of his daughters),[61] he became captivated at the exiled queen's court by Margaret Lucas, a young, bashful lady-in-waiting to the queen and the wealthy heiress of Sir Thomas Lucas of Colchester. She was then just twenty-two years of age, close to the age of Newcastle's own three surviving daughters, who in due course became her stepdaughters.

2. William Cavendish and Margaret Lucas Cavendish

It was, then, a worldly and middle-aged man, newly widowed, badly defeated in battle, much impoverished by his support of his sovereign, who became infatuated with Margaret Lucas, the young maid-of-honor to Henrietta Maria who later described herself in her autobiography as having been so "bashful" at court that she "was thought a Natural Fool."[62] As readers of the future Margaret Cavendish's writings learn, however, the self-description immediately following this, while not often cited by scholars, is equally insightful and accurate: "Yet, she writes, "I was not an idiot, my Wit was according to my years, and though I might have learnt more Wit, and advanced my Understanding ... I rather chose to be accounted a Fool, than to be thought rude or wanton" (374). Her self-presentation, whether a result of deep calculation or of social insecurity, was just the bait needed to catch the very eligible Cavendish: "my Lord the Marquis of Newcastle did approve of those bashfull fears which many condemn'd, and would choose such a Wife as he might bring to his own humours, and not such a one as was wedded to self conceit, or one that had been temper'd to the humours of another, for which he wooed me for his Wife" (375).[63] As Grant has shown (*Phanseys*),

---

[60] According to Trease (*Cavalier*, 141–42), these included one Mark Anthony Benoist, tutor to his sons and, it seems, the author of a touching document written at a difficult moment in Elizabeth Egerton's later life (below, 117–18).

[61] Bodl. MS Rawl. Poet. 16: 4, 13; Beinecke MS Osborn b.233: 6, 15.

[62] In her *True Relation of My Birth, Breeding, and Life* [appended to her] *Natures Pictures* (London, 1656), 374.

[63] The passage continues, "and though I did dread Marriage, and shunn'd Mens companies, as much as I could, yet I could not, nor had not the power to refuse him, by reason my Affections were fix'd on him, and he was the onely Person I ever was in love with: Neither was I ashamed to own it, but gloried therein, for it was not Amorous Love,

this wooing included the composition—almost daily—of love verses titled, not insignificantly I believe, "The Phanseys of the Marquesse of Newcastle Sett by him in verse att Paris the [ ] 1645."[64]

Whether or not Mendelson is correct in attributing shrewdness and calculation to the young Margaret Lucas, who—as she correctly points out— "transformed each apparent disadvantage into a strategic advantage," finally landing her man,[65] we can agree that this witness to courtly behavior in Paris and, later, in the domicile of her urbane husband was fully capable of appreciating the sophistication around her. Certainly, she later managed a parallel twist in her writings, turning the disadvantages of her poor early formal education[66] into a justification for the superiority of her unlearned, but fresh, ideas, as in the prefatory letter "To His Excellency the Lord Marquis of Newcastle," in her *Philosophical Letters*, when she was to justify her ideas by stating,

> my opinions being new, are not so easily understood as those, that take up several pieces of old opinions, of which they patch up a new Philosophy, (if new may be made of old things,) like a Suit made up of old Stuff bought at the Brokers: Wherefore to find out a Truth, at least a Probability in Natural Philosophy by a new and different way from other Writers, and to make this way more known, easie and intelligible, I was in a manner forced to write this Book.[67]

In the *Life* of her husband that she published in 1667, the duchess stated that she was given in childhood to solitary musing and to recording her

---

I never was infected therewith, it is a Disease, or a Passion, or both, I onely know by relation, not by experience; neither could Title, Wealth, Power or Person entice me to love; but my Love was honest and honourable, being placed upon Merit, which Affection joy'd at the fame of his Worth, pleas'd with delight in his Wit, proud of the respects he used to me, and triumphing in the affections he profest for me, which affections he hath confirmed to me by a deed of time, seal'd by constancy, and assigned by an unalterable decree of his promise, which makes me happy in despight of Fortunes frowns."

[64] The manuscript was purchased by the British Library in 1885. Lucas's letters have been edited from Portland MSS. List I B by R.W. Goulding as *Letters written by Charles Lamb's Princely Woman* (Lincoln, 1909).

[65] Mendelson, *Mental World*, 18–24, esp. 24.

[66] *True Relation*, 371.

[67] *Philosophical Letters: or Modest Reflections upon some Opinions in Natural Philosophy, Maintained by Several Famous and Learned Authors of This Age, Expressed by Way of Letters: by the Thrice Noble, Illustrious, and Excellent Princess, the Lady Marchioness of Newcastle* (London, 1664), sigs. a–a^v.

musings: "it pleased God to command his Servant Nature to indue me with a Poetical and Philosophical Genius, even from my Birth; for I did write some Books in that kind, before I was twelve years of Age, which for want of good method and order, I would never divulge."[68] Although these juvenilia remained in manuscript, however, her oft-repeated desire for recognition and even fame took wing after her marriage, when she became the very indulged wife of a man of expansive habits, himself in the habit of composing light verses. Their exchange of poetry and letters during courtship, noted earlier, may have revived her juvenile interest in writing. William Cavendish may never have imagined, or intended, that his child-wife would attempt to publish her writings, or achieve notoriety by so doing, but it is my contention that he provided her the same sort of encouragement he had earlier provided his own children, and that the tenor of her writings, like the tenor of his daughters' early writings, is consistent with the tenor of his worldly lifestyle (i.e., of the lifestyle in which Elizabeth Egerton had been reared). An opportunity for Margaret to achieve recognition through her inclination to write arose after she was dispatched from the continent, in 1651, in the company of her brother-in-law, Sir Charles Cavendish, to attempt to compound for her husband's estates. (Occasional replenishing of his exchequer was necessary, since Cavendish could well have served as the model after whom Thackeray wrote his famous chapters on "How to Live Well on Nothing a Year."[69]) In London she returned to the habit of writing down her thoughts and, in 1653, she took the further daring step of putting *Poems and Fancies*,[70] her first book, to the press.

It seems to me significant that Margaret Cavendish first put her work into print when she was separated from her husband, for she could not, after all, have done so against his express wishes, and she could not have been certain in advance that he would approve the step. Her comment in one of the prefaces to this volume, "An Epistle to Mistris Toppe" (Elizabeth Champlain Toppe, a waiting maid who had been her friend from childhood days), is revealing. Cavendish makes both her awareness of her breach of convention and her calculated thinking public when she states, "in this Action of setting out of a Booke, I am not clear without fault, because I

---

[68] *Life of the Thrice Noble, High and Puissant Prince William Cavendish*, sigs. a^v–a2^r.

[69] William Makepeace Thackeray, *Vanity Fair* (New York: Rinehart & Co., Inc., 1958), 375–90.

[70] *Poems and Fancies Written by the Right Honourable Margaret Marciones Newcastle* (London, 1653).

have not asked leave of any Freind thereto; for the feare of being denied, made me silent: and there is an Old saying; That it is easier to aske Pardon, then Leave: for a fault will sooner be forgiven, then a suite granted" (sig. A4ᵛ). What a world of suggestion lies in this passage! And what further self-possession, and possibly clever strategizing, is suggested by Cavendish's well-known homage to her husband in the same volume:

> A Poet I am neither borne, nor bred,
> But to a witty Poet married:
> Whose Braine is Fresh, and Pleasant, as the Spring,
> Where Fancies row, and where the Muses sing.
> There oft I leane my Head, and list'ning harke,
> To heare his words, and all his Fancies mark;
> And from that Garden Flowers of Fancies take,
> Whereof a Posie up in Verse I make.
> Thus I, that have no Garden of mine owne,
> There gather Flowers that are newly-blowne. (214)

Known to students of early modern women chiefly as the supportive husband of this eccentric second wife who was to become one of the most prolific women writers of the seventeenth century in England, William Cavendish is commonly dismissed as a benign but negligible male figure.[71] But as we have already noted in connection with his appointment as guardian of the young Charles II, the "witty Poet" to whom Margaret was "married" should not be underestimated. Cavendish consorted with such men of polite letters as James Shirley, John Dryden and Thomas Shadwell; he himself wrote original plays and poems, in addition to translating Molière.[72] One should not forget, either, that guests at his dinner table included the scientific illuminati of the age.[73] Renowned for his mastery of horsemanship, he

---

[71] Grant, *Phanseys*, xxi. This evaluation has recently been repeated by Ruth Perry, *The Celebrated Mary Astell: An Early English Feminist* (Chicago, Univ. of Chicago Press, 1986), who describes Newcastle as "a man thirty-four years older than she [Margaret], harmlessly addicted to horsemanship and swordsmanship. . . . There were no children. He appreciated and encouraged her writing" (114–15).

[72] See, for example, Francis Needham, ed., *Welbeck Miscellany* 1–2 (Bungay, Suffolk: Richard Clay & Sons, Ltd., 1933–1934); Graham Parry, *The Golden Age Restor'd: The Culture of the Stuart Court, 1603–42* (Manchester: Manchester Univ. Press, 1981).

[73] Letters he exchanged with Hobbes are abstracted in *The Portland Papers*, 2: 124, 125–26, 128, 129–30. Alluding to the letter on 126 of this calendar, Strong reprints, as his Appendix II (237–40), "Considerations on the Motions of a Horse by Hobbes,"

composed, during his years in exile, an elaborately illustrated work, often reprinted, on the subject.[74] And he would be dubbed "our English Mecaenas
[sic]" by Langbaine.[75] Few persons studying women writers of the seventeenth century have either questioned Cavendish's benignity or noted his
influence on the other women writers in his family, his daughters—including, of course, Elizabeth Cavendish Egerton, the subject of this study who
was to become the wife of John Egerton, the second earl of Bridgewater.
Yet I believe that Cavendish's influence on his daughters—suggested in the
extracts from manuscripts at the University of Nottingham cited earlier—was
profound and that the evidence of this influence underpins one of the theses
promulgated here: that the varied extent and nature of a dominant male's
influence on the women writers and other subordinated writers in his family
(as well as that of other men) sheds light on their lives and writings and, by
extension, on those of other early modern women and other subordinated
persons. Because Margaret Cavendish's writings shed light on the very different direction taken in the writings of Elizabeth Cavendish Egerton, I will
pause briefly now to consider the duchess's *oeuvre* from that perspective.

§

It seems possible, even probable, that the juvenile habit of composition
would not have been revived for Margaret Cavendish without the encouragement provided in her earlier married life, and that it perhaps would not

---

which he describes as a "little treatise . . . in the handwriting of Thomas Hobbes of Mal-
mesbury, the philosopher." See Lisa Sarasohn, "A Science Turned Upside Down," *Huntington Library Quarterly* 47 (1984): 289–307 (here 290).

[74] *La methode et Invention Nouvelle de dresser les Chevaux* (Antwerp, 1657); *A New
Method and Extraordinary Invention to Dress Horses, and Work them, according to Nature;
as also to Perfect Nature by the Subtlety of Art; which was never found out but by the thrice
noble, high, and puissant Prince, William Cavendish* (London, 1677). Sir William claimed
that the 1677 book was a new work. According to Parry, Newcastle "was the leading
theorist and practitioner in England . . . in the art of horse-manship" (*Golden Age*, 181).
The illustrations in the 1657 edition are discussed below. Sadly, Cavendish, who had
been the benefactor of so many writers in his more prosperous earlier years, was forced
to depend on the generosity of friends to bring out his own book (Trease, *Cavalier*, 176).

[75] Gerard Langbaine, *An Account of the English Dramatick Poets* (Oxford, 1691), 386:
"No Person since the Time of *Augustus* better understood Dramatick Poetry, nor more
generously encourag'd Poets; so that we may truly call him our *English Mecaenas*." Since
Langbaine was writing after the death of the duke, the remark was not intended as mere
flattery.

have been resuscitated without the immediate impetus provided by her relatively unsettled, relatively isolated state in London in 1652/53. Her own reflections are both affecting and enlightening:

> The time I have been writing them, hathnot [sic] been very long, but since I came into England, being eight Yeares out, and nine Months in; and of these nine Months [a significant period of gestation!], onely some Houres in the Day, or rather in the Night. For my Rest being broke with discontented Thoughts, because I was from my Lord, and Husband, knowing him to be in great Wants, and my selfe in the same Condition; to divert them, I strove to turne the Stream. ("To the Reader," sig. A7)

At this time, she could not have been absolutely certain that her husband would indulge her incursion into print, and she clearly realized that putting her work to press was daring. Her comment to Mistress Toppe implies her realization that her impulse could have been denied—a reflection of patriarchal constraint in her privileged, pampered, and supported life. Equally clearly, such a denial would have been definitive: it would have preempted this independent action. Extremely eccentric Margaret Cavendish undoubtedly was, but her idiosyncrasies combined with a cold-eyed, hard-nosed realism that is certainly very intelligible to the late twentieth-century reader.

In the multiple prefatory epistles to this first work, much of the highly individual mix of qualities that informs her corpus as a whole is already present, and the discussion that follows will therefore draw heavily on this volume. Significantly, in terms of my argument in this introduction, she begins by addressing her brother-in-law, her male guardian of the moment. Cavendish notes, inter alia, when she asks him "to accept of this Booke" (otherwise termed her "Garment of Memory" created by "Spinning with the braine") that his "Bounty hath been the Distaffe, from whence Fate hath Spun the thread of this part of my Life" (sig. A2ᵛ). She thereby employs an extended metaphor that is more famously, and surely more dexterously, employed by her contemporary Anne Bradstreet ("My hand a needle better fits"),[76] one, moreover, that goes back to Isabella Whitney, the earliest pro-

---

[76] In "The Prologue" to *The Tenth Muse* (1650), a volume first printed by Bradstreet's brother-in-law without her knowledge, Bradstreet writes "I am obnoxious to each carping tongue, / Who sayes, my hand a needle better fits, / A poets Pen, all scorne, I should thus wrong; / For such despight they cast on female wits: / If what I doe prove well, it wo'nt advance, / They'l say its stolne, or else, it was by chance" (sig. B2ᵛ).

fessional woman poet in England.[77] Returning to this metaphor in the last
of her epistles in the volume, one addressed "To the Reader," Cavendish
notes that with her "Lords Estate being taken away," she is unable to exercise "huswifery, or thrifty Industry to imploy my selfe in; having no Stock to
work on," although "Thrift weight, and measures out all Expence. It is just
as in Poetry: for good Husbandry in Poetry, is, when there is great store of
Fancy well order'd, not onely in fine Language, but proper Phrases, and significant Words. And Thrift in Poetry, is, when there is but little Fancy,
which is not onely spun to the last Thread, but the Thread is drawne so
small, as it is scarce perceived. But I have nothing to spin, or order, so as I
become Idle" (sig. A7).

In her second dedicatory epistle, addressed "To All Noble, and Worthy
Ladies," Cavendish distinctively expresses her consciousness of herself as a
woman and as a writer, her awareness of other women, of what is conventionally expected of women and of conventional criticisms of women, and
her awareness of the handicap she struggles under by reason of an education
inferior to that of men combined with an unabashed desire for fame. Her
consequent arguments sometimes take unexpected turns, as in the following
comments in the letter "To His Grace the Duke of Newcastle" prefixed to
her *Life of ... William Cavendish*:

> As for my being the true and onely Authoress of them, your Lord-
> ship knows best, and my attending Servants are witness that I have
> had none but my own Thoughts, Fancies and Speculations to assist
> me; and as soon as I have set them down, I send them to those that
> are to transcribe them, and fit them for the Press; whereof since there
> have been several, and amongst them such as onely could write a
> good hand, but neither understood Orthography, nor had any Learn-
> ing (I being then in banishment with your Lordship, and not able to
> maintain learned Secretaries) which hath been a great disadvantage to
> my poorworks, and the cause that they have been printed so false,
> and so full of Errors; for besides that, I want also the skill of Schol-
> arship and true writing, I did many times not peruse the Copies that

---

[77] In "To Her Sister Misteris A. B.," one of the verse epistles to members of her
family in her *Sweet Nosgay* (1573), Whitney alluded to the same expectations when she
wrote: "Had I a husband, or a house, / and all that longs thereto / My selfe could frame
about to rouse / as other women doo: / But til some houshold cares mee tye, / My
bookes and Pen I wyll apply" (sig. D2).

were transcribed, lest they should disturb my following Conceptions.
(sigs. a2^v–b)

While there is some disagreement as to whether Margaret Cavendish, like
her husband, in fact disdained revision, as she claims here,[78] this often reiterated disclaimer, related to the distinction she draws between learned and
inspired ways of knowing, can profitably be contrasted with the disclaimer
of the learned Elizabeth Cary in her prefatory letter "To the Reader" of her
translation of Jacques Davy Cardinal du Perron:

> I desire to have noe more guest at of me, but that I am a Catholique
> and a Woman; the first serves for mine honor, and the second, for
> my excuse, since if the worke be but meanely done, it is noe wonder,
> for my Sexe can raise noe great expectation of anie thing that shall
> come from me: Yet it were a great follie in me, if I would expose to
> the view of the world, a work of this kinde, except I judged it to
> want nothing fitt, for a Translation. Therefore, I will confesse, I
> thinke it well done, and so had I confest Sufficientlie in printing it:
> if it gain noe applause, hee that writt it faire hath lost more labour
> then I have done for I dare avouch it hath bene fower times as long
> in transcribing, as it was in translating."[79]

In her very individual way Cavendish also both extols and censors women.
Apparently acting, for example, on the motto that the best defense is a good
offense, she states, "I imagine I shall be censur'd by my owne Sex; and
Men will cast a smile of scorne upon my Book, because they think thereby, Women incroach too much their Prerogatives" (*Poems and Fancies*, sig.
A3^{r-v}). Her approach to the gender wars, in other words, is somewhat com-
plex: she both signals an awareness of commonplace misogyny and seems in
part to accept it. Her plays—in form almost outside the limits of the

---

[78] Mendelson points out that the duke makes the same disclaimer, and theorizes that
the duchess employed a drudge to do her revisions (*Mental World*, 42). But, noting
changes in *The Second Impression, much altered and Corrected* of *Poems and Fancies* (1664),
Germaine Greer, et al., state, "Given the Duchess's personal involvement in the production of her books of poetry, many of the variants in the second edition must represent direct authorial intervention" (*Kissing the Rod: An Anthology of Seventeenth-Century Women's
Verse* [New York: Noonday Press, 1989], 166).

[79] Elizabeth Cary, trans., *Reply of the Cardinall of Perron to the Answeare of the King
of Great Britaine* (Douay, 1630), sig. C2.

genre—consider and feature extraordinary women, and her utopian fantasy centers on a young woman, rescued miraculously from an attempted rape, who becomes empress of an imaginary world and befriends none other than Margaret Cavendish, her hand-picked secretary and confidante who occasionally becomes homesick for her "lord."[80] Despite such seeming oddities, there is no gainsaying that the dominant theme of her work is feminism. As Smith has stated, "Her greatest contribution to feminist thought was the degree to which questions of sex division dominated her work. No matter what her subject, no matter what the context of a particular piece, the duchess introduced the fact that she was a woman and explained how this influenced her work" (*Reason's Disciples*, 78). Mendelson perhaps succeeds in making some sense of Cavendish's inconsistencies when she notes that Cavendish's "underlying theme [is] ... a power struggle between the sexes" (*Mental World*, 23).[81]

It is surely an indication of her strong awareness of this struggle that Cavendish surprisingly alludes, in 1653, to a literary quarrel in which Lady Mary Wroth ("the Lady that wrote the Romancy") had been engulfed over thirty years before, paraphrasing angry lines addressed to Wroth by Lord Denny: "Work Lady work, let writing Books alone, / For surely wiser Women nere wrote one" (sig. A3ᵛ).[82] Women writers of the early modern period commonly tried to excuse their boldness in writing, and Cavendish is no exception, though her reasoning, again, is very individualistic. The early humanists had claimed that *learned* women would be virtuous; Cavendish, with no claim for learning, yet states that *writing* women will be virtuous, indeed will "employ their time no worse then in honest, Innocent, and

---

[80] *Playes Written by the Thrice Noble, Illustrious and Excellent Princess, the Lady Marchioness of Newcastle* (London, 1662); *Plays, Never before Printed* (London, 1668); *The Description of a New Blazing World* (London, 1666), also published with her *Observations upon Experimental Philosophy* (1666). There are also orations by women within other volumes.

[81] Wiseman, "Gender and Status," provides a powerfully nuanced discussion of Cavendish's "slippages."

[82] Cavendish alludes to this quarrel elsewhere as well (e.g. "To His Excellency the Lord Marquess of Newcastle," *CCXI Sociable Letters, Written by the Thrice Noble, Illustrious, and Excellent Princess, the Lady Marchioness of Newcastle* [London, 1664], sig. b.) The late Josephine A. Roberts brought this episode to the attention of literary scholars in "An Unpublished Literary Quarrel Concerning the Suppression of Mary Wroth's *Urania*," *Notes & Queries* 222 (1977): 532–35; she also discussed it in the introduction to her edition, *The Poems of Lady Mary Wroth* (Baton Rouge: Louisiana State Univ. Press, 1983).

harmlesse Fancies; which if they do, Men shall have no cause to feare, that when they go abroad in their absence, they shall receive an Injury by their loose Carriages" (*Poems and Fancies*, sig. A3ᵛ).

To return, though, to the most important of these considerations for a study centering on one of Margaret Cavendish's stepdaughters, the duke's positive attitude and support were determining factors in establishing Cavendish's continued pattern of publication; her output in print, successfully initiated through this indirection, was approved, and his approval underlay its later profusion. In addition to the early poem cited above, Cavendish acknowledged this support in a dedication to her *Orations of Divers Sorts*: "I cannot chuse but declare to the World how happy I and my works are in your Approvement, which makes me confident and resolute to put them to the Press."[83] This support was to be affirmed again and again in her *oeuvre*; her husband's supportive posture was critical to her writing, as Mendelson has pointed out (*Mental World*, 31). Her *Philosophical and Physical Opinions*[84] contains a strong example. In it, the marquis prefixed both a signed commendatory poem "To the Lady Marquesse of Newcastle On her Book intitled her Philosophicall, and Physicall Opinions," affirming (in remarks that could be read as an extension of his devaluation of book learning to Prince Charles) the value of her work above that of earlier authorities:

> Were the old Grave Philosophers alive,
> How they would envy you, and all would strive
> Who first should burn their Books; since they so long
> Thus have abus'd the world, and taught us wrong. (sig. A)

Not only that, but the marquis also substantiated his wife's protests against those who claimed that her ideas were not her own (a misappropriation experienced by other early modern women, as well),[85] and the terms in which he did so are extremely interesting: the detractors are motivated by envy of women (an argument reminiscent of More's and Hyrde's comments some 150 years earlier[86]); the truth of her claim to composition is attested

---

[83] *Orations of Divers Sorts* (London, 1662), sig. a.

[84] *Philosophical and Physical Opinions* (London, 1655).

[85] It was not uncommon to ascribe anything well written to a male writer, on the grounds that women were incapable of writing well. Writing in 1621, Rachel Speght notes in the front matter of her *Mortalities Memorandum* (sig. A2ᵛ) that her *Mouzell* had been ascribed to her father on such grounds.

[86] Sir Thomas More, "Letter to William Gonell" (1518) in *St. Thomas More: Selected*

to by a male and based on the code of honor. These intriguing comments
are here abstracted at some length:

> some ... she hath heard from me, but not the fortieth part of her
> book, all the rest are absolutely her own in all kindes, this is an
> ingenious truth, therefore beleeve it. As for the Book of her Philo-
> sophical opinions, there is not any one thing in the whole Book that
> is not absolutely spun out by her own studious phancy. ... Truly I
> cannot believe so unworthily of any Scholer, honouring them so
> much as we both do, that they should envie this Lady, or should have
> so much malice or emulation, to cast such false aspersions on her,
> that she did not write those Books that go forth in her name, they
> will hardly finde out who else writ them, and I protest none ever writ
> them but her selfe; You should rather incourage her, then by false
> suppositions to let her see the world is so ill natured, as to beleeve
> falshoods before truths. But here's the crime, a Lady writes them, and
> to intrench so much upon the male prerogative, is not to be forgiven;
> but I know Gown-men will be more civil to her, because she is of the
> Gown too, and therefore I am confident you will defend her and
> truth, and thus be undeceived. I had not troubled you with this, but
> that a learned Doctor, our very noble friend, writ is [sic] word of the
> infidelity of some people in this kinde; whatsoever I have write is
> absolutly truth, which I here as a man of Honour set my hand to.
> (sig. A3)

As witnessed by the opening sentence of Margaret Cavendish's dedication
to her husband in her *Philosophical Letters* (1664), his support was constant:
"you have allways encouraged me in my harmless pastime of Writing," she
states there (sig. a). The apparent dynamics of this supportive relationship
seem to have been crucial to her writing, and, as will be argued below, are
also very useful for an understanding of the writings of her stepdaughter,
Elizabeth Cavendish Egerton.

Other impetuses that underlay the *oeuvre* of the Duchess of Newcastle
were her childlessness and the political disappointments of the duke. As to
the first, Margaret Cavendish employs the conventional tropes of women
writers, alluding in the earliest of her volumes to her writings as her off-

---

Letters, ed. Elizabeth F. Rogers (New Haven, 1961), 103–4; Richard Hyrde, "Unto the
moost studyous," in *Devout Treatyse*, trans. Margaret Roper (1524), sig. A2.

spring, her childlessness serving both as an excuse for her devoting time to her writing and as an explanation for her defensiveness about her books.[87] She alludes, also, to the duke's (initially) great desire that she bear him additional children (*Life*, 55), and she writes apparently envious criticisms of women who expected to be fussed over while bearing children, reflecting on the lack of tangible good reason for a woman to wish for children.[88]

Political disappointment, specifically disappointment over the duke's exclusion from the inner court circle after the Restoration, also seems to have fed into her writing. As Mendelson puts it, "The only way to revenge herself was to pour her energy into her works. It was no accident that Margaret's literary activities waxed as Newcastle's political influence waned" (*Mental World*, 40). There is certainly no question that both Margaret and William Cavendish were eager for fame and recognition as well as for the means to support a very high standard of living. Margaret expresses an awareness of the bars to direct wielding of power by women and of the traditional ways that women developed power over men,[89] and Mendelson brings suggestive support for her thesis that Margaret indeed gained the ascendancy over her husband towards the end of her life, avariciously acquiring control over larger and larger portions of his estates. The earliest of the duchess's acquisitions is dated October 1662, i.e., before Elizabeth Egerton's death. We do not have any reference by Elizabeth to the situation, though we do know of the distress this state of affairs would cause other surviving children from Cavendish's first marriage and some of his retainers a few years later.[90] Strong prints one letter from William's heir (dated 10 August 1671) expressing these dissatisfactions.[91] In later years, a disaffected servant

---

[87] E.g., "If any do read this Book of mine, pray be not too severe in your Censures. For first, I have no Children to imploy my Care"; "True, it may taxe my Indiscretion, being so fond of my Book, as to make it as if it were my Child, and striving to shew her to the World, in hopes Some may like her, although no Beauty to Admire, yet may praise her Behavior, as not being wanton, nor rude" ("To the Reader," *Poems and Fancies*, sigs. A7–A7ᵛ). Of course, men had long used such images as a pregnant wit, teeming brain, etc.

[88] *CCXI Sociable Letters*, Letter XCIII (183–87).

[89] *CCXI Sociable Letters*, Letter XVI (26–28).

[90] Mendelson, *Mental World*, 42, 57–58. These events occurred in 1667 and 1668.

[91] "I am very mellencholly, finding my Father more perswaded by his Wife then I could thinke it possible. ... I thanke God my little fammily are in health the joy I take in it cannot be taken away from me by yᵉ unkindness to us at Wellbeck" (*Catalogue*, 63–64, "The Earl of Ogle to the Earl of Danby").

of Newcastle drew direct parallels between Margaret and Bess of Hardwick, claiming that Margaret herself had noted the parallel.[92]

What I find most fascinating here, as well as most significant for the present study, are the multiple oscillations. In Margaret's writings there are shifts between comments critical of women and gender-conscious remarks expressing an awareness of women's relative powerlessness; between remarks showing a consciousness of her daring and others showing the great support her husband provided her. In Margaret's life there is a contradiction on the one hand between the protectiveness of her husband, her gratitude for it, and her statement that he chose her as someone he could mold, and, on the other, an acted-on consciousness, nevertheless, of women's powerlessness (a consciousness that may account for the unattractive acquisitiveness that she exhibited in her old age). Perhaps these contradictions merely reflect the contradictory realities of her time: as Elaine Hobby comments (*Virtue of Necessity*, 82), the rationale Margaret Cavendish gives for composing her own life is that she not be subsumed so totally in her husband's identity that she be confused in aftertimes with his first wife or with another wife who might follow her.[93] This notion bespeaks deep insecurity about herself— about her chances at achieving the fame she so much desired and about the durability of her husband's feelings for her combined with the knowledge that as a "feme covert" she was indeed subsumed within her husband's legal persona.

It is possible that her insecurity—and bravura—were exacerbated by the less than cordial attitude taken towards her by her close-knit stepchildren and their spouses (an attitude that may have included some anger at, or

---

[92] University of Nottingham MS Portland Collection Pw 1 315–317. Trease, *Cavalier*, 200–3; Mendelson, *Mental World*, 58.

[93] "I hope my Readers, will not think me vain for writing my life, since there have been many that have done the like, as Cesar, Ovid, and many more, both men and women, and I know no reason I may not do it as well as they: but I verily believe some censuring Readers will scornfully say, why hath this Ladie writ her own Life? Since none cares to know whose daughter she was, or whose wife she is, or how she was bred, or what fortunes she had, or how she lived, or what humour or disposition she was of? I answer that it is true, that 'tis to no purpose, to the Readers, but it is to the Authoress, because I write it for my own sake, not theirs; neither did I intend this piece for to delight, but to divulge, not to please the fancy, but to tell the truth, lest after-Ages should mistake, in not knowing I was daughter to one Master Lucas of St. Johns neer Colchester in Essex, second Wife to the Lord Marquis of Newcastle, for my Lord having had two Wives, I might easily have been mistaken, especially if I should dye, and my Lord Marry again" (*True Relation*, 390–91).

disappointment with, William Cavendish for his remarriage), and one which she must have perceived, despite the polite veneer that usually covered it. For the early family ties between the Cavendish siblings did not end with their marriages and the remarriage of William Cavendish. Letters in the Portland Collection at the University of Nottingham demonstrate deep affection and strong family feeling that continued in later life among the Cavendish children and their spouses (Plate 6). Elaborately courteous, although they deal with homely family matters, these missives are informed with gentleness and redolent of kindly feelings.[94] Other extant documents also demonstrate continued association among them and attest as well as to Cavendish's attempts to remain in contact with them.[95]

Despite efforts to present Margaret in harmony with Cavendish's children and their spouses, however, her relationship with them sometimes became severely strained, and the strains sometimes were sounded beyond the family. As we will see when considering Elizabeth Egerton's life as a married woman, to take this one example, John Egerton's meticulous family records of their children's christenings witness that William and Margaret Cavendish never—even when they were in England—stood as godparents. Similarly, Margaret and William Cavendish are notably omitted from Elizabeth Egerton's anxious reviews of the relatives for whom she prays God's protection in "On ye same occasion," one of the entries in her "Loose Papers" mourning her daughter Catherine. And lines penned by Elizabeth's young daughter in later years would sneer, "Mongst Ladyes let Newcastle weare ye Bayes."[96]

---

[94] These include University of Nottingham Library MS, Portland Collection Pw 1 83 and 84 (letters written by Charles Cheyne to John Bridgewater, his brother-in-law, in April and May 1656); Pw 1 86, 87, 88 and 89 (letters written by Jane Cheyne to her brother, Viscount Mansfield in March and April and May 1656); Pw 1 118–20 (letters written by Elizabeth Bridgewater to her brother Viscount Mansfield in March, April, and May 1656); and Pw 1 121–22 (letters written by John Bridgewater to Mansfield in June 1656).

[95] *Portland Papers*, 2: 141, 142: Lord Henry Cavendish to Viscount Mansfield (1656); 143: Marquis of Newcastle to Viscount Mansfield (1659); 145: Henry Viscount Mansfield to William Cavendish (1663); 147: William Cavendish to Countess of Ogle (1665); 149: William Cavendish to Earl of Ogle (1669–70); 151: Earl of Ogle to William Cavendish (1675). There were certainly efforts to maintain family ties, both from exile, under a pseudonym (Pw 1 77–79) and after the Restoration. We have a record, for example, of a visit by Cavendish's grandchildren to Welbeck in 1670 (Trease, *Cavalier*, 201–3), and the abstract of a letter the duchess wrote expressing cordial feelings towards her step-grandson (*Portland Papers*, 2: 152).

[96] It is also difficult, for example, to read the effusive complimentary letters by Jane's husband, Charles Cheyne (78–79), and Elizabeth's husband, John Egerton (77–78), in a

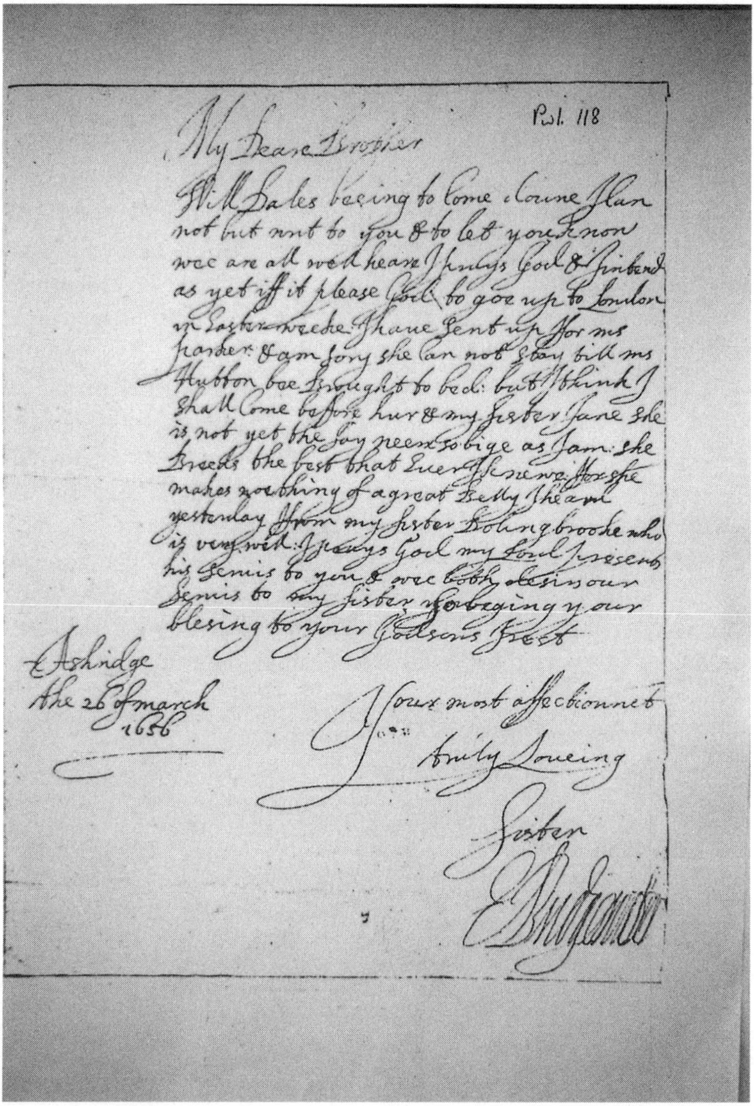

Plate 6: Letter from Elizabeth Egerton to her brother, 26 March 1656.
Portland Collection, Pw 1 folio 118.
Reproduced by permission of The University of Nottingham Library.

However much dismay this rift may have occasioned him, William Cavendish certainly was supportive of his wife. I disagree, in this connection, with Hobby's analysis of the rather peculiar bonding in print between husband and wife that occurs in both editions of Cavendish's *Natures Pictures*,[97] where some materials by the duke are incorporated into the text without a statement to this effect on the title page and where the frontispiece (to the first edition) suggests a close relationship between William and Margaret Cavendish and his children (Plate 7). "At one level," Hobby comments, "she might have been subsumed by him. *Natures Pictures* includes some passages identified in the text as written by the Duke; they are unacknowledged on the title page, however, and incorporated into the text as part of the body of Cavendish's work" (*Virtue of Necessity*, 82). I suggest that rather than subsumption, this interesting text instances a legitimizing and idealizing of Margaret Cavendish. A remarkable instance of this effect and—I believe—this intention is afforded by the frontispiece of the first edition, an idealized group portrait of the marquis and his second wife together with the children of his first marriage and their spouses, prepared at a time when William and Margaret Cavendish were in fact living in exile abroad and his (adult) children were in England.[98] The suggestion is of a harmonious family, respectful of Margaret Cavendish's creativity, and I view the interpolations of material by William Cavendish (interpolations that are

---

1666 volume honoring Margaret (*Letters and Poems In Honour of the Incomparable Princess, Margaret, Dutchess of Newcastle*), as untinged with irony. Egerton's praise of Margaret's publications, written in December 1662 (just six months before the death of the wife he would memorialize so strongly for "Modesty in Concealing" her writings) seem patently insincere. And in this light, as noted in June 1997 by Elizabeth Clarke, Victoria Burke, and Marie-Louise Coolahan of the PERDITA Project, in an as yet unpublished paper, "Margaret Cavendish: Family Context, Literary Contexts," Margaret's rather tart comments on devotional writings by women in 1664, the year following Elizabeth Egerton's death (in her *Sociable Letters*, 225–26) suggest intra-familial sparring in particularly bad taste. I thank the authors for sharing their findings with me.

[97] *Natures Pictures Drawn by Fancies Pencil To the Life*. The second edition was printed by A. Maxwell in 1671.

[98] The group portrait, which is not included in the second edition of the work (printed after their return to England), was after an illustration by Abraham van Diepenbeke and, alas, suggests William's desire for an intact family rather than the fact that his children and his second wife related cordially to one another. Similarly, another idealized group portrait (also after an illustration by Abraham van Diepenbeke) showing the family gathered at a display of menage (Plate 8), was included in Newcastle's work on horsemanship (Antwerp, 1658), while William and Margaret Cavendish were in fact in exile abroad (they returned to England in late 1660).

Thus, in this Semy-Circle, wher they Sitt,
Telling of Tales of pleasure & of witt.
Heer you may read without a Sinn or Crime,
And how more innocently pass your tyme.

Abr. à Diepenbeke delineauit.

Pet. Clouet sculp.

Plate 7: Margaret Cavendish, William Cavendish, and William's Children. The frontispiece of The Huntington Library copy (RB120144) of Margaret Cavendish's *Nature's Pictures* (1656). Reproduced by permission of The Huntington Library, San Marino, California.

Plate 8: The frontispiece of Francis Bickley's *The Cavendish Family* (1914).
Reproduced by permission of United States History, Local History & Genealogy Division,
The New York Public Library, Astor, Lenox and Tilden Foundation.

always signaled in print to the reader) as part of a thread of interminglings throughout the work with this effect in mind. I suggest that these features were intended to aggrandize Margaret Cavendish, rather than to diminish or subsume her. The inclusion of Margaret's autobiography at the end of this first edition, replete as Hobby notes (*Virtue of Necessity*, 84), with constant deferential references to the marquis, is consonant with such an interpretation. Including a husband's additions to a work and acknowledging them as his could be termed subsuming only when the authority of the entry was left in question. The point is worth attention, because, as we will see, an instance of such subsumption of the author does occur in the unpublished manuscripts of Elizabeth Cavendish Egerton. In *Natures Pictures*, however, the wife is ceded additional credit by association, not subsumed or silently edited, precisely the reverse of what we will recognize as the effect of John Egerton's tampering with his wife Elizabeth's manuscripts.[99]

Given the intellectual intermeshing of William and Margaret Cavendish, the question I find puzzling is not Margaret Cavendish's own query "Why hath this Ladie writ her own Life" (*True Relation*, 390), but rather why this lady, with so supportive a husband, nevertheless frequently wrote so strenuously—if sometimes contradictorily—from what can accurately be called a proto-feminist perspective, raising (in Smith's terms), the issue of "women's subordinate role in society" (*Reason's Disciples*, 79). What made her so conscious of the woman question when her husband was so supportive? Mendelson poses the question somewhat differently, asking, "Why did the majority of her fictional heroines condemn wedlock in the strongest possible terms, resolving never to marry? And why, on the other hand, did these same heroines always break their resolution and marry anyway?" (*Mental World*, 32). Perhaps, as Smith hypothesises, "her incipient feminism"—and, I would add, her fantasies of acclaim and success—resulted from the stunting of the "talents and aspirations" that were nurtured in her at home, but that languished in the "thin soil" of "a society that provided women with little education and even less opportunity for public use or display of intellect" (*Reason's Disciples*, 86). Mendelson, less sympathetic, posits that the

---

[99] Similarly, in the case of the *Life*, I do not altogether agree with Hobby's evaluation as subsumption of Margaret Cavendish of the duke's having "dictated what should be included and what omitted" (*Virtue of Necessity*, 84), because it was, after all, *his* life that was being related, a subject in which he could legitimately take a commanding interest, and the subject was politically sensitive, as well, touching as it did on major public personalities and events.

duchess was an "egoist who happened to be of the female gender" (*Mental World*, 55) and who was interested in her own distinction rather than in that of women in general (ibid., 56–57). Such underlying contradictions in Margaret Cavendish's own statements find, even more interestingly, a parallel in the contradiction between a husband who strongly supported her writing—as evidenced both by statements in print (like those quoted above) and by her assertion (also quoted earlier) that this much older man had courted her as "such a wife as he might bring to his own humours, and not such a one ... that had been tempered to the humours of another." Her oscillating life circumstances and opinions, in other words, provide an outstanding instance of the individual early modern woman's dependence on male approval for publication.

The importance of such approval is also demonstrated in the writings of her stepdaughter, Elizabeth, which oscillated, as the authority figure in her life changed, from an early courtliness to a later piety.

3. Bodleian MS. Rawl. Poet. 16 and Beinecke MS Osborn b.233

That Cavendish's affectionate nurturing of his young children's creativity (as shown in the documents cited earlier) bore fruit in the form both of strong affection for him on the part of his daughters and of efforts at composition is perhaps most strongly demonstrated by a bound manuscript miscellany by his daughters Jane and Elizabeth, most parts of which are extant (with some variation) in two similar witnesses housed in two far-flung locations, the Bodleian (Oxford University) and the Beinecke libraries (Yale University).[100] "POEMS SONGS a PASTORALL and a PLAY," the

---

[100] The longer of the two manuscripts was bequeathed to the Bodleian in 1755 by Richard Rawlinson. The Bodleian catalog entry for the manuscript reads, " 'Poems, Songs, and a Pastorall [and a play] by the rt. hon^ble the lady Jane Cavendish and lady Elizabeth Brackley,' copies, made later, probably for the duke of Newcastle, whose initials 'W. N.' are on the binding. The play is 'The Concealed Fansyes.' In the pastoral the two authors' parts are indicated by initials, not elsewhere. The period of the original poems must be later than 1641 but before 1649." A notation states, "In English, on paper: written in about 1670 (?): 12 3/8 x 8 1/4 in., viii + 168 pages." The Beinecke acquired its witness much more recently, in 1951, from the bookseller Emily Driscoll. Regrettably, I have been unable to trace its provenance prior to Driscoll's offer of the manuscript for sale, a particularly frustrating gap since much of the remaining portion of the Bridgewater family library was sold through Sotheby's in 1951, and it is not impossible that this manuscript had found its way to Ashridge during Elizabeth Egerton's lifetime and was

Bodleian Library witness (Bodl. MS Rawl. Poet. 16), has received some critical attention (particularly the last portion of it, the "PLAY"); the less complete, untitled witness held at the Beinecke Library (lacking the play and a few poems) has, to the best of my knowledge, been briefly noted in print only by Kelliher.[101]

The relationship of these two witnesses to each other is itself an interesting puzzle, though I believe not one whose solution is altogether essential to an understanding of Elizabeth Egerton. The Beinecke witness is not a fragment, though it lacks a title page, a table, several of the verses comprising the "Poems" and "Songs,"[102] and perhaps most dramatically, "The concealed Fansyes," the play comprising the final section of the Bodleian manuscript that has seen print and even performance in this century and that has attracted most critical attention till now of any of Elizabeth Egerton's

---

one of the items put to auction in 1951. Driscoll Catalog No. 13 (1951), describes the manuscript as follows: "Cavendish, Lady Jane. A.Ms.S. Poems. With one long poem by Lady Elizabeth Brackley, her sister. 74 pp., folio. c. 1640. Bound in contemporary morocco, gilt." This description, alas, is partially incorrect, and the Beinecke's own catalog perpetuates the mistake: the manuscript contains two short poems by Elizabeth (also present in the Bodleian witness). The Beinecke catalogue entry reads as follows: "MS. Osborn b.233 Cavendish, Lady Jane [Poems, mid 17th century]. 74 p.; 29 x 19 cm. Autograph manuscript, with one poem by Lady Elizabeth (Cavendish) Egerton, Countess of Bridgewater (ca. 1626–63), her sister. Dedicated to her father, William Cavendish, Duke of Newcastle (1592–1676). English poetry; Cheiney, Lady Jane (Cavendish)."

[101] In their discussions of the miscellany, Ezell and Greer, et al., refer only to the Bodleian witness. Kelliher notes that "A further manuscript, apparently copied in the same hand but comprising the poems and pastoral only, survives in New Haven, Yale University Library, Osborn MS b.233" ("Newcastle Manuscript," 171, n. 55). The hand he tentatively identifies in both witnesses is that of John Rolleston, William Cavendish's long-time secretary, who—Kelliher suggests—may have remained at Welbeck while Cavendish was in exile, although, as Kelliher notes, Rolleston is not named in "The Carecter," a verse (on Bodl. 23; Os. 25) that names other male members of the household at Welbeck. Aside from these very tentative assessments, the relationship between the two witnesses and the dates at which they were transcribed is undetermined. The complete Bodleian copy is far neater, and the hand far more ornamental; the Beinecke witness bears many cancelled lines and contains many blank pages. The manuscript is also discussed by Clarke, et al. ("Margaret Cavendish"), who seem to interpret Kelliher's evaluation less tentatively than I do. In the current text, the transcriptions of extracts follow the Bodleian copy of the manuscript, but the modern page numbers for the extracts are supplied for both witnesses (the first cited page number refers to the Bodleian copy; and page numbers in the Osborn manuscript are designated "Os.")

[102] The Bodleian witness contains the following verses not included in the Beinecke copy: "The angry Curs" (25), "A songe" ["A man and a wife when once they marry"] (26), "The Speakeing Glass" (42), "Loues conflict" (43), "On my Worthy friend Mr Richard Pypes," "On my Worthy freind Mr Haslewood" (44), and "Hopes Still" (45).

writings.[103] Intriguingly, this last section of the Bodleian manuscript may
not have originally been planned as part of the Bodleian miscellany, either.
For on the title page of the Bodleian witness, the word "SONGS" is
followed by a cancelled "and," and following the word "PASTORALL" the
words "and a PLAY" have clearly been squeezed onto the page (Plate 9).
(Or perhaps, if the copyist used the Beinecke witness as copytext, the
section was accidentally elided, initially). The Beinecke manuscript seems
more hastily written than the Bodleian copy, with cancelled lines on several
leaves, and it is certainly less aesthetically pleasing.[104] Yet MS Osborn
b.233 contains two important entries that are lacking in the Bodleian copy:
a preface, signed by Jane Cavendish alone and addressed to William
Cavendish, and an unsigned poem at the end of the manuscript praising her.
Why, one might well ask, does one witness lack a table of contents and a
major entry; why is that entry noted, seemingly as an afterthought, on the
title page of the longer witness; why does the order of a few of the "Poems"
vary in the two manuscripts; and why does the more complete witness lack
several entries? The answer is not the obvious one, for the Beinecke
exemplar is still intact in a contemporary binding. Is it possible that the
Beinecke witness, containing both a dedication by Jane Cavendish to her
father and a final set of verses commending her writing, was copied
hurriedly to be sent to the exiled William Cavendish without the "Play"
(which cast aspersions on his then ongoing courtship of Margaret Lucas)?
That the more carefully copied Bodleian witness, prepared after Cavendish's
return from exile in Rolleston's mature hand, included the play, which was
no longer offensive since Cavendish had long since married Lucas? That it
lacks the dedicatory epistle and the concluding commendatory verses because
these were not an integral part of the contents of the manuscript? Regrettably, these possibilities are merely conjectural; I am unable at this moment

---

[103] Nathan Starr published an old-spelling edition ("The Concealed Fansyes: A Play
by Lady Jane Cavendish and Lady Elizabeth Brackley," *PMLA* 46 [1931]: 802–38); and
more recently, S. P. Cerasano and Marion Wynne-Davies a modern spelling edition
(*Renaissance Drama by Women*, 131–54), following an introduction to the play (127–30);
while Women and Dramatic Production 1570–1670 has produced a video of an actual,
recent production, directed by Alison Findlay and Jane Milling. Studies of the play are
listed in n. 109.

[104] The Bodleian copy contains two tables of contents, one on the last pages (159–62)
in the same hand as the rest of the manuscript, and the second a roughly written, partial
listing (sans page numbers) that was apparently added on pages iii–iv at a later date. The
Beinecke witness lacks any table of contents.

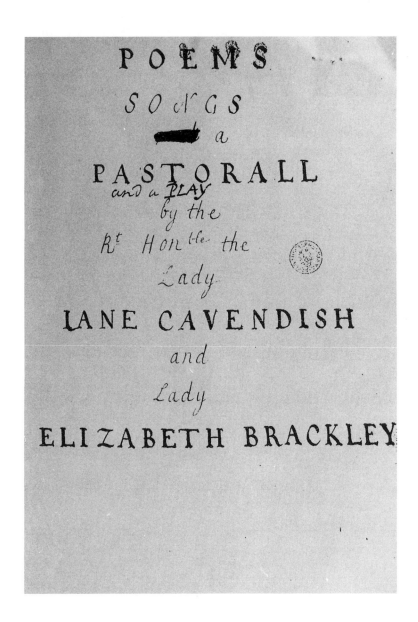

POEMS
SONGS
~~——~~ a
PASTORALL
and a PLAY
by the
Rt Honble the
Lady
JANE CAVENDISH
and
Lady
ELIZABETH BRACKLEY

Plate 9: The title page of Bodleian MS. Rawl. Poet. 16.
Reproduced by permission of The Bodleian Library, Oxford.

to shed further light on the relationship of the two witnesses, on the reasons for the differences in the contents, and on the authorship of some of the individual pieces. I can, however, note some of the major differences between the two witnesses briefly before considering their common contents for the assistance these provide to our understanding of Elizabeth Brackley.

The two manuscripts—the more complete 176 pages and the shorter seventy-four pages—vary at the outset. The miscellany is attributed on the title page of the Bodleian copy to "the Rt. Honble the Lady Jane Cavendish and Lady Elizabeth Brackley," William Cavendish's two older daughters (whose individual contributions, as discussed below, are not always certain).[105] The Beinecke witness, lacking a title page, begins with a dedicatory paragraph (lacking in the Bodleian copy) that establishes the significance of William Cavendish to his daughters, but that, if read literally, would deny Elizabeth Cavendish any part in the miscellany, clearly an error, given the presence of her initials on some of the pages of the pastoral, her signature to one of the prologues, and (in the case of the Bodleian exemplar) her name on the title page (Plate 10):

> My Lord
>
> As nature ownes my creation from you, & my selfe my Education; soe deuty inuites mee to dedicate my workes to you, as the onely Patterne of Judgement, that can make mee happy if these fanceys may owne sense, they wayte vpon your Lor^{pp} as the Center of witt. I humbly thanke yor Lo:^{pp}; & if a distinction of Judgement, God reward your Lo^{p.} For in a word, what I haue of good, is wholly deriued from you, as the soule of bounty and this booke desires noe other purchas, then a smyle from yo:^{ur} Lo^{pp} or a word of Like, wch will glorifie your creature; That is affectionately
>
> > Your Lo^{pps.} Most obliged obedient
> >
> > Daughter
> >
> > Jane Cauendysshe. (Os. 1)

---

[105] Kelliher states merely, "The poems themselves seem to be mostly of Lady Jane's composition. ... Only the pastoral and the play ... are demonstrably joint enterprises, written at Welbeck" ("Newcastle Manuscript," 153). In their unpublished paper ("Margaret Cavendish"), Clarke, Burke, and Coolahan posit (more definitely), "That Jane is the sole author of the poetry." For differences between Ezell and Greer, et al., see 78–79.

Plate 10: Letter addressed by Jane Cavendish to her father.
Page 1 of Osborn MS b.233. Reproduced by permission of the
James Marshall and Marie-Louise Osborn Collection,
The Beinecke Rare Book and Manuscript Library, Yale University.

The Beinecke manuscript ends with a short, unsigned poem addressed to Jane Cavendish that is not present in the Bodleian exemplar (Plate 11):

Vpon the right honourable the Lady Jane Cauendish her booke of verses

> Madam at first I scarsely could beleiue
> That you so wittyly could tyme deceiue
> Or that a garrison your muse durst stay
> When that shee heard the drumms and cannon play
> Shee knew her modest and most innocent straine
> Could with none better then your self remaine
> The Issue of your braine I Lyke soe well
> That whether I shall your other see yett cannot tell
> It hath proue Lyke soe modest chast and witty
> That you should want an equall match t'were pitty[106]

Each section of both manuscripts begins with a dedication to William Cavendish, then "Marquess of Newcastle" (1; Os. 1): the poems and songs, some addressed to members of the family (1–46; Os. 1–41); the pastoral masque, in which individual pages are alternately initialled by each of the two sisters—presumably by the one who authored each page (49–83; Os. 43–76); and in the case of the Bodleian exemplar, the play, followed by epilogues (84–157; lacking in the Osborn manuscript).

Several details help to date the composition of this volume—or at least most of its pages—to the early 1640s, when Elizabeth Cavendish Egerton became a very young bride. That she is styled Lady Brackley, for example, dates the title page (and some verses addressed to her, 11, 19, 22, 28; Os. 13, 21, 24, 28) after her marriage to John Egerton, then Viscount Brackley, on 22 July 1641 at the sumptuous, recently built Newcastle House in Clerkenwell (London) and the adjoining St. James Church (Trease, *Cavalier*, 88).[107] A memorial poem to her mother, Elizabeth Basset (31; Os. 31), was of course written after Basset's death in April 1643. Frequent mentions of the danger William Cavendish is in and references to his absence (e.g., 1, 3, 4, 7, 8, 10, 15, 20, 21, 29, 42, 43, 45; Os. 5, 6, 9, 10, 12, 14, 15, 17, 22,

---

[106] This verse does not follow immediately upon the earlier text, but lies on a page in the midst of many blanks at the end of the manuscript, with the modern pagination "77."

[107] She is styled Brackley throughout the volume, signs pages of "A Pastorall" with the initials "E. B.", and probably most conclusively, signs herself "Elizabeth Brackley" in the dedicatory verses to "A Pastorall" (50; Os. 44).

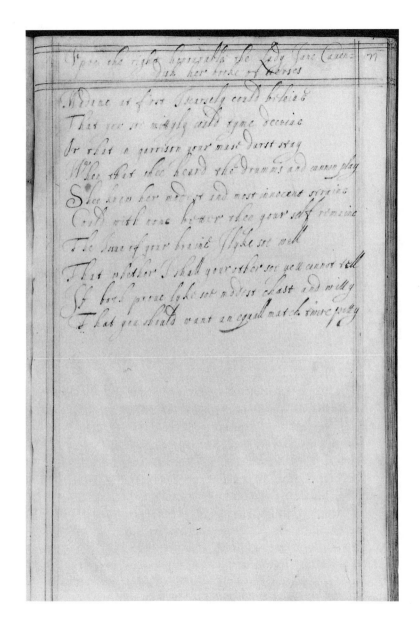

Plate 11: Poem addressed to Jane Cavendish.
Page 77 of Osborn MS b.233. Reproduced by permission of the
James Marshall and Marie-Louise Osborn Collection,
The Beinecke Rare Book and Manuscript Library, Yale University.

29) seem to allude to his military service in the early 1640s; of these, one poem, "On the 30th of June to God" (38; Os. 38), as Greer, et al., note (*Kissing the Rod*, 107), refers to a victory by the royalist forces on 30 June 1643 at Adwalton Moor. References to Cavendish's voyage and landing (4, 7, 8, 15, 41; Os. 6, 9, 10, 17) allude to the period of his exile on the Continent. The play that comprises the concluding section of the manuscript is commonly read as topical: some allusions point to the siege of Welbeck Abbey, the Cavendish seat in which the authors were living during that difficult time, and others seem to express their reactions to Cavendish's courtship of Margaret Lucas in 1645. Since we know that the father and daughters were communicating with each other during this time, it seems plausible that their very title for this drama (as well as the title of their volume as a whole) may have been a play on the "Phanseys" he was at that very time composing for Lucas.[108]

Each of the three portions of this volume provides insights into the inner dynamics of the Cavendish family, and particularly into Cavendish's relationships with the rest of his family. Although records of this closeness appear thoughout, one particularly rich poem, "A recruted joy upon a L're from your Lo^{pp}," expands most helpfully on the joy of the poet on receipt of a letter from her father:

> Thou happy Tuesday since that now I see
> My Fathers hand that happy now I bee
> For in his health, I doe confess I Live
> And soe my prayers I retorneinge giue
> For your sweete gallant selfe for soe you are
> The best of man, & soe all sex will sweare
> Husband, your Loue, unto your wife was such
> As shee, did thinke shee could not Love too much
> For Father, your Children wishes every day
> That in their Life, or death, they truely may
> Your kindnes to deserue, & soe, thus wee
> Our dayes will make to onely studdy thee
> Servants doe say their Loue to you makes feare

---

[108] In "The First Female Dramatists," (*Women and Literature*, ed. Wilcox) 267–89, Ros Ballaster notes that "the term 'fancy' is . . . [Margaret Cavendish's] most frequently cited aesthetic category" (276). This may be yet another indication of the influence of William Cavendish on the women writers in his family.

And soe their service they doe hold most deare
For generall each one may euen truely say
That souldiers soe serue you, not valews pay
For freindship all that knowes you will this owne
That you for trueth of freind doth stand alone
And when you Like in kind for to appeare
Each youths brings you their springes of each sweet yeare
Thus Husband, Father, Maister Louer are
The onely one that is without compare
And soe for Generall, & a faythfull freind
All cheweseth you their fortunes free to Lend
Therefore thou Roman spiritt stand to bee
Example for eternities to see
As patterne for great soules to practize thee
And soe thy selfe will euer valleued bee. (29)

Most scholars who have cited Bodl. MS Rawl. Poet. 16 at all devote their attention to "The concealed Fansyes," the last item in the miscellany, and one that is not included in Beinecke MS Osborn b.233.[109] While it is certainly not my intention to minimize this play's significance, my interest in the manuscript relates to what it can tell us about the Cavendish family and the evolution of Elizabeth Cavendish Egerton as a writer. I shall therefore work backwards through the manuscript, considering only those aspects ger-

---

[109] Among those who have noticed "The concealed Fansyes" are Ballaster, "Female Dramatists"; Nancy Cotton, *Women Playwrights in England, c. 1363–1750* (Newark, Del., and London: Associated Univ. Presses, 1980), 40–41; Margaret J. M. Ezell, *The Patriarch's Wife: Literary Evidence and the History of the Family* (Chapel Hill: Univ. of North Carolina Press, 1987), 67; and " 'To Be Your Daughter' "; Greer, et al., *Kissing the Rod*, 106–18; Alfred Harbage, *Cavalier Drama, An Historical and Cultural Supplement to the Study of the Elizabethan and Restoration Stage* (New York: MLA, 1936), 229; Hopkins, "Teaching *The Concealed Fancies*"; Sophie Tomlinson, " 'My Brain the Stage': Cavendish and the Fantasy of Female Performance," *Women, Texts, & Histories 1575–1760*, eds. Clare Brant and Diane Purkiss (London: Routledge, 1992), 138 and 145; and Wiseman, "Gender and Status." Three other essays on the play are forthcoming: Alison Findlay, "Playing the 'scene self' in Jane Cavendish and Elizabeth Brackley's *The Concealed Fancies*," in *Enacting Gender on the English Renaissance Stage*, eds. Anne Russell and Viviana Comensoli (Urbana: Univ. of Illinois Press); and " 'She gave you the civility of the house': Household Performance in *The Concealed Fancies*," *Readings in Renaissance Women's Drama*, eds. Marion Wynne-Davies and Susan Cerasano (London: Routledge); and Alison Findlay, Gweno Williams, and Stephanie Wright, " 'The Play is Ready to be Acted': Women and Dramatic Production 1570–1670," *Women's Writing*.

mane to study of Egerton of first the play and then the pastoral, and shall end by commenting on the first section, the "Poems and Songs."

§

As commentators have uniformly pointed out, "The concealed Fansyes" seems to be an autobiographical outgrowth from the period of the troubled residence of the Cavendish daughters in a country seat garrisoned by soldiers. The central characters are a number of women of rank whose major preoccupation is the management of their suitors. Two sisters, Lucenay and Tattiney, daughters of Monsieur Calsindow, are usually understood to represent Jane and Elizabeth Cavendish, while three cousins under siege are usually interpreted as the three Cavendish sisters. The flirtatious and designing Lady Tranquillity, courted by Monsieur Calsindow, is believed to represent Margaret Lucas, at that juncture actually courted by Cavendish in France; the threat posed by Tranquillity is eliminated at the end of the play—though not in real life—when she marries the far less exalted Corpolant. While it conveys a sense of the usually carefree existence of women of rank living in the country, the play does not escape the somber touches of military occupation. It also attends—as Nathan Starr first demonstrated ("Concealed")—to a consideration of the position of women in courtship and marriage. Alison Findlay deftly draws attention to the interest of the playwrights (and of the female characters in their play) in "courtship, betrothal, and marriage from a female perspective" ("Playing"). As noted below, given the identification of the actors with the Cavendish sisters, this "enactment of gender," as Findlay terms it, and particularly the conscious tilting by Monsieur Calsindow's daughters at the traditional domestic hierarchy, indeed resonates interestingly with comments about Elizabeth and John Brackley in other parts of Bodl. MS Rawl. Poet. 16.[110] It is clear that the nature of courtship and marriage was a subject deeply of interest to marriageable young aristocratic women like the Cavendish sisters, and one which would particularly have exercised them in the mid-1640s, following

---

[110] Dr. Findlay very generously shared her thought-provoking essay ("Playing") with me before it appeared in print. She argues for a more liberated reading of a portion of Elizabeth Egerton's "Loose Papers" (her "Considerations Concerning Marriage") than I posit in my "Down-Home Bacon, or, a Seventeenth-Century Woman's 'Considerations concerning Marriage,'" in *American Notes & Queries* 5.1–2. [*Renaissance Texts*, ed. Anne Lake Prescott] (1992): 134–37.

the marriage of Elizabeth in 1641 to John Egerton, Lord Brackley, and the courting by their father of a young woman their own age in 1645, after the death of their mother in 1643.

The London theatres had, of course, been closed in 1642. Therefore, the writing by the sisters of a play and of a masque, at a time when the theatres had been closed by parliament, constituted a political statement of loyalty to the royal side, in addition to giving vent to their personal interests in aristocratic marriage and courtship. And, if it was performed, it also participated, as Harbage has noted (*Cavalier Drama*, esp. 191–214), in a continuation of courtly performances in private aristocratic houses during the interregnum (when the court was essentially banished). We might also note that a play like "The concealed Fansyes" on the theme of ideal and married love is an exposition of a constant preoccupation of the royalists who repeatedly honored and celebrated the marriage of Charles and Henrietta Maria,[111] as in the masque by Ben Jonson commissioned by William Cavendish for presentation at Bolsover in 1634 on the occasion of a visit by the royal couple.[112] Harbage believes that "it is nearly certain that among ... groups [of exiles from court] theatricals helped to while away the days of separation and waiting" (*Cavalier Drama*, 207). As explained above, however, in the case of "The concealed Fansyes" (and the other contents of Bodl. MS Rawl. Poet. 16 and of Beinecke MS Osborn b.233), the teen-aged Cavendish sisters, in their father's garrisoned Nottinghamshire seat, were doing more than whiling away idle time; they were living very much under the sword while their estates were literally being seized and released by royalist and parliamentary troops in turn, before being finally taken by parliamentary forces in Novem-

---

[111] This was true of the court masques that aroused the opprobrium of the Puritans, of course, and also of other works connected to the court, like Mary Fage's *Fames Roule* (1637) that cloyingly celebrated the union of Charles and Henrietta Maria, "Carolus-Maria-Stuarte" (sig. B3). Recent additions to the vast literature on Stuart court culture include J.S.A. Adamson, "Chivalry and Political Culture in Caroline England," in *Culture and Politics in Early Stuart England*, eds. Kevin Sharpe and Peter Lake (Stanford: Stanford Univ. Press, 1993), 161–97; Leeds Barroll, "The Court of the First Stuart Queen," in *The Mental World of the Jacobean Court*, ed. Linda Levy Peck (Cambridge: Cambridge Univ. Press, 1991), 191–208; and Caroline Hibbard, "The Role of a Queen Consort: The Household and Court of Henrietta Maria, 1625–1642," in *Princes, Patronage, and the Nobility: The Court at the Beginning of the Modern Age*, eds. Ronald G. Asch and Adolf M. Birke (London: Oxford Univ. Press, 1991), 393–414.

[112] Parry, *Golden Age*, 180–81.

ber 1645.[113] While they were not bereft of male attendants (23; Os. 25), the sisters were also without (what one would assume to be) the comforting presence of their father and brothers who had left the country in July 1644, and their writing certainly merits the description by Germaine Greer, et al., as "the work of two brave young women, who cannot conceal [one might note—who indeed make no attempt to conceal] their desperate longing for their father's return or their distrust of the unknown woman he married."[114]

Consideration of these precise circumstances may lead to some enlightenment about the creation and production of the play, a largely speculative issue over which scholars disagree and about which I would like to proffer a new suggestion. The known facts can be summarized briefly: In July 1644 Cavendish left his daughters under the protection of royalist troops at Welbeck Abbey. By mid-August 1644 the Parliamentarians had taken control of both Welbeck and Bolsover Castle (Cavendish's seat in Derbyshire), at which time Edward earl of Manchester wrote to the Committee of Both Kingdoms that he found it "very regularly fortified; and the Marquis of Newcastle's daughters and the rest of his children and family are in it, unto whom I have engaged myself for their quiet abode there, and to intercede to the Parliament for a complete maintenance for them."[115] There was a brief period, from July 1645 till—at latest—November, when the estate was again under royalist control, and during which, on 15–17 August and on 13 October, Charles I stopped there. In mid-November 1645 Welbeck was again in Parliamentarian hands, and Bolsover was ordered destroyed. At this juncture, Elizabeth Brackley may have removed to Ashridge,[116] a former

---

[113] Cerasano and Wynne-Davies believe that [t]he play exists . . . at a point of transition. It . . . paid lip service to a devalued court ideology, but . . . cannot help but represent the authors' sense of loss, as well as their sharp disillusionment" (*Renaissance Drama by Women*, 130).

[114] There seems to be a minor error in this chronology: as Greer, et al., note, the estate was "finally given up to Parliamentarian forces in November and disgarrisoned by mutual agreement" (*Kissing the Rod*, 107). However, the marriage of William Cavendish and Margaret Lucas took place later, in December 1645.

[115] *Calendar of State Papers Domestic Series—Charles I*: 6 August 1644. An earlier record exists in the *Calendar* of Jane's communications with the royalist military leadership (21 April 1644) and another of the daughters' salvaging of family plate (University of Nottingham, Portland Collection Pw 1 367 & 368). Starr ("Concealed") quotes yet another letter from Jane and Frances Cavendish, dated 17 April 1645, in which the "humble service" of their "sister Brackley" is presented to Fairfax.

[116] 9 November 1646, the birthdate of her oldest child, John, later third earl of Bridgewater, establishes that she took up residence with her husband close to the end of

monastery and royal residence straddling the border of Hertfordshire and Buckinghamshire (granted in 1605 to Sir Thomas Egerton), that served as the seat of the large Egerton family (Plate 12).[117]

It is at this point that the evidence becomes particularly spotty. The whereabouts of Elizabeth's unmarried sisters, Jane and Frances Cavendish, after this time, are uncertain.[118] Starr speculates that they were unlikely to have remained at Welbeck without Elizabeth and may have removed to Ashridge with their sister ("Concealed," 804).[119] A later document by Jane Cavendish concerning "2 pare of holland sheets which I used to lie in at Welbeck, I brought with mee to Ashridge, & from thens to Chellsey [her home after marriage]" has been located (HN MS EL 11143) and cited by Greer, et al., (*Kissing the Rod*, 107), and does, in fact, suggest that the two may have accompanied their sister to Ashridge at this time. Starr further speculates that "The concealed Fansyes" may have been written at Ashridge during a hypothetical visit there of the Cavendish sisters in 1646, when, "to pass time which must have hung heavily on their hands, and perhaps to amuse the old Earl of Bridgewater, [they] dashed off a Comedy" ("Concealed," 836). He also posits a performance of the play at Ashridge.

As to dating, Starr ("Concealed") takes the expansive view that Elizabeth Brackley would have been styled countess of Bridgewater on the title page of the manuscript had it been completed after 1649 (when her husband succeeded his father as second earl of Bridgewater), and that the play therefore can be dated no more precisely than between 1642 (when she became

---

1645. Trease states (*Cavalier*, 114) that Elizabeth was away from Welbeck in 1643. One cannot know the basis for this assumption since he does not give his source. Possibly he merely assumed that as a married woman she had removed to her husband's home. But he seems to be mistaken in this case, since the evidence cited earlier in this text establishes her presence there.

[117] The second earl had fourteen siblings, ten of whom survived into adulthood. For histories of Ashridge, see Samuel Egerton Brydges, "History of Ashridge Abbey, Bucks," *The Topographer* 12 (March 1790) No. 3 of Vol. 2: 131–54; also Henry John Todd, *History of the College of Bonhommes, at Ashridge.*

[118] Both, however, are known to have been married in 1654, Jane to Charles Cheyne, Esquire, later Viscount Newhaven, and Frances to Oliver St. John, later second earl of Bolingbroke. It was in 1654 that William Cavendish's older brother, Sir Charles, died, having willed his estates to his nephew to be held for the exile. Given matrimonial economics, this bequest may have facilitated the marriages of Cavendish's two daughters.

[119] In an otherwise persuasive argument about the play, Cerasano and Wynne-Davies mistakenly consider this "an unnecessary hypothesis, since there is clear evidence to show that Elizabeth and Jane were living together at Welbeck, while none exists to link them to Ashridge" (*Renaissance Drama by Women*, 127).

Plate 12: Ashridge. From the March 1790 issue of *The Topographer* (Shelf-mark 982.d.3–6), facing page 131. Reproduced by permission of The British Library.

Lady Brackley, as she is styled throughout the manuscript) and 1649 (when she became countess of Bridgewater). Cerasano and Wynne-Davies reject this expansive hypothesis, noting, surely correctly, that "it is clear from the contemporary allegory that the play was written, and probably performed, before Newcastle remarried in December 1645." They further object to Starr's "romanticized version of events [which] transfers the authors from their isolated imprisonment at Welbeck, which certainly demanded both independent fortitude and ingenuity ... [so that] the play itself becomes a recreational pursuit devised for the amusement of others" (*Renaissance Drama by Women*, 128–29). Since, as Starr notes, at least portions of Bodl. MS Rawl. Poet. 16 were written in collaboration, and since (as already shown) events in it cannot be dated past that month, I suggest November 1645 as a likely *terminus ad quem* for composition of the volume. I think, along the lines suggested by Cerasano and Wynne-Davies, that the ending of the play, with Lady Tranquillity (by general agreement an unflattering representation of Margaret Lucas) marrying not Monsieur Calsindow (by general consent, a representation of William Cavendish) but Corpolant, a person of much lower degree, would hardly have been penned after the marriage of Cavendish and Lucas, and that the *terminus ad quem* is therefore November 1645, before their wedding. I agree with Starr "that the siege in Act III must reflect directly the course of events at Welbeck in 1644–45" ("Concealed," 836). Like Cerasano and Wynne-Davies, I believe that "the play was written, and probably performed, before Newcastle remarried in December 1645, and that this would suggest a date commensurate with the sisters' residency at Welbeck" (*Renaissance Drama by Women*, 127).

Finally, I advance yet another possibility—similarly wholly speculative—that Charles's first visit to Welbeck in 1645, from 15–17 August, may have provided the occasion for a performance of "The concealed Fansyes": such entertainments were, after all, courtly and wholly in the tradition of regal entertainment familiar to the Cavendish sisters, and the topical allusions to Cavendish's courtship of Margaret Lucas also fit this time frame, as noted earlier. I think that the suggestion of a performance for Charles and his entourage during his first visit at Welbeck in August 1645 is at least as plausible as the notion of one for the first earl of Bridgewater, then mourning his dead at Ashridge. While a determined search has yielded no allusions to a performance during Charles's first visit, it has shown clearly that Charles was greatly refreshed by his visit.[120] Given the history of royal entertain-

---

[120] During what was to become a tiring, dangerous period of marches to evade his

ments by the Cavendish family, the possibility that the sisters would have ventured to perform the play for him is not unlikely.

Whatever the specific occasion of its composition and performance, the writing of a play also participated in the Cavendish family tradition. William Cavendish's verses to his daughters concerning the masque he had written demonstrate that, as Harbage notes, he had himself composed comedies in pre-civil war days which were performed and which "anticipate the actual atmosphere of Restoration comedy of manners" (*Cavalier Drama*, 74). "The concealed Fansyes" therefore demonstrates the general filial feeling and intellectual indebtedness to William Cavendish of the other materials in Bodl. MS Rawl. Poet. 16 (and Beinecke MS Osborn b.233). I think it is reasonable to posit even more direct influence than this. In addition to scattered references to and poems about William Cavendish throughout the compilation, each section of the manuscript is introduced and ended by verses addressed to Cavendish by his daughters. Cerasano and Wynne-Davies, excerpting lines from "In perticuler to your ᴸᵒʳᵖᵖᵉ," the final epilogue of "The concealed Fansyes," note, surely correctly, that this verse "calls for his [Cavendish's] approval" (*Renaissance Drama by Women*, 129). Given the circumstances of composition, with Cavendish abroad and his daughters

---

Parliamentary pursuers, Charles twice stopped at Welbeck. His second stay, on 13 October, was barely a reprieve, and surely not a rest. But during his first stop of 1645, from 15–17 August, Charles does not seem to have yet realized that he had lost the game. And in fact events just might have evolved differently, though his chances were already slim. Clarendon reports that Charles "with very little rest passed through Shropshire and Derbyshire, till he came to Welbeck, a house of the marquis of Newcastle in Nottinghamshire, where was then a garrison for his majesty; where he refreshed himself, and his troops, two days" (*History of the Rebellion* [Oxford: Clarendon Press, 1827], 4: 1989). The stop at Welbeck in August was unquestionably a very heartening one. Among the documents listed in the *CSPD—Charles I*, dated between 15–17 August 1645, is "The King's proclamation of grace and pardon to all such of the county and of the city of York as shall submit to his Majesty's mercy and return to their allegiance." Dated 17 August, this proclamation is most tellingly addressed from "Our Court at Welbeck," a signal, to my mind, that Charles was feeling very much at ease by the end of his stay at the Cavendish seat. A letter dated 18 August that Charles sent to Sir Edward Nicholas from Doncaster confirms this impression: "Nicholas," he writes, "I haue sent this bearer expresly to giue you a particular account of my present condition, wᶜʰ considering what it was at the beginning of this monthe, is now (I thanke God) miraculously good" (*Diary of John Evelyn*, ed. William Bray [London: Bickers and Son, 1906], 4: 169). Neither Clarendon nor any other of the contemporary sources that I have examined mentions a bagatelle like an amateur performance by the Cavendish sisters, but it seems to me—in light particularly of the history of regal entertainments at Welbeck—no less extravagant a possibility than Starr's hypothetical performance at Ashridge for the earl of Bridgewater.

under siege, I think such verses suggest more than the fact that Cavendish was expected to read and pronounce on the play and that his approval was very important to his daughters:

> Lu: Now since your Excellence hath thought it fitt
> Ta: To stay a three howres Comedy of sitt
> Lu: And soe but speake of it as Like
> Ta: Then are our Sceanes euen happy in your sight
> Lu: And though wee haue, smyles & hats if yo^u dislike
> Ta: Wear'e totally condemned, for to night. (156)

> Haue you now read my Lord, pray doe not speake
> For I'm already growne, soe faint & weake
> Not knoweing how you will now sensure mee
> As rash to thinke, noe witt a present bee
> But if you Like not, I pray Let mee knowe
> The Pen and Inke shall haue a fatall blowe
> If you not pleas'd, it will impression make
> In my vaine selfe, for indiscretion sake
> But if you Like you will mee Cordyall giue
> And soe as witty, I shall euer Liue. (157)

Direct addresses of this type suggest to me that composition of this manuscript was thoroughly connected to Cavendish, and may perhaps even have been suggested by him to his daughters as a way of distracting them from the danger of their situation and of helping them to maintain a sense of connection with him at this stressful time. It seems, in other words, a direct continuation of the earlier compositions (among the Cavendish family papers now housed at Nottingham) that Cavendish had assigned his daughters as children and that were noted above.

One other feature of this play merits notice: the prologues. The third prologue, a direct address to Cavendish, falls within the bounds of the epilogues considered above. The first two, however, address the propriety of a woman's public speech. It is fascinating that the Cavendish sisters express an awareness and anticipation of the outrage their auditors might experience and pronounce on this form of "public speech."[121] When we remember

---

[121] Wiseman does not mention the prologues in her otherwise interesting comments on the play and pastoral, and while it is true, as she states, that we do not have a "cast list" and therefore that "they [i.e., non-existent cast lists] cannot be the basis for a full

the prologues that Aphra Behn was to compose *after* the Restoration on this very subject, one is almost forced to acknowledge a general concern over women's public speech and public place.[122] The later intra-familial reactions to Margaret Cavendish's publications and publicity-seeking behavior by women of the Cavendish family also take on another light when we recognize that these women had, in fact, a strong, conventional sense of decorum:

> A Prologe to the Stage
> Ladyes I beseech you blush not to see
> That I speake a Prologe being a Shee
> For, it becomes as well if votes cry Ey
> Why then should I, a Petticote cry fye,
> Gentlemen if soe you allow; is witt
> Why then not speake, I pray your patience sitt
> And now to tell you trueth of our new Play
> It doth become a womans witt the very way
> And I did tell the Poett plainely trueth
> It Looks like 18. or .22. youth
> Or els it could not bee, as t'is but well
> I'le say noe more untill yor hands Playes tell

> The second Prologe spoke by a Woman.
> Though a second Prologe spoke to our Play
> I will speake trueth, 'tis woman all ye way
> For you'll not see a Plott in any Act
> Nor any ridged, high, ignoble fact
> Feareing you'll sensure mee now full of Tongue
> It is not fitt, that I should speake too longe. (87)

> A perticuler Prologe to your Lor^{pp}.
> My Lord

argument about women's acting during the Interregnum" ("Gender and Status," 163), these prologues demonstrate that women did indeed act in the private theatre of that period.
  [122] See, for example, the "Epistle to the Reader" in Behn's *Dutch Lover* (1673); the "prologe, Spoken by Mrs Gwin" to her *Sir Patient Fancy* (1678); and the "Preface" to *The Lucky Chance* (1687). In "Teachng *The Concealed Fancies*," Hopkins comments aptly on the closeness of these comments to Rosalind's epilogue (5, 4, 198–209) in *As You Like It* (London: Methuen, 1975), and to comments in dramas by some of Shakespeare's contemporaries (400–1).

If that your iugement doth approve of mee,
I pray you smile, that all may truely see,
You Like, & doe approve, of what wee say,
And then each one will freely give their pay.
If then your quicker witt doth crowne our Play
Your health shalbee our word today. (88)

As this last prologue clearly shows, the writing of "The concealed Fansyes" participates in the general demonstrations of filial feeling and of intellectual indebtedness to William Cavendish of the other materials in Bodl. MS Rawl. Poet. 16.

§

Within the last decade, Germaine Greer, et al., have published parts of the highly topical penultimate section of Bodl. MS Rawl. Poet. 16, "A Pastorall," preceded by masque and antimasque (*Kissing the Rod*, 109–15). Among features of interest are witches, introduced in the masque and antimasque, who confess to creating a mayhem clearly connected to that in the England of civil-war days. We are left to wonder whether, as the authors cleverly suggest, these witches delude themselves into a sense of agency ("our pride to our selues makes us thinke wee are Actours") or whether, as one hag, Bell, insists, their "mischeife made warr, and that a miserable one, to make Brother hate brother," and "Lords wee send beyond Seas at our pleasure" (52; Os. 46). But one insinuation is clear: the civil war, because of which the authors' own father has been sent (beyond seas), is hellish. Since, as Harbage and Greer, et al., have noted, the scenes in the masque and antimasque introducing the pastoral are initialled by each sister, persumably to indicate authorship, we know that these lines are Jane Cavendish's.

As in the last part of the manuscript, in "A Pastorall," too, evidence abounds of the perceived presence of Cavendish, in signed prologues and concluding verses addressed to him by both his daughters. Jane Cavendish, for example, writes before the pastoral (and—the reader is reminded—following the section of Poems and Songs):

My Lord

After the deuty, of a Verse,
Give Leave now to rehearse;
A Pastorall; then if but giue

Your smile, I sweare I Liue,
In happynes; ffor if this may
Your fauour have, t'will ne're decay
Now Let my Language speake, & say
If you bee pleas'd I haue my pay.

That passionately am

Your Lo:^{pps}

most affectionate and obedient

Daughter

Jane Cavendysshe. (49; Os. 43)

Her sister (our subject) states:

My Lord

This Pastorall could not owne weake
But my intrest which makes mee speake.
To begg you'l not condemn the best
For th'ill: but chase it, to it rest
Where I shall owne the word submitt
Vnto your Judgement of pure witt.

Your Lo^{pps} most affectionate

and obliged

Daughter

Elizabeth Brackley. (50; Os. 44)

It takes no great skill to unravel the pastoral. Three shepherdesses (a.k.a. Jane, Elizabeth, and Frances Cavendish), wooed by three shepherds, are too desolated by the absence of their father and brothers to be able to entertain their would-be lovers' suits. As if to underline the unity of tone of the entire volume, some of the lines are repeated from earlier pages in the first section of the manuscript. There is perhaps room to note one other allusion of particular interest in lines spoken by one shepherdess to another: "You owne your selfe," she says, "to bee a wife / And yet you practice not that Life" (73; Os. 65). These lines, which fall on a page bearing Elizabeth Brackley's initials, presumably refer to Elizabeth Brackley, married but—as her redoubtable stepmother would later inform us—"too young to be bedded" (*Life*, 95) and therefore living still on her father's estate in 1644/45.

The pastoral ends with verses from both J.C. and E.B.
J.C. writes,

> My Lord it is your absence makes each see
> For want of you what I'm reduc'd to bee
> Captiue or Sheppardesses Life
> Giues envy leave to make noe strife
> Soe what becomes mee better then
> But to bee your Daughter in your Penn
> If you're now pleased I care not what
> Becomes of mee, or what's my Lott
> Now if you Like, I then doe knowe
> I am a Witt, but then pray' whisper't Low.

E.B.'s verse is briefer:

> My Lord your absence makes I cannot owne,
> My selfe to thinke I am alone
> Yet sheppardesses can see to read
> And soe upon your stock of wit I feede
> Soe beggs your blessing to Like this
> Then am I crown'd wth hight of bliss. (84; Os. 76)

§

Bodl. MS Rawl. Poet. 16 (and Beinecke MS Osborn b.233) are character-ized throughout by a uniformly courtly tone in which idealized pronounce-ments or portrayals are made of persons or situations. The tone is con-gratulatory; criticism is nonexistent. Dissonance is hinted at in the masque and antimasque which touch on civil disorder; and a mournful tone is intro-duced only in commemorating deceased relatives and in worry over the safety of the absent William Cavendish. Although the abundant personal entries perhaps detract from Margaret Ezell's evaluation of the manuscript as a "pub-lic proclamation," I agree with her assessment that the contents are "patterns of abstract values" and the whole a statement "reaffirming bonds between members of a threatened society" (" 'To Be Your Daughter,' " 285–87).

The quality of the verses in the first part of Bodl. MS Rawl. Poet. 16 is not higher than in the rest of the manuscript: some verses are sprightly and refreshing, others turgid. The sentiments, though, are of a piece with the courtly, even idealized sentiments of the pastoral and play: there are many celebrations of William Cavendish—his person, his manner, his courage, his writings; of other members of the Cavendish family and of the royal family. There are commentaries on imaginary occasions and on significant contemporary events and the general turn of affairs, pronouncements on idealized, courtly subjects like friendship and nobility, and less frequently on such light subjects as "On the least finger of hir hand" (14; Os. 16). Alternately, there are solemn, frightened, and hopeful verses about the safety of William Cavendish: "Great God and universe I pray bee true / All these I doe invoke, to safe land you" (4; Os. 6). There are also occasionally proud descriptions of his courtliness and attractiveness: "My Lord your Picture speakes you this to bee, / A Courtier & a souldier each may see" (4; Os. 6). This last was composed, the title suggests, on receipt of a sketch of Cavendish ("The trueth of Pensell" 4; Os. 6), as other verses are occasioned on receipt of a letter from Cavendish or in response to his "Sayter" [i.e., satire].

Therefore, despite extensive personal and topical allusions in the second and third parts of Bodl. MS Rawl. Poet. 16, it is the first section of "Poems and Songs" that is richest for reconstruction of Cavendish family dynamics. Local references and subjects are legion and are undisguised. Beginning (not unexpectedly) with two prefatory poems to the Marquis of Newcastle ("The Greate Example" and "Passions Le^tre to my Lord my father" 1; Os. 3), the verses are also addressed to and concern virtually every member of the extended Cavendish family (both living and dead!): the authors' "sweete brother Charles" [Viscount Mansfield, d. 1659] and "sweete brother Henry" [later earl of Ogle and second duke of Newcastle, d. 1691] (2; Os. 4); "Noble Uncle Sir Charles Cavendysh Knight" [d. 23 Feb 1653/4] (3; Os. 5); "sweete Nephew Henry Harpur" (10; Os. 12);[123] "sweete Sister Brackley" [Elizabeth Cavendish, our author] (11; Os. 13); "sweete Sister Fraunces" [Frances Cavendish, later countess of Bolingbroke, d. 15 August 1678], wife of Oliver St. John; most significantly, "the Peart one, or otherwise, my Sister Brackley" (11; Os. 13); and "the Lord Viscount Brackley" [John Egerton, later second earl of Bridgewater] (19; Os. 21); "Noble Grandfather, Sir Charles Cavendysh" [paternal grandfather, d. 1617] (30; Os. 30); "Lady Ogle my deare Grandmother" [Katherine, baroness Ogle, second wife of Sir Charles, d.1629] (30; Os. 30); "My deare mother the Countess of Newcastle" [Elizabeth Basset, d. 1643] and "deare brothers and sister" (30; Os.

---

[123] Son of their half-sister, Elizabeth (daughter of Elizabeth Basset and Henry Howard, her first husband) who married Sir John Harpur of Swarkston in Derbyshire (Collins, *Peerage*, 1: 318).

31); "Grandfather Mr Basset" [William Basset, great-grandfather] (32; Os. 34);[124] "Grandmother the Lady Corbett" (32; Os. 32);[125] "sweet Sister the Lady Harpur" (32; Os. 32); "Gilbert Earl of Shrewsbury" [seventh earl of Shrewsbury, son of their great-grandmother and husband of their great-aunt, Mary Cavendish, 1553–1616] and "Hon:[ble] Aunt Mary Countes of Shrewsbury" [wife of Gilbert, d. 1632] (33; Os. 33); "good Aunt Jane Countes of Shrewsbury" (34; Os. 34);[126] "good and true freind M[r] Henry Ogle

---

[124] Determined search has yielded only sparse information about William Basset, the maternal grandfather of the Cavendish sisters, and what little has emerged is somewhat contradictory. The second husband of their maternal grandmother, the Lady Corbet (who is also memorialized by them), he was styled 'Esquire' (i.e., Gentleman); he is usually said to have resided in Blore, Staffordshire; and he was very wealthy (since his daughter is invariably styled an heiress). The following epitaph ("Vpon a Tombe att Bloore in Staffordshire as aBoue" [sic]) is preserved among the papers in the Portland Collection at the University of Nottingham (Portland Collection Pw 1 654):

> Here lyes a Courtier Souldier handsom Good
> Witty wise valient and of Pure Blood
> from Willams Conquest and his potent sword
> in the Sam lyn Many a Noble lord
> That tim: hath lost in paying thus Deaths Sett
> as this unparaleld William Basset
> But thy High virtues with thy antient nam
> Shall Ouer Swell the cheekes of Glorious fam

In the one printed source I have found to depict the Basset arms, a source in which a family tree shows him married to Judith Austen (later Lady Corbet), he is, however, styled as William Basset of Fole, county Stafford, grandson of "[Sir] Will. Basset of Blore [and] Grendon [in Com. Stafford] & Langley [in Com. Derby]," (*Staffordshire Pedigrees Based on the Visitation of that county made by William Dugdale esquire, Norroy King of Arms in the years 1663–1664*, ed. Sir George Armytage and W. Harry Rylands [London: Harleian Society, 1912], 63: 19–20). *The Visitacion of Staffordshire, A.D. 1583* (ed. H. Sydney Grazebrook, Esq. [London, 1883]) identifies two grandsons of Sir William, both a William Basset of Blore and one of Fole as "nowe livinge, 1583" (45), but gives no information that could indicate which was Elizabeth Basset's father. Goulding states in his *Catalogue* that Basset "died at Blore, 9 December 1601" (363). He also mentions that Elizabeth Basset, mother of Elizabeth Egerton, "is represented in a kneeling posture" on Basset's tomb (363).

[125] Daughter of Sir Thomas Austen of Oxley, Judith Austen (ca. 1580–28 August 1640), the mother of Elizabeth Basset, married three times: first William Boothby, second William Basset (the father of Elizabeth Basset), and last Sir Richard Corbet, a member of the Middle Temple. (*International Genealogical Index* [Salt Lake City, Utah: Church of Jesus Christ of Latter-Day Saints, 1981–]; *Burke's . . . Peerage and Baronetage*, 105th edition [London: Burke's Peerage, Ltd., 1975], 641). Goulding notes that she and Basset married "in May 1598" (363).

[126] Jane Ogle Talbot (d. 1625/6) was the daughter of Cuthbert Ogle, seventh lord

[uncle, d. 1635]" (34; Os. 32);[127] and "Hon:^ble Grandmother, Elizabeth Countess of Shrewsbury" [actually their great-grandmother, Bess of Hardwick, d. 1608] (35; Os. 35). The sentimentality that pervades this section is underlined when we recognize that many of the persons named and addressed were already dead. Knowing the threatening circumstances in which these poems were written, poems to such personages seem almost a species of invocation, a harking back to memories of less threatened times, an emotional hugging by the sisters of those who protected them.

Given the hint from earlier documents that Elizabeth had been a timid child, her characterization here as "peart," meaning "lively, brisk, sprightly, active, clever, intelligent, sharp of comprehension,"[128] takes on particular interest. The altogether positive description of Elizabeth blends liveliness and quieter virtues. She is the "quinticence, of beauty, goodnes, trueth"; she is "pritty, younge and witty ... fitt for nothinge, but a Citty"; indeed, she "for wiues ... [is] the onely syse" (11; Os. 13); her "natures onely fitt for Casars wife" (19; Os 21). She "can tell, how to bee free and wise," and, in sum, is "pritty, faire, & witty, to bee kised" (11; Os. 13). But her beautiful face reveals "the trueth of vertues booke" (19; Os 21). Interestingly, "The sweetnes of [her] ... face may euen controll / Our weakest Animall or Liueinge soule" (19; Os. 21). Descriptions of her are complemented by lines about her new husband, John Egerton, the subject of one verse, "On the Lord Viscount Brackley" (19, Os. 21). Brackley is a "Patterne," who "desire[s] but your wife to kisse, / ... wise, & that our Sex doe Loue, / A loueinge Mate, ... iust Like a Doue." Clearly, then, Elizabeth Egerton was not reduced at her marriage to the nullity we associate with the pitifully subordinated wife, but we note that the possibilities of ranging are associated with her new husband (who does not, as it happens, take them up), and therefore the greater restrictions applied to married women are lightly suggested here. If we sense the continued hold over a husband sketched by the Cavendish daughters in "The concealed Fansyses" (as Findlay argues in "Playing"), we

---

Ogle, and the wife of Edward Talbot, eighth earl of Shrewsbury (1560/1–1617/8), brother of the seventh earl.

[127] Mr. Henry Ogle was one of the Ogles of Kirkley, a collateral branch of the family of Katherine Ogle, William Cavendish's mother. In the early seventeenth century, Ogle acted as trustee of the estate of William's parents (Turberville, *Welbeck Abbey*, 16). Henry Ogle died on 23 December 1635 at the advanced age of 76 years, and was commemorated in verse by William Cavendish.

[128] *Oxford English Dictionary*, eds. James A. H. Murray, Henry Bradley, W. A. Craigie, C. T. Onions (Oxford: Clarendon Press, 1961), 7: 594.

do not find any suggestion that the comic inversions of the play were en-
acted by Elizabeth and John Brackley. Instead, there is movement towards
the subordinated position even a cherished wife would hold in a seventeenth-century aristocratic household. Above suspicion, endowed with fine
parts, she is "fitt for Casars wife," a moon to his sun.

Verses are also addressed to unnamed, occasionally "noble" or "worthy" or
"honourable" acquaintances (possibly sometimes imaginary and certainly
idealized): to the "sacred" king, queen, and Prince of Wales, to a number of
"worthy" friends, and in two cases, to a chambermaid, these last fellow "in-
mates," one assumes, at Welbeck. The cumulative effect is of a sense of deep
embeddedness in a family and social order about which the poets express
great pride. The brief verse on the recently deceased Elizabeth Basset ("On
my deare mother the Countess of Newcastle"), paged together with a memorial verse on four Cavendish brothers and a sister who did not live to ma-
turity, merits quotation in full in this connection:

> I had a mother which to speake was such
> That would you prayse, you could not prayse too much
> For what of woman could bee perfect Lov'd
> But shee was that, & the true side of good
> Then in a word shee was the quinticence of best
> And now sweete Saint, thy happy soule's at rest. (31)

As noted earlier, verses addressed to and verses about William Cavendish
are also interspersed throughout this section, witnessing his centrality to his
daughters even in his physical absence. Clearly no blame attached to his
leaving them behind in July 1644 when he embarked for France; they were,
after all, protected by royalist troops. Their concern for him, rather than for
themselves, is a recurring theme, as in "Passions Contemplation": "The fire
makes mee on a battle thinke / Seeinge you deepe ingaged, I then doe
winke / Water doth make mee justly for to see / Your selfe att S'ea I weepe-
ing teares for thee" (4; Os. 6). In fact, some verses imply that Cavendish
had left on command: "But now our Kinge calls you a way / I pray thee
come, & make noe stay" ("A Songe," 10; Os. 12). This is certainly not the
commonly held understanding of Cavendish's exile, which was unpopular in
some quarters (as we know from Pepys' comments). Perhaps these verses
reflect a layer of intrigue that has not come down to us; his second wife also
celebrates his wartime behavior, and his "loyalty" *was* widely recognized. (Of
course, Cavendish may also have misrepresented his behavior to his female
dependents.)

Greer, et al., Kelliher, and Ezell have commented on the first portion of the manuscript within the last decade, although only Kelliher seems to be aware of the existence of the Beinecke witness. There is a difference of opinion among them concerning the authorship of its contents, however, a difference worth considering at length because it is germane to this study. Greer, et al., claim (without, however, providing either a reason or substantiation) that "[a]ll the occasional poems" in Bodl. MS Rawl. Poet. 16 are by Jane Cavendish" (*Kissing the Rod*, 116).[129] Kelliher comments more moderately: "The poems themselves seem to be mostly of Lady Jane's composition. ... Only the pastoral and the play ... are demonstrably joint enterprises, written at Welbeck" ("Newcastle Manuscript," 153). In contrast, Ezell notes that "since the individual pieces, with the exception of the scenes in the pastoral, were not signed, the volume suggests a collaborative and cooperative effort rather than pieces of individual workmanship. This implies the authors did not seem to have felt much anxiety over being recognized, or not, for individual literary accomplishments. Poetry here is not the unique, original product of a lone artistic soul; with only a few exceptions, the poems do not 'belong' to an individual" ("'To Be Your Daughter,'" 284). This is an important issue, but Ezell is doing more than attributing the poems, as well as the pastoral and play, to both sisters. It is on the more general issue of private and public authorship that she is focusing: "[t]his seemingly casual approach to authorship, infuriating to modern editors, is not necessarily a modest gender characteristic. One need think only of the efforts required to untangle the lyrics of the Sons of Ben or the later Restoration court poets to recognize that a larger issue of attitudes toward authorship and audience is involved" (ibid.). (Of course, as Anne Lake Prescott has mentioned to me, untangling joint authorship in the drama is even more spectacular.) Ezell is making the important point that Bodl. MS Rawl. Poet. 16 is not merely a private document, but that it is also like the manuscripts of "gentleman-amateurs" of the time who composed for and circulated their works among "coterie readers."[130] That the readers of

---

[129] Though I don't think the point is proven by the imprecise signals in the manuscripts themselves, the fact that none of the verses directed to family members (in the first part) are addressed to Jane is a lacuna that could suggest she was the sole author of these verses and of course did not write to herself. The dedication to William Cavendish is also signed only by Jane. However, the pastoral and play are patently by Elizabeth and Jane both.

[130] In "'To Be Your Daughter'" (284), Ezell cites Arthur F. Marotti, "Women and

these manuscripts would include members of the Cavendish family and that William Cavendish himself would judge them certainly does not reduce the level of this audience to that, say, of the friendly auditors at a kindergarten recital; Cavendish and his family, as already noted, were discriminating readers themselves, and were intimately associated with the important literary figures of his time.

These associations, we might note, did not end for the Cavendish children after they left their childhood home. Among a plethora of proofs of continued interaction with such figures is a poem by Davenant on the marriage (in 1654) of the Lady Jane Cheyne, Cavendish's oldest surviving daughter,[131] who would herself compose a poem on her sister Elizabeth's death.[132] And Lady Jane's own death would be memorialized by Richard Flecknoe and Thomas Lawrence.[133] In sum, although William Caven-

---

the Manuscript System," 48–61, in his *Manuscript, Print, and the English Renaissance Lyric* (Ithaca, N.Y.: Cornell Univ. Press, 1995), who describes the many ways in which early modern Englishwomen participated in manuscript culture. In *The Patriarch's Wife*, interested in demonstrating that the activities of seventeenth-century women writers were not necessarily different from those associated with male writers, Ezell characterizes Bodl. MS Rawl. Poet. 16 as "a charming collection of . . . literary efforts designed strictly to entertain," containing "types of items . . . comparable in nature to the amateur verse and dramas composed by other lively young wits such as Henry King and Dudley, Lord North. . . . There is no textual evidence that either of these books was meant to be read by those outside a circle of friends and relatives, yet the books' contents demonstrate that these young women, as much as the young men, were actively engaged in literary activities, exploring the literary conventions and forms of their day, and believing that their final productions were worth preservation in formal, bound copies so that in the future others might read them" (67). That a second copy was made underlines this point.

[131] In a section of his *Works* (1673), with the separate title page *Poems on Several Occasions, Never before Printed* (1672), 293–94:

"Upon the Marriage of the Lady Jane Cavendish with Mr. Cheney."
Why from my thoughts, sweet rest; sweeter to me,
Then young Ambition's prosp'rous Travails be,
    Or Love's delicious progresses;
    And is next Death the greatest ease?
Why from so calme a Heav'n,
Dost call me to this World, all windy grown;
    Where the light Crowd, like lightest Sand is driven,
And weighty greatness, even by them, to Air is blown?

[132] Held in facsimile at the Huntington as HN MS EL 8353, "On the death of my Deare Sister the Countesse of Bridgewater dying in Childbed, Delivered of a dead Infant a Son, the 14:th day of June 1663."

[133] Flecknoe (d. 1678), a protégé of Newcastle's, commemorated her in his *Epigrams*

dish's daughters—and, as we have already noted, his granddaughter as well—consciously eschewed the notoriety associated with Margaret Cavendish, they did not eschew the act of composition. Moreover, their contrasting references to her lack of conformity and their own quieter mode of composition underlines the association of such continued creativity with early Cavendish family roots, which—as we have seen—ran deep.

The same associations hold true for members of Elizabeth Egerton's family by marriage, a family of at least equal literary sophistication to the Cavendishes, numbering among its members patrons of Shakespeare, Spenser, and Milton. In the 1630s, Milton's *Comus* was performed before the Egerton family; among persons to whom verses in MS Bodl. Rawl. Poet. 16 are addressed is the Lady Alice Egerton, one of the sisters-in-law of Elizabeth Cavendish Egerton (then Lady Brackley). Alice Egerton was a student of Henry Lawes and a performer, with two of her brothers (one of them Elizabeth Egerton's husband), in Milton's *Comus*. And several other masques were performed by members of the Egerton family in the same decade.[134] Aside from Milton, who composed two masques for the Bridgewaters, the Egertons were closely associated with other prominent men of letters: John Donne served for many years as Sir Thomas's secretary, remaining close to the family after he left that post, and other longtime Egerton family dependents included Abraham Fraunce and the celebrated musician Henry Lawes (1596–1662), who composed verses on Elizabeth Egerton's wedding and on many of her anniversaries (107–8). The courtly tenor of the Cavendish household, reflected, as we have seen, in Bodl. MS Rawl. Poet. 16 and Beinecke MS Osborn b.233, was consonant with the tone of the Egerton household in the early thirties. Indeed, I think that attention to Bodl. MS Rawl. Poet. 16 (and Beinecke MS Osborn b.233) is extremely important for a study of Elizabeth Cavendish Egerton *because* there is a marked divergence between the compositions it contains and those written later in her life.

---

of all Sorts, Made at Divers Times on Several Occasions (1670), 6–7. Lawrence, who might be either of the persons by that name listed in Donald Goddard Wing (*Short title catalogue . . . 1641–1700*. 2nd ed. New York: MLA, 1972–1988), wrote a lengthy "An Elegy on yᵉ death of the thrice Noble and Vertuous Lady the Lady Jane Cheyney Eldest daughter to William Duke of Newcastle Oct: 9 1669" (University of Nottingham, Portland Collection Pw V 19: 1–3).

[134] See Lady Alix Egerton, *Milton's Comus, Being the Bridgewater Manuscript with Notes and a Short Family Memoir* (London: J. M. Dent & Sons, 1910). Lady Alix notes the existence of a group of "maskin cloathes" in the 1630s (28).

After a review of this background information, it is at last time to supplement such earlier recognitions as Ezell's as to the evidence in Bodl. MS Rawl. Poet. 16 and Beinecke MS Osborn b.233 of an affectionate and high-spirited family atmosphere, of pronounced literary and courtly tastes and inclinations, and of the intellectual debt to their father the daughters evince in this manuscript, and to analyze the changes that occur in Elizabeth Egerton's writings in later years when the dominant personal and intellectual influence on her life was no longer William Cavendish.

METAMORPHOSIS

Of those who have noticed Elizabeth Egerton at all, Ezell and Cerasano and Wynne-Davies have mentioned this change. "Lady Elizabeth," Ezell states, "continued her literary pursuits after she became the Countess of Bridgewater, but her tastes shifted from pastorals to more serious matters. She left behind an enormous volume of *Meditations on the Several Chapters of the Holy Bible* in the Bridgewater Library" (*Patriarch's Wife*, 67).[135] Cerasano and Wynne-Davies, writing of Elizabeth Brackley and Jane Cavendish, take this one step further: "When the two sisters left their father's home, they inevitably ceased to benefit from his open encouragement of their literary skills. Although Elizabeth and Jane continued to write, in future their work would consist of private meditations and personal poetry, not the public drama they had produced with the encouragement of their father, and the freedom which, somewhat ironically, their imprisonment at Welbeck had given them" (*Renaissance Drama by Women*, 130). In their otherwise very useful account of the play, Cerasano and Wynne-Davies do not pronounce, and have no interest, one infers, in pronouncing, on Jane Cavendish,[136] but neither they nor Ezell proceed beyond preliminary observation to draw the inference that I wish to emphasize: that the shift to another authoritative male figure in Elizabeth Egerton's life determines this change in tone and interest. Moreover, as I will show, this is not only a matter of waning and changing influence; less benignly, the shift can be attributed to interference that can be documented in extant Egerton family manuscripts.

When Elizabeth Egerton first entered the tradition of noteworthy women as a married woman, i.e., as an Egerton, through the good offices of George Ballard,[137] she was dissimilar to the "peart" young woman of Bodl. MS.

---

[135] Although Ezell correctly identifies this facsimile holding at the Huntington as HN MS EL 8374 (35/C/16), she apparently is not aware of its connection to another Huntington holding, RB 297343 (or 2/G/8).

[136] They state, "The only evidence of Jane's continued writing is from a poem on her death by Thomas Lawrence (University of Nottingham Portland MS Pw V 19)" (*Renaissance Drama by Women*, 209, n.16).

[137] His pioneering recovery of English women writers in his *Memoirs* is still valuable. Perry's rich "Introduction" (*First Duchess*, 12–48) provides useful information on the friendships of this eighteenth-century antiquarian with early women bluestockings. Another useful source is Ada Wallas, *Before the Bluestockings* (London: George Allen & Unwin, Ltd., 1929), especially Chap. 5, "Elizabeth Elbstob," 133–89.

Rawl. Poet. 16 and Beinecke MS Osborn b.233, manuscripts that Ballard did not mention. In her *Writing Women's Literary History*, Margaret J. M. Ezell comments on what she aptly terms the "homogenization" of accounts of women writers by male memorialists.[138] As Ezell notes, Ballard felt called upon to explain his inclusion of Elizabeth Egerton in his catalogue of women "celebrated for their writings or skill in the learned languages, arts and sciences" despite the fact that he had uncovered no evidence of such distinction. Instead, his reason for a notice of Elizabeth Egerton was that she

> Has such an extraordinary character given of her in her monumental inscription that being come to that period of time in which she lived, I am unwilling to pass her over in silence. I have searched very carefully, though ineffectually, for some concurrent testimonies of her merit. But as I cannot add anything to the account given in her epitaph, so neither will it be thought much wanting in the opinion of those who are so candid as to suppose that inscription to have been drawn up with a view of doing justice rather than of honour to her memory. I shall therefore transcribe it as I find it printed in Sir Henry Chauncey's *History and Antiquities of Hertfordshire* and Mr. Collin's *Peerage*. (84)

Transmitted from these antiquarian sources, the long and extraordinary inscription that Ballard then published, composed by John Egerton, the second earl, shaped the historical understanding of Elizabeth Egerton (partly through Ballard's own publicizing of it). Because of its importance to our understanding of the evolution of Elizabeth Egerton, the epitaph is presented here, although it is out of chronological order, for the convenience of the reader:

> To the sacred memory of the late transcendently virtuous Lady, now glorious Saint, the Right Honourable *Elizabeth* Countess of Bridgewater.

---

[138] Margaret J. M. Ezell, *Writing Women's Literary History* (Baltimore: The Johns Hopkins Univ. Press, 1993). Ballard is discussed on 78–89, Elizabeth Egerton on 84. A splendid example of this tendency is Ballard's summation of the character of the extraordinary, exhibitionist Margaret Cavendish as "naturally reserved and shy, and she seldom said much in company, especially among strangers. She was most indefatigable in her studies, contemplations and writings. She was truly pious, charitable and generous. She was an excellent economist, very kind to her servants, and a perfect pattern of conjugal love and duty" (281).

She was second Daughter to the Right Honourable *William* Marquiss of Newcastle, and Wife to the Right Honourable *John* Earl of Bridgewater, and whose Family she had enriched with a hopeful issue, six Sons; *viz. John* Viscount Brackley her eldest, Sir *William Egerton* second Son, both Knights of the Honourable Order of the Bath, Mr. *Thomas Egerton* a third, Mr. *Charles Egerton* her fourth; Mr. *Henry Egerton* her fifth, Mr. *Steward Egerton* her sixth Son, and three Daughters, *viz.* Mrs. *Frances Egerton* her Eldest, the Lady *Elizabeth* her second, and the [sic] *Katherine Egerton* her third Daughter, all of which Children three, *viz.* Mr. *Henry Egerton* her fifth Son, Mrs. *Frances* her eldest, the Lady *Katherine Egerton* her third Daughter lye here interred, dying in their Infancy, the rest are still living Pictures of their deceased Mother, and the only remaining Comforts of their disconsolate Father.

She was a Lady in whom all the accomplishments both in Body and Mind did concur to make her the Glory of the present, and Example of future Ages, her Beauty was so unparalleld that 'tis as much beyond the Art of the most elegant Pen, as it surpasseth the skill of several the most exquisite pensils (that attempted it); to describe and not to disparage it; she had a winning and an attractive Behaviour, a charming Discourse, a most obliging Conversation; she was so courteous and affable to all persons that she gained their Love, yet not so familiar to expose herself to contempt; she was of a Noble and Generous Soul, yet of so meek and humble a Disposition that never any Woman of her Quality was greater in the Worlds opinion, and less in her own, the rich at her Table daily tasted her Hospitality, the poor at her Gate her Charity; her Devotion most Exemplary if not Inimitable, (witness) besides several other occasional Meditations and Prayers full of the holy transports and rapture of a sactified [sic] Soul) her Divine Meditations upon every particular Chapter in the Bible, written with her own hand, and never (till since her death) seen by any eye but her own, and her then Dear but now sorrowful Husbands, to the admiration both of her eminent Piety in Composing, and of her Modesty in Concealing, then she was a most affectionate and observing Wife to her Husband, a most tender and indulgent Mother to her Children, a most kind and bountiful Mistress to her Family; in a word she was so Superlatively good, that Language is too narrow to express her deserved Character; her Death was as religious as her

Life was vertuous, on the 14th day of *June* in the year of our Lord 1663. of her own age 37. she exchanged her earthly Coronet for an heavenly Crown.

Pro. 31. 28.29

Her Children rise up and call her Blessed, her Husband also and he praiseth her: Many Daughters have done vertuously but thou excellest them all[139]

Although this memorial will be considered in greater detail below, it is useful at this juncture to recall that two of Elizabeth Egerton's later writings on religious subjects are mentioned in this epitaph. The exacting, indefatigable Ballard, who cites the epitaph in full, was clearly aware of Elizabeth Egerton as a writer, but despite his searching "very carefully," he was unable to find copies of her writings to examine and judge. This "ineffectual" search underlines the success with which John Egerton maintained what he commends as his late wife's "Modesty in Concealing" the writings that he nevertheless, simultaneously, describes as "*witness*" to the "holy transports and rapture of a sactified [sic] Soul [emphasis added]." And Egerton's words of approbation can be taken as a general formula for the male authority figures who have widely obscured the subjectivity of even the pious (read approved) early modern *feme covert*, i.e., the married woman who, under law, was subsumed within the legal persona of her husband and was therefore without legal agency. As Egerton unblushingly states, the countess's thoughts, although her sorrowing widower describes them approvingly as "written with her own hand," were "never (till since her death) seen by any eye but her own, and her then Dear but now sorrowful Husbands." As analysis of the manuscripts indicates, even this approbation masks some part of Elizabeth Egerton's subjectivity.[140]

---

[139] Since the epitaph is quoted by Ballard from Chauncy (*Hertfordshire*, 488–89), the spelling and punctuation in this text follow Chauncy, rather than Ballard.

[140] This privatization and its attendant "success" was long continued by descendants of the family. In a remarkable passage alluded to earlier in this volume (*Gentleman's Magazine* 62 [1792]: Second Part [Supplement]: 1163), Sir Samuel Egerton Brydges (a descendant of the third son of the second earl) responded to the life of Elizabeth Egerton "inserted" by Ballard in his *Lives of Learned Ladies*, to announce that he possessed "a MS 8vo volume, intituled, 'True Coppies of certaine loose Papers.' . . . All which is evidently the fair hand of an Amanuensis; and under it is the Earl's attestation and subscription, in these words, 'Examined by J. Bridgewater.' This MS. which has never been out of the hands of the Countess and her descendants, is certainly proof of a very uncommon piety

Nonetheless, it would be unduly cynical to discount Egerton's praise altogether, particularly when we couple these lines with the epitaph—perhaps even more extraordinary—that he composed (in advance) for himself:

Here lies interred

John Earl of Bridgewater, Viscount Brackley, Baron of Elesmere, and one of the Lords of the Privy Council, and Lieutenant of the County of Bucks and Hertford, and

Custos Rotulorum of both, to King *Charles* the second and King *James* the second. Who desired no other Memorial of him but only This, That having (in the 19th year of his age) married the Lady *Elizabeth Cavendish*, Daughter to the then Earl since Marquess, and after that Duke of Newcastle he did enjoy (almost 22 years) all the happiness that a man could receive in the sweet society of the Best of Wives, till it pleased God in the 44th year of his age to change his great Felicity into as great Misery, by depriving him of his truly loving and intirely beloved Wife, who was all his worldly Bliss; after which time humbly submitting to, and waiting on the Will and Pleasure of the Almighty, he did sorrowfully wear out 23 years, 4 Months and twelve days, and then on the 16th day of *October*, in the year of Lord 1686. And in the 64th year of his own age, yeilded

---

at least, which in the accounts of her has not been at all exaggerated, and which, combined with her beauty, her accomplishments, her youth, her descent, and the pathetic epitaph on her death, of that husband, who was himself distinguished for all learned and amiable qualities (and for whom, as the elder brother in COMUS, all lovers of Milton feel peculiar respect) appears to me, who, however, confess myself a partial judge, eminently curious and interesting. Yet I am aware that the unusual strain of religion, which breaks forth on every occasion, is open to the jests and sneers of light-hearted and unfeeling people; for which reason it is a treasure that shall never, with my consent, be unlocked to the profane eyes of the public at large." In a paradigm of the transmission of the model of the pious woman, these comments are quoted by Horace Walpole, *Catalogue of the Royal and Noble Authors of England, Scotland, and Ireland* Vol. 3 (London, 1806), 73. Ironically, it is Brydges's copy—bearing his handwritten reproduction of his family tree on a preliminary leaf (as well as his mother's mark of ownership and the signature of an unidentified C. Hammond), that is now housed in the British Library as BL MS Egerton 607. (See Plate 32.) Brydges's copy was featured in Thomas Thorpe's "Catalogue of Ancient Manuscripts," 1835, item 224, and was purchased by the British Library. I thank Dr. Kelliher for confirming this identification of the BL manuscript in correspondence in 1993 and 1997.

up his Soul into the merciful hand of God who gave it.

Job 13. 15.

Though he slay me, yet will I trust in him.[141]

§

Before searching for specific explanations for these discordant records in Elizabeth Egerton's own life, we can gain some understanding of this puzzling metamorphosis by generalizing a bit. It is a given that, at all times in her life, the chief quality looked for in any early modern woman was chastity, the quality in which all others were subsumed.[142] Taking Elizabeth Egerton as our case in point, we recall that as a young adult, married but as yet living apart from her husband, she contributed to Bodl. MS Rawl. Poet. 16 (and Beinecke MS Osborn b.233), a compilation containing writings that while certainly not improper, are distinct in tone and content from those John Egerton and George Ballard would memorialize. Later, as a wife, or *feme covert*, she would constantly have been exhorted to subordinate herself to her husband.[143] We can identify this attitude in the epitaph itself. And Ballard is consonant with other male memorialists "in his principles of selection, which in turn effectively create a narrative of female experience," as Ezell states (*Writing Women's Literary History*, 84), by celebrating women who fit the pattern of virtuous or innocuous. Elizabeth Egerton, in other words, is typical of women praised by men (the writers, until very recently of most histories) for having been a virtuous, conventional woman. Her case, as Ballard's difficulty shows, illustrates the typical difficulty of locating information about such women—a situation that obtained in early modern

---

[141] Chauncy (*Hertfordshire*, 488). Chauncy, of course, takes this from the monument itself, but HN MS EL 8164, a facsimile of the composition (quoted below) is also extant among the Bridgewater papers at the Huntington, with instructions for filling in the dates and engraving it on the stone. There is a mistake in the arithmetic, as Anne Lake Prescott has pointed out to me, and I do not know whether Chauncy transcribed incorrectly or whether the earl's descendants were guilty of a miscalculation.

[142] As the highly influential Vives stated, "chastyte is the principall vertue of a woman and countrepeyseth with all the reste: if she haue that, no man wyll loke for any other: & if she lacke that no man wyll regarde other" (Juan Luis Vives, *Instruction of a Christen Woman*, trans. Richard Hyrde [London, 1529], sig. L4ʳ).

[143] As I note in "Down-Home Bacon," she assimilated this ideal so thoroughly that she reiterated it in her own writings.

reality and, we might pause to observe, one that is reflected in its imaginative literature.

Consider, for example, Shakespeare's portrayals of many strong, single young women, as opposed to far less powerful older women. Even in her newly expanded role as a mother inculcating piety in her children—for which function, in a departure from earlier times, contemporary theorists exhorted women to develop their minds[144]—the mother is essentially invisible in these plays. Musing about the paucity of mothers in early modern drama, Mary Beth Rose has recently concluded that "the best mother is an absent or a dead mother."[145] More broadly, Rose suggests that "examining the drama's strategies of participating in certain sexual discourses while avoiding others can illuminate the process by which women's voices are marginalized in the transmission of texts, and, therefore, of knowledge" ("Where Are the Mothers?" 314). The subject of grieving comments by her husband after her death (like her extraordinary epitaph), Elizabeth Egerton exemplifies Rose's observation. Her sprightly, youthful manuscript writings are passed over by her memorialists in silence. Moreover, these writings, even though she composed them as a young married woman, have been identified with the Cavendish family, and not with her later life and writings. This division has impeded investigation of Elizabeth Cavendish Egerton as a whole person.

Occasionally, early modern men are on record as having considered writing by an early modern Englishwoman acceptable (though a form of public speech). An outstanding instance of such approval is the work of Thomas Bentley, "of Graies Inne Student," compiler of an enormous folio volume of "Seven severall Lamps of Virginitie, or distinct treatises ... the woorthie works partlie of men, partlie of women; compiled for the necessarie use of

---

[144] I first brought attention to this new approach in my doctoral dissertation, "The New Mother of the English Renaissance," St. John's Univ., 1976. For a recent treatment, see Valerie Wayne, "Advice for Women from Mothers and Patriarchs," *Women and Literature*, ed. Wilcox, 56–79.

[145] Mary Beth Rose, "Where Are the Mothers in Shakespeare? Options for Gender Representation in the English Renaissance," *Shakespeare Quarterly* 42 (1991): 291–314 (here 301–2). See also Myra Glatzer Schotz, "The Great Unwritten Story: Mothers and Daughters in Shakespeare," *The Lost Tradition: Mothers and Daughters in Literature*, eds. Cathy N. Davidson and E. M. Broner (New York: Frederick Ungar, 1980), 44–54; Betty S. Travitsky, "The New Mother of the English Renaissance: Her Writings on Motherhood," 33–43. More broadly, such treatments relate to the development of female subjectivity, as discussed, inter alia, by Belsey, *Subject of Tragedy*.

both sexes."[146] A further instance of such approbation contained within Bentley's *Monument of Matrones* is the preface by William Cecil that precedes the reprint of Katherine Parr's *Lamentacion of a Synner*, commending Katherine's printing of her moving work: "to put on the spirite, the cause of sanctification: forsakyng ignorance wherin she was blind, to come to knowledge, wherby she may see: remoovyng supersticion, wherwith she was smothered, to enbrace [sic] true regilion [sic] wherwith she may revive."[147] Keeping Ezell's comments on the public nature of manuscript writing in mind, let us note that Bentley included both manuscript and print writings by women in his *Monument*, and that Elizabeth Egerton's later writings—unpublished and generally unremarked manuscripts—clearly fit the acceptable mold as established by traditional and contemporary authorities (read men).

Until quite recently, in consonance with this traditional pattern, those few references to Elizabeth Egerton that have appeared in print since her lifetime have, like Ballard's, relied on and tended to repeat John Egerton's extraordinary post-mortem remarks and have concentrated on her pious writings. Her earlier writings, although acceptable to her coterie public, as we have seen, do not seem to have become known beyond that exalted, and exclusive, personal circle.[148] Given their current physical location, it is probable that most of the extant manuscripts she composed as a married woman never passed outside the hands of the Egerton family. Until very recently, therefore, the brief notices of Elizabeth Egerton and her writings that appeared in print were primarily comments by antiquarians, county

---

[146] Bentley has not yet been further identified. Parts 1–5 were published in 1582 by H. Denham; parts 6–7, in the same year, by Thomas Dawson. Two early studies of writings by early modern Englishwomen that emphasize their dominantly religious tone are Elaine V. Beilin's *Redeeming Eve* and *Silent But for the Word: Tudor Women as Patrons, Translators, and Writers of Religious Works*, ed. Margaret P. Hannay (Kent, Ohio: Kent State Univ. Press, 1985). A selection is included in my *Paradise of Women*. For valuable listings of books by and for women, see Suzanne W. Hull, *Chaste, Silent & Obedient: English Books for Women, 1475–1640* (San Marino, Calif.: The Huntington Library, 1982), and Hilda L. Smith and Susan Cardinale, comps., *Women and the Literature of the Seventeenth Century: An Annotated Bibliography based on Wing's Short-title Catalogue* (Westport, Conn.: Greenwood Press, 1990).

[147] "William Cecil hauing taken much profit," in Lamp 2 [Bentley's term for the second book], sigs. Hv'–Hvi.

[148] This may be an instance of the retention of older ideals of aristocratic propriety in connection with relatively secular work. For a recent discussion, see Margaret W. Ferguson, "Renaissance Concepts of the 'woman writer,'" (*Women and Literature*, ed. Wilcox), 143–68.

historians whose comments were picked up by literary historians (some connected to the Cavendish and Egerton families), and by family retainers.[149] Although members of both her prominent birth family (including, once, her sister Jane) and her family by marriage are frequently mentioned in the *Calendar of State Papers Domestic Series,* she is mentioned there only posthumously, and then indirectly,[150] while the *DNB* incorporates brief mentions of Elizabeth Egerton within its longer entry for her husband. Significantly, such notices have not mentioned her contributions to Bodl. MS Rawl. Poet. 16 (and Beinecke MS Osborn b.233). Elizabeth Egerton's earlier writings have been noticed, however, by more recent literary and social historians (as part of a general tendency in the latter part of this century to recover and to study manuscript materials about "invisible" parts of the early modern population) who devoted their attention to the most literary of her writings, Bodl. MS Rawl. Poet. 16 (and Beinecke MS Osborn b.233).[151] No one, to my knowledge, has yet attempted to piece together these early and later writings to form the composite—if, alas, still incomplete—profile of Elizabeth Cavendish Egerton, countess of Bridgewater, that I hope to create here, in large part from the writings that she and other members of the Egerton family left behind them. I believe that studying the subsumption of

---

[149] Antiquarians memorializing the family who included notices of the countess include Chauncy; Robert Clutterbuck, *History and Antiquities of the County of Hertfordshire* (London, 1815); Cokayne, *Peerage* (1: 312); Collins, *Peerage.* As noted earlier, Henry John Todd recorded valuable tidbits of Egerton family history both in his *History of the College of Bonhommes, at Ashridge* and in introductory comments to his successive editions of Milton, which built on Thomas Warton (ed.), *Poems upon Several Occasions . . . by John Milton, with notes* (London, 1791). Notices on Elizabeth Egerton alone—largely repeating the excerpts in Chauncy—include Ballard; *Biographium faemineum* (London, 1766); Samuel Egerton Brydges, "Letter to Mr. Urban, December 21, 1792," 1163; and "History of Ashridge Abbey, Bucks," in *The Topographer* 12 (1790); Horace Walpole, *Catalogue of the Royal and Noble Authors of England, Scotland, and Ireland*; and Jane Williams, *Literary Women of England* (London, 1861). An exception to the idealizing tenor of these studies on the Bridgewaters is Bernard Falk's rather racy *The Bridgewater Millions: A Candid Family History* (London: Hutchinson and Co., 1942). Falk, however, seems to have been writing for a sensation-hunting audience.

[150] In the *Calendar of State Papers Domestic Series of the Reign of Charles II, 1661–1685* (London, 1860–1939), on 10 November 1663, there is an entry concerning a letter from Lord Rochford, noting that the earl is "too incensed against them by others for their malice to him and his late dear wife to be instrumental for their release, but he will obey orders" (334).

[151] Several, as noted earlier, have commented on "The concealed Fansyes." Ezell, Greer, et al., and Kelliher have written on the manuscript as a whole.

Elizabeth Cavendish within the Egerton family, a family badly shaken in the years immediately prior to her marriage in 1641 to John Egerton, will provide the key to these changes. Accordingly, I will now sketch the relevant Egerton family backgrounds as well as the tenor of daily life within the household of John and Elizabeth Egerton. It is possible to do so by analyzing dozens of manuscript holdings—most, originally, in the Bridgewater family library, now dispersed. Some of these documents have been noticed, fleetingly, in the past; some, though noticed, have been incorrectly identified; many of them have not garnered any attention until now.

Fortunately, although study of Elizabeth Cavendish Egerton, like that of most early modern women, is often frustrated by gaps and silences, extant materials about Elizabeth Egerton can be made to speak suggestively about her voice and about its differing notes at different times in her life. It is instructive, for example, to note that, as Greer, et al., mention (*Kissing the Rod*, 106), William Cavendish's initials appear on the binding of Bodl. MS Rawl. Poet. 16, an indication, certainly, that he was intended as a reader (and perhaps, as Ezell suggests, as "final" reader of the manuscript ["Daughters," 293]), an indication, certainly, of his influence. When we come to consider the significance of John Egerton's initials on manuscripts by his dependents—including those of his wife, Elizabeth Cavendish Egerton—we may decide that William Cavendish's initials are open to another, less innocent but illuminating, interpretation. More pointedly, these dual sets of initials remind us that Elizabeth Cavendish Egerton was subordinated both as an unmarried woman (under her maiden name) and as a married woman, under her various married names and titles.

ADULT YEARS: ELIZABETH EGERTON

1. The Egerton Family, Its History and Its Library

The sumptuous wedding of Elizabeth Cavendish, on 22 July 1641, in the splendid town house her father had recently built, signalled her entry into adulthood at fifteen years of age, even though she did not immediately take up residence with her husband. In perfect harmony with her privileged background is the partial receipt, signed by "JBridgewater," the first earl of Bridgewater, and dated 19 July 1641, "for marriage portion [of] the full summe of sixe thowsand pounds of lawfull money of England,"[152] on the occasion of Elizabeth's betrothal to his son, John, Lord Brackley (Plate 13).

Prominent in their own right, major patrons of the arts themselves, associated with first performances of important courtly productions, their family library rife with presentation copies of important works, the Egertons were also, however, at the time of Elizabeth Cavendish's marriage, still reeling from their close connection to one of the most sensational and sordid of the scandals to touch the aristocracy in seventeenth-century England, the Castlehaven scandal, so called after the name of the villain of the piece, Mervyn Touchet, Lord Audley, earl of Castlehaven.[153] This association would have profound effects on Elizabeth Egerton.

In 1624, Touchet, a widower, had married Anne Stanley, daughter of the earl of Derby and widow of Grey, Lord Chandos; in 1628, Castlehaven's eldest son by his first wife was married to his stepdaughter, his wife's daughter Elizabeth by her first husband. Anne Stanley was the oldest daughter of the dowager countess of Derby, third wife of Sir Thomas Egerton, Lord Ellesmere; Anne was also the sister of Frances, countess of Bridgewater, wife of the first earl. The connection to the Egertons was therefore extremely close and doubly strong.[154] According to complaints lodged in 1630,

---

[152] University of Nottingham MS, Portland Collection Pw 1 628. This was just half her portion according to Margaret Lucas's *Life* (2: 95).

[153] For lucid summaries of the case, see Caroline Bingham in "Seventeenth-Century Attitudes Toward Deviant Sex," *Journal of Intellectual History* 1: 3 (Spring 1971): 447–72 and, more recently, Cynthia Herrup, "The Patriarch at Home: The Trial of the 2nd Earl of Castlehaven for Rape and Sodomy," *History Workshop Journal* 41 (1996): 1–18.

[154] As noted above, a witness to the piety of Elizabeth Hastings is held at the Huntington Library as HN MS EL 6871, the fair copy of a manuscript, "Certaine Collections of the Right hon:ble Elizabeth late Countesse of Huntingdon for her owne private use 1633." The piety of Frances, wife of the first earl and mother of the second and (as we will note) annotator of a manuscript by Donne, is the subject of the last entry by Eliza-

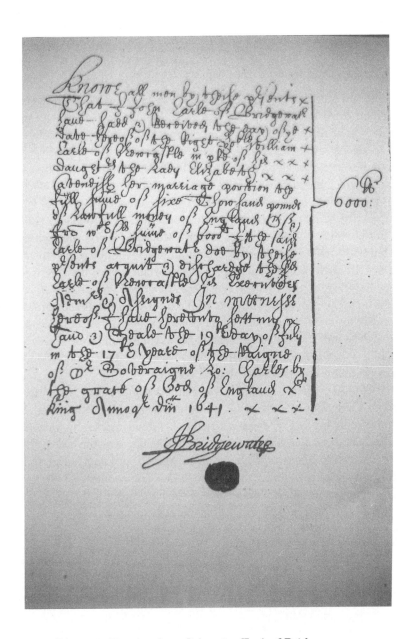

Plate 13: Receipt from John, 1st Earl of Bridgewater,
for part of the marriage portion of Elizabeth Cavendish.
Portland Collection, Pw 1 628.
Reproduced by permission of The University of Nottingham Library.

the Castlehaven menage had been indeed a scandalous one. Shortly after his second marriage, Castlehaven had instigated a rape of his own countess by one of his servants and favorites. After the marriage of his son, Castlehaven had repeatedly forced one of his favorites on his daughter-in-law so that his estates would be inherited by this favorite's child. Following a sensational trial by his peers for the rape he instigated of his wife and the sodomy he committed with his servants, the earl of Castlehaven was executed in May 1631; his servants, brought to trial despite their having been assured that they would not be convicted on the basis of their own testimony, were executed in July. The mud slung around during these trials did not stick only to Castlehaven. Even the dowager countess refused to assume that her daughter and granddaughter were altogether free of taint, and although she sued to the king for pardons for them, she refused to take them in until pardon was granted. After pardon was granted, in November 1631, Castle-haven's widow, Anne, sister-in-law of the first earl of Bridgewater, took up residence with her mother, the dowager countess of Derby (and widow of Sir Thomas Egerton), as did her daughter, Elizabeth Stanley Audley, John Egerton's niece. Widely described by contemporaries as a "whore," Elizabeth Audley apparently never overcame this early disgrace, although she lived till 1679.[155] Her husband did not live with her after 1631.[156]

Although Castlehaven's sisters and his son tried to intercede on his behalf,[157] the first earl of Bridgewater, then a member of the Privy Coun-

---

beth Cavendish Egerton in her "Loose Papers" ("Made on a Sight of the Countesse of Bridgewaters Picture"). Both Frances and Elizabeth Stanley had died before Elizabeth Cavendish married John Egerton, as had their mother, the dowager countess of Derby. As the memorial verses to Frances and the manuscript that follows testify, both sisters were remarked for their piety. The only survivor among the Stanley sisters by the time of Elizabeth Cavendish's marriage to John Egerton was the oldest, Anne, who had married Mervyn Audley, earl of Castlehaven and become a party to the Castlehaven scandal.

[155] According to Falk, *Bridgewater Millions*, 61 n, who cites *The Complete Peerage*.

[156] James Touchet was created Baron Audley of Hely on 3 June 1633, suggesting that the scandal had abated a bit by then, and certainly that Touchet was considered exonerated. Memory of the scandal had not, however, been lost in 1637, when Mary Fage created the anagram "You meet chast" for Touchet (*Fames Roule*, Acrostic 292, sig. 2c^v).

[157] In her biography of Mervyn's sister, Lady Eleanor, a mid-seventeenth-century prophet, Esther S. Cope details the efforts of Castlehaven's sisters and Sir Archibald Douglas, Lady Eleanor's husband, on Mervyn's behalf. A brother, Ferdinando, testified against him. Lady Eleanor later wrote a number of tracts supporting her brother (*Handmaid of the Holy Spirit* . . . [Ann Arbor: Univ. of Michigan Press, 1992], 53–56). Two are included in Cope's edition of many of these documents, *Prophetic Writings of Lady Eleanor Davies* (New York: Oxford Univ. Press, 1995).

cil, apparently attempted to distance himself from the scandal. He is not recorded to have made any effort to have Castlehaven pardoned, and he does
not seem to have attended any sessions of the Council while the scandal
played itself out. Nor was he asked by the king to attend the trial as did the
other members of the Council.[158] It is plausibly because of the continuing
odium surrounding the affair that Bridgewater did not take up his important
and welcome nomination as Lord President of the Council of Wales in
1631, or even in 1633, when it was confirmed. His move to Ludlow Castle
in September of 1634 to take up the position was marked by the performance on the twenty-ninth of that month of one of the greatest masques in
a century of great masques, Milton's *Comus*, first produced on that occasion
with three of the children of the first earl as performers to music composed
by their music teacher, Milton's friend, Henry Lawes, who also performed
the part of the Attendant Spirit (Plates 14, 15, 16).[159]

Comus, of course, enacts the triumph of a young lady, separated from her
family and lost in a wood where she is imprisoned by an enchanter, over the
temptations of this enchanter; she is so innocent that his temptations do not
hold any appeal for her. It is now generally agreed, as Barbara Breasted first
argued persuasively, that *Comus*, "a lovely compliment to the family of the
Earl of Bridgewater," provided more than "an opportunity for the Bridgewater children to display their skills at memorizing poetry, singing, and
dancing, [that] *Comus* may also have expressed the family's need to see its
last unmarried daughter enact sexual virtue and restraint" (202).[160] It was
particularly important that this daughter, Alice Egerton, sister of that fellow
performer John Lord Brackley who would marry Elizabeth Egerton in 1642,
be contrasted with and distinguished from her young cousin, Elizabeth
Stanley Audley, so notoriously styled a "whore."[161] The enactment of Alice

---

[158] Barbara Breasted, "*Comus* and the Castlehaven Scandal," *Milton Studies* 3 (1971):
201–24.

[159] Citing Chauncy's description of John Egerton, Warton suggests that Milton's
"panegyric" in *Comus* (l. 298 ff.), alludes to the beauty of the Egerton children: "Their
port was more than human, as they stood:/ I took it for a faery vision / Of some gay
creatures of the element, / That in the colours of the rainbow live, /And play i' th'
plighted clouds. I was awe-struck, / And as I past, I worship." (Warton, *Poems upon Several Occasions*, 12: 125–26). This suggestion is repeated by other nineteenth-century commentators.

[160] Breasted analyzes the cuts in the version of *Comus* performed at Ludlow Castle
and suggests that they were occasioned by the proximity of the family to the Castlehaven
scandal.

[161] The Lady Alice (d. 1689) became the third wife of Richard, Lord Vaughan, earl

Plate 14: John Egerton, Lord Brackley (afterwards 2nd Earl of Bridgewater).
Facing page 20 in Lady Alix Egerton, *Milton's Comus:*
Being the Bridgewater Manuscript with Notes and a Short Family Memoir
(1910). Reproduced by permission of J. M. Dent.

Plate 15: Thomas Egerton, youngest son of John, 1st Earl of Bridgewater.
Facing page 32 in Lady Alix Egerton, *Milton's Comus:*
Being the Bridgewater Manuscript with Notes and a Short Family Memoir
(1910). Reproduced by permission of J. M. Dent.

Plate 16: Lady Alice Egerton, youngest daughter of John,
1st Earl of Bridgewater (afterwards Countess of Carberry).
Facing page 30 in Lady Alix Egerton, *Milton's Comus:*
Being the Bridgewater Manuscript with Notes and a Short Family Memoir
(1910). Reproduced by permission of J. M. Dent.

Egerton's chastity, and of her family's concern for chastity, amounted to a public affirmation of "the Bridgewaters' possession of the aristocratic virtues which their relatives so notoriously lacked" (Breasted, "*Comus*," 201). In the second part of the masque, the sister and brothers are led to "Ludlow Town and the President's Castle." As Breasted notes, this public presentation of "the Lady, the Elder Brother, and the Younger Brother to their actual parents in the audience ... confirms the public identities of the three children that the masque has been idealizing all along," thus constituting "the masque as a ritual purification of the entire family" ("*Comus*," 211).[162] We might note that the children of the first earl did not, after the presentation of *Comus*, act in further masques, although an older sister, Penelope, had performed in Jonson's *Chloridia* at Shrovetide 1630, and the two brothers in Carew's *Caelum Britannicum* on Shrove Tuesday 1633.[163]

Only seven years after the celebrated first perfomance of *Comus*, Elizabeth Cavendish and the young John Egerton who had played the first brother on that occasion were married. During those intervening years, in addition to

---

of Carbury, whose seat, Golden Grove, would provide a place for Jeremy Taylor while he wrote his *Holy Living* and *Holy Dying*. The marriage was childless, but apparently quite happy to judge from a poem the earl addressed to her that was published in Lawes's *Select Ayres* (1669). A manuscript of advice by Carbury ("The R:ᵗ Hon:ᵇˡᵉ Richard Earle of Carbery his Advice to his Sonn"), is among the Bridgewater family papers at the Huntington; an edition by Virgil B. Heltzel was published as "Richard Earl of Carbery's Advice to His Son" in *Huntington Library Bulletin* 11 (1937): 59–105.

[162] In "The Vision," the manuscript country house poem by a late seventeenth-century female dependent of the Egerton family reproduced in Appendix II, there is a description of the Lady Mary, the eldest daughter of the third earl, that is particularly resonant in this connection:

> ... Oft haue I seen
> How blest the Sight! How ravishing t'has been!
> Her pass along Like some triumphing Queen,
> Thro these fam'd Woods, as well to Hunt the Deer,
> As take her Solitary foot walks Here.
> Att whose Approach the Birds in Consort Sing.
> And Woods expect an Everlasting Spring.
> The horned Beasts oerjoy'd forsake their Shade,
> And Gaze, as if She was to be obey'd.
> Oft haue I heard the Sylvan Goddess prays'd;
> How Men admir'd, & Temples to her rais'd,
> The Beast admire here, but Men adore,
> Diana much deserved, Maria more.

[163] As noted by Brydges in his "History of Ashridge Abbey, Bucks," 142.

their unhappiness over the Castlehaven scandal, the Egerton family had been sobered by losses—the death in 1635 of Frances, wife of the first earl, for whom he experienced a prolonged mourning (and after which he increasingly withdrew from larger affairs), and the death of her mother, the dowager countess of Derby, in 1636. Yet Elizabeth Cavendish was fortunate in joining a soundly affectionate, large family.[164] As we have seen, she had been raised—to tease Lawrence Stone's phrase—in a "companionate" *household*; she would witness her father in a second "companionate marriage"; she had entered a family that was similarly close-knit, and she would build a warm, loving relationship with her own husband.[165] As we shall see below, from her own writings, she would prove a very pliant wife—not a surprising development in a very young married woman schooled in conventional obedience, recently bereft of her mother, left to fend for herself with her sisters for at least eighteen months on a garrisoned estate, separated from a hitherto protective father who was courting a woman of her own age, and totally dependent on her new husband and his family at a time when the country was becoming engulfed in civil disorder. There is every reason to believe that the prudent and pious cast that had been adopted by the Egertons after the Castlehaven scandal became deeply and receptively engrafted in her, that her youth, her position, and the precepts of obedience in which she, like any woman of the period, was trained combined with the affectionate family life into which she was absorbed to encourage her to embrace this essentially unobjectionable stance. Such an attitude is captured in the detail of a print after Diepenbeke showing her as a modest wife gazing demurely aside as her husband speaks to her (Plate 17). Consonantly, the Countess's writings as a married woman are measurably more staid than those she had written earlier in her life, while under the protection of her

---

[164] In "Scribal Publication and the Countess of Bridgewater," a paper presented on 9 May 1997 at the Renaissance Conference of Southern California, Professor Ted-Larry Pebworth posited that Frances Egerton, the first countess of Bridgewater, is the "source" of an interesting annotation to Donne's "On His Mistress Going to Bed" in her copy of what is today "the Bridgewater Manuscript of John Donne's Poetry and Prose (Huntington MS EL 6893)." This comment, "why may not a man write his owne Epithalamion if he can doe so modestly," is echoed, as shown below, by her son's description of his late wife as "wife, mother, *misteris*, & Freind" (emphasis added). I thank Professor Pebworth for sharing a copy of his forthcoming paper with me and for allowing me to cite this information, and Professor Shari Zimmerman for bringing it to my attention.

[165] For his definitions of a variety of early modern marriage patterns, see Lawrence Stone, *The Family, Sex and Marriage in England 1500–1800* (New York: Harper and Row, 1977), 3–10.

Plate 17: "Happy Egerton Couple."
Facing page 97 in Bernard Falk, *The Bridgewater Millions* (1942).
Reproduced by permission of United States History, Local History
& Genealogy Division, The New York Public Library,
Astor, Lenox and Tilden Foundation.

father, William Cavendish, or than those that would be written by her step-mother, wife and dependent of William Cavendish, in succeeding years.[166]

Evidence of the transformation of the "peart" young Elizabeth Cavendish into Elizabeth Egerton, the pious matron, can be drawn from the family library developed at Ashridge by three succeeding generations of Egertons—including her husband—and we must, accordingly, pause briefly to describe this important site.

§

The Bridgewater Library was founded by Sir Thomas Egerton (1540?–1617), the remarkable, illegitimate son of Sir Richard Egerton of Cheshire. Sir Thomas (Plate 18) trained as a lawyer and rose under Elizabeth and James I from Governor of Lincoln's Inn (1580), Solicitor-General (1581), and Attorney-General (1592), to a member of the Privy Council and Lord Keeper (1596), and Lord Chancellor (1603). He was created first Lord Ellesmere (1603) and later Viscount Brackley (1616). A very learned man, Sir Thomas amassed a fine collection of law books—many of which he heavily annotated—as well as a rich literary collection, much of it comprised of presentation copies from such writers as Sir John Davies, Ben Jonson, Samuel Daniel, and Joshua Sylvester. John Donne served as his personal secretary. Sir Thomas' son, John Egerton (1579–1649), second Viscount Brackley, created first earl of Bridgewater in 1617 after his father's death, inherited his father's literary tastes, a predisposition no doubt strengthened by his step-grandmother's, Alice Stanley's, connections, since he married Frances Stanley, her daughter.[167] The first earl also continued the family

---

[166] One unanswerable question, from the extant evidence, is whether the shift in her tone resulted from anger with or disappointment in her father or disapproval of her step-mother, as well as from the dominance of the Egertons. Did she willingly acquiesce in shifting in the Egertons' direction because of disappointment over Cavendish's second marriage and over the deportment of her stepmother?

[167] Sir Thomas's long-lived third wife, Alice Stanley, dowager countess of Derby, widow of Ferdinando fifth earl of Derby, was herself an important patron of literary figures; it was to her ("Ladie Strange") that Spenser's *Teares of the Muses* was dedicated, and before her that Milton's *Arcades* was first presented. (See French R. Fogle, " 'Such a Rural Queen': The Countess Dowager of Derby as Patron," in *Patronage in Late Renaissance England*, eds. French R. Fogle and Louis A. Knafla [Los Angeles: William Andrews Clark Memorial Library, 1983], 3–29.) According to Falk, "at one time or another she was hostess to Spenser, Shakespeare, Ben Jonson and Milton, as well as other contributors to that radiant flowering-time of the English imagination" (62).

Plate 18: Sir Thomas Egerton. An engraving (1616) by
Simon van de Passe (kindly identified by A. V. Griffiths, Department of
Prints and Drawings, The British Museum, as Hind, No. 11)
that serves as frontispiece to BL MS Egerton 607 (folio 1ᵛ).
Reproduced by permission of The British Library.

habit of annotating his library holdings. Possibly the most outstanding of his connections with the literary personages of his time was the performance before him in 1634 of *Comus*, a performance in which his son, John Egerton, Lord Brackley (later second earl), and his daughter, Lady Alice Egerton, appeared, and an event and occasion with deep social and literary significance for the Egerton family as a whole, as well as for Elizabeth Egerton, in particular. Elizabeth's husband, John Egerton (1622–1686), the second earl, was also celebrated as a literary man.[168] Happily for later generations, he, too, had the deeply ingrained habit of annotating his books, although in his case these annotations tended to be judgmental.[169] Perhaps even more happily for twentieth-century readers, the second earl had a most distinctive hand, making his marks very easy to recognize. As we will see, his habit will prove to be an essential help, or at least an essential signal, in the effort to recover Elizabeth Egerton's voice.

Here we must seemingly digress yet again to discuss the permutations in the acquisition of the Bridgewater family library by Henry E. Huntington (although the reader will soon understand their importance to this account). Mr. Huntington, a lifetime collector of rare books and objects of art, made his en bloc purchase of the greater part of the Bridgewater family library in 1917, towards the end of his life, close to the date of his establishment of the Huntington Library. The net result of the transaction was that scholars wishing to study a variety of early modern topics would—when the Huntington was opened in 1919—have ready access, in San Marino, California, to much of the Bridgewater family library. But at the time of the sale, the descendants of the Bridgewaters retained books and manuscripts that they deemed either private or otherwise personal. These included less traditionally valued treasures (the manuscript edited in this volume among them). As a result, there were some frustrating gaps in the listings of the collection in the multivolume folio catalog that had been drawn up by family librarians,[170] a catalog made available to readers at the Huntington (even

---

[168] In Chauncy's words, quoted at greater length below, "He was a learned Man, delighted much in his Library" (*Hertfordshire*, 484).

[169] One of the most notorious—on Milton—is cited in Espinasse's notice in the *DNB*, and discussed below.

[170] Through the after centuries, the Bridgewater library was placed in the care of a number of prominent curators, among them Henry John Todd, cited earlier, and the notorious John Payne Collier. A number of forgeries in the collection have been traced to Collier. Mr. Nicholas Barker, an authority on Collier to whom I put the question (in a conversation at the British Library in 1990), was confident that Collier had tampered

though some entries in it were still in the United Kingdom). These gaps tended to be particularly frustrating for students of social history, or family history, or of such submerged groups as early modern women. A great improvement was effected in mid-century, when a Huntington reader arranged to have facsimile copies made in Edinburgh of the materials that had been retained by the family; these facsimiles were sent to the Huntington so that scholars who needed access to these materials could study them in San Marino. Unfortunately, however, these copies sometimes are incomplete and sometimes are unable—by their very nature—to illuminate the nature of the original, tantalizingly hinting at information that could probably be extracted from the originals but that cannot be extracted from a copy.[171]

There is one further complication that should be mentioned, this one primarily concerning the printed volumes of the Bridgewater library. Before the opening of the Huntington's research institution, in 1927, in what would now be considered an ill-advised series of moves, Mr. Huntington held a series of auctions, selling some so-called duplicate *STC* books,[172] and thereby dispersing some Bridgewater books.[173] On the other side of the water, descendants of the family have also sold some of their remaining holdings since 1917.[174] In strict accuracy, therefore, one can report that at this time the great bulk of the Bridgewater Library (but not the whole of it) is housed at the Huntington (in either original or facsimile form), and that most—but not necessarily all—of the remaining, original holdings of the family are at Mertoun.

The Huntington holds scores of letters, literary compositions, deeds, and other legal documents and family papers connected with Elizabeth Caven-

---

only with famous materials, and that manuscripts of the type studied in this volume would have been beneath his notice.

[171] To alert readers to this limitation, materials cited in this essay that are held only as facsimiles at the Huntington will be so described.

[172] So called after *A Short Title Catalogue of Books Printed in England, Scotland, & Ireland and of English Books Printed Abroad 1475–1640*. 2nd ed. revised and enlarged. Begun by W. A. Jackson and F. S. Ferguson. Completed by Katharine F. Pantzer. 3 vols. (London: Bibliographical Society, 1986–1991); hereafter *RSTC*.

[173] The series of sales, which began in 1918, were held at the Anderson Galleries in New York City, and continued through the early 1920s.

[174] As detailed below, in connection with the manuscript of Elizabeth Egerton's "Meditations," a large sale was held in 1951 at Sotheby & Co., London, to which the catalogue is titled, "Catalogue of the Remaining Portion of the Bridgewater Library Sold by Order of the Rt. Honble the Earl of Ellesmere."

dish Egerton, wife of the second earl. Hundreds of pages—both facsimile and original—witness to details of her life at Ashridge among the Egertons: verses in celebration of nuptials and anniversaries; sermons—some dedicated to her—on both happy and sorrowful occasions; books bearing her inscriptions and inscriptions about her; records describing the dramatic events leading to her death; the death certificate her husband composed; memorial poems written after her death.[175] In addition to two facsimiles of her "Loose Papers" (facsimiles of radiating copies of BL MS Egerton 607 unidentified as such before I began this study), the library also owns a fair (not altogether complete) copy of Elizabeth Egerton's "Meditations," which—as a result of the scattering of important Bridgewater documents— had been first misidentified as her mother-in-law's and then mislaid altogether, as well as a facsimile of the holograph of the "Divine Meditations" that John Egerton recorded that his wife had composed "upon every particular Chapter in the Bible."[176] This last is a compilation of crowded sheets in a cramped hand, often heavily annotated, not to say corrected, in the hand of the second earl. (The holograph from which this copy was made is presumably still at Mertoun.) This state of affairs is extremely frustrating and confusing to a scholar. To take the "Loose Papers" as an example, no connection has ever been made before between BL MS Egerton 607, the best known of the writings of Elizabeth Egerton, and the related facsimiles at the Huntington. Unfortunately, although one of the Huntington facsimiles contains unique annotations by the second earl that are germane to this study, the relationship between the Huntington facsimiles and the BL manuscript cannot be assessed through examination of the facsimiles alone. Many questions about other facsimile holdings also cannot be resolved at present. Yet the extant Bridgewater documents do yield a great deal of in-

---

[175] Ancillary documents include "The Vision," a poem by a female family retainer transcribed in Appendix II of this volume, that contains a long encomium to the second earl and his wife, and a manuscript book of devotions by an earlier female relative, "Certaine Collections of the Right Honorable Elizabeth late Countess of Huntingdon for her owne private use 1633."

[176] This misidentification has been accepted even by Clarke, Burke, and Coolahan, in their study of the Cavendish "family context" ("Margaret Cavendish"), who thereby fail to recover part of Elizabeth Egerton's *oeuvre* and fail to appreciate her husband's intention to perpetuate her. Commenting on the copying of "The Loose Papers," they note that "Bridgewater himself mentions her biblical prose writing, 'Meditations on the generall Chapters of the Holy Bible,' a multivolumed work which he chose not to publish in this way."

formation, and it is largely from them that the following account has been pieced together.

2. The Household of John Egerton and His Wife

Although she had been married very young—indeed, in her stepmother's memorable phrase, "too young to be bedded"—once Elizabeth Egerton's married life began at Ashridge, its tenor seems to have been genuinely affectionate.[177] Evidence in the Egerton papers is plentiful, including compositions by Henry Lawes, the prominent musician and member of the Egerton household who created celebratory pieces for many Egerton family events, including historically insignificant ones.[178] A sprightly instance is "A Hymneall Songe on a celebration of the nuptials of the Right Honorable John, Lord Brackley, and his vertuous Lady after the Byrth of their First Sone: performed by the Lady Alice Egerton, his Lordships sister, and Henry Lawes, an humble Servant to that Honorable Family."[179] This first son, later the third earl, was born in very troubled times, on 9 November 1646, and Lawes' celebratory poem alludes to these troubles, in lines assigned to "HL," describing the innocence of the newborn boy "That knows not yet / what this Lewd Age hath done." Yet the general serenity of daily life at Ashridge during the lifetime of the first earl—despite the upheaval throughout the realm—is suggested by the instant retort to this allusion: "Touch not on Sorrow," "La" rejoins to this comment, "till to Morrow, / this day I dedicat to Joy / to Grandsyr, Syr and his sweet boye." While we are not very surprised by what at first seems an erasure of the new mother in this celebration of patrilineage, "HL" indeed amplifies these lines and indicates the respect with which Elizabeth Egerton was treated by asserting, "Let us in-

---

[177] The only writer on the family to have questioned this is Falk, whose goal, as already noted, seems to have been rather muckraking.

[178] Lawes describes his relationship to the Egertons in the dedication to Book I of his *Ayres and Dialogues, for One, Two, and Three Voyces* (1653) "To the Right Honourable, The two most Excellent Sisters, Alice Countesse of Carbery And Mary Lady Herbert of Cherbury and Castle-Island, Daughters to the Right Honourable, John Earle of Bridgewater, Lord President of Wales, etc" (sig. a2), where he states that he wishes to record the "Honour I bear to the Memory of Your deceased Parents," and notes that most of the contents of the volume were "Composed when I was employed by Your ever Honour'd Parents to attend to Your Ladishipp's Education in Musick."

[179] HN MS EL 8342 (facsimile).

clud the Bryd." Ending in a chorus of good wishes, and in praises of "theyr good deeds [which] / Sett them A boue [sic] all prayse," the poem epitomizes the warmth that seems to have genuinely characterized the marriage of Elizabeth Cavendish and John Egerton. Other extant anniversary poems to this couple (both by Lawes and unattributed) suggest a consistently peaceful and settled domestic state.[180]

The Egertons were able to defer such unpleasant thoughts because the first earl increasingly secluded himself at Ashridge, distancing himself as much as possible from either side. His temporizing cost him the Lord Presidency (granted again to his son after the Restoration), but gained him some credibility with the Parliamentarians, and Ashridge itself was spared all but very minor incursions by the soldiery during his lifetime. Despite the political and religious upheaval in the country at large, life at Ashridge, therefore, was generally serene. The change for Elizabeth from the state of siege at Welbeck to the serenity at Ashridge must have been profound (Falk, *Bridgewater Millions*, 65–67). Yet "to Morrow" did eventually come. There was to be some trouble—relatively minor, considering that the country was in a state of war, and certainly minor compared to the disruption of the affairs of her natal family—during the lifetime of the second earl. In 1651, Egerton was arrested, imprisoned, and fined.[181] As mentioned earlier,

---

[180] These include three facsimiles, HN MS EL 8343, "Anniversary On the Nuptials of the Right Honorable The Earl and Countess of Bridgewater, Set into Musique for 2 voices, by their Honours most humbly devoted servant H. Lawes—July 22—51," HN MS EL 8345 (an unsigned text) "Anniversary on my lords nuptiall day July 22th 57," and HN MS EL 8363 (also unsigned) "To my good lady & lord Bridgewater, July 22 1659." Yet another set of verses, entitled "An Anniversary on the Nuptials of John Earle of Bridgewater, July 22. 1652," written by Thomas Birkenhead and set to music by Lawes, was printed in Lawes's *Ayres and Dialogues, For One, Two, and Three Voyces*; this celebrates their tenth anniversary ("This Day Ten years to Him and Her did grant/ What Angels joy, and Joyes which Angels want," 33). A number of unattributed and undated celebratory poems on the nuptials of an unnamed lord and lady Bridgewater, although numbered in the same sequence in the Bridgewater family catalogue (i.e. as dating from the time of the second earl), cannot with certainty be said to refer to this couple. To further amplify the embeddedness of the Egertons in a literary coterie, we might note that Abraham Fraunce seems to have performed a similar function for the previous generation of Egertons, having composed epithalamia for at least six of the first earl's eleven sisters (G.C. Moore Smith, ed., *Victoria, a Latin Comedy by Abraham Fraunce* [Louvain: A Uystpruyst, 1906], xxxix–xl).

[181] *Calendar of State Papers Domestic Series, 1649–1660*: 18 April 1651: "12. The Committee for Examinations to give order for securing the Earl of Bridgwater, Lord Mansfield, and the others taken prisoners with them, take their examinations, and report them to Council" (155). And 22 April 1651: "9. Lord Bridgwater to be bailed, on bond

Elizabeth was to compose a prayer on this occasion that would be "Collected" after her death from among her "Loose Papers." A number of documents abstracted in the *Calendar of State Papers Domestic Series* and held at the Huntington relate to outbreaks of disorder involving the Egerton family, but these also underline their relatively painless experiences.[182]

The celebratory verses are not our only evidence of married devotion. In 1659, the earl settled on his countess some jewels (not legally under her own control), for her independent disposal during her lifetime "as well for the considerations aforesaid as alsoe for the intire love and affection that he hath and beareth to the said the Countesse of Bridgewater his wife."[183] That close family feeling did not exclude Elizabeth Cavendish's natal family is demonstrated by letters that passed among herself, her husband, her brother (Viscount Mansfield), her sister (Lady Jane Cheyne), and her brother-in-law (Charles Cheyne). These letters and poems show Elizabeth Cavendish Egerton both as the object of affection and as a person capable of expressing warmth, concern, and affection herself. A further indication of continued ties is the fact that portraits of many of the members of her natal family were displayed at Ashridge.[184]

Another facet of these documents, their attention to, indeed their emphasis on, decorum and piety, should be noted in view of the Castlehaven scandal. Facsimiles of two undated sermons preached in the chapel at Ashridge by Robert Hitchcock, identified as a "Bachalor in Deuinity, and Preacher of Gods word at Wingraue in Buckingham shire," suggest both the settled tone of Elizabeth Egerton's daily life and the deference shown the countess as a godly woman of rank: "The Thankfull Leaper or Samaritan" was addressed to "the right Hon:ˡᵉ the Countesse of Bridgwater, & that noble familie,"

---

for 10,000*l.*, with two sureties in 5,000*l.*, to appear before Council on summons, and not to do anything prejudicial to the present Government" (162).

[182] Among documents held at the Huntington are facsimiles of two letters from Parliament dealing with the unwarranted intrusion of troops at Ashridge and of exchanges between Protector Cromwell and the second earl (HN MS EL 8044–45 and 8179–8184). *Calendar of State Papers Domestic Series 1649–1660*, 19 January 1652: "1. The petition of the Earl of Bridgewater referred to the Committee for Examinations" (108); 12 March 1652: "To All whom it may concern. Not to embezzle, spoil, or waste the materials of Holt Castle, co. Denbigh, belonging to John Earl of Bridgewater" (554); 25 January 1655–6: "9. The petition of the Earl of Bridgewater referred to Major Gen. Worsley, to enquire and report" (138).

[183] HN MS EL 8226.

[184] As enumerated by Brydges in his "History of Ashridge Abbey, Bucks," 150, among the portraits hanging "Over the fourth side of the Cloyster."

and "The Pilgrims Staffe" to "the right Hon^le the Earle & Countesse of Bridgwater."[185] That concern for religious duties was not merely a matter of form is shown by a series of dispensations for her to eat meat during Lent in 1660, 1661, and 1662.[186] Finally, we see something of such proclivities in the books bearing her annotations, though they are but a small harvest in comparison to those annotated by Egerton men: Robert Southwell's *S^t. Peters Complaint*[187] bears the unique inscription "The Lady Elizabeth Cauendish her Booke" (Plate 19), and John Downame's *The Christian Warfare* (Plate 20)[188] carries her elegant, delicate signature from a later time in her life, the "E Bridgewater," unmistakably the same as in her correspondence. As noted below, her mark is less directly made on a copy of *Certain Sermons*[189] in which her oldest son memorialized her. We must remember that such artifacts demonstrate a turn from the relative indifference towards religion that characterized the household in which she grew up. Concentration on religion, however, is the characteristic of Elizabeth Egerton's extant writings as a married woman, and I believe that this shift in emphasis stems from her openness to absorbing the anxiousness of the Egertons at distancing themselves from the notoriety of the Castlehaven scandal. If the personhood of the subordinated individual is—as I am suggesting—problematic, the dramatic change in her *oeuvre* could indeed be attributed to the Egerton family's style and authority (however gently expressed), and in particular to John Egerton's authority. His interference in the writings of his dependents—including Elizabeth—i.e., his assumption of control over them, will be demonstrated below.

Evidence of her espousal of wifely subordination can be drawn not only from the writings of others, but from Elizabeth Egerton's own writings. Since this was a belief to which both she and the second earl subscribed, it caused no discernible friction between them. Both products of large and warm families, both highly committed to shared sets of principles, they lived their privileged lives placidly, in consonance with each other and with their ideals, sharing and recording pleasures—and some sorrows—in the raising of their large family. Both spent some time in compiling pious records as

---

[185] HN MS EL 34/A/20 and 35/B/29.
[186] MS HN EL 8087, and (facsimiles) 8089, 8090.
[187] (1620), HN RB 69508; *RSTC* 22965.
[188] (1608), HN RB 60168; *RSTC* 7134.
[189] (1627), HN RB 473000; *RSTC* 22965.

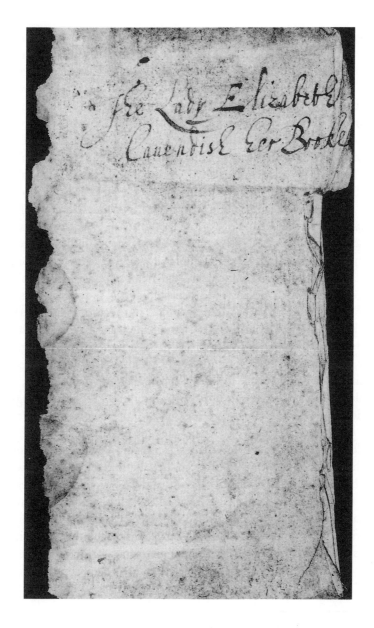

Plate 19: Ownership mark of Elizabeth Cavendish
in The Huntington Library copy (RB 69508) of
Robert Southwell, *St. Peters Complainte* (1620). Reproduced by
permission of The Huntington Library, San Marino, California.

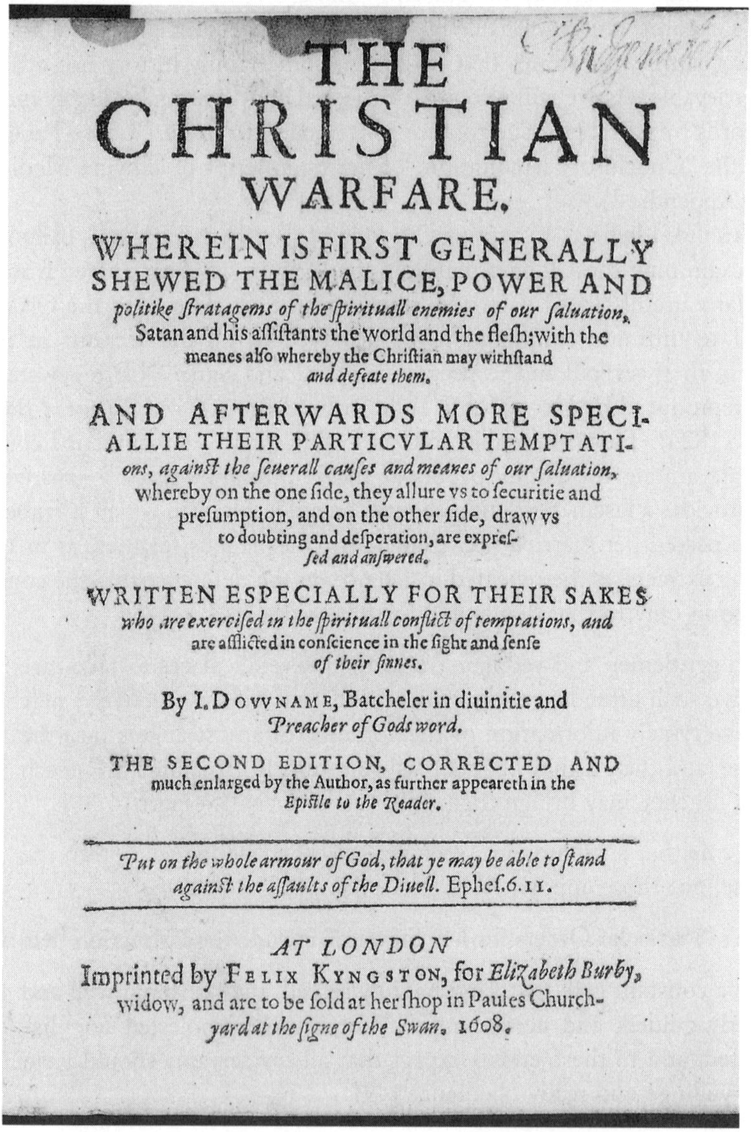

THE
CHRISTIAN
WARFARE.

WHEREIN IS FIRST GENERALLY
SHEWED THE MALICE, POWER AND
politike ſtratagems of the ſpirituall enemies of our ſaluation,
Satan and his aſſiſtants the world and the fleſh; with the
meanes alſo whereby the Chriſtian may withſtand
and defeate them.

AND AFTERWARDS MORE SPECI-
ALLIE THEIR PARTICVLAR TEMPTATI-
ons, againſt the ſeuerall cauſes and meanes of our ſaluation,
whereby on the one ſide, they allure vs to ſecuritie and
preſumption, and on the other ſide, draw vs
to doubting and deſperation, are expreſ-
ſed and anſwered.

WRITTEN ESPECIALLY FOR THEIR SAKES
who are exerciſed in the ſpirituall conflict of temptations, and
are afflicted in conſcience in the ſight and ſenſe
of their ſinnes.

By I. Dovvname, Batcheler in diuinitie and
Preacher of Gods word.

THE SECOND EDITION, CORRECTED AND
much enlarged by the Author, as further appeareth in the
Epiſtle to the Reader.

---

*Put on the whole armour of God, that ye may be able to ſtand
againſt the aſſaults of the Diuell. Epheſ.6.11.*

AT LONDON
Imprinted by Felix Kyngston, for *Elizabeth Burby,*
widow, and are to be ſold at her ſhop in Paules Church-
yard at the ſigne of the Swan. 1608.

Plate 20: Ownership mark of Elizabeth Egerton
in The Huntington Library copy (RB 60168) of
John Downame, *Christian Warfare* (1608). Reproduced by
permission of The Huntington Library, San Marino, California.

well. The most concretely informative—though relatively the most dry— of these records are marginalia by the earl in one of his printed books recording family milestones that document some family history not other- wise retrievable. As we will also see, occasional and sometimes deeply mov- ing records by Elizabeth Egerton are contained both in her "Loose Papers" and in the "Conclusory Meditation" of her manuscript of "Divine Medita- tions" (Appendix I).

It is useful, I believe, to capture the tone of Elizabeth Egerton's daily life before examining these longer manuscripts. Insights can be garnered from a particularly useful record dated 24 June 1652, titled "These are the Orders which I require and command to be observed by all the servants in my Family in their severall and respective degrees," and signed "J.Bridgewater," that is reproduced by Henry John Todd in his *History of the College of Bon- hommes* (1823). This "household roll" as Todd calls it—a document I could not locate among the family papers at the Huntington Library—inadver- tently provides a fascinating glimpse into the golden cage in which Elizabeth Egerton passed her married life. One of its conspicuous features, as in the following extracts, is the repeated insistence on the deference due the coun- tess, second only to that demanded for the second earl:

> Both gentlemen and yeomen are in their severall places to take care
> to give such attendance, that my selfe or my wife, respectively, may
> receive tymely information of the cominge of any strangers into the
> house, and that, if they bee such as we thinke fitt to admitt to speech
> with us, they may bringe them in to us with civill respect (47)

> 8. ... neither shall any one, stranger, or other, be lodged within the
> house, but those appoynted by me, or my wife ... (48)

Egerton's "Particular Orders for My Steward" include the instruction that he

> have a constant care that God be duly served, the houshold well and
> orderly guided, and neither myself nor my wife molested nor dis-
> quieted; and to these ends I expect that all my servants should yield
> him willinge and ready obedience (49)

Egerton's "Orders for my Yeoman Husishar" include the command that he

> [g]ive diligent attendance, that strangers that come in may be
> courteously entertained, but must not suffer such as come in to have
> access immediately to myselfe, or my wife, but must take care, that
> wee be first made acquainted with their cominge in (50)

He must also

> [s]ee that the Table be covered in due time, and assist the Buttler in it; and, in the absence of the Gentleman huisher, must give myself, and my wife, notice when the time for prayers is come (50)

> ... and if myselfe, or my wife, be out of our private Chambers, must then bring in lights to us at a seasonable time wheresoever we are; and before bed-time must take care that noe hurt come either by fyre or candle. (51)

His "Orders for the Clerke of my Kitchen" instruct that person

> [e]very Saturday morning weekly [to] present a declaration of whatsoever hath come in and what hath been spent that week, and what remayned the night before in every severall Office in the house, that the steward may examine it, and it may be ready for myselfe or my wife to view whensoever we think fit to call for it (51)

We can sympathize with the sentiments that lie behind a "Memorand" instructing "that so, as much as is possible, abuses may be redressed without disturbance to myself or my wife" (51), but we may also suspect that we detect a weak spot in administration here. There is, however, certainly specificity in the "Orders for my Buttler," who must

> keepe his office Sweet and cleane; and give curteous entertainement to such strangers as are sent thither by myselfe, or my wife, or by our allowance; not sufferinge any others to come within the office. (51–52)

Finally, "Orders for my Wardrobe Keeper" include the instruction that that functionary must

> be ready to carry a light, to light myselfe, and my wife, and such company as goe alonge with us to and from the Chappell. (52)

These instructions, drafted at mid-point, as it happens, in Elizabeth Egerton's marriage, convey the clear message that her comfort and well-being were provided for—indeed insisted upon—by her husband, even if she always was listed as an appendage to him. Her daily needs were attended to by what seems a small army of servants; her desires were clearly considered at every moment; her daily routine was cushioned at every moment by service and deference; authority restricted her with silk gloves.

Moreover, her life was passed in the midst of a close community of kin; there was emotional as well as economic cushioning, a quality of life that can be inferred from several artifacts, mainly at the Huntington, artifacts, we might note in passing, that constitute further evidences to undermine Lawrence Stone's theory of low affect.[190]

The surviving letters—largely on layings-in and late pregnancies—that passed among the adult Cavendish siblings and John and Elizabeth Egerton and, as we will see, the impressive standing as godparents by siblings from both families detailed in John Egerton's marginalia, testify to the importance accorded to family affairs and to the ties maintained among these relations. Even the bare descriptions of these ceremonial occasions in John Egerton's annotations conjure up an aura of excitement and community, glittering with the presence of high-ranking persons, most notably in the case of the one child born after the Restoration, to whom Charles II stood as godfather. (This occasion is reminiscent of the 1520 christening at Newcastle House of the young Charles Cavendish, to whom the future Charles I stood as godfather.) Also below, in the review of John Egerton's library, mention will be made of juvenilia presented to his father on the education of children, a subject clearly important in this family.

Extant documents at the Huntington provide brief glimpses of some of the children as subjects interacting with their parents. Perhaps the most amusing is a set of verses, dated in the Bridgewater family catalogue merely "In the time of John, second Earl of Bridgewater, 1649–1686," addressed to Elizabeth and John Egerton by their daughter Elizabeth Egerton (b. 1653), and suggesting—if not quite the playfulness experienced by the Cavendish children—yet some sort of verbal interplay between the generations, possibly in a suit for pardon for some unspecified reason. That the younger Elizabeth Egerton expresses herself in graceful verse is certainly of interest. The lines to her father (HN MS EL 8366), perhaps disingenuously, use a familiar deprecatory metaphor to describe her writing:

---

[190] Stone maintains that a low level of emotional attachment characterized parent-child relationships in early modern England (*The Family, Sex and Marriage in England 1500–1800*). Strong contestants of this theory are Lois G. Schwoerer, "Seventeenth-Century English Women Engraved in Stone?" *Albion* 16 (1984): 389–403; Ralph A. Houlbrooke, *The English Family, 1450–1700* (New York: Longman, 1984); and Alan MacFarlane, "The Family, Sex and Marriage in England 1500–1800: Review Essay," *History and Theory* 18. 1 (1979): 103–26.

Honoured <u>Sir</u>

> <u>Pardon these</u> rude lines from a hand, whose skill
> Can <u>use a</u> Needle better; then a Quill
> My <u>duty, and</u> affectiones nere the lesse
> Though <u>it</u> appeare in a mere homely dresse
> A Bill, <u>or</u> Obligationes still the same,
> Signed <u>with the</u> Party's Marke, as with his name.

Yo^r most dutyfull Daughter

E Egerton

Those to her mother, Elizabeth Cavendish Egerton (HN MS EL 8367), are still more revelatory—of interfamilial intercourse, of interfamilial modelling. "Apparently," as Greer, et al., suggest, "the Duke's family" indeed "found her [Margaret Cavendish] embarrassing" (*Kissing the Rod*, 165):

To the Right Honble my most Honoured Mother Elizabeth countesse of Bridgwater.

> Madam, I Dedicate these Lines to you
> To whom, I doe confesse, Volumes are due;
> Hoping your wonted Goodnes will excuse
> The errours of an Infant Female Muse.
> Mongst Ladyes let Newcastle weare ye Bayes,
> I onely sue for Pardon, not for Praise.

Madam I am

Your most obedient Daughter

Elizabeth Egerton/

William Cavendish's daughters—and his granddaughter—then, consciously eschewed the notoriety associated with Margaret Cavendish, but they did not eschew quiet composition.[191]

---

[191] Although we cannot date the verses by this young Elizabeth Egerton (held at the Huntington as facsimiles) more precisely than to say that they had to have been written between 1653 and 1663, we do know that resentment of Margaret Cavendish grew as she succeeded in wresting larger and larger financial gifts from Newcastle. After her death, which surprised everyone by preceding Newcastle's, she was reviled by many (Mendelson, *Mental World*, 60). On the other hand, as Mendelson notes, "while she was condemned or ridiculed by conventional women . . . , Margaret also created feelings of envy which

As precious as children can be demonstrated to have been to the Cavendish and Egerton clans, one of the hard facts of early modern life was the high rate of infant mortality, and a number of documents witness grief over the loss of young lives. HN MS EL 8373, a facsimile annotated by the second earl with the words "Mr. Heylin, at ye buriall of my sonne Henry Egerton, July:1 mo-56," attests to the trauma of the loss of the Egertons' seventh child. The "Loose Papers" themselves include very moving statements on each of the Egerton children who died in infancy, including at least one section that, as we shall see, was in fact written by the second earl. And great pathos attaches to yet another facsimile, HN MS EL 8347, this one, unusually, bearing annotations that I would identify (on the basis of other known writing in her hand) to be by Elizabeth Egerton herself. "Keate," as we learn from several heart-rending entries in the "Loose Papers," was a beloved daughter (aged one year and ten months) who in 1660 succumbed to death from smallpox. HN MS EL 8347, a long facsimile document, is titled "This following Meditation was written at Ashridge & made the 18:th of August 1660 as I was goeing in the Coach to the buriall of the right Ho:^{ble} the Lady Katherine Egerton my most honored Valentine." On the outer fold, Elizabeth Egerton has identified the writer by noting, "Made by Mr Benoyst of my Deare Child Keate, upon my Grieffe of her Death."[192] While much of this meditation is a conventional effort to draw the distinction between the blessings of eternity and the disadvantages of earthly life, the first sentences, like the heading, radiate empathy

---

were sometimes transformed into clandestine emulation" (ibid., 61). Conceivably, then, her example may have enabled compositions like this one and like the country-house poem reproduced in Appendix II, replete with a preface breathing fiery feminist thoughts.

[192] Although "Mr. Benoyst" is not identified further in this document, his closeness to the countess and the tone of his comments make plausible an identification of him with the Cavendish family retainer whose name appears in documents in the Portland Collection at the University of Nottingham (Pw 1 12–Pw 1 24), and in a notation recorded by Strong in "a MS. Note by [Frances Pierrepont] the Duchess of Newcastle: The Gift [of] Marke Anthony Benoyst Esq: To my Lord Henry Duke of Newcastle att the New Building of his Chapell att Wellbeck. Oct. 1677 Hee was Gouenouor to my Lord to his Elder Brother and to my Lords only sonn. F. Newcastle" (*Catalogue*, 117). This would certainly seem to be the same Mark Anthony Benoist described by Trease (*Cavalier*, 33) as the tutor to the Cavendish brothers in 1641 who went into exile with William Cavendish and his sons in 1644, and the same Mr. Benoist who conveyed a book of Margaret's to John Egerton sometime before Egerton addressed a letter to her in December 1662 and who himself addressed a letter to her that appeared in the same volume as Egerton's (*Letters and Poems*, 77).

and love, and the turn to consolation is very skillful:

> If we may by the Budde iudge of the Blossome, or by the Spring
> guesse the Summer, I can boldly say, that there is not in the world a
> more perfect Lady then my Sweet valentine would haue been in all
> respects. Some Fancies esteeme the Fayre, others commend the
> Browne, but Reason itself is ravish'd by Symmetrie & Proportion,
> which did already exactly appeare in euery Part of her Body, & in-
> comparably in the Whole. As to her Minde; with ye & no, with
> Baba, & other such pretty words of her owne inuention, She did
> expresse the Sense of double her Age, & was so forward, that euen
> her vntimely End hath prou'd her like to those fine Fruits, which
> being too soone ripe doe not last long. She was deseruedly the Joye
> of her Parents, a greate Satisfaction to her Kindred, & an vnspeakable
> Pleasure to their Friends & Acquaintances; leauing to them all by her
> Death the contrary of what her Life did plentifully afford them. Such
> losses are deeply felt, & highly lamented; but whether in our Griefes
> there is not more Partiality than Affection, is not so commonly
> Known; as it is palpably evident. Does it not seeme that we had
> rather they should want at that time euerlasting happinessse, then we
> their Company?

As we continue to explore Elizabeth Egerton's personal relationships, we
can extract traces of filial feeling, dating after her death, from documents
connected with her oldest son, John. While not surprising, they further confirm this sense of what we would today term a loving, highly functional, and
intact family. An elegy by one Samuel Holland (possibly the minor writer
listed in Wing) is "Dedicated to the Flourish of youth the most incomparable Lord, John Lord Brackley her most pious and much lamenting
Son."[193] And annotations in John Brackley's hand to the same effect are
extant in two printed works from the Bridgewater family library. The first
of these is in RB 473000, an association copy of *Certain Sermons Or Homilies* (1627) bearing a Bridgewater bookplate, the initials of John Egerton's
seven sisters, and, touchingly, the notation in the third earl's hand "JBrackley
Ex dono Matris suae 1663." The second, discussed below at greater length,
is the far more extensive series of annotations in Christopher Sutton's *Godly*

---

[193] HN MS EL 8350, held in facsimile at the Huntington.

Meditations upon the most holy Sacrament of the Lords Supper,[194] a book in which the second earl recorded family milestones and in which the third earl continued his father's practice, beginning with a record of the second earl's death.

Finally among these records of intergenerational relations, we should note "The Vision," a striking and, to my knowledge, hitherto unremarked country-house poem of 1699, preceded by a striking feminist manifesto,[195] in which Marie Burghope, a dependent of the Egerton family,[196] described

---

[194] *RSTC* 23493.5 (London, 1622).

[195] On the country house poem as a genre attractive to women, see the revisionist work on Aemilia Lanyer initiated by Barbara K. Lewalski, the first scholar to have noted that the genre, traditionally thought to have its inception in Jonson's "To Penshurst," may have been initiated by Lanyer's *Salve Deus Rex Judaeorum* ("Of God and Good Women: The Poems of Aemilia Lanyer," in *Silent But for the Word*, 203–24; 283, n 3). Lewalski has amplified her findings in several later studies ("The Lady of the Country-House Poem," *The Fashioning and Functioning of the British Country House* [Washington: National Gallery of Art, 1989]: 261–75; "Re-writing Patriarchy and Patronage: Margaret Clifford, Anne Clifford, and Aemilia Lanyer," *Yearbook of English Studies* 21 [1991]: 87–106; and "Imagining Female Community: Aemilia Lanyer's Poems," in her *Writing Women in Jacobean England* [Cambridge, Mass.: Harvard Univ. Press, 1993], 213–41). Others who have written about Lanyer's transformation of the genre include Lynette McGrath, " 'Let Us Have Our Libertie Againe': Amelia Lanier's 17th-Century Feminist Voice," *Women's Studies* 20 (1992): 331–48; Ann Baynes Coiro, "Writing in Service: Sexual Politics and Class Position in the Poetry of Aemilia Lanyer and Ben Jonson," *Criticism* 35.3 (Summer 1993): 357–76; Susanne Woods, who has edited the poem in modern spelling (for Oxford Univ. Press, 1993), "Aemilia Lanyer and Ben Jonson: Patronage, Authority, and Gender," *Ben Jonson Journal* 1 (1994): 15–30. For a less widely-known instance in Latin by Elizabeth Jane Weston, see Donald Cheney, "Westonia on the Gardens of Barvitius," in *American Notes & Queries* 5: 2–3 [*Renaissance Texts*, ed. Anne Lake Prescott] (1992): 64–67.

[196] Marie Burghope is identified in the Bridgewater folio catalogue as "daughter of [the] Vicar of Ashridge" (Volume 10: 8); internal evidence in her manuscript dates it to 1699. The George Burghope listed in Volume 4 (757) of the same catalogue ("in the time of the second earl"), as "a Priest of the Church of England," who is credited with (the undated) facsimile, HN MS 35/B/38 "A seasonable Discourse to the Clergy and Laity in a Visitation Sermon," is presumably her father. He is also presumably the same George Burghope described as "Vicar of Ashridge" in HN MS 35/B/4, "A Consolatory Discourse written to the right Hon[ble] John, [third] Earl of Bridgewater, upon the losse (by burning) of his two eldest sons" (in the tragic fire at Bridgewater House, 1678) and in Volume 5 (785) of the catalogue ("in the time of the third earl"), as the "G.B., Chaplain to the Rt. Hon. The Earl of Bridgewater," who delivered "A sermon preached at the opening of the new Chapel at Ashridge, Aug. 27. 1699" (HN MS 35/B/42, facsimile). He must be the George Burghope named by Chauncy in 1700 (*Hertfordshire*, 485) as rector of the deanery of Berkhamsted in the Diocese of Lincoln (in the gift of the Egertons), but is probably not the same George Burghope "Of Buckinghamshire" who

John, the late, second earl of Bridgewater and his wife, Elizabeth, countess of Bridgewater (the parents of *her* employers), as almost a casebook illustration of the nature of early modern marriage in England, and particularly of the subsumption of the early modern married woman, or *feme covert*, in the person of her husband. Although Burghope signals only approval of the conventional hierarchies observed by the Egerton family she celebrates in her "Vision," the "Dedication" she addresses to "the Lady Mary Egerton," Elizabeth Egerton's granddaughter, fulminates against male aspersions on the education of women and on women's writing. Burghope exhibits no consciousness of the disjunction between her protests at the denigration of women and the models she praises. As demonstrated by the following extract from this unusual country-house poem (reproduced in full in Appendix II of this volume), Burghope describes the relationship between the second earl and his wife as it was perceived, articulated, and celebrated in their own circle during their lifetimes and in after years:

> ... [the earl] so well had known
> To raise his Country Honours, & his own.
> For by Paternal Care He first was taught,
> Ev'n all that StatesMen knew, or Nobles ought.
> He Soon the depth of Learneing did attaine,
> And seem'd to haue (nor is't a Poets Strain)
> The Vniversall System in his Brain.
> He rose all Loyall, & all Loyall Sett.
> Both Piety & Prudence in Him mett.
> And for's Devotion. Cou'd I but aspire
> To Sett it forth with such Seraphic Fire
> As He perform'd it, I Shou'd never fade,
> But as Imortall as himselfe be made.
>
>   . . .
>
> Near in that Church doth His Lov'd Consort rest.
> Her Soul in Heaven, Her Image in his Breast.
> In Natures gifts She did all far excell,
> And in all Graces had no Parrallell.
> Tho Her Memorialls great, Yet words by far

---

was admitted sizar at Emmanuel College Cambridge in 1695/6 (John Venn, *Alumni Cantabrigienses* [Cambridge: Cambridge Univ. Press, 1922]: Part I, Vol. 2: 364).

Too Scanty are to Speak her Character.
So when the Objects raised out of Sight
We are not able to describe the flight.
So when the Sun Shines bright, we quickly find
That the bold Gazers Eyes are soon struck blind.
She was His Life, No Joys He had beside.
To Live with Her He Liv'd, to follow Her He dy'd.
He dy'd————[197]

While we might judge that the "23 years 4 Months and 12 days" that the second earl "did sorrowfully wear out" as a widower after his wife's death hardly signify, as Burghope suggests, an alacrity that "to follow Her He dy'd," the tenor of the celebratory anniversary poems, the epitaphs, the epithalamia, the bequest, and this memorial poem all support the view that the marriage of Elizabeth and John Egerton was a most peaceful, most proper, and most affectionate one, albeit governed by his undisputed control—however loving—over her.[198] I believe that extant documentation demonstrates both the second earl's deep affection for his wife and his autocratic ways. We have all come to recognize that the sensibilities of one age are not those of another, and it is therefore clear that twentieth-century readers should read and interpret seventeenth-century artifacts (such as family documents) with an awareness of this difference. The basis for evaluation of a powerful seventeenth-century nobleman was different in his own time from what it would be today. Specifically, what seems arrogant behavior on John Egerton's part may have appeared quite different to his peers. Nevertheless, Elizabeth Egerton's life as a married woman seems to have been thoroughly disempowered despite the respectful treatment accorded her and despite the histories of a number of extraordinary women in both her natal family and the family into which she had married. Given the evidences of John

---

[197] "The Vision. Or A Poeticall View of Ashridge in the County of Bucks. The ancient Seat of the Right Honorable John Earle of Bridgewater. Together with the History & Characters Of the most considerable Members of that Noble Family. Written by one of the Female Sex In the Year 1699 To the Right Honorable The Lady Mary Egerton" (HN MS EL 35/B/62), ff. 16–17 (a facsimile).

[198] Moreover, we have the following wry comment by Todd, writing in the posture of family retainer: "His grief appears to have been indelible, however it might have admitted temporary consolation" (*Poetical Works of John Milton*, 5: 200). The statement is repeated in each of the succeeding editions. If we needed a reminder of the ubiquity of the double standard this would serve admirably.

Egerton's interference with her writings that we will examine shortly, it is appropriate, even essential, that we pause to consider his character and habits.

§

The second earl was indeed well thought of. The standard appraisal by a contemporary (written in 1700) is the following character by Sir Henry Chauncy, the antiquarian writer on Hertfordshire who first preserved the wording of the epitaphs in Little Gaddesden church:

> He was a Person of middling Stature, somewhat corpulent, had black Hair, a round Visage adorn'd with a modest and grave Aspect, a sweet and pleasant Countenance, a comely Presence, and allowed free Access to all Persons who had any Concerns with him; He was a learned Man, delighted much in his Library; and was endewed [sic] with all the rare Accomplishments of Virtue and Goodness; very temperate in eating or drinking, complaisant in Company, spoke sparingly but always very pertinently; he was very pious to his God, most devout in his Acts of Religion, and firm to the Church of England; he was very loyal to his Prince; wary in Council, most affectionate to his Lady, very tender to his Children; remarkable for Hospitality to his Neighbours; his Charity to the Poor; his Liberality to Strangers; true to his Word, faithful to his Friend, strict in his Justice, and punctual in all his Actions.[199]

As Chauncy commented, the second earl "delighted much in his Library." Consequently, many holdings in the Bridgewater family library testify, in different ways, to the range of his scholarly and personal inclinations and to changes in his interests at different stages of his life. These evidences, in turn, bear on his relationship to his wife and their children and afford us some information about their life together.

A number of manuscripts now held at the Huntington—both bound ones that seem to be the exercises of his school days and loose papers (including business and estate papers) that he generated in later life as paterfamilias—

---

[199] Warton amplifies this account in his foreword, "John Earl of Bridgewater and his Family," by noting that the Bridgewater sons were most comely, citing lines in *Comus* that purportedly refer to the beauty of the Egerton child performers (*Poems*, 125).

are his own compositions and translations. Attesting to his scholarly predilections, as well as to his family-centered ways, his juvenilia include a catechism translated from Latin to English for presentation to his father—annotated by the first earl "by my sonne J.B."—and a translation into French of Raleigh's instructions to his son, with a preface of Egerton's own composition (also in French) addressed to his father.[200]

Manuscripts dating later in the second earl's life can be classified under three heads: political, business, and religious. The least numerous are political. A long and very attractive work on heraldry (HN MS EL 34/A/4) reflects his concern for rank, and a political argument, dated 1643, which includes descriptions of the military situation, reflects his deep concern over the "present Warre" (HN MS 34/B/3). As relatively minor as the involvement of the Egerton family was in the unrest of the mid-century, there are letters (and responses) between the earl and Cromwell concerning county matters (HN MS EL 8044, 8045); letters, petitions, and certificates concerning marauding soldiers and the threatened sequestration of his estates (HN MS EL 7770–7771; 8179–8184); and state papers: a commission for the lieutenancy of Buckinghamshire, after the Restoration (HN MS EL 8082–83); and facsimiles of a petition to Charles II for restitution of money expended on behalf of Charles I (HN MS EL 8122)[201] and of an appointment to an honor at the coronation of James II (HN MS EL 8172).

The second earl's predisposition to micromanaging, a quality that emerges also in his relationship with his family and that is important in considering Elizabeth Egerton's subordination, is demonstrated by the most extensive of these categories: assorted business and estate papers. There are far too many such documents to discuss in any detail, but a few should be singled out for the clear glimpses they provide into John Egerton's penchant for recordkeeping, particularly since many of them are entirely in his own hand. The earl clearly supervised the ordering of his accounts: moneys paid and to be settled on his family (HN MS EL 8130 and facsimiles HN MS EL 8131–8138; 8141; 8142); rents and leases (HN MS EL 8009, 8010, facsimiles 8215 & 8218); letters concerning game and poachers (HN MS EL 8084–8086, 8118). Reminiscent of the household book transcribed by Todd are a number of later documents particularly suggestive of a martinet-like person-

---

[200] HN MS EL 34/A/23 and HN MS EL 34/A/6, both facsimiles.

[201] As Todd notes, the second earl was divested of his offices under Cromwell but restored to them under Charles II (*History*, 44–46).

ality. "Directions wch I require to be obserued not onely by my Clarke of ye Kitchen, & my Cooke, but likewise by all my Servants whatsoeuer, in such measure as they may be any way therein concern'd" (HN MS EL 8041; also facsimile), dated 1670, begins as follows: "That good Care be taken, that there be no Cutting of any meate ... before it come up to my Table." Similar directions are contained in the facsimile "Memorialls ... to be put in Execution, when I am gone to London" (HN MS EL 8139), intended to "suddenly stop y^t resort, which hath hitherto, beene so very expensive to me." Other facsimiles, HN MS EL 8142, eleven pages of cramped records in Egerton's hand constituting carefully kept accounts of "Moneys paid by me since the 4:th day of 10: ^{bris} 1649 ..." and HN MS EL 8094, an inventory of moveables at Ashridge dated 1663—listing, inter alia, eleven Bibles kept in the chapel—further suggest the earl's desire to maintain control over his estates, although there is also reason, as we will now see, to believe that he did not succeed as he wished. Detailed evidence of his unsuccessful involvement in financial management can be extrapolated from an unhappy document first dated in 1668 (and amended several times, the latest March 1674), entitled "Some reasons given by me why I am in debt" (HN MS EL 8117, facsimile). Intended as an apologia to his heir for the condition of the estate he would one day inherit, this floundering list of the many liabilities and responsibilities that the second earl grappled with—including the huge encumbrances on the estate that he had himself inherited—includes, most extraordinarily, a long justification for the very expensive monument he erected in memory of his wife and parents in which he expresses both the dutifulness and respect he intended and a self-centeredly self-righteous, and self-serving, state of mind. The monument was erected in honor of:

> my Father, & my Mother, & that most unaualuable, & unpriseable Jewell, with which God once blessed me, my entirely beloued, & truly louing Wife; of whose excellent goodnesse, & of that great happinesse which I enjoyed by it, whilst it pleased God to Continue her Life, I should haue thought myselfe totally unworthy, if I should not (in some measure) haue endeauoured to perpetuate the remembrance of so admirable a Person, so neerely related to me, & who had beene so many yeares my whole felicity; I cannot therefore conceiue that this Expence, whatsoeuer it was (& that it was considerable, I belieue whosoeuer lookes upon it cannot doubt) can fall under any hard Censure by any Friend of mine; & for my deare Children, I cannot thinke any of them so unworthy, as to grudge the Charge of

such a Memoriall of their worthy Ancestors, & particularly of their owne unparallelled, & incomparable Mother.

Versions of his will containing the remarkable inscription he composed for his monument—one (HN MS EL 8164) signed and sealed, another a facsimile of a copy, yet another a facsimile of a probated copy (HN MS EL 8163–8165)—give a cumulative sense of the managerial quality of a personality that attempted direction even beyond the grave. The earl precisely instructs the details of his burial "amongst my Deare Relations, And as neer to the Body of my Deare Wife, as may be," and the setting up of the memorial stone on "a Table of White Marble, no bigger then to hold conveniently, in a Legible, but not very large Character, the Inscription, ... which Inscription (the Blankes in it being first filled according to the truth of the time of my death ...), I would haue to be Engraven on the Table, and the Letters afterwards Painted Black: About the Table I would haue a Border of Black Marble." More endearingly, although he bequeaths all his goods to his eldest son, he details a few (presumably cherished) possessions: "my Collection of Coynes, And all my Bookes, both all those in my Library at my house at Ashridge, and those belonging to my Chappell there, and all those in my Library at Bridgewater-house in Barbacan, and those belonging to my Chappell there; And likewise all the Gunns, Crossebowes, and all other Armes whatsoever that are mine at Ashridge, And all such mony and plate as I shall leaue, at the time of my Decease."

Numerous manuscript compositions on religious subjects (both by and addressed to the second earl), reflecting his deep commitment to God, afford knowledge of yet another facet of his character. These are of particular relevance to students of Elizabeth Egerton because of her turn to deep piety after her marriage. One of these manuscripts is a copious "Collection of all those places of the Holy Scriptures which may be found in more bookes of the Holy Bible then one" (HN MS EL 34/B/18), a facsimile that might prove of particular interest if examined in conjunction with the manuscript commentary on all the chapters of the Bible drafted by Elizabeth Egerton. Yet others contain copies of sermons and hymns dedicated to Egerton and preached before him, some annotated by him. A facsimile of his holograph "A Preparatory Prayer upon ye receiving of ye Lord's supper" (HN MS EL 8372) is a culminating instance of the degree to which the earl's micromanagement interferes with our efforts to recover the writings of his wife, for this "Preparatory Prayer" is included in her "Loose Papers"—in the case of all but one of the copies of the manuscript without any indication of its true authorship (Plate 21). A volume of notes (HN MS EL 34/B/18), similar to the annotations in Sutton (*Godly Meditations*)—some in French, some cursory, others quite lengthy—records information on sermons heard between August 1645 and June 1650: the dates when sermons were heard, the name of the preacher, and the text on which the sermon was based.

The second earl's personal characteristics and interests can also be extrapolated from parts of the printed portion of the family library bearing his annotations. A bookish man, he included some of his volumes in his baggage when he travelled from one of his residences to another. One particularly unusual holding is the Bridgewater "travelling library," a set of miniature books made to fit within a lovely case in the form of a folio volume bound in leather, produced for the convenience of book owners who wished to carry reading matter with them with some ease, and one of only four known sets from the seventeenth century. The Bridgewater travelling library was made originally for Sir Thomas and descended to his heirs. The forty-four volumes, many in Latin, are housed within the case on three wooden shelves; they deal mainly with theology and philosophy but include some ancient literature. These could constitute the preferred reading only of a truly erudite person.[202] In addition, Sutton's *Godly Meditations* also seems to have travelled with the second earl to and from his various residences, and his marginalia appear to have been added to it periodically, when he had it at hand.[203]

Like his father and grandfather before him, the second earl added to the holdings of the family library. It was his penchant to collect civil war tracts, many of which bear his copious annotations. Of these, none is better known than Milton's *Defensio Pro Populo Anglicano* (1651), on the title page of which the second earl—who had, as a young boy, acted in this author's *Comus*—wrote the dismissive comment: "Liber Igne, Author Furcâ dignissimi" (fit to be burnt and its author fit for the gallows!).[204] Sagely uncom-

---

[202] For a discussion of the seventeenth-century travelling library, including the Bridgewater exemplar, see Howard M. Nixon and William A. Jackson, "English Seventeenth-Century Travelling Libraries," *Transactions of the Cambridge Bibliographical Society* 7.3 (1979): 294–321.

[203] His not having it always at hand would constitute one explanation for what seems to be an incomplete record of sermon attendance; of course, another possibility is that he did not always attend.

[204] A celebrated Huntington holding, discussed by Ingoldsby (in "Intramuralia," 90), who corrects a traditional mis-rendering of the earl's comment ("Liber igni, Author furcâ,

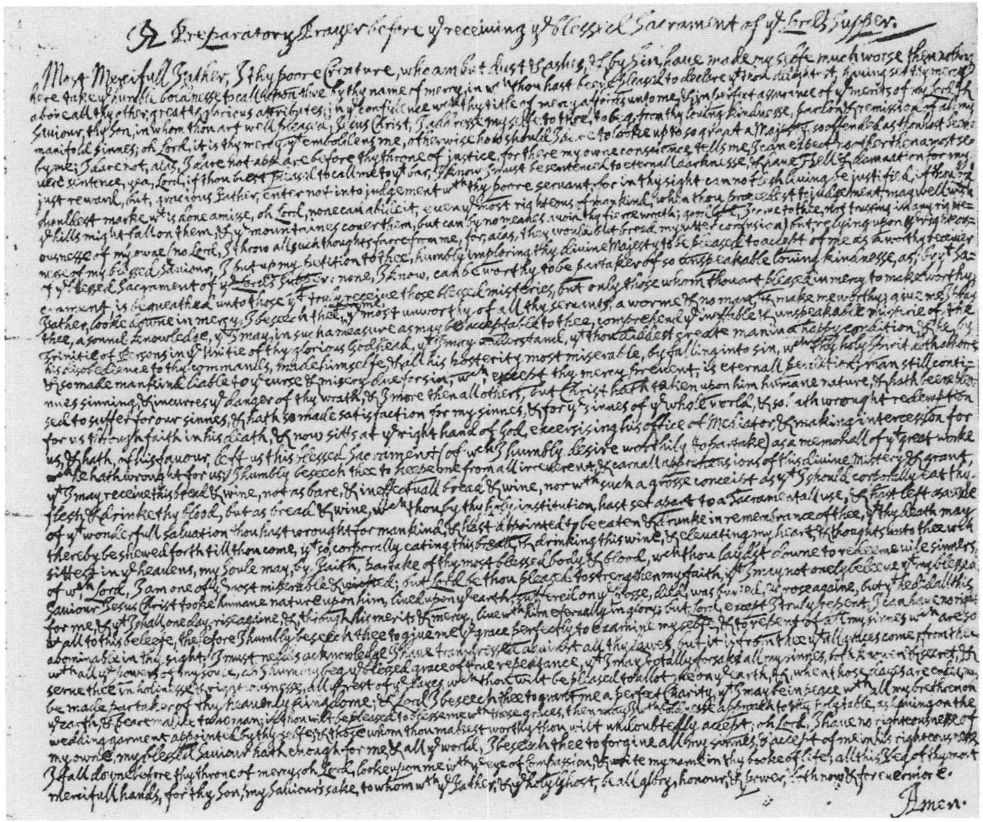

Plate 21: "A Preparatory Prayer before yᵉ receiving yᵉ blessed Sacrament of yᵉ Lord's Supper." Reproduced by kind permission of His Grace, Sir John Sutherland Egerton, sixth Duke of Sutherland, from MS EL 8372 housed at The Huntington Library, San Marino, California.

mitted to the actual furor of his time he may have been, but the second earl was not neutral in his sentiments![205] Not only political materials carry his annotations, and not surprisingly, the printed works bearing evidences of his reading fall into the same categories as his manuscripts. One long and annotated holding is RB 80066, James Peele's *Pathewaye to perfectness* (1569), a work in the form of a dialogue on the keeping of accounts the tables of which are similar to manuscript accounts in the earl's hand. A number of printed works straddle the political-religious divide: RB 61607, a heavily annotated copy of James Howell's *Dodona's Grove, or the vocall forrest* (1640), a religious political, geographical, and historical allegory in the form of a dialogue among trees; RB 61848, a heavily annotated copy of James I's *Basilikon Doron* (1604); RB 61859, *God and the King* (1615); and RB 62838, Ephraim Pagitt's *Christianographie* (1635), a geographical survey of Christians who are not under the sway of the papacy. Like the following instance, discussed at length, these materials underline the earl's piety.

The last, and certainly the most revealing by far, of the many artifacts from the Bridgewater family library that help show the second earl as man, husband, and father, is a document that, as housed at the Huntington, must be described as falling between the categories of manuscript and printed book. Held at the Huntington as unbound facsimile copies of individual, copiously annotated pages, these revealing—and tantalizing—sheets derive from the earl's copy of Christopher Sutton's *Godly Meditations*, a printed volume to which the second earl seems to have felt particular attachment (Plate 22).[206] In addition to holograph transcriptions of a number of per-

---

dignissimi"). It is interesting, but perhaps not surprising, that in the second edition of his minor poems (1673), Milton omitted Lawes's dedication of *Comus* to Brackley.

[205] Similar holdings, bound in groups by the Huntington as "Historical and Political Tracts" in which the second earl's annotations appear, include RB 6144–RB 6154; RB 8199; RB 8232; RB 8304–8311. The opinionated comments by the second earl are occasionally in Latin and are usually indignant.

[206] The Huntington holds facsimile copy of some pages from this printed book in its manuscript department, as HN MS EL 22/F/39. The location of the original of this heavily annotated copy is unknown. It is not one of the three copies recorded in *RSTC*, and the Huntington does not have any record of it as a holding as a printed book in San Marino. It is unlikely, therefore, that the original was among the items included either in the en bloc purchase of 1917 or among the "duplicates" sold subsequently by the library (and indeed it is not listed in the auction catalogues). The probability, instead, is that it was retained among the more "personal" family holdings at the time of the original purchase, was copied in the 1960s along with the rest of the holdings retained by the family, and is still at Mertoun. I did not, however, locate it during my visit there in 1990.

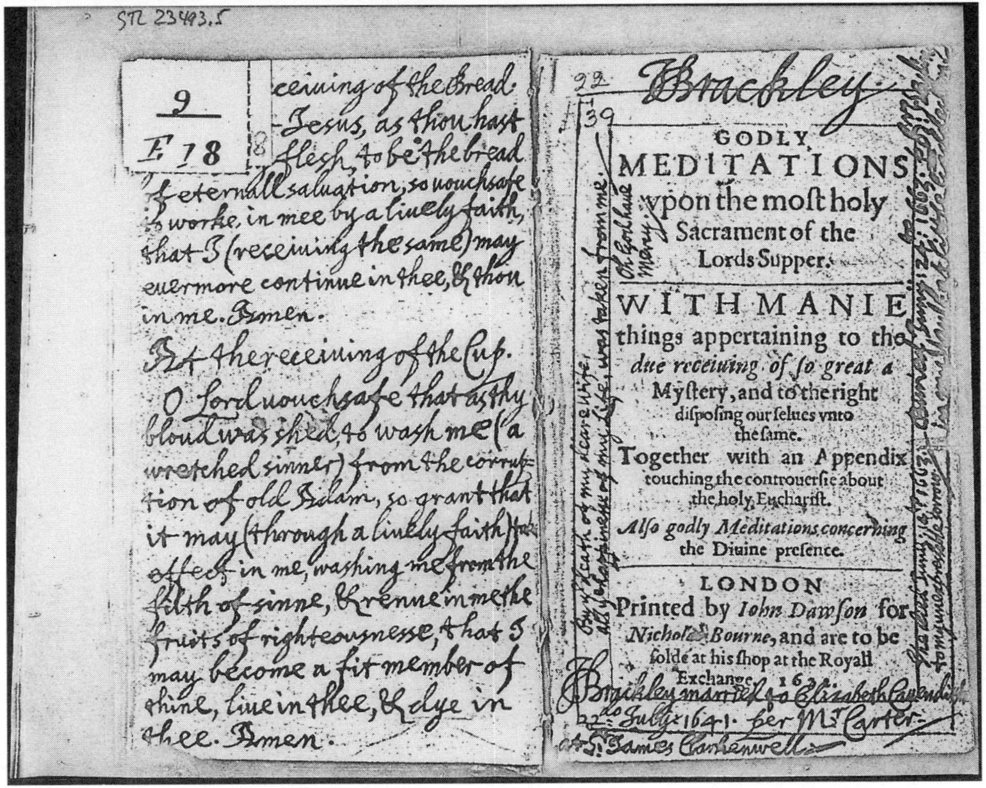

STC 23493.5

9
F 18

ceiuing of the Bread.
Jesus, as thou hast
flesh, to be the bread
of eternall saluation, so vouchsafe
to worke in mee by a liuely faith,
that I (receiuing the same) may
euermore continue in thee, & thou
in me. Amen.

At the receiuing of the Cup.
O Lord vouchsafe that as thy
bloud was shed, to wash me (a
wretched sinner) from the corrup-
tion of old Adam, so grant that
it may (through a liuely faith) ha
effect in me, washing me from the
filth of sinne, & renue in me the
fruits of righteousnesse, that I
may become a fit member of
thine, liue in thee, & dye in
thee. Amen.

Brackley

GODLY
MEDITATIONS
vpon the most holy
Sacrament of the
Lords Supper.

WITH MANIE
things appertaining to the
due receiuing of so great a
Mystery, and to the right
disposing our selues vnto
the same.
Together with an Appendix
touching the controuersie about
the holy Eucharist.
Also godly Meditations concerning
the Diuine presence.

LONDON
Printed by *Iohn Dawson* for
Nicholas Bourne, and are to be
solde at his shop at the Royall
Exchange. 1622.

Brackley married to Elizabeth Cavendish
22 July 1641. per Mr Carter
at St James Clarkenwell

Plate 22: Title page of Christopher Sutton,
Godly Meditations upon the most holy Sacrament of the Lords Supper (1622).
Reproduced by kind permission of His Grace, Sir John Sutherland Egerton, sixth Duke of Sutherland,
from MS 22/F/39 housed at The Huntington Library, San Marino, California.

sonal prayers and meditations on aspects of the receiving of the sacrament, some quite lengthy, the second earl made use of the margins of this text for recording important family events at different times in his—and consequently in his wife's—life.[207] Although, very regrettably, not all of this important artifact is available at the Huntington, I have identified six sequences in those portions housed there, recognizing that it is possible that some of these could be differently divided or further subdivided if more of the leaves could be studied. Four sequences, recording the marriages, births, christenings, and deaths in the families of Egerton's married children, are peripheral to this study, and are sometimes difficult to follow since in some cases they are inserted late in the text and work backwards, towards the earlier pages. These sets of records nevertheless attest to the second earl's methodical habits, however idiosyncratic, and however unavailing.

Another set of records, beginning on the first page of the first chapter of the text (1), notes church services the second earl attended, beginning on Whitsunday 1638, recording in each case the calendar date, the place, and the preacher who officiated. As befitted a man of studious inclinations, the earl recorded these events in Latin. The records uniformly show the member of the family with whom the earl attended services, thereby also quietly attesting to his strong ties to his family. The sequence merits our attention because, beginning on "The 16:[th] Sunday after Trinity: 13:[tio], 7:[bris] 1646" (17) the earl initiated what would become the habit throughout his married life of adding the words "cum uxore" to these entries. As noted earlier, we do not know precisely when Elizabeth Cavendish removed to Ashridge from Welbeck, and can therefore say with certainty only that the date is roughly close to this first entry, since John Egerton, their oldest son (later the third earl), was born on 9 November 1646. Poignancy enters this set of records on page 52 of the volume, with a variant: "Christmas day. 25:[to] 10 [bris]: 1663 . . . cum filio Johanne./" A different poignancy attaches to the culmination of the sequence. Following a note in the hand of the second earl on the Christmas day sermon 1685, we find what seems a most filial effort to continue the record: "John Earle of Bridgwater died in Bridgwater House in Barbican London the 26 . . . day of Octo: 1686 & was buried in his owne vault in Littell Gadsden the 4 . . . novemb: 86:" (114).[208]

---

[207] While in the notes to the marginalia that follow I have been able to identify family members, I regret that I have not been able to identify all of the officiating clergymen since in several cases more than one possible identification exists.

[208] Although I think it would be unnecessarily confusing to detail all of his annota-

The title page bears a mark of ownership and records of the two events that we may fairly judge to have been the most momentous—to him—in the life of the second earl. At the foot of the page he wrote,

Jbrackley married to Elisabeth Cauendish 22:^{do} July: 1641. per Mr. Carter. at S:^{t} James Clarkenwell.^{209}

And in the left and right margins respectively, he recorded the following,

By ye death of my deare Wife, all ye happinesse of my Life, was taken from me./ Oh God haue Mercy." [And] "She died June: 14to: 1663. to my unexpressable sorrow./ Buried Juny. 24to: 1663. per Mr. Heylin. in my Vault at Little Gaddesden."^{210}

This note serves to introduce the most significant, the first in place, and the earliest of the sequences of records in the volume, beginning on the first page of the preface (sig. A3), in which the second earl (then Lord Brackley) began to chronicle the growth of his own family. The earl's penchant for order is apparent from the observable fact that he continued these records throughout his married life, augmenting them when appropriate by adding details of later events to earlier records. These comments in some cases provide us with details that cannot be found anywhere else: the dates, for example, of some of his children's births and deaths (especially of those who died young), and consequently their precise places in the family.^{211} It is deeply frustrating that we do not have access to the original book and must content ourselves with a sometimes illegible facsimile, and also frustrating that not all the pages in the volume are available at the Huntington. Yet

tions in the text as well as his father's, the third earl, as mentioned earlier, did continue his father's habit of annotating this volume.

^{209} Presumably the same Mr. John Carter who had preached a funeral sermon at the death of Frances, countess of Bridgewater in 1636 (HN MS EL 35/B/23, facsimile).

^{210} Presumably the Richard Heylyen who gave the first earl a copy of *RSTC* 23917+ (Tesauro, Emmanuele, *Reverendi Patris Emanuelis Thesauri e Societate Iesu Caesares* [Oxford, 1637]), RB 69660. This would seem to be the same Richard Heylyn of Salop (d. 1669) who is listed in Joseph Foster's *Alumni Oxonienses ... 1500–1714* (Oxford, 1891), 2: 701.

^{211} Clutterbuck gives a fairly detailed family tree (*History*, 392), but does not show such details as the places of the three daughters in the order of births (Plate 23). Thus, without these marginalia, it would be impossible, generally, to know that the entries in the "Loose Papers" are not in chronological order, and impossible, specifically, to date such entries as the sequence about the dying Katherine.

John Egerton=Elizabeth Cavendish.

1 ux. Eliza-=1. John, born 9th=2 ux. Jane, | 2. Sir William, born 15th August, | 4. Charles, born 12 March, 1654,
beth, dau. | Nov. 1646, made | eldest dau. | 1649, seated at Worsley, in the | seated at Newborough, in the
and heiress | one of the knights | of Charles | county of Lancaster, made one | county of Stafford, M. P for the
of James | of the bath at the | Paulett, | of the knights of the bath at the | town of Brackley, in Northamp-
Cranfield, | coronation of King | dukeofBol- | coronation of King Charles the | tonshire, ii. eight several parlia-
earl of Mid- | Charles the Second, | ton; ob. 22, | Second; M. P. for Aylesbury 1 | ments in the reigns of King Wil-
dlesex, ob. | a knight in Parlia- | and bur.* | Jac. II. ; ob. Dec. 1691, bur. at | liam and Queen Anne; ob. 11th
3d March, | ment for Bucking- | 30th May, | Hemel Hempsted; he married | Dec. 1717; he married Eliza-
1669, æt. | hamshire in that | 1714, æt. | Honora, sister of Thomas lord | beth, widow of Randolph Eger-
22, and bu- | called by James the | 61. | Leigh, of Stoneley, who was re- | ton, of Bettley, in Staffordshire,
ried * | Second; ob. 19th, | | married to Hugh lord Willough- | esq. and daughter and heiress of
 | and buried* 31st | | by, of Parham. | Henry Murray, esq. one of the
 | March, 1700-1. | | 3. Thomas, born 16 March, 1651, | grooms of the bedchamber to
 | | | seated at Tatton Park, in | King Charles the First; ob. 30th
John born 11th | A daughter, who | | Cheshire; he married Hesther, | Jan. 1712.
Jan. 1668; ob. | died as soon as | | onlydaughter of Sir John Busby, | 1. Frances, was buried *
31st March, | she was born, | | of Addington, in the county of | 2. Elizabeth, born 24 Aug. 1653;
1670, and bu- | and buried* | | Bucks, knt. ; ob. and was bur * | she was married to Robert Sid-
ried * | | | 2d Nov. 1685-ʌ. | ney, earl of Leicester, who died
 | | | 5. Henry, born 2d and ob. 29th | 1702, æt. 53 ; she died 1709, æt.
 | | | June, 1656, and was buried * | 57, bur. at Penshurst, co. Kent.
 | | | 6. Stewart, born the 8th March, | 3. Katherine, ob. unmarried, and
 | | | 1660 ; ob. unmarr. A. D. 1678. | was buried *

1 ux. Elizabeth=3.Scroop,bo.=2 ux. Rachael | 1. Charles, born 7 May, 1675 ; & | 5. Henry Eger-=Elizabeth-1. Mary,
Churchill,third | 1681; he was | Russel, dau. | 2. Thomas, born 15th Aug. 1679, | ton (fifth son of | Ariana | born 14th
daughter and | on the 18th | of Wriothes- | both unfortunately burnt by the | John third earl | Bentinck, | March,
coheiress of | of June, | ley, second | great fire at Bridgewater House, | of Bridgewa- | daughter | 1676,ma.
John Duke of | 1720, cre- | Duke of Bed- | Barbican, London, and were | ter) born 10th | of William | A.D.1703
Marlborough ; | ated by pa- | ford; married | buried * 14th April, 1687. | Feb.1688,D.D. | earl of | William
ob. 22d, and | tentMarquis | on the 4th of | 4. William, born 5th Nov. 1684, | canon of Christ | Portland; | lord By-
was buried * | of Brackley | August,1722, | M.P. for Bucks in the first Par- | Church, in Ox- | marr. 18th | ron ; ob.
29th March, | and Duke of | and re-marr. | liament of Great Britain con- | ford, rector of | Dec. 1720, | of the
1713-14, in | Bridgewa- | December | stituted by the Union, and af- | Whitchurch, in | ob. 8th | small pox
the 26th year | ter; ob 11th, | 1745 to | terwards in six others for the | Shropshire,and | Nov.1765, | 12 April,
of her age. | andwasbur.* | Sir Richard | town of Brackley, in North- | A. D. 1706, one | buried at | 1703.
 | 20th Jan. | Lyttelton, | amptonshire; ob. 9 July, 1732, | of his majesty's | Bruton, | 2. Eliza-
 | 1744-5. | K. B.; ob. 22, | being then colonel of the 20th | chaplains, con- | co. Somer- | beth,born
 | | and was | reg. of foot; he mar. Anna-Ma- | secrated 2 Feb. | set. | 6th Nov.
 | | buried* 28th | ria, dau. of Sir George Saunders, | 1723-4, bishop | | 1687; ma.
 | | May, 1777. | and left issue Jane, Henrietta, | of Hereford ; | | 3d May,
 | | | and Anne. | ob. 1st April, | | 1718,
 | | | 6. John, born 1st Sept. 1690, page | 1746. | | Thomas
 | | | to the Duke of Gloucester, ob. | | | Catesby
 | | | unmarried; bur.* 25 June,1707. | | | lord Pa-
 | | | 7. Charles, born 14th April, 1694, | | | get, eldest
 | | | M. P. for Chipping Wycombe, | | | son and
 | | | co. Bucks ; ob. 7th Nov. 1725 ; | | | heir to
 | | | he mar. Katharine sister to Wm. | | | Henry earl
 | | | lord Brooke; ob. July, 1735. | | | of Uxbridge.

1. John, born 3d | 1. Charles, born 27th July, 1725, | 1 ux. Anne=1. John Eger-=2 ux. Ma- | 2. William, a Major in the
Feb. 1703-4; ob, | ob. 2d May, 1731. | Sophia Grey, | ton,LL.D.born | ry, sister | second troop of horse-
at Eton 30thJan. | 2. John, born 29th April, 1727, | dau. and co- | 30th Nov. 1721, | to Sir Ed- | guards,M.P.forBrack-
and was bur.5th | succeeded as second Duke of | heiress of | consecrated4th | ward | ley 1768 and 1774;
Feb. 1718-19. | Bridgewater; ob. 26th Feb. | Henry duke | July, 1756, Bi- | Bough- | ob. 26th March, 1783.
2. Charles, ob. an | and bur.* 4th Mar. 1747-8, s. p. | of Kent, by | shopofBangor; | ton, bart. | He married the 15th of
infant, and was | 3. William, born 15 Jan. 1728-9, | Sophia, dau. | translated 12th | | August, 1751, Mary,
buried in St. | and died 19th Feb. following. | of William | Oct. 1768, to | | daughter of Robert
James'sChurch, | 4. Thomas, born 18th April, 1730, | Bentinck, | these of Litch- | | Kirke, esq. and left
London. | and ob. 1st May following. | earl of Port- | field and Co- | | issue three daughters.
Anne, married in | 5. Francis, born 21st May, 1736, | land; ob. | ventry ; and, | | 3. Henry, D.D. Preben-
the year 1725 to | succeeded his brother John as | 24th March, | on the 8th of | | dary of Durham. He
WriothesleyRus- | third Duke of Bridgewater ; ob. | 1780 | July,1771,pre- | | married the sister of
sell,thirddukeof | 8th, and was buried * 16th | | ferred to that | | Sir James Lowther ;
Bedford;second- | March, 1803, s. p. | | of Durham ; | | ob. s. p.
ly, William earl | 6. Louisa, born 30th April, 1723, | | ob. 18th Jan. | | 4. Charles, a Lieutenant
of Jersey ; ob. | marr. 29th March, 1748, Gran- | | and was buried | | Colonel in the army;
15th April,1763. | ville Leveson, viscount Trent- | | 30th Jan. 1787, | | ob. at Bath 13th of
 | ham, afterwards Earl Gowerand | | at St. James's | | May, 1793. He mar-
 | Marquis of Stafford; ob. 14th | | Church, West- | | riedMissSkinner,niece
 | March, 1761. | | minster. | | of the late William
 | 2. Caroline, born 21st May, 1724, | | | | Melmoth, esq. and left
 | ob. unmar; bur.* 18 Sept. 1792. | | | | issue two daughters.
 | 3. Diana, born 3d March, 1731-2, | | | | 5. Francis, ob. s. p.
 | married 9 March,1753, Frederic | | | | Anne, died unmarried.
 | lord Baltimore ; ob. 18th Aug. | | | |
 | 1758. | | | |

John, born 18th | 5. JohnWilliamEgerton,born=Charlotte-Catherine- | 3. Francis Henry, Rector | Amelia, married 25th
August, and was | 14th April, 1753, M. P. for | Anne, only dau. | of Whitchurch and | April, 1771, to Mr.
bu. at Ross, co. | Brackley; succeeded the | and heiress of Sa- | Middle, in the county | afterwards Sir Abra-
Hereford, 11th | late Duke as 7th Earl of | muelHaynes,esq. | of Salop, and Preben- | ham Hume, of
Nov. 1749. | Bridgewater 8th March, | married 14th Ja- | dary of Durham. | Wormley-bury, in
 | 1803, a general in the | nuary, 1783. | | the county of Hert-
 | army and colonel of the | | | ford, bart.
 | 14th reg.of light dragoons. | | |

* At Little Guddesden.

Plate 23: A partial Egerton family tree from Robert Clutterbuck,
History and Antiquities of the County of Hertford (1815), page 392.
Reproduced by permission of The Folger Shakespeare Library.

these comments, incomplete though they therefore are—given these limitations—nonetheless are invaluable, and some extracts are therefore reproduced here, sometimes, unfortunately, with gaps when the facsimile is illegible:

Sig. A3 [outer margin] 1. John Egerton borne 9.no 9^{bris} 1646. & Christned 12 ^{mo}: 9: ^{bris} 1646. per Dr. Fowler. Godfather, my Father, the Earle of Bridgwater, & M^r: Thomas Egerton, my brother representing, the Earle of Newcastle, Godmother, the Lady Jane Cauendisshe./ [foot of the page] At Barbacan in my Father, the Earle of Bridgwater his Chamber./^{212}

Sig A3^v [outer margin] Frances Egerton borne 9:^{mo}April: 1648 & Christened the same day per M^r: Jones. Godfather < > Stanley representing my Father the Earle of Bridgewater; Godmothers, the Lady Frances Cauendysshe & the Lady Alice Egerton, my Sister./ [foot of the page] At Barbacan, in my owne chamber./ [top of the page] She died 13$^{< >}$: 7^{bris} :1648. Burie< >^{213}

Sig A 4 [outer margin] 3. William Egerton borne 15 ^{to}: Augusti: 1649. & Christened 16to: Augusti, per Mr. Jones. Godfathers my Father the Earle of Bridgwater & the Lord Viscount Mansfield representing the Marquesse of Newcastle, Godmother the Lady Alice Egerton, my Sister./ [foot of the page] At Barbacan in my Father the Earle of Bridgwater his Chamber./^{214}

---

[212] This information can be supplemented by Clutterbuck's chart: The third earl was born 9 November 1646 and died 19 March 1700/01. All the family members are familiar figures: the earl of Bridgewater, of course, was John Egerton, father-in-law of Elizabeth Cavendish Egerton, who was still alive in 1649; Thomas Egerton was the younger Egerton son who had also performed in *Comus*; William Cavendish, the earl of Newcastle, Elizabeth's father, of course, was still in exile; Jane Cavendish was Elizabeth's older sister, the co-author of the anthology discussed at some length earlier.

[213] If a number precedes this entry in the original (as one does in most of this series of annotations), it is not visible on the facsimile page. This is the only evidence we have for Frances Egerton's dates; Clutterbuck lists her as first among the daughters but provides no other data. Frances Cavendish was Elizabeth's younger sister, and Alice Egerton, the young lady of the performance of *Comus*. The facsimile is so smudged at this point that the name (or abbreviation) before "Stanley" is illegible. Possibly the person named was James Stanley, earl of Derby (executed in 1651), who was related to the Egertons (both through the mother of the second earl, a Stanley, and her mother, third wife of Sir Thomas).

[214] William died, according to Clutterbuck, in December 1691. The Viscount Mans-

Sig. A4^v [outer margin] 4. Thomas Egerton borne 16:^{to} Marchi: 1651. & Christned 18 < > Marchi: per Dr. Fowler. Godfathers Charles Viscount Mansfield & S:^{r} Charles Cauendysshe, Godmother ye Lady Arbella S^t. John, my Sister./ [foot of the page] At Barbacan in my owne Chappell. [top of the page] He dyed 8:^{bris} < > 1685. 9^{bris} 2: ‹ › 1685, Buried by < >, in my Vault at < >^{215}

Sig. A5 [outer margin] 5. Elizabeth Egerton borne 24 ^{to} Aug^{ti}: 1653. & Christned 27 ^{mo} Aug ^{ti}: 1653. per Mr. Heylin. Godfather S: ^{r} Charles Cauendysshe, Godmothers ye Lady Jane Cauendysshe representing ye Countesse of Exeter my Sister, & ye Lady Penelope Napier my Sister./ [foot of the page] At Barbacan in my owne Chappell./^{216}

Sig. A5^v [outer margin] Charles Egerton borne 12: ^{mo} Mar< >: 1654. & Christned 21: ^{mo} Mar< >: per Mr. Heylin. Godfathers John Earle of Exeter, & Oliver Earle of Bolingbrooke, Godmother, Frances, Countesse of Bolingbrooke./ [foot of page] At Ashridge, in my owne Chappell./ ^{217}

---

field was Elizabeth's brother Charles, who was to die in 1659; we note that William Cavendish is now styled "marquesse."

[215] Although Thomas predeceased his father, and the date of his death is recorded (here) in the volume, it is illegible in the facsimile. Clutterbuck, however, gives the death date as 2 November 1685. By the time of this christening the first earl of Bridgewater had died, and Elizabeth's husband had become second earl and she countess of Bridgewater. The Sir Charles Cavendish mentioned here was William's brother who had returned to England to attempt to compound for his estates; it is interesting that Margaret Lucas Cavendish, who had accompanied him to England, did not stand (and possibly was not asked to stand) as godmother. Lady Arbella, sister of the second earl, had been married (before 1628) to Oliver, lord St. John (d. 1642), son of the first earl of Bolingbroke.

[216] Elizabeth Egerton, author of the mocking juvenile verses quoted earlier, married Robert Sidney, Viscount Lisle, in 1672. She was the only one of Elizabeth Egerton's daughters to live till adulthood. She died, according to Clutterbuck, in 1709. The countess of Exeter was the earl's sister Elizabeth, married to David Cecil, Esq., later earl of Exeter; the Lady Penelope, another sister, was wife of Sir Richard Napier (Bart.) of Luton Hoo in Bedfordshire.

[217] John Cecil, fourth earl of Exeter (1628–1677/8), was the son of Davil Cecil (c. 1604–1643) and Elizabeth Egerton (sister of the second earl of Bridgewater). David Cecil had become third earl of Exeter in 1640; on his death, in 1643, John became fourth earl. Frances, countess of Bolingbroke, was Frances Cavendish, sister of Elizabeth Cavendish Egerton. She married Oliver St. John, later second earl of Bolingbroke, grandson of the first earl of Bolingbroke, who succeeded to the earldom following the death of Oliver St. John, son of the first earl, who was married to Arbella Egerton. Charles Egerton died,

Sig. A6 [outer margin] 7. Henry Egerton borne 2: ‹ › 1656. &
Christned the same day per Mr. Heylin. Godfathers Richard Earle of
Carbery, & Charles Cheyne Esq. Godmother y ᵉ Lady Magdalene
Cutler, my Sister. / ‹ › Hinton./ [inner gutter] M:ʳ Cheyne stood for
my Lord Henry Cauendysshe./ [foot of page] At Barbacan in my
owne Chappell./ [top of the page] He died ‹ ›: 29: 1656./ Buried
July: 1 ᵐᵒ 1656. Per Mr. Heylin, in my vault at little ‹ ›[218]

Sig. A6ᵛ [outer margin] 8. Catherine Egerton borne 8: ᵇʳⁱˢ : 17 ᵐᵒ
1658. & Christned 25:ᵗᵒ 8 ‹ › : 1658. per Mr. Heylin. Godfather,
Charles Cheyne, Esq., Godmothers yᵉ Lady Anderson, representing
yᵉ Lady Mary Herbert my Sister, & yᵉ Lady Paulet St. John./ M:ʳˢ
Levinston./ ‹ › Hinton./ [inner gutter] Died, Aug: 16. Buried, 18.
[foot of page] At Barbacan in my owne Chappell./ [top of page] She
died Aug: ‹ › 1660./ Buried ‹ › 1660. in my Vault ‹ ›[219]

Sig. A7 [outer margin] 9. Stuart Egerton borne Mar‹ ›: 8 ‹ ›: 1660.
Christned 31:ᵐᵒ Mar‹ › 1661. per Dr. Sanderson Bᵖ of Lincolne,
Godfathers, Charles yᵉ Second King of England, & yᵉ Lord Hyde of
Hindon Lord Chancellor of England, Godmother, Frances Countesse
of Bolingbrooke./ [foot of page] At Barbacan in my owne Chappell./
[top of page] He died 10 ᵇʳⁱˢ 20ᵐᵒ 1678. Buried by ‹ ›10 ᵇʳⁱˢ 24 ‹ ›
1678./ in my Vault, at Gadsden ‹ ›./[220]

---

according to Clutterbuck, on 11 December 1717. Like the entry for Frances Egerton, this
entry, too, is unnumbered in the facsimile.

[218] Richard, Lord Vaughan, earl of Carberry, was John Egerton's brother-in-law,
having taken, as his third wife, the Lady Alice Egerton. Charles Cheyne was the husband
of Jane Cavendish. The earl's sister Magdalen (d. 1664) was married to Sir Gervase Cutler of Stainburgh. Lord Henry Cavendish was the younger son (and eventually the heir)
of William Cavendish. Clutterbuck shows that Henry Egerton was born 2 June and died
29 June 1656. Possibly "Hinton" is Sir John Hinton (1603?–1682), a prominent royalist
physician who is known to have been in London in 1655.

[219] Several entries in Elizabeth Egerton's "Loose Papers" supplement this entry, as
does HN MS EL 8347, as discussed above. Lady Mary Herbert, another sister of the
second earl of Bridgewater, had been married to a prominent royalist, Richard, second
Lord Herbert of Cherbury (d. 1655), a nephew of the poet. I have been unable to identify Lady Anderson or Mrs. Levinston.

[220] This christening, of course, follows the Restoration of Charles II. The participants
are very impressive. Robert Sanderson, Bishop of Lincoln (1587–1663), was onetime
chaplain to Charles I, and Regius Professor of Divinity at Oxford. Edward Hyde (1609–
1674), the trusted adviser of Charles I and Charles II, was created first earl of Clarendon
after the Restoration. The name chosen for the child, and the presence of these august

We now pass to the most somber of these entries, surely to be taken at
face value, given all we have found to substantiate the sentiments recorded
by the second earl:

> Sig. A7ᵛ [outer margin] 10. After yᵉ birth of her last Child, who was
> a Sonne, borne dead, 14: ‹ › Juny: 1663 (about a quarter of an houre
> after) my deare Wife, who was yᵉ Joy of my heart, yᵉ delight of my
> Eyes, & yᵉ Comfort of my Life, deceased, to my irreparable losse, &
> unasswagable grieffe, & left me, who was formerly yᵉ most happy, in
> her sweet Society, now, being depriv'd of her, yᵉ most miserable of
> Men./

It remains to note a comment on a tantalizing slip of paper in the folder
containing these facsimile pages—possibly the copy of a flyleaf: "A Bible
bearing the Derby Arms (& probably belonging to Frances Stanley mother
of the Second Earl of Bridgewater) is in the Library. It is marked throughout in coloured inks—probably by the Second Earl."[221]

3. "The Meditations"

The appealing and often illuminating annotative habits of the second earl
take on another complexion, however, when we find them not in the margins of the printed holdings in his library, but interpolated into the
manuscript writings of members of his family. A particularly pointed
example is provided by Elizabeth Egerton's "Divine Meditations upon every
particular Chapter in the Bible." This composition, mentioned by the second
earl, we may recall, in his epitaph for his wife, has meandered in recent
years a bit more than the rest of the family library. As we have seen, the two
copies of what the earl termed Elizabeth Egerton's "Divine Meditations"
were part of the Bridgewater family library, Todd establishes, in 1809, and
they are apparently the very manuscripts listed (in reverse order) in volume
10 of the folio catalogue of the Bridgewater family library now at the
Huntington Library:

---

persons at this christening, the only one of the Egerton children's christenings to have
taken place under a peaceful monarchy, signals the movement of the second earl securely
into the royalist camp after the Restoration. Stuart Egerton died unmarried in 1678.

[221] The hand is that of Henry John Todd, librarian to later Egertons and family me-
morialist. The most likely location of this Bible is at Mertoun, but I did not find it during my visit there.

Meditations on consecutive chapters of the Bible & Apocrypha. 4to. With clasps, lock & key. A fair copy. "Examined by J. Bridgewater."[222]

Meditations on the Severall Chapters of the Old Testament. Folio. With clasps & lock. Ornamentally bound — leather covering wood. Edges tooled and gilt. Fair copy.[223]

Todd does not mention seeing a holograph of the countess's Meditations, also meticulously described in the folio catalogue:

Meditations on the generall Chapters of the Holy Bible, by the Right Hon[ble] Elizabeth, Countess of Bridgewater, who died the 14th of June in y[e] year of our Lord, 1663. 313 leaves, in several books. Vellum binding. In the handwriting of the Countess, and corrected for copying by her husband.[224]

Among the Bridgewater holdings that were, in 1951, sold through an auction at Sotheby's[225] was a beautifully bound fair copy of a manuscript of "Meditations" in a lovely slipcase, attributed by Sotheby's merely to a seventeenth-century countess of Bridgewater. This artifact was purchased by Maggs Brothers for resale.[226] The author was mistakenly identified by

---

[222] Listed in volume 4 (754[a]) and in volume 10 of the folio catalogue (7) under the call number 32/C/9. This quarto witness could not be located in San Marino and may still be housed at Mertoun.

[223] Listed under the call number 8/G/8 in the folio catalogue (10: 7), a number corrected in volume 4 of the catalogue (754[a]) to 2/G/8. As described below, the holding was shelved as RB 297343.

[224] Listed in both volume 4 (754[a]) and volume 10 (7) under two call numbers: HN MS EL 8374 and 35/C/16.

[225] The sale was held on 19 and 20 March 1951 according to the catalog, which is titled "Catalogue of the Remaining Portion of the Bridgewater Library Sold by Order of the Rt. Honble the Earl of Ellesmere." One manuscript, sold as lot 46 on the first day's sale, was listed as follows: "[Bridgewater (Countess of)] MEDITATIONS ON THE SEVERALL CHAPTERS OF THE OLD TESTAMENT, MANUSCRIPT on paper, 190 ll., ruled in red throughout, contemporary English gilt calf over wooden boards, border formed by fillets, irregularly-shaped corner and centre ornaments stamped in relief, the field filled with a seme of rosettes, tooled and panelled back, three metal clasps and catches, the middle one with a lock (key missing), fine gilt and gauffered edges, slightly worn in three or four places, but otherwise in very good condition, folio. First third of the 17th Century [Watermarks, cf. Heawood-Labarre, nos. 1199, 1201, and 1202]" (10).

[226] The title listed by Maggs, "Meditations on consecutive chapters of the Old Testament," is not altogether correct; it is actually, as given in the Sotheby catalogue, "Meditations on the Severall Chapters of the Old Testament." The manuscript was first offered

Maggs as "[Bridgewater (Frances, Countess of)]," and the manuscript was most fortunately sold to the Huntington—most fortunately because the purchase seems to have been made by the Huntington not to gain a Bridgewater document, but because the binding is particularly lovely.[227] Most unfortunately, it was miscatalogued and misshelved at the Huntington as a rare book until May 1993.[228] In fact, this is clearly the folio copy of the manuscript described by Todd (Plate 24).

The purchase of the beautiful folio from Maggs Brothers was particularly fortunate because among the items retained in the Bridgewater family library that had been copied in facsimile for the Huntington was a long, bound holograph, undoubtedly the third volume described in the Bridgewater family catalogue, now available at the Huntington for study as 313 loose, acid-free pages in an acid-free folder. In fact, these two holdings are intimately related to one another: the fair copy being not the work of Frances, countess of Bridgewater, but rather an incomplete copy of her daughter-in-law Elizabeth Egerton's "Divine Meditations," reported by her grieving husband to have been "written with her own hand, and never (till since her death) seen by any eye but her own, and her then Dear but now sorrowful Husbands, [sic] to the admiration both of her eminent Piety in Composing, and of her Modesty in Concealing." Some of the confusion about the titles assigned these two manuscripts is eliminated if we note the earl's prefatory annotations to the holograph, seemingly made as he had corrected the manuscript for copying and provided it with both a general title and part titles.[229] Particularly illuminating when the two documents are studied

---

by Maggs Brothers in June 1951 in a catalogue titled "Mercurius Britannicus or Mercuries Swift Messenger . . . [including] A selection of Association Books from the Great Bridgewater Library." Apparently not selling at that first offer, it was featured again in 1953, in Maggs Brothers' Centenary Catalogue No. 812, "A Selection of Books Manuscripts and Autograph Letters of Special Interest and Rarity."

[227] Although a record of the purchase could not be located there when I inquired about it, the Huntington apparently purchased the manuscript in 1953. With the assistance of Edward Baynton-Coward of Maggs Brothers, W. H. Kelliher, curator of manuscripts at the British Library, and Kimball Higgs of the Grolier Club, I secured a copy of the pages from the 1953 Maggs catalogue identical to pages stored in the slipcase containing the manuscript at the Huntington.

[228] According to a note dated Saturday, 20 July 1991 addressed to me by Mary Robertson, curator of manuscripts at the Huntington.

[229] The titles, in the hand of the earl, are printed on a blank leaf facing the first page of the countess's holograph meditations. As indicated by the photograph of this page, the first title reads "Meditations on the Seuerall Chapters of the Holy Bible, by the Right

Plate 24: Binding of the folio fair copy of Elizabeth Egerton's
"Meditations." Reproduced from *Mercurius Britannicus or Mercuries Swift
Messenger* ... [including] *A selection of Association Books from the Great
Bridgewater Library* (1951), facing page 77, by permission of Maggs Bros. Ltd.

Meditations on the Seuerall Chapters of the Old Testament.

Meditations on the Booke of Genesis.

On the 1st Chapter of Genesis.

The first thing we read of is Gods Creation of the World: God Created the Heaven and the Earth, and it was darke, and he made light,
So gaue he us light, that we might not liue in darkneße, and so diuided
the light from darkneße: and for euery day he made Something that was
good and conuenient for Man before he made Man; to let him see he
ought not to liue in Idleneß, but to follow the care of those Creatures
God had made for him. And let us euer giue God our thankes for his goodnes
to us in prouiding all things for us: in giuing us light to desire his bleß-
ings to us./

On the 2d Chapter.

Here we see God rested the 7th day from all his Workes, to show Man an
Example of his day of rest, wherein he might praise him and dedicate himselfe
in prayer unto the Lord for his great goodnes in giuing him so great a Sub-
sistance, and the Gouernment of all Creatures. And the Lord seeing he wanted
a Companion for himselfe, made Woman; so formed he Eue out of Adam, to make
the freedom amity and affection between them. So ought we euer to be louing to
our Husbands. Since the Lord appointed it: and it belongs to them euer to praise
the Lord for his bleßing in Creating them happy, if they could haue so continued:
Let us euer study to obey the Lord, and not bring upon us his high displeasure; but let us
seeke him with our whole hearts and Soules./

On the 3d Chapter.

Here we see that no Sooner wert Adam and Eue made happy, but this Euill Spirit
did tempt them in making them Sinners, in disobeying the Lords command, and not
only Eue Sinned, but the Euill Spirit was so great as he made Adam yeild to his
Wife's folly, in committing the Same Sinne, in eating of what the Lord forbid them,
and when they had Sinned, then was they ashamed to see the Lord whom he called unto
them; yet for all their Sin God was mercifull in his Anger, and did not utterly destroy
them, nor did he take their knowledge from them, of knowing good and euill, but bid
them, and would not let them goe to the Tree of life to liue for euer, but yet
he gaue them the bleßing of Children; and let us euer praise him for that bleßing,
and for Sending us his Sonne our Saueiour Jesus Christ to dispose us to unth us and
our Children cleane; that through baptisme they are washed from this Originall
Sin, and by our Saueiours death from our actuall Sinns; and who beleeues in him
hath euerlasting life, so came he to purchase for us life for euermore; which Adam
lost: Oh let us euer be his faithfull Disciples, and Creatures, begging his Compassion
on us in pardoning our offences; and let us euer say O beleiue, Lord helpe my
unbeleife; and euer fortifie our faith that this Deuill may neuer haue
power to make us forfeit our Soules to him, from our Lord and Saueiour Jesus
Christ; but that we may be faithfully his, that he may bring us to life euerlasting./

On the 4th Chapter.

Here we see Eue brought a Son, and declared the goodnes of the Lord; and God
gaue to her another Son; but Cain was so Sinfull that he kild his brother Abell,
which action displeased the Lord; and thus we see though they knew both good
and euill, yet had they not power to choose either, Since their Parents lookt
it before the Lord appointed them; thus did their griefe come upon them; and
here

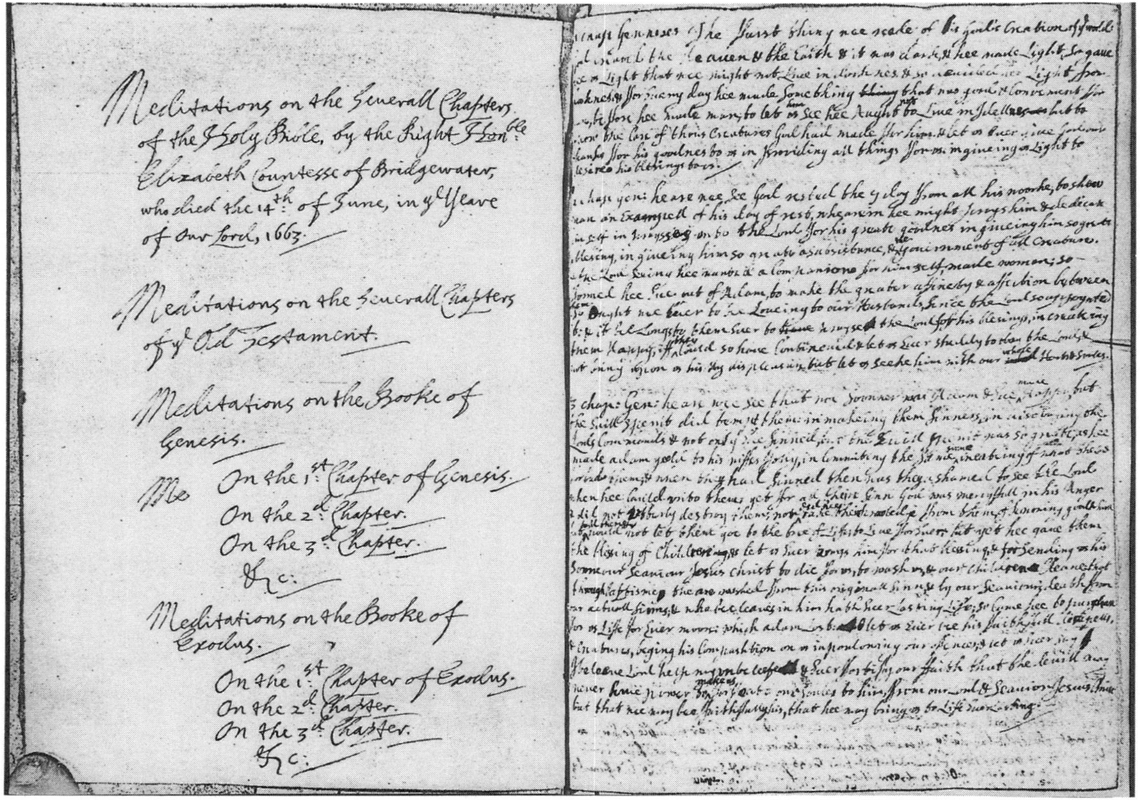

Plate 26: Headings and the opening page of the corrected holograph of Elizabeth Egerton's "Meditations." Reproduced by kind permission of His Grace, Sir John Sutherland Egerton, sixth Duke of Sutherland, from (the unpaginated) MS EL 8374 housed at The Huntington Library, San Marino, California.

together are the cancellations and interpolations on the holograph—in the earl's hand—changes that are reproduced in the fair copy without any sign that a hand other than the countess's had composed them (Plates 25 and 26).

Although one witness seems to have disappeared, and although copies, alas, cannot speak as clearly as originals, the presence of both the facsimile of the holograph and the fair copy at the Huntington is indeed a happy chance. Given the many gaps in our knowledge and evidence about the countess's writings, it is worth considering these two witnesses at some length, since it seems reasonable to assume that they may provide a parallel to the processes that obtained in the examining and copying of all her manuscripts—including the "Loose Papers," the best known of her writings, of which we possess only fair copies. The photographs of corresponding pages of text in the fair and holograph copies presented here, therefore, indicate the degree to which Egerton altered his wife's words. These corrections are not limited to comments on the Bible that could be construed as matters of fact, but are made even in the final entry in the holograph, called a "Conclusory Meditation on all the other Meditations," an enunciation of personal religious and domestic beliefs transcribed in Appendix I, that alas is not included in the incomplete fair copy, and therefore is not available for comparison. Yet this "Conclusory Meditation"—like the rest of the manuscript described in the Bridgewater family catalogue, "In the handwriting of the Countess, and corrected for copying by her husband," and replete with corrections in the distinctive hand of the second earl—is, I believe, as close as we can come today to the unadulterated thinking of Elizabeth Egerton. Since the earl's interpolations appear in those entries that are included in the incomplete fair copy, we can reasonably assume that those in the "Conclusory Meditation" would also would have been incorporated in this entry had the fair copy been completed (Plate 27).

As mentioned earlier, the copies of the holograph also include several pages of directions in the hand of the second earl (like the sample reproduced above) that appear to list the headings he wished the scribe to include in the final copy. These, as can be seen on the reproductions, match the headings in the fair copy of the manuscript. Lists on still other pages, in the

---

Hon:^ble"; the next reads "Meditations on the Seuerall Chapters of y^e Old Testament." There are further sub-titles, which seem clearly to be in the form of directions, and which are not present in the facing original.

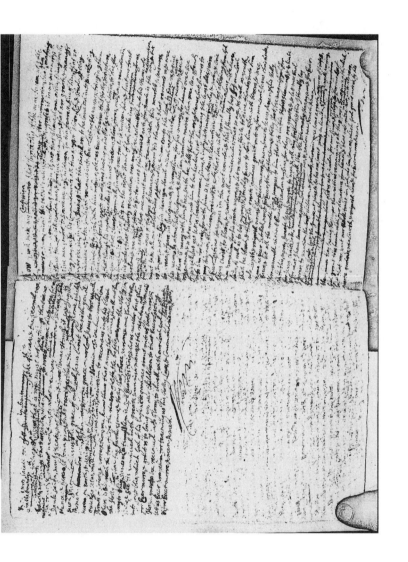

Plate 27: Elizabeth Egerton's "Conclusory Meditation on all the other Meditations," as it is titled by the second earl. Reproduced by kind permission of His Grace, Sir John Sutherland Egerton, sixth Duke of Sutherland, from (the unpaginated) MS EL 8374 housed at The Huntington Library, San Marino, California.

second earl's hand, but in minuscule, are more cryptic (Plate 28). These may possibly have been a schedule for the copying process, or perhaps for the correction process. Unfortunately, the beginning of the series is not present: the first of the slips, with the beginning date 7:^{bris} 20:^{quo}—70, begins "ex: to ye end of ye 16th Psalme." These lists do, however, continue through the end of the book of Revelation and include (for 9:^{bris}13:^{tio} 1677) the final entry in the holograph, the "Conclusory Meditation." It is impossible from examination of the uniformly oversize facsimile leaves to determine whether the originals of these sheets were tiny scraps of paper, appropriate to such memoranda, and dictating the use of such a tiny hand. It is also uncertain why the schedule ends in 1677; and why the fair copy ends at the middle of page 379, in the middle of Luke, with the heading, "On the 21:st Chapter." An intention to complete the fair copy is conveyed by the continuation of pagination through page 570, with eight leaves ruled but otherwise blank at the very end. (Although the corrected fair copy is incomplete, however, the earl's corrections extend throughout the entire holograph.) I have found only one record correlating with the interruption in the earl's design: the entry for the countess in Cokayne includes the comment, "M.I. [monumental inscription] Admon. [testamentary letters of administration] 27 Apr. 1677" (I: 312).[230]

As inappropriate and even impertinent as interpolations in a personal document seem to a twentieth-century reader (or at least to this twentieth-century reader) holding twentieth-century conceptions of the integrity of personhood and authorship, such notions of personhood may be anachronistic when applied to the early modern period.[231] In any event, the interference of the second earl in the papers of subordinated members of his family did not stop with corrections of his dead wife's papers. Facsimiles of several other documents (HN MS EL 8598, 8601, 8603)—copies of various states of an epitaph written by John Egerton, later the third earl, after the death of his first wife, Elizabeth Viscountess Brackley, eldest daughter of

---

[230] According to Robert C. Yorke, the archivist of the College of Arms (letter, 31 May 1997), "the gap of 14 years" between the death of the countess and the administration "may indicate litigation involving the Countess's estate." I have as yet been unable to determine the nature of this litigation, however.

[231] There is some parallel with what Mary Sidney did to her dead brother's manuscripts, so the determinant is not only gender, it is true. Perhaps our modern sense of authorship as a unique self-expression of a uniquely owned private and mysterious mind stems from the Romantics.

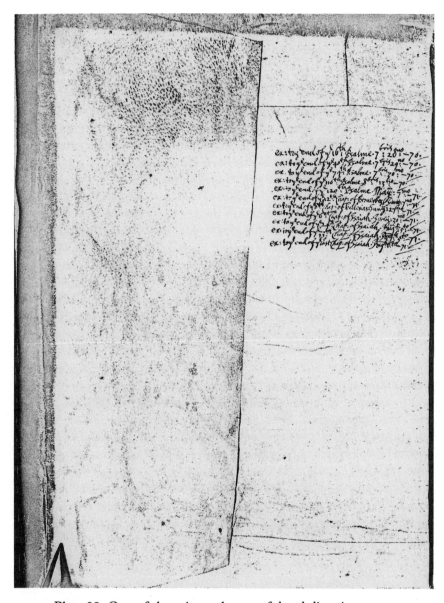

Plate 28: One of the minuscule sets of dated directions
in the handwriting of the second earl.
Reproduced by kind permission of His Grace, Sir John Sutherland Egerton,
sixth Duke of Sutherland, from (the unpaginated) MS EL 8374 housed at
The Huntington Library, San Marino, California.

James, earl of Middlesex, who died after childbirth in 1669/70—are also replete with the second earl's emendations, which are incorporated into the final copy silently (Plates 29, 30, 31). As in the case of the "Meditations," described by the second earl as "written with her own hand, and never (till since her death) seen by any eye but her own, and her then Dear but now sorrowful Husbands, to the admiration both of her eminent Piety in Composing, and of her Modesty in Concealing," the final epitaph is attributed to the viscount in the outer seal of the final copy, HN MS EL 8598, despite the alterations in his father's hand: the label describes the document as "A certificate of *my* wifes & child death" (emphasis added).

True, the changes—as the reproduced copies show—do not altogether shift the basic meanings of these texts. But cumulative differences do change a tone, and in any case, deviate from the author's original intentions. It is interesting, and to me astonishing, that the earl did not hesitate to impose corrections on intimate and extremely private compositions of subordinated members of his family. And it is valuable to ponder the interesting light—or shadow—cast by these documents on a center of controversy in editorial circles, the issue of authority. This controversy rages with particular strength over the editing of Renaissance drama—the original site of much early twentieth-century editorial activity, with scholars arguing over the relative authority of various states of texts, and over the identification of texts as single authored or socially constructed documents.[232] Clearly, however, as the above exemplars indicate, the question of authority is also applicable to the quieter area of private forms. Among the questions that these documents raise, to my mind at least, are the following: Can we generalize from these documents to other questions about authority in private documents? Was the second earl unusual in his editorial intrusiveness? Were his interventions considered appropriate in his time and to his social unit (family) and class (nobility)? Or to his gender? Alternately, were they a facet of an unusually domineering or intrusive personality? How can we know—indeed can we know—the actual authorship/authority of even intimate documents from the early modern period?

---

[232] For recent overviews, see D.C. Greetham, "Criticizing the Text: Textual Criticism," esp. 323–46 in his *Textual Scholarship: An Introduction* (New York: Garland Press, 1994), and Tanselle, "Varieties."

Plate 29: "A certificate of my wifes & childs death," corrected by the second earl.
Reproduced by kind permission of His Grace, Sir John Sutherland Egerton, sixth Duke of Sutherland,
from MS EL 8598 housed at The Huntington Library, San Marino, California.

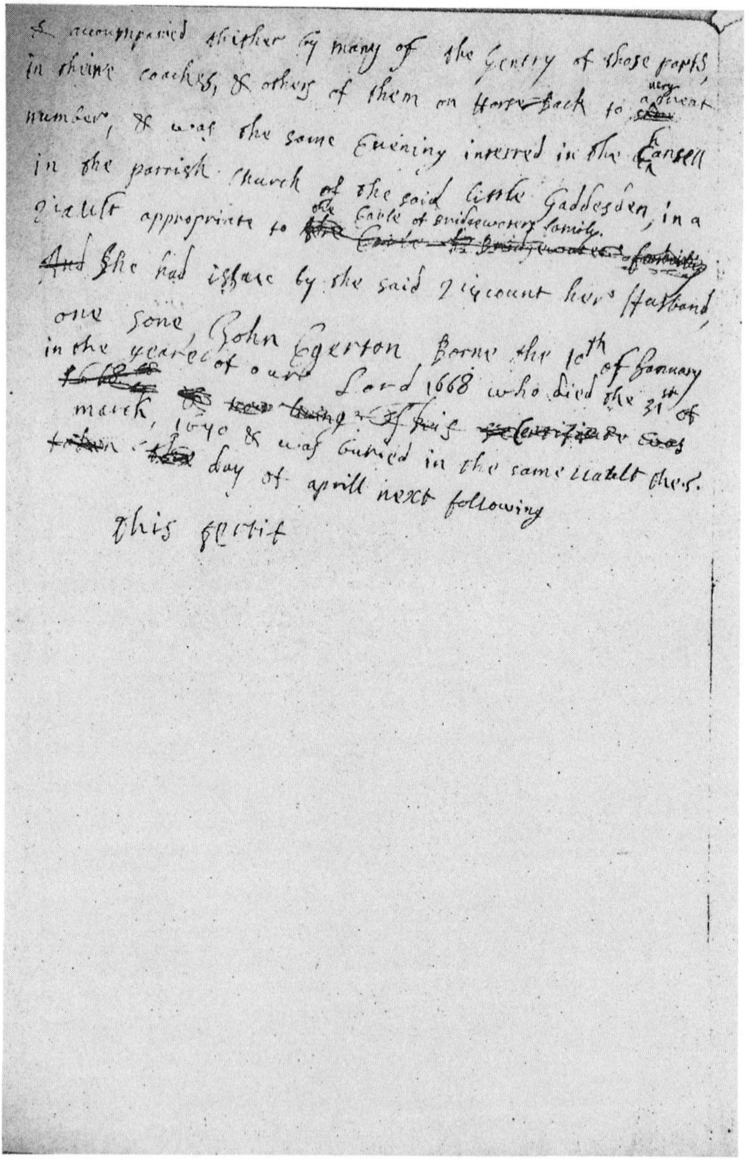

& accompanied thither by many of the Gentry of those parts
in their coaches, & others of them on Horse-back to a very
great number, & was the same Evening interred in the Chancell
in the parrish church of the said little Gaddesden, in a
quire appropriate to the ~~Earle of Bridgewater~~ family.
~~And~~ She had issue by the said Viscount her Husband
one sone John Egerton Borne the 10th of January
in the yeare of our Lord 1668 who died the 31 of
march, 1670 & was buried in the same vault there
... day of aprill next following

This certif

Plate 30: "A certificate of my wifes & childs death,"
corrected by the second earl. Reproduced by kind permission of
His Grace, Sir John Sutherland Egerton, sixth Duke of Sutherland, from
MS EL 8598 housed at The Huntington Library, San Marino, California.

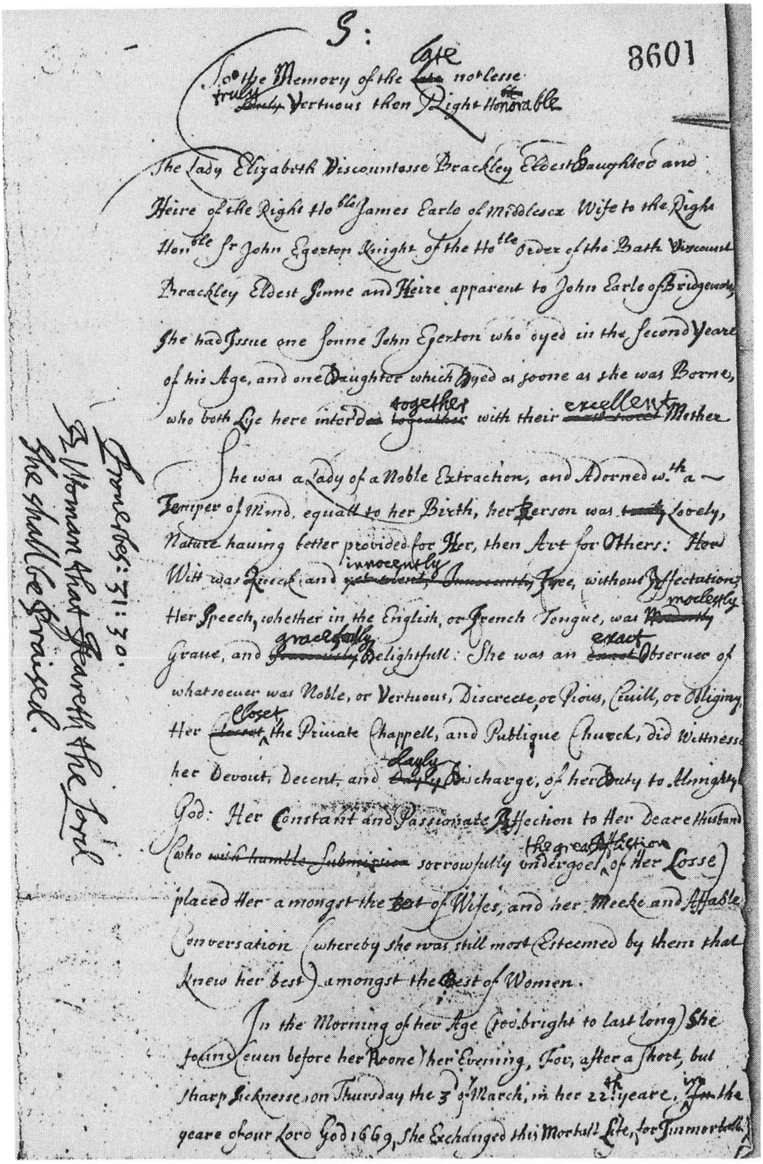

8601

S:

To the Memory of the late not lesse
truly Vertuous then Right Honorable

The Lady Elizabeth Viscountesse Brackley Eldest Daughter and
Heire of the Right Ho[nora]ble James Earle of Middlesex Wife to the Right
Hon[ora]ble Sr John Egerton Knight of the Ho[norab]le Order of the Bath Viscount
Brackley Eldest Sonne and Heire apparent to John Earle of Bridgewater,
she had Issue one Sonne John Egerton who dyed in the second Yeare
of his Age, and one Daughter which dyed as soone as she was Borne,
who both Lye here interred together with their excellent Mother

She was a Lady of a Noble Extraction, and Adorned w[i]th a
Temper of Mind, equall to her Birth, her Person was lovely,
Nature having better provided for Her, then Art for Others: Her
Wit was Quicke and innocently free, without Affectation,
Her Speech, whether in the English, or French Tongue, was modestly
grave, and gracefully Delightfull: She was an exact Observer of
whatsoever was Noble, or Vertuous, Discreete, or Pious, Civill, or Obliging,
Her Closet the Private Chappell, and Publique Church, did Wittnesse
her Devout, Decent, and Lowly Discharge, of her Duty to Almighty
God: Her Constant and Passionate Affection to Her deare Husband
(who with humble Submission sorrowfully undergoes the great Affliction of Her Losse)
placed Her amongst the Best of Wives, and her Meeke and Affable
Conversation (whereby she was still most Esteemed by them that
knew her best) amongst the Best of Women.

In the Morning of her Age (God bright to last long) She
found even before her Noone her Evening, for, after a short, but
sharp Sicknesse, on Thursday the 3 of March, in her 22th yeare, In the
yeare of our Lord God 1669, she Exchanged this Mortall Life, for Immortall.

Proverbs: 31:30. A Woman that feareth the Lord, she shall be praised.

Plate 31: "To the Memory of the late not lesse truly Vertuous then
Right Honorable . . . ," corrected by the second earl. Reproduced by
kind permission of His Grace, Sir John Sutherland Egerton,
sixth Duke of Sutherland, from MS EL 8601 housed at
The Huntington Library, San Marino, California.

4. Death and the Posthumous "Loose Papers"

We have reviewed the extant documentation about the background, childhood, young adulthood, and married life of Elizabeth Cavendish Egerton. Glimpsing her at both serene and difficult periods, examining her juvenilia, and referring occasionally to her later writings, we have caught fleeting records of this person: timid as a child; "peart," and indeed, "pritty, younge and witty . . . fitt for nothinge, but a Citty," as a young adult; sheltered and deferred to though herself obedient as a married woman: at every stage of her life enclosed within a privileged, close-knit, concerned, loving and supportive family circle, and herself expressing and conveying love and concern to those around her (as her letters and Conclusory Meditation indicate). A moon to John Egerton's sun. We have now reached the final crisis and premature end of her life at the age of 37.

Her death was sudden, shocking. After the disruptions of the civil war years, at what must have seemed just the barest beginning of a resumption of the peaceful, conservative lifestyle in which she had been reared, just three years after the birth of her ninth child had been graced by the presence of Charles II and his Lord Chancellor, life at Ashridge was rudely disrupted. In May 1663, responding to a plea from the Lady Elizabeth Cranfield, daughter of James, late second earl of Middlesex (d. 1651), and having obtained a judgment permitting him to do so from Sir Richard Newdigate,[233] John Egerton agreed to act as guardian for the Lady Elizabeth, who had run away from her appointed guardian, her paternal grandmother.[234] The Lady Elizabeth's uncle Lionel (ca. 1625–1674), who in 1651, on his brother's death, succeeded as third earl, challenged Egerton in

---

[233] (Facsimile) HN MS EL 8093, dated May 1663. Sir Richard (1602–1678), a judge, had been called to the bar at Gray's Inn in 1628, and elected an ancient in 1645 and a bencher in 1649. After having been made serjeant-at-law in 1653–4 and a justice of the upper bench in 1654, he suffered a number of checks during the Commonwealth, being removed from the bench in 1655 for declining to serve on a special commission, and being reinstated in 1657. After the Restoration he was remade an old serjeant, and his career was very prosperous.

[234] HN MS EL 8093. Lionel Cranfield, the first earl of Middlesex (1575–1645), was of humble origin. Having been apprenticed as a boy to a merchant adventurer of London named Richard Shepherd, the young Cranfield married his master's daughter Elizabeth (c. 1596) and was forgiven two years of his apprenticeship. His success as a merchant adventurer led to political successes and appointments, and after a second marriage (before 1619/20) to Anne Brett, a relative of Buckingham's wife, to an earldom. Although he suffered reverses for a time in the 1620s, he was restored to favor by 1640. The grandmother was Anne Brett, who survived the first earl until 1670.

very insulting terms[235] under the erroneous impression that he had been privy and party to the running away of his niece. Except in the sense that violence breeds further violence, the final result was unforeseen and unintended. Charles, learning of the intended duel, referred the matter to Parliament as a breach of the peace, with the result that on 12 June 1663 Middlesex was committed to the Tower and Bridgewater to the custody of John Ayton (d. 1676), later Sir John, nephew and heir of the courtier and poet Sir Robert Ayton,[236] who was then the Gentleman Usher of the Black Rod.[237]

The consequence of what had begun as a serio-comic episode was unexpectedly tragic, when the pregnant Elizabeth Egerton, having joined her husband, fell into premature labor and died on the fourteenth of the month, as recorded in the earl's marginalia in Sutton, quoted above, but repeated here to underline its heavy significance to the second earl:

After ye birth of her last Child, who was a Sonne, borne dead, 14: ‹ › Juny: 1663 (about a quarter of an houre after,) my deare Wife, who

---

[235] To wit: "My Lord, I must forget youre quality, sence you haue onely a title, and no honnour, therefore I must let you know, that you are the basest, and the most unworthyest person, that euer owned him selfe, a gentleman, and as for the injury that you haue done mee, know that there is nothing but youre sowrd shall euer giue mee a satisfaction for it, which if suddenly you refuse to giue mee, expect in print, on euery post in ye towne to find youre selfe an infamous coward, this is all from him that scornes you, Middlesex." A facsimile copy in the handwriting of the second earl is held at the Huntington as HN MS EL 8092. On this document, the second earl characterized this challenge as "my Lord of Middlesex his Challenge in ye Billingsgate dialect," seemingly an aspersion on Cranfield's origins.

[236] According to Charles B. Gullans, ed., *The English and Latin Poems of Sir Robert Ayton* (Edinburgh: William Blackwood & Sons, Ltd., 1963), John Ayton apparently first came to court (in 1630), "under the protection of his uncle." John Ayton "claimed the Office of the Black Rod" in 1641, but did not secure it till 1660, when he returned to England at the Restoration of Charles II. After the Restoration, his holdings "were united into the barony of Kippo, and he was styled Sir John Ayton of Kippo." In 1700, his nephew John Aytoun of Kinnaldie was "retoured heir to Sir John in the lands and barony of Kippo" (101 n.1).

[237] The Gentleman Usher of the Black Rod, an officer of the Order of the Garter and of the House of Lords, is the chief gentleman usher of the Lord Chamberlain's department of the royal household, an office that can be traced back to 1348, and that is so called because the incumbent carried his black rod as a symbol of authority. By 1640, one of his functions was apprehending delinquents and bringing them before the House of Lords. (Maurice Bond and David Beamish for the House of Lords Information Office, *The Gentleman Usher of the Black Rod* [London: Her Majesty's Stationery Office, 1976]). I thank Anne Lake Prescott and Jay Shuman for their help in clarifying this reference.

was ye Joy of my heart, ye delight of my Eyes, & ye Comfort of my
Life, deceased, to my irreparable losse, & unasswagable grieffe, & left
me, who was formerly ye most happy, in her sweet Society, now,
being depriv'd of her, ye most miserable of Men. (Sig. A7^v).

The political and ceremonial consequences of this mischance stretched out
for a number of weeks.[238] The grief of John Egerton—compounded, one
speculates from this distance, by a sense of guilt—has been demonstrated
above in such witnesses as this annotation in Sutton and the epitaphs for his
wife and himself. A number of elegies were composed in Elizabeth Egerton's memory; some have already been mentioned, including those by Samuel Holland, writing to her grieving son, John Lord Brackley, and her sister,
the Lady Jane Cheyne; others are unattributed. They testify to widespread
admiration and affection.[239] Other pitiful remains include a fair copy of a
document described by Egerton as "The Exact Coppy of ye Certificate,
entred into ye Heralds booke upon ye death of my intirely beloued Wife,
whose departure hath made her disconsolate Husband irrecouerably Miserable," a "Coppy of ye Inscription on ye Brasse plate on y^e <K>rest of ye Coffin
of my Deare, & neuer to be forgotten Wife."[240] A holograph letter written by Egerton from Ashridge to John Halsey of Lincoln's Inn[241] in August 1663, held in the Hertfordshire Record Office, shows Egerton already
bent on the expensive tomb-building he was to undertake, asking Halsey to

endeavour, if it be possible, to find out those papers wch concerne y^e
Tomb, my father intended for my Mother for my thoughts beate not
so earnestly upon anything in ye World, as upon my intention of
making a Tomb for them both, & my incomparable Wife, & without
those papers my designes will be but lame, I hope therefore yt you

---

[238] Recorded at length in a series of facsimile documents now at the Huntington
(HN MS EL 8091–8093).
[239] Facsimiles of still other extant elegies among the Bridgewater papers (HN MS EL
6888, 11653, 11654, 11655, 11656), although they seem probably to have been composed
about her, cannot be said absolutely to refer to this countess of Bridgewater.
[240] HN MS EL 8348; 8349 (facsimiles).
[241] Sir John Halsey, esquire (1615–1670), the son of William Halsey of Great Gaddesden, was matriculated at New College in 1632, became barrister at law at Lincoln's
Inn in 1641, master in chancery in 1669/70, and was knighted in 1670. (Joseph Foster,
Alumni Oxonienses, Vols. 1–2: 637.)

will haue ye good fortune to find them, yt I may see them, when I see you next.[242]

In another letter (also primarily of a business nature) dated "9:^bris 2:^to 63," from Ashridge and addressed to an unidentified "Sir," he writes heartrendingly of,

Another occasion of Charge I haue had of late (God helpe me) wch was y^t y^t hath made me truly miserable, & poore indeed, ye losse of ye best Wife y^t euer Man was blest w^th: her funerall was Chargeable; Oh, y^t it had pleased God by granting me her Life, to haue preuented y^t Charge, & I shuld haue underualued all other Charges in ye world; for all other Charges do but breake ye purse, but this hath broke my heart; but of ye Charge of it (since it hath pleased God to make me so unhappy as to loose her (I can least of all repent, for I can neuer do enough to testifie ye true loue y^t I did beare to her (who so well deseru'd it of me) & do still beare to her Memory, who was not to be parallelled by any Creature upon Earth[243]

Remembered as a martinet of a patriarch, leaving behind himself some evidences of this firmness, or steadiness, in his directions, in his intricate involvement in family matters, the grieving earl is perhaps most appropriately remembered in the terms he himself established in his epitaph and for his constant visits as recorded by Burghope, on the fourteenth of the month, to his wife's tomb. He never remarried.[244] A long elegy in rhymed couplets, which he composed, of course, sometime between 1663 and 1678, and in which he pays measured tribute to Elizabeth Egerton's memory, as "wife, mother, misteris, & Freind," recalls "The Strange place where she did resigne her Breath," and affirms that "With such a Wife 'tis Heaven on Earth to dwell, / And with her Contrary (a bad one) Hell."[245]

---

[242] HRO AH 1074.

[243] HRO AH 1075.

[244] As noted earlier, Todd—presumably privy to family legend—commented, "His grief appears to have been indelible, however it might have admitted temporary consolation" (*Poetical Works of John Milton*, 5: 200. The statement is repeated in each of the succeeding editions.

[245] HN EL MS 8354 (facsimile). The outside dates are established by the line "Her children (Ten in all) but Foure are gone / Two of each sex ...": the countess died in labor with her tenth child, an unnamed son, in 1663; in 1678, the next of her surviving children (Stuart) died.

In sum, the family tradition about the earl and his wife, echoed in Marie Burghope's lines, seems to perpetuate the nature of their actual relationship, a relationship which was consonant with the ideals of their time about both companionate marriage and the dominance of the husband. There is no trace of the scandal that had rocked the Bridgewater family earlier in the century, or of the unconventional women relatives to whom Elizabeth Egerton could have been constructed as a foil. At every turn in her life, she emerges as an individual deeply rooted in family and in tradition, capable of inspiring the admiration and affection of others towards herself. We also find the hint, although such factors as wealth, status, and affectionate family ties would ordinarily have led her to develop great self-confidence, of a somewhat timid young girl (or perhaps of a person who understood her own limitations) as well as the traces of a "peart" young adult and of a mature individual capable of inspiring the admiration and affection of others towards herself, and as we shall see as we continue to examine her later writings, of experiencing and expressing concern and affection for others.

§

It remains for us to attempt, finally, to recover bibliographic and editorial control of Elizabeth Cavendish Egerton's recorded voice as it is both sounded and muffled in the private memorial her husband constructed for her, the "Loose Papers" that were the starting point for this investigation.[246]

Let me repeat that a reader of the standard twentieth-century notices of this artifact would assume BL MS Egerton 607 to be a lone, chance survival

---

[246] Deborah Rubin has eloquently argued that the recovery of past women's voices is a "work of mourning," but that "we as women/survivors/scholars, especially if we are exploring periods or individuals for whom records are scarce, must move beyond grief over irrevocable loss, and beyond a yearning for the actual person—whose remains will never adequately or surely reconstruct her—to the mediated pleasures of speech, both the dead's and ours" (conversation). Sara Jayne Steen states firmly that "women's scholars want to bring women from behind the arras of a male-determined canon and let them share the stage. The emphasis is on the writer, the woman, her education, her varied roles within her culture, how she perceived herself in relation to her society, how she constructed her everyday reality, how she shaped herself in words, how her roles changed over time, and on us as readers, on how we can interpret what she has to say" ("Behind the Arras: Editing Renaissance Women's Letters," in *Voices of Silence: Editing the Letters of Renaissance Women, 1990 MLA Panel*, ed. Josephine A. Roberts [Amherst, Mass.: RETS, 1990], 6–20).

from the countess's hands. And a hypothetical reader would not be dis-
abused of this notion by the *DNB* or by the description in the *List of Additions to the Manuscripts in the British Museum*, which (omitting the fact that
the manuscript is not a holograph) reads as follows:

> Prayers, Meditations, and devotional pieces, by Elizabeth, Countess
> of Bridgewater, daughter of William Cavendish, Duke of Newcastle;
> collected after her death in 1663, and certified by her husband, John,
> second Earl of Bridgewater. Octavo. [Bibl. Eg. 607.].[247]

It was therefore a great surprise to me to discover listings of what seemed to
be two other copies of the "Loose Papers" in the folio catalogue to the
Bridgewater family library:

> True Coppies of certaine loose Papers left by the Right Hon[ble] Eliza-
> beth, Countesse of Bridgewater. Collected and transcribed together
> here since her death, anno Dni 1663.
>   'Examined by J.Bridgewater'. 84 fos. Bound in leather. 6 3/4" x 4
> 3/8".

and

> do.   do. (Another Copy)
> 4 of the pieces are by Lord Bridgewater. 158 fos. 7" x 4 1/2".[248]

These holdings at the Huntington proved to be among the copyflo facsimile
copies, made in the 1960s, of documents retained at Mertoun. Having
visited Mertoun with the gracious permission of the duke of Sutherland, and
having examined the originals of these facsimiles, I can attest to their existence, but I must also report that I did not find the holograph originals of
the "Loose Papers."

The first public intimation I have been able to trace of the existence of
more than one "transcript" (as Espinasse terms it in the *DNB*) of the "Loose
Papers" appeared in 1790, in Samuel Egerton Brydges's description of Ashridge and the Egerton family in *The Topographer*. In this article, Brydges

---

[247] The manuscript at the British Library is so described in *List of Additions to the
Manuscripts in the British Museum in the Years MDCCCXXXVI–MDCCCXL* (London,
1843), 42. Spelling, etc., for the "Loose Papers" in the text of this volume is, however,
supplied from another witness (reproduced in this volume and described below).

[248] These are HN MS EL 8376 and HN MS EL 8377, respectively. (In volume 10:
7.)

supplemented his description of his own copy of the countess's "Loose Papers," her "occasional meditations and prayers" ("a pretty thick 8vo. fairly written out by an Amanuensis, and certified to be a true copy by the Earl himself with his own hand.—")[249] with the following words:

> The copy in question came from his 3d son the Hon. Thomas Egerton, of Tatton-Park. Probably a copy, so written out and sign'd, was deliver'd by the Earl to each of his children (143).

Emanating from a descendant of the family (indeed, as shown on the reproduction of his family tree, handwritten on a preliminary leaf of the BL exemplar, from a descendant of the Hon. Thomas Egerton, Plate 32) and a well-respected bibliographer, this statement suggesting that multiple copies of the "Loose Papers" had been created at one time from one original seems more than idle supposition.[250] Bibliographically, it suggests that the multiple manuscripts of the "Loose Papers" are what Fredson Bowers termed "equidistant radiating documents" (84), or documents "not genetically related to each other in a linear or derived manner but instead . . . in some manner from the lost archetypal manuscript" (96).[251] Editorially, it suggests that this is a case in which we do not have a "copy-text," or one version of the text clearly more authoritative than the others that should serve as the base copy, so to speak, for an eclectic, or critical, edition.[252] Additional notice of the existence of more than one copy of the "Loose Papers" was provided

---

[249] "History of Ashridge Abbey, Bucks," 142–43 n. The fact that only two copies are described suggests that one was separated early from the family library.

[250] The statement does not, however, altogether match the recovered materials. If a copy was made for each child alive after the death of Elizabeth Egerton (but before the death of the second earl), either six copies would have been made before 1678 (when Stuart died), or five copies between that date and 1686, the date of the death of the second earl. Several therefore would be unaccounted for. Aside from the holographs, a *record* of the same number of copies of the "Meditations" (i.e., three) has surfaced, although only two of these three recorded witnesses has been located), and it is possible either that only three copies of each of these documents were transcribed or that the others are intact or non-extant for identical reasons.

[251] Fredson Bowers, "Multiple Authority: New Problems and Concepts of Copy-Text," *The Library*, 5th series 27. 2 (June 1972): 81–115.

[252] The ultimate implications of the issue are detailed in a recent essay by G. Thomas Tanselle, "Editing Without a Copy-Text," *Studies in Bibliography* 47 (1994): 1–22, in which he discusses eclecticism particularly on 16–18. As Tanselle notes, Bowers considered eclecticism in editing at length in his "Remarks on Eclectic Texts," in his *Essays in Bibliography, Text, and Editing* (Charlottesville: Univ. Press of Virginia, 1975), 488–528.

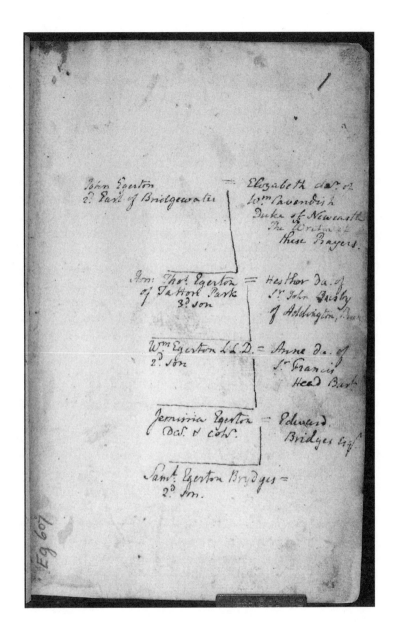

Plate 32: An Egerton family tree ending with Samuel Egerton Brydges
from BL MS Egerton 607, folio 3ᵛ.
Reproduced by permission of The British Library.

by Henry John Todd in his *Poetical Works of John Milton*, where Todd cited Brydges's letter to the *Gentleman's Magazine* describing the contents of the "Loose Papers," and noted, "Among the late Duke of Bridgewater's manuscripts are two attested copies of these pious and tender Meditations; which I have read. They answer the character of them, already given." Despite these notices by Brydges and Todd, it is Espinasse's description in the *DNB* of BL MS Egerton 607, innocent of any reference to other copies of the manuscript, that has achieved the greatest currency.

It is time to describe this perplexing survival. The "Loose Papers" consist of forty-four separate compositions, most of which seem to have been composed at moments of stress, perhaps providing relief of that stress through private transcription. While writing, as noted above, was a problematic activity for respectable early modern women, poised as it was on the verge of a breach of that silence prescribed for women, the contents of these pages all have a personal dimension and therefore fall within the limits allowed women. The tone is uniformly sober, and religious concerns permeate almost every section. More than half deal directly with personal, domestic or interpersonal concerns: childbearing; marriage and widowhood; the "Socyety of Deare and Neere friends;" the domestic occupation of the "vnwinding of a Skeane of silke;" the illnesses of three of Egerton's children; reflections on her mother-in-law's portrait, on her husband's birthday, and on her fear of his impending arrest. Although the recurring prayers connected with child-bearing and childrearing are akin to those in Bentley's *Monument*, the brief essays on marriage and widowhood are, to my knowledge, unique artifacts by a woman of the period, all the more interesting because they were not intended to argue a public case.[253] It is a great pity that we cannot know to what extent John Egerton may have altered them. A prayer on the feared arrest and imprisonment of her husband, while verging on the political, is nonetheless essentially domestic as well. Other prayers and confessions, presumably composed in connection with her exercise of religion within the confines of the family estates, also are in part personal and domestic, not least because they express Egerton's mind, rather than purely "objective" verities.[254] Only the reflections on the "Skeane of silke" and on the "sight

---

[253] In this, as well as in the position they take, they are unlike Mary Astell's later *Some Reflections upon Marriage* (1700).

[254] While the force of her meditations on her children's death is unquestionable, I differ, in my evaluation of these other prayers and meditations, from Clarke, et al., who state that "It is only in the agonising encounters with tragedy in the form of the deaths

of the Countesse of Bridgewater's Picture" could be said to have any affinity
with the literary, and their quality is poor.

Although one would ordinarily assign some weight to the single date
("June.1.day 1648", Plate 33) at the beginning of all three of the manuscripts
(as I did in my first study of the document), and although, again, the
description of the manuscripts as "*True* Coppies" (emphasis added) tends to
a modern reader to suggest that this dating is meaningful, there is no certainty that the earliest of the "Collected" papers are those that begin the
bound manuscript. That this entry dating some seven years after the marriage of Elizabeth and John Egerton is the earliest one datable among the
"Loose Papers" may be merely coincidental. For a number of entries can be
dated, and these (listed here in their order in the "Table" appended to the
manuscript) are not in chronological order in any of the copies. "A prayer in
ye Sicknesse of my Girle Franck" (and the earl's corresponding "A Prayer in
the sicknesse of my Girle Franck") were clearly written between the birth of
Frances in April and her death in July 1648. "A Prayer when I was w.th
Child of Stuart" was written in late 1659 or early 1660, before Stuart's birth
on March 8, 1660. "Vpon occasion of my Husband's Birth-day" (on which
Egerton [b. 1622] "was blest ... to see 27 yeares") was written in June 1649;
"A Prayer for my Husband," beseeching God "to protect him from their
hands of Cruelty, seeking to arrest him" presumably refers to his arrest in
1651, rather than to his final imprisonment by the Black Rod—which surely
would not have merited the term "hands of Cruelty." "Vpon occasion of y^e
Death of my Boy Henry" was written on June 29, 1656, and "On my Boy
Henry," mourning the death of the twenty-nine day-old infant, near that
date. "When I lost my Deare Girle Kate," and "On the same occasion," and
"On the same" were written near the date of the death on 16 August 1660
of Catherine, the "most honored Valentine" of Mr. Benoyst (HN MS EL
8347). (Internal clues date the third entry, which is not out of chronological
order, as it happens: "A Prayer when I was with Child" refers to "my last
Babe Frances," and therefore was composed during her third pregnancy,
with William, who was born on 15 August 1649.)

The "Loose Papers" present us with a number of puzzles. One is the
classification of the manuscript, a document outside traditional, canonical
forms. In an earlier essay, I attempted to place BL MS Egerton 607 within

---

of beloved children that Elizabeth Brackley's individual experience struggles with received
truth to produce a distinctive rhetoric" ("Margaret Cavendish").

Page
1.
June 1st day
1648

A Confeßion of Faith,
w:th Meditation and
Prayer.

My Beleife is in God
the Father, Sonne, and
Holy Ghost, which three
hath beene my Maker, my
Redeemer, and my Sanc=
tifier, and by Faith I may
be saved, though a Sinner,
for there is nothing impoſ=
w:th God; for Jesus Christ saith,
verily

Plate 33: "Page 1" of the Mertoun copy of "The Loose Papers"
reproduced in full in this volume. Reproduced by
kind permission of His Grace, Sir John Sutherland Egerton,
sixth Duke of Sutherland, from MS EL 8377 housed at
The Huntington Library, San Marino, California.

the newly recognized genres of private writings by women with the assistance of some of the useful theoretical work on women's writings of writers like Margo Culley, Sidonie Smith, and Mary Mason,[255] classifying it as representative of that rather amorphous, non-traditional category, the private form, and specifically as the "marginalized" literary form termed by Margo Culley a "periodic life record."[256] It was my assessment then that the "Loose Papers" were related to autobiography, a genre that had its inception in English through a woman (Margery Kempe), that seems to have had great appeal to women, and that took wing in the seventeenth century. Certainly many of the entries in this manuscript, even though their sequencing is indeterminate, seem related to life writing. They also take the particularly female form, discussed by Mary Mason, of "self-discovery of female identity [through the] recognition of another consciousness and . . . the identification of some 'other.'"[257] There is commonality between the qualities of this manuscript and what Brodski and Schenck usefully distinguish in autobiography as a "tension between life and literature, between politics and theory, between selfhood and textuality" (14).[258] In reading it, we can recognize an instance of what Brodski and Schenck term "nonrepresentative, dispersed, displaced subjectivity" (6). In those relatively innocent days, before I discovered the existence of other copies of the British Library manuscript, before I had learnt of and studied other manuscripts by Elizabeth Egerton, and before I had learnt of John Egerton's editorializing practices, I did envision some possible difficulties for the student of this document: "that its contents were assembled, after Egerton's death, apparently at her bereaved husband's direction, and were recopied, possibly by an amanuensis"; [that it] "may be shorter—even considerably shorter—than Egerton's original corpus"; [that it may be] "either incomplete itself or . . . merely one of the countess's compositions"; [that it] "may have been edited by the 'sorrowful'

---

[255] " 'His wife's prayers and meditations': MS Egerton 607," in *The Renaissance Englishwoman in Print*, 241–60.

[256] Margo Culley, *A Day at a Time* (New York: Feminist Press, 1985), 15–17. Her comments on posthumous editing are extremely useful. I provide citations of Culley and other critics (both named in this paragraph and not referred to directly here) in " 'His Wife's Prayers,' " nn. 14–18 and the "Sources, Secondary: Theory, Mainly Feminist."

[257] Mary G. Mason, "The Other Voice: Autobiographies of Women Writers," in James Olney, ed., *Autobiography: Essays Theoretical and Critical* (Princeton: Princeton Univ. Press, 1980): 207–35 (here 209–10).

[258] Bella Brodski and Celeste Schenck, eds., *Life/Lines: Theorizing Women's Autobiography* (Ithaca: Cornell Univ. Press, 1988).

'J. Bridgewater' who examined it, or, alternately, may contain the only scattered papers that he discovered among his wife's effects"; "that these (now)
bound papers do not represent the total range of the countess's thinking";
[and that] "they may not represent the evolution of her thinking either,
since the papers may have been deliberately—or even carelessly—disordered
by Egerton or by his scribe" (" 'His Wife's Prayers,' " 244–46). These poten-
tial difficulties have in fact been substantiated by the further recoveries
reported above.

    These recoveries force us to conclude that while such associations of the
manuscript with the genre of life writing correspond to it as it exists, they
cannot be said to describe it in the form in which Elizabeth Egerton presumably composed its discrete, component parts. And given the further
information about John Egerton's editorial practices that I have now uncovered, it is more precise to note that while this classification fits the manuscript *as it stands*, it is misleading to assign an intention of creating such a
form to Elizabeth Egerton. We have no basis for assuming that the "Loose
Papers" are in a final form that corresponded to her intentions. We are, in
other words, confronting the major editorial issue that G. Thomas Tanselle
has called "The Editorial Problem of Final Authorial Intention" (n. 8). The
fact that Elizabeth Egerton's loose papers were assembled by another hand
after her death, put in an order that she did not authorize, possibly—even
probably, given his earlier practice—revised by her husband, and inevitably
altered—however unintentionally—by the scribe who copied them, necessi-
tates some re-evaluation of the bound manuscript into which they were
collected.

    Before considering this difficulty further, we might note another useful
context for consideration of the "Loose Papers," one that is particularly relevant since the document is deeply tinged with religious sentiment: the Protestant meditative tradition, particularly as it had taken shape in Protestant
books of devotion by Elizabeth Egerton's time, a tradition that has been
studied very usefully by Helen C. White.[259] The "Loose Papers" are con-

---

[259] *English Devotional Literature [Prose] 1600–1640* (New York: Haskell House,
1966). Her *Tudor Books of Private Devotion* (Madison, Wis.: Univ. of Wisconsin Press,
1951) provides useful background information. Another overview of Protestant forms of
meditation that I have found very helpful is Barbara Kiefer Lewalski's "Protestant Meditation: Kinds, Structures, and Strategies of Development for the Meditative Lyric," 147–
65 (Chap. 5) in her *Protestant Poetics and the Seventeenth-Century Religious Lyric* (Princeton, N.J.: Princeton Univ. Press, 1979). A recent study that sheds light on the devotion

sonant with key Protestant beliefs in conscious avoidance of any trace of
Roman Catholic doctrine, in heavy concentration on biblical citation, and in
application of methods of self-analysis in order to bring about penitence and
purification. Elizabeth Egerton is squarely within the boundaries of the form
of meditation developed by such writers as Thomas Rogers, Edward Bunny,
and Joseph Hall, a form that differed from Catholic meditations stressing
ascent to God through meditation on His qualities, and that instead centered on such central Protestant beliefs as "Justification by Faith, Predestination and Election, and the reliance on Scripture as the final authority"
(White, *English Devotional Literature*, 187). Elizabeth Egerton's meditations
focus on such typical Protestant subjects and concerns as signs of regen-
eration (connected, often, with the taking of communion); considerations of
sinfulness; and experiences that manifest God's involvement in her life. In
consonance with Protestant practice, she is deeply concerned with the question of her salvation, and her many meditations on communion (as well as
her husband's[260]) concentrate on the stirring up of appropriate responses.
Egerton constantly employs two Protestant systems of meditation: those
occasioned by meditation on objects in the world and those originating in
the conscious choice of a subject in a time set aside for that purpose; in both
cases she draws connections between the Bible and her own life. These foci
are clear in a reading of the text of the "Loose Papers," as in the meditation
"Vpon occasion of ye Death of my Boy Henry," when the countess beseeches
"let me never goe so farre, o Lord, as David did, would God I had dyed for
thee my Child, as he said of his sonne Absolon."[261]

In a series of observations that seem very suited to the tenor of Elizabeth
Egerton's "Loose Papers," White observed,

> Like prayer[,] meditation is one of the gentler arts of the religious
> life and one of the more purely inward. Like prayer it is not likely to
> flourish in a clash of points of view. Like prayer its processes are not
> discursive, and its findings are of scant avail for argumentation. It

---

of lay persons like the countess is Judith Maltby, *Prayer Book and People in Elizabethan
and Early Stuart England* (Cambridge, 1998). I thank Leslie S. B. MacCoull for bringing
this study to my attention.

[260] Aside from the portions of the "Loose Papers" on communion that are actually by
John Egerton, the second earl's many pages of annotation and reflection in Sutton (*Godly
Meditations*) indicate a similar preoccupation on his part.

[261] An allusion to 2 Sam 18: 33.

grows rather out of accepted premises; its peculiar service to the life of the mind and spirit lies not in any aptitude for the discovery or establishment of truth but rather in the fullness of its realization of truth. It has little in it of the Church Militant and much of the Church Triumphant. When the strifes of this world of uncertainties are over, and their swords are laid away, meditation will keep her gentle way over the heavenly fields. (*English Devotional Literature*, 153–54)

In contrast to those by her two kinswomen—Elizabeth Hastings and Bridget Egerton— Elizabeth Egerton's meditations are distinctively informal and even unpolished. It is impossible to know whether this distinction results from the unreadiness of the material to be collected and transcribed at the time of her sudden death or from a relative lack of sophistication on the part of the countess. As the reader will see, a final, arresting quality that sets them apart from the manuscripts of the meditations by her kinswomen[262] is their deep individuality. These are not collections of cherished texts or approved summaries of the writings of others; instead, they read as though they were being penned as they were formed in Elizabeth Egerton's mind, and are therefore tinged by the personal, even when they consider impersonal, eternal questions. In their informality and intensity, her prayers more closely resemble the fervent, reported words of two other seventeenth-century women, the uneducated Bessie Clarksone and the noblewoman, Helen Livingston.[263]

Like her "Meditations" on the Bible, Elizabeth Egerton's "Loose Papers" clearly demonstrate that the text of the Bible was central to her thinking, and the glosses that I have supplied demonstrate some of that indebtedness. Yet we are reminded of a clear irony if we contrast the "Loose Papers" with

---

[262] Elizabeth Egerton's prose lacks the resonance characteristic of the more firmly paraphrasical "Certain Collections" of Elizabeth Hastings and of the "Forme of Confession" of Bridget Egerton, but it is only fair, after all, to consider these "Loose Papers" a work in progress, left scattered at Elizabeth Egerton's death. Her anchorage in the Bible is very clear.

[263] Both women are reported to have originated confessional materials that appeared in print in the first half of the seventeenth century. Clarksone's *Conflict in Conscience* (*RSTC* 16611) was put to press by her minister, William Livingstone, in 1631. *The Confession and Conversion* of Eleanor Hay Livingston appeared in print in 1629. Both texts are among those reproduced in *Brief Confessional Writings*, ed. Mary Ellen Lamb, in the Ashgate Press series, *The Early Modern Englishwoman: A Facsimile Library of Essential Works* (forthcoming 1999).

Elizabeth Egerton's "Divine Meditations," which are not noted in the *DNB* and were not accorded much attention in those traditions about the countess that did survive. For unlike the "Loose Papers," the "Divine Meditations" descend to us as a relatively plentiful and revealing record: an original document, the editing of that record by another hand, and the final folding of the editing into the equivalent of a published document. In other words, in the "Meditations," the tampering with Elizabeth Egerton's words by John Egerton is overtly before us: we have both her holograph—bearing his corrections—and a fair copy—incorporating them. However, the authority of her "Loose Papers"—the manuscript for which she has been most remembered (and for that reason, the root of this attempt to study her)—is far more problematic: the "Loose Papers," the manuscript mentioned by Espinasse in the *DNB*, is a fair copy without the benefit of any witnesses in anterior or intermediate states.[264]

Alas, there is therefore no way to penetrate beneath the surface of this British Library manuscript to ascertain exactly what Elizabeth Egerton wrote and what was altered, although I wish to emphasize that we do have the direct testimony of the title page of the document (reproduced above, on p. 4) to point us in the correct direction for understanding it. The *bound* BL MS Egerton 607, "Examined by JBridgewater," as the title page shows us, consists of "True Coppies of certaine *Loose Papers* left by ye Right ho.^{ble} ELIZABETH Countesse of BRIDGEWATER Collected and Transcribed together here since Her Death Anno Dni. 1663" (emphasis added). The "Loose Papers" did not exist in their present physical state in the lifetime of Elizabeth Egerton. There is no basis for assuming that Elizabeth Egerton would have joined these particular "Loose Papers" together or that she would have bound them in this particular order, much less that she would have wished them preserved—or altered. There is no basis for establishing the extent of the original body of her "Loose Papers," although the impulse that seems to have underlain John Egerton's collecting, copying, and binding of them suggests that he was motivated by a wish to perpetuate his wife's memory and activities and therefore that he included more, rather than less,

---

[264] Light does not emanate from Espinasse, who (aside from not mentioning the existence of different manuscripts of meditations by Elizabeth Egerton) does not describe BL MS Egerton 607 as one of a number of copies of the "Loose Papers" of Elizabeth Egerton (and who may, indeed, have been unaware of the existence both of other manuscripts and of other copies of this one).

of her scattered papers. That the contents of the manuscript are dubbed "*True* Coppies" (emphasis added) suggests at least an intention to transcribe them accurately and exactly. Modern assumptions about the integrity of another's wishes and awareness of the contamination of the historical record do not seem to have obtained in the mind of the second earl. Yet although one might cautiously hypothesize that a desire to perpetuate would be coupled with care in preserving an original document, we know that these papers are not bound in the order in which they were composed, and, as we have seen, we have—in the case of Elizabeth Egerton's "Meditations" and in the case of the memorial documents by Egerton's son—clear evidence of tampering by the second earl with the writings of subordinated members of his family. To assume that similar tampering did not take place in the case of these "Loose Papers"—attested to have been "Examined by JBridge-water"—would be to fly in the teeth of the evidence. It would belie the unconscious irony of the desire John Egerton expressed in his epitaph that there be "No other Memorial of him" beyond a record of his joy in his marriage to Elizabeth Cavendish and of his sorrow as a widower; a desire that distorts and even conceals the invisibility of assumptions of male priority by John Egerton, Elizabeth Egerton, and others, then and since: i.e., of the underlying status of a moon to his sun.

Assumption of the muddled authority of BL MS Egerton 607 is substantiated by comparison of the three scribal witnesses. On examination, none of the three surviving fair copies has proved to be precisely the same; even though each of the three bears on its title page the attestation "Examined by JBridgewater," the number of lines per page (and hence the number of pages) varies in each; the accidentals and occasionally the order of the entries in the manuscripts are not constant from copy to copy. Therefore, Egerton's approbation suggests either a less perfectionist standard than ours for copying or less than careful scrutiny. Far more significantly, in addition to such accidental variants as those sketched above, one of the manuscripts now housed at Mertoun, as the Bridgewater family catalogue notes, contains a comment that informs us that some of the entries were not written by Elizabeth Egerton at all (Plate 34). This witness, the one that is in facsimile at the Huntington labeled HN MS EL 8377, carries towards its end the notation, "The 4 following pieces were made by JB" (269). While these four entries ("Spoken Vpon the receiving a Cake of perfume made up in the Shape of a Heart," "A contemplation on the sight of a Cushion," "A Prayer in the sicknesse of my Girle Franck," and "A Preparatory Prayer before y^e receiuing of y^e Blessed Sacrament of the Lords Supper") are included in all

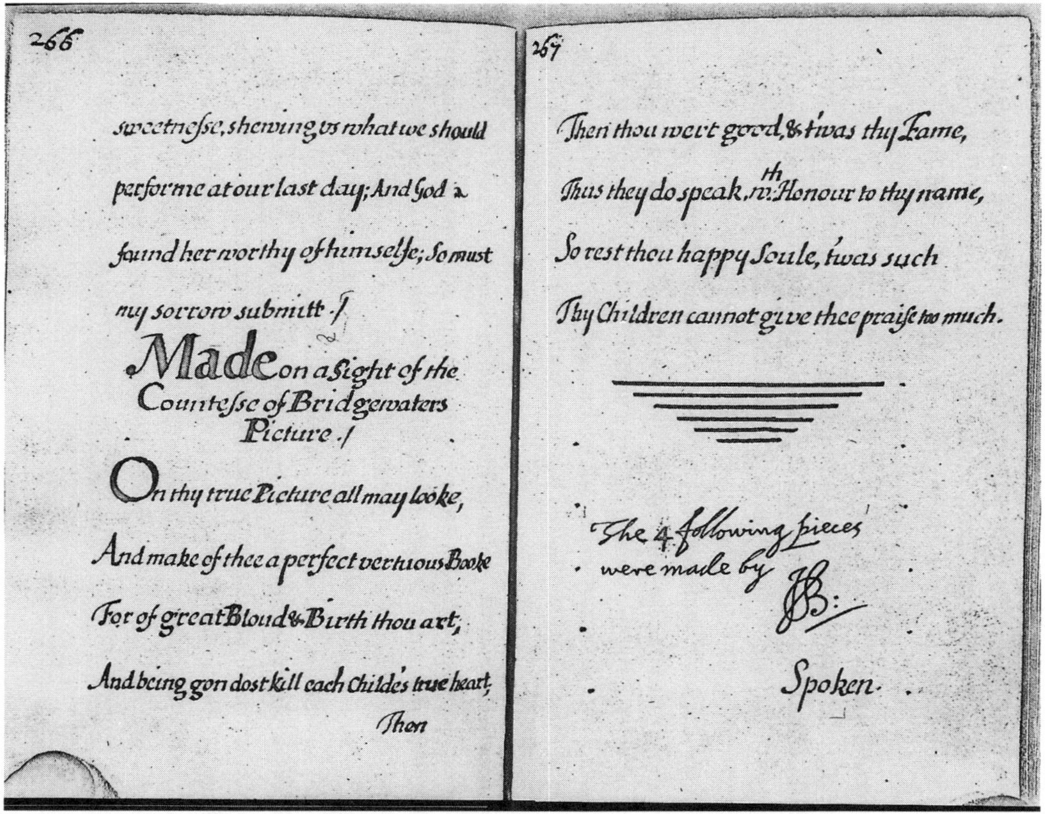

...weetneße, shewing to whatwe should

performe at our last day. And God a

found her worthy of himselfe, so must

my sorrow submitt ./

Made on a sight of the
Countesse of Bridgewaters
Picture ./

On thy true Picture all may looke,

And makes of thee a perfect vertuous Booke

For of great Bloud & Birth thou art,

And bring gon dost kill each childes true hart.

Then

Then thou wert good, & t'was thy fame,

Thus they do speak, in Honour to thy name,

So rest thou happy Soule, t'was such

Thy Children cannot give thee praise too much.

The 4 following pieces
were made by JB:/

Spoken.

Plate 34: "The 4 following pieces were made by JB:/."

Reproduced by kind permission of His Grace, Sir John Sutherland Egerton, sixth Duke of Sutherland, from page 267 of MS EL 8377 housed at The Huntington Library, San Marino, California.

three copies of the manuscript, in BL MS Egerton 607 and in HN MS EL 8376 they are simply incorporated into the manuscript with no indication that they were not written by Elizabeth Egerton. In other words, in two of the copies, including the most publicly accessible (the one at the British Library), all the entries in the manuscript are seamlessly attributed to Elizabeth Egerton, while the third witness (reproduced in this volume) testifies that some are not hers. As noted earlier, this problematization is further underlined by the existence (at the Huntington, as HN MS EL 8372) of a facsimile of the last of these four entries, "A Preparatory Prayer," in the hand of the second earl (Plate 21, above).

Some of the limitations we face in interpreting and attributing the "Loose Papers" by Elizabeth Egerton are individual: connected to the editorial practices of her husband and the date at which the document was assembled. Yet we are realistically compelled to assume that the editorializing was intended to "improve" and "refine," to preserve and not to erase, and that it did not altogether alter her intentions, that in these pages, however fuzzily, we have at least an approximation to the actual thinking of a respectable, conventional wife and mother, speaking her own thoughts (somewhat refined and perhaps reordered by her posthumous editor) but supporting conventional religious and domestic values. And if considered from another standpoint, the four most problematic entries, as I suggested in an earlier study, offer future students an exciting opportunity to consider the differences between male and female writing on the same subject, a subject of great interest to students of the rhetoric that was not taught early modern women, since each can be associated with a similar entry by Elizabeth Egerton.[265] To say this is not to gainsay two further distinctions. One is the possible dissimilarity in capacity between this particular man and this particular woman—a dissimilarity we cannot measure from this distance. The second is that John Egerton's added entries presumably were honed to a form he considered finished, while the entries by Elizabeth Egerton may not have been so revised and indeed have an unsophisticated flavor (what Sidonie Smith terms "amateur writing"[266]), appropriate to compositions on

---

[265] "Reconstructing the Still, Small Voice: The Occasional Journal of Elizabeth Egerton," 198. On early modern women and instruction in rhetoric, see Walter J. Ong, "Latin Language Study as a Renaissance Puberty Rite," *SP* 56 (1959): 103–24.

[266] *A Poetics of Women's Autobiography: Marginality and the Fictions of Self-Representation* (Bloomington: Indiana Univ. Press, 1987), 42. Smith usefully discusses the silencing and passivity attendent on a "self-representation structured in the fictions of goodness and

"loose" papers that might have been revised by the author had she lived to do so.

A final limitation that we must recognize in studying this document is the reality that we all come to recognize: that there is, ultimately, no way absolutely to penetrate all the veils that separate us from persons and events we study in the past (or even in our own time) with absolute authority. Yet however dim the light these bound "Loose Papers" shed, however dubious their current condition as a bound manuscript, they constitute an extremely rare type of record. For the musings originating with Elizabeth Egerton that these pages contain bring us close to—if not absolutely in touch with—the thinking of an early modern woman. We can assume that efforts at recovery will bring other such documents to light, but at present the "Loose Papers" remain a rarity and merit our serious, if cautious, attention.

§

The documentary edition of the "Loose Papers" that follows reproduces the text of one of the witnesses at Mertoun, the copy catalogued at the Huntington as HN MS EL 8377, hereafter styled "77," because this manuscript bears the interesting and unique annotation "The 4 following pieces were made by JB." This unique annotation might today suggest that additional attention had been paid to 77, but given the editorial habits of the second earl described above, we cannot infer that 77 is generally a more reliable copy than the others. Rather, each of these three clearly written witnesses seems to fit the category of radiating copies, none requires extensive emendation, and none seems to carry greater authority than the others. It therefore seemed more logical to reproduce one of the three texts that could equally be argued to be a contemporary version, close to the intentions of the countess, rather than to produce the eclectic edition I had originally intended to create. The documentary edition is followed by a unified "Record of Variants" in which the copy from the British Library is styled "BL," the second copy at Mertoun (designated at the Huntington as HN MS EL 8376), "76," and as already noted, the copy reproduced here, "77."[267]

---

self-effacement," (55) a form of "*self*-representation"(emphasis added) to which the present analysis of the "Loose Papers" adds an extra degree of irony.

[267] I employ the system created by G. Thomas Tanselle in his "Editorial Apparatus for Radiating Texts," *Library*, 5th Series, 29 (1974): 330–37.

I have opted to present the text of 77 in clear reading form, unemended, except for the following interventions: The page numbers from the manuscript of 77 are supplied in square brackets for the ease of readers who may wish to check the transcription against the facsimile at the Huntington. (The differing page breaks in the other two manuscripts, however, are not reported.) Headings, which are centered in 77, are, for ease in reading, regularized here as single lines beginning at the left margin, and a few sample pages of 77 are reproduced here to convey the design of the original manuscript. The one date found at the beginning of the first entry of 77 (where it is placed in the margin) is also printed here as a separate line at the very beginning of the transcription. When words are broken at the end of a page, the hyphen is not reported and the word is printed after the page number. The slanted line at the end of some headings has been treated as a matter of design and has not been reproduced.

Catchwords are reported in the "Record of Variants" only when they differ from the first word of the next page. Hyphenation in the "Record of Variants" is given in the form of the double hyphens employed in each of the witnesses to signify word breaks at the end of lines. Hyphenation is not reported when there is no possibility of retaining the hyphen in the spelling of the word. Similarly (because I am not attempting to report such nontextual details), a small number of citations of biblical passages that appear in the margins of the pages of the first meditation are printed here as footnotes (inserted at the end of the line at which they are positioned in the manuscript) rather than in the margins, since this seemed to me the clearest way to present them to the reader. Because these citations are substantively the same in all three witnesses, I have not reported the minor variants in punctuation among them. In addition to these footnotes, I have supplied a relatively small number of citations of biblical allusions as footnotes, distinguishing these additions from the marginalia present in 77.

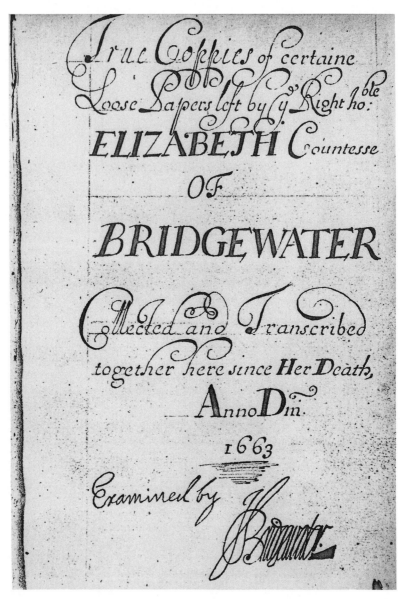

Plate 35: The title page of the Mertoun copy of "The Loose Papers" reproduced in full in this volume. Reproduced by kind permission of His Grace, Sir John Sutherland Egerton, sixth Duke of Sutherland, from MS EL 8377 housed at The Huntington Library, San Marino, California.

True Coppies of certaine
Loose Papers left by y Right ho.[ble]
ELIZABETH *Countesse*

OF

BRIDGEWATER

Collected and Transcribed
together here since Her Death,

Anno Dm.

1663

Examined by

JBridgewater./

[1] Page 1 June.1ˢᵗ. day 1648

A Confeſsion of Faith, w.ᵗʰ Meditation and Prayer.

My Beleife is in God the Father, Sonne, and Holy Ghost, which three hath
beene my Maker, my Redeemer, and my Sanctifier, and by Faith I may be
saved, though a Sinner, for there is nothing impoſ wᵗʰ God; for Jesus Christ
saith, [2] verily if you haue Faith[1] as a graine of Mustard-seed, you shall
say vnto this Mountaine, remove hence to yonder place, and it shall remove,
and nothing shall be impoſsible vnto you: neither do I hold I can merit, by
my works, but by Gods mercy, for I am a Sinner, [3] and such a Sinner,
that without his great goodneſse, I can hope of no redemption, yet he sent
our Saviour, to dye that bitter death, wᶜʰ he suffer'd for me vpon the Croſs;
and his bloud shed for me washeth my sinnes a way, though they be as red
as Crimson, makes [4] them as white as Snowe;[2] yet still, without his grace,
my life can not owne a place in Heaven, but it must be his mercy, which
must save me: neither do I hold Predestination, so as to think I shall be
saved though I be the vilest Creature on earth, but God hath [5] given vs
the Spirit of prayer, for Jesus saith, Watch you[3] and pray, least you enter
into temptation, the Spirit is ready but the flesh is weake we can challenge
no goodneſse, but what is given vs from God, and 'tis he that hath given vs
prayer to acknowledge [6] him, for Christ saith vnto you, aske, and it shall
be[4] given you, Seeke, and ye shall find, knock, and it shall be opened vnto
you, for every one that asketh, receiveth, & he that seeketh, findeth, and to
him that knocketh, it shall be opened: for [7] God left Adam to himselfe,
and he sinned in eating of the forbidden Tree, & though God suffered him
to know both good and evill, yet he would not suffer him to tast of yᵉ Tree
of life;[5] From hence are we born in sinne, and without Christ's birth [8]
and death we could not haue hope of a resurrection; thus if God leaues vs
to our selves, we are leſs then nothing, and though we know good and evill,
yet are we subject to do ill, but not to do good, without his grace, for he
saith, my[6] [9] grace is sufficient for thee. For fasting; 'tis not that I think
there is any merit in it, but that I hold a day of Fasting, and prayer, is

---

[1] The following citation appears in the margin of 77: 17. Mat. 20.
[2] Is. 1.18.
[3] 77 marg.: 14 Mark.38.
[4] 77 marg.: 11: Luke.9&.10.
[5] Gen. 3.
[6] 77 marg.: 12.2.Cori.9.

fitting to goe together; and in many places you shall read where Fasting and prayer goes [10] together. But the dayes[7] will come, when the Bridegroome shall be takē away from them, and then shall they Fast in those dayes; and who is the Bridegroome, but our Saviour? and now he is gone from vs on earth, haue we not reason to Fast, since he hath [11] commanded vs? and sure, especially before we receive him (which is the Seale of our salvation, wrought by him) in the communion. Besides our Saviour tells vs, How be[8] it this kind goes not out, but by prayer, and fasting, which was concerning [12] the Devill he cast out of the Child, which you may[9] read: and if he fasted to cure vs, haue not we great cauſe to fast for our sinnes? and surely the Devill was the Childe's crying Sinne; and can we owne to have none? ô no! I may cry wᵗʰ the Prodigall Sonne, Father[10] [13] I haue sinned against Heaven, and in thy sight, and am no more worthy to be called thy Sonne, & I may cry with the blind man, Thou Sonne of David[11] haue mercy on me; and by Faith he was made whole, from that very houre; now we may see that by [14] faith, prayer, and fasting, we may obteyne favour with God our Heavenly Father; yet we must haue repentance, but it must come from the bottome of our heart, and then doubtleſs we may be saved; For Christ saith vnto vs, that[12] likewise Joy shall be in [15] heaven over one Sinner that repenteth, more then over Ninety and Nine just persons, that needs no repentance; and though we know our sinnes to be so great, yᵗ they cry against vs yet lest we should goe into the sinne of desperation, [16] our Saviour comforts vs, looking vpon vs saith wᵗʰ[13] men it is impoſsible, but not with God, for with God all things are poſsible: his anger is but[14] for a moment; there is no vnrighteousneſse in him; he is mercifull and[15] gracious, after many sinnes [17] he invites, and accepts of our repenting; he shews loving kindneſs vnto Thousands, his bowells yernes vpon vs, vpon our repentance; he afflicts, vntill we know him to be the Lord; he is[16] slow to

---

[7] 77 marg.: 2:Marke.20.
[8] 77 marg.: 17.Mat:21.
[9] 77 marg.: 17 Mat: 18.
[10] 77 marg.: 15.Luke.21.
[11] 77 marg.: 10.Mark.47.
[12] 77 marg.: 15 Luke:7.
[13] 77 marg.: 10.Mark.27.
[14] 77 marg.: Psal: 30.5.
[15] 77 marg.: Psal: 103.8.
[16] 77 marg.: Nahum.1.3.

anger, and great in power, he reteyneth [18] not his anger for ever, becauſe he delighteth in mercy, he is just, and having salvation. I beleeve in the Holy Ghost, who is my Sanctifyer, he is Gods Meſsenger to infuse the Spirit of Grace into vs, he was our first spirit of good tyedings, for he [19] brought the knowledge of his Spirit to the virgin Mary: with which she conceived a Sonne; vnto the Lord:[17] then John said he Baptized with water, but one mightyer then I commeth, he shall Baptize you with the Holy Ghost, and with Fyer;[18] [20] then our Saviour commanded John to Baptize him, and when he was Baptized, the Heavens were opened vnto him, and he saw the Spirit of God descending like a Dove and lighting vpon him, saith this is my beloved Sonne in whom [21] I am well pleased:[19] So when we haue grace, we haue Gods spirit, wch is the Holy Ghost; you see he was the first knowledge of our Saviour, and still he is the first Sacrament we receive after our birth from our Parents, for then we are Baptized, to wash [22] a way our originall sinne, then Christ dyed to redeem vs from our actuall sinne, he descended into Hell, then he rose from the dead, he ascended into Heaven, and there he sitteth on the right hand of our heavenly Father, and eternall God, to judge [23] to save, or to condemne vs; and I beleeve the Holy Catholick Church, the Communion of Saints, the resurrectiō of the dead, which why should I doubt, when Christ shewed vs on earth an Example in Lazarus, in raiſing [24] him out of the Grave, when we receive the Sentence of death, it is because we should not trust in our selves, but in God, who raiſeth the[20] dead; when we are delivered to death for Jesus sake, it is that the[21] life of Jesus might be [25] manifest in our mortall body. And I beleeve there is a life everlasting, for after our sufferings indured, God refresheth vs with many adorning mercyes, he taketh pleasure in vs & beautifies vs wth salvation; we are saved by the [26] Lord with everlasting Salvation, not to be ashamed, or confounded world without end; God gives vs affliction to confirme vs vnto ye end, that we may be blamlesse in the day of his appearance, which is the day of [27] Judgment, and when we see him, we shall sing prayses; for you may read that when the body rises againe, and is not left in the grave, it is matter of

---

[17] Lk 2:10.
[18] Acts 1:5.
[19] Mt 3:17; 12:18.
[20] 77 marg.: 2:Cor:1:9.
[21] 77 marg.: 2.Cor:4.10:.

gladne∫se, rejoycing and confidence; and when the Lord descends, [28] he comes with the voyce of Archangells, which is the voyce of Joy and gladne∫s; and ô Lord grant to me that I may not be guilty, but innocent, when I come to thee, but how can I a sinner, be cleare from sinne? [29] therefore ô Lord rebuke me not in thy anger, neither chasten me in thy displeasure, but hear my prayer, ô God, and hide not thy selfe from my petition, which is, ô Christ, that I may never want oyle in [30] my lamp, to meete thee, and so to be shutt out of Heavenly comfort, but give me I beseech thee ever a watchfull knowledge of thy truth, that I may not suddenly be taken, when thou ô God, shalt call me, but that I may [31] be ready to see thee yᵉ light of my salvation;²² Lord give me and continue me in Holy devotion to thee, and yᵗ I may not be led by yᵉ Devill, to any vile actions, or thoughts against thy divine Majesty, still keepe [32] me from all sinne and prophane∫se against thy Holy Church; make me to heare of Joy and gladne∫s, that the bones which thou hast broken may rejoyce, let thy mercyfull kindne∫s [33] be ever vpon me, & make me still more and more put my whole trust in thee, Ô God, in thee, ô Father, Sonne, and Holy Ghost.

[34] A Prayer in the Sickne∫se of my Girle Franck.

O Almighty and eternall God, I with an Humble Heart to thee, beseech thee that am now greeved for my poore sick Child, I beg of [35] thee, ô God, and of thy Sonne my Saviour, to heale her, from her great paine, and sickne∫se, thou that art the God of all Gods, and of all things, have mercy, and compa∫sion of my dear Infant, restore [36] her I beseech thee, to be a healthfull child, and bring her out of the jawes of death; Lord Jesus look vpon my affliction and hear my prayer and let it be as thou hast said, that whatsoever [37] you aske in prayer, beleiving you shall receive;²³ Lord I beleeve that thou art the only true God, and without thee wee are nothing, and with thee, and thy grace, we are to feare and [38] magnifie thy name; ô sweet Jesus, say vnto me, as thou didst to the woman of Canaan, ô woman great is thy faith, be it vnto thee even as thou wilt, and immediatly the Child was made [39] whole, from that houre;²⁴ Lord there is nothing impo∫sible wᵗʰ thee; as thou rai∫edst Lazarus from the grave, so rai∫e my

---

²² Mt 25:3.
²³ Jn 16: 24.
²⁴ Mt 15:22.

deare Babe to long life, that shee may enjoy the Honour of Age,[25] and w.th
thy [40] spirit take her by the hand, as thou did'st the Damsell Tabbitha,
saying ariſe,[26] so I beseech thee say to her, & I humbly desire thee, ô
Lord, to have mercy on her, and lay not my sinnes [41] to her innocent
charge, neither punish me ô Lord in taking her from me; I know ô Sweet
Jesus, and beleive, that thy power is as great in Heaven, as it was on earth,
therefore I beg it [42] of thee, to have compaſsion on her in this world, but
if it please not thee to give an eare, nor say Amen to these my fervent
prayers, I beg wth my teares, to have mercy of her in y^e [43] world to come,
and to make her one of thy Elect in Heaven, which is a glorious Saint, and
to give me patience for the loſse of her, and to take this affliction, without
grudging, at thy [44] holy will, but yet Lord let me say wth Abraham, let not
my Lord be angry, and I will speake but this once,[27] wch is to grant her
long life, which is the prayer of me, that prayes in this most [45] holy and
direct prayer, wch Christ thy only son hath taught vs. Our Father w:^{ch} art in
Heaven &c:[28]

[46] A Prayer when I was with Child
O God to thee I give all praiſe and glory, that thou hast beene pleased to
bleſse me, that I have conceived againe with Child, and hast [47] of thy
great goodneſse, given it the Spirit of life, so I beseech thee infuse the Spirit
of thy grace into it, and give it, all perfect shapes, that I may see w.th
comfort, thy mercyfull [48] hand to me, in this Child I am now wthall; yet
ô Sweet Jesus, let me not only petition thee in prayer, but acknowledge a
thanksgiving; for that thou did'st send me the comfort of [49] two, a Male,
and Female, and madest me Joyfully to behold them and they to receive the
Sacrament of Baptisme, I humbly beg the same goodneſse to this, and still
[50] replenish thy loveing kindneſse to me, in the life of my deare Babes,
thou art pleased to send me; and give them true knowledge and vnderstanding
in all things and [51] especially in thee, and in thy most holy word, where
they shall not faile of true vertue, and if it be thy good will lay not thy heavy
hand of Justice and affliction on me, in [52] takeing a way my Children in
their youth, as thou wast pleased to take my last Babe Frances, but Ô Lord

---

[25] Jn 11: 1–12:19.
[26] Acts 9:36–42.
[27] Gen 18:30.
[28] Mt 6:9.

my God, look downe with thy mercyfull eye and bleſse them, as thou didst
[53] Abraham, and Jacob, Sarah, and Rebekah[29] and when t'is thy pleasure
to call them, make them joyfully to see thee, in thy Cælestiall Kingdom,
where they are purifyed from all their sinnes. [54] Now ô deare God, Father
of all truth, I beg of thee to have compaſsion on me in the great paine I am
to feele, in the bringing forth of this my Child, and I beseech thee lay no
more on me, [55] then thou wilt enable me to beare, and let the sufferings
of thy sonne, my Saviour ease my paine, as his bloud shed on the Croſse
washed me from my sinnes; ô Sweet Jesus, when that I come to the [56]
cruell grones of labour, in this my travaile giue me patience, and sure
confidence in thee, and in thy mercy, and to beleive thy most holy words,
come vnto me all yee that are heavy [57] laden, and I will ease you, and I
will refresh you, and you shall find rest vnto your Soules;[30] ô Lord Christ,
giue me no vntimely Birth, but that it may be Borne to vs it's parents joy,
[58] and be made a living member of thy most holy Church; My Sinnes ô
God, bury in thy Sonne's grave, and make them never to riſe in judgment
against me, but be yᵘ ever President, [59] resident with me, and in this
great danger, Lord leave me not, but instruct me how to vndergoe it, in the
feare and love of thee, and turne not, I beseech thee thy eare from me, when
that in [60] my bitter paines and cryes, I call vnto thee, but send thy holy
Angell to guard me that begs the remiſsion of all my sinnes, and that my
Children be not punished for my offences; this [61] ô deare Lord, grant for
thy Sonne my Redeemer's sake, to whom be glory & honor. Amen.

[62] A Prayer in time of Labour
Lord Jesus since thou art pleased my time is come, to bring forth this my
Babe, thou hast made in me, give me a heart full of all truth and [63]
obedience to thee and that I may take this height of paine patiently, without
grudging at thy holy will and pleasure; I beg, oh heare, Three persons ease
me, and that soone; [64] Lord be not angry, that I should limitt thee a time,
but sweet Christ bring me out of this my extremity, and fill my mouth with
honor and praiſe to thee, that I may see this my deare Child wᵗʰout [65] any
deformity, wᶜʰ sight is of the wonderfull mercy of my God, far beyond my
sinnes; thus thy name is to be praiſed wᵗʰ a Song, and magnified w.ᵗʰ
thanksgiving, ô Lord heare, ô Lord forgiue, and [66] suffer me not to

---

[29] The histories of the patriarchs and matriarchs are recounted in Genesis.
[30] Mt 11:28.

accompany my sinnes in the deepe, but part vs, and make me become a new Creature,[31] and if it be thy will, ô God, that I shall be no more in this world, Chriſt raiſe me to [67] life everlasting in the true beleife of thee, who art my only Saviour. Amen.

A Prayer after I was brought to Bed.

My Lord and my God, to thee I give all praiſe, and [68] thanks, that thou hast beene pleaſed to deliver me out of the great paine of Childbirth, and hast of thy great goodneſse given me so perfect a Child; ô Lord continue thy owne work, [69] and give it a lively faith in thee, to love, obey, and feare thee, and to beleive in thy Sonne my Saviour Jesus Chriſt; and I beg that thou wilt be pleaſed to grant it a long life. ô Lord, [70] I know thou mightest have smothered this my Babe in yᵉ Wombe, but thou art ever mercyfull, and hast at this time brought vs both from great dangers, and me from the great [71] torture of Childbirth; in trouble and distreſse the Saints forgett not their thankfulneſse, & should I that am a Sinner forgett to praiſe & magnifie thy most holy name? in that it was thy [72] most bleſsed pleasure to be present with me in my greatest extremity, and heard the Cryes of me the vnworthyest of thy Servants; and I beseech thee o Father give this my Sonne true [73] Baptiſme, that it may wash him from all originall sinne, and from vs his parents sinnes, who without thy infinite kindneſse, might haue sunck, had it not beene for thy immediate [74] hand, therefore wᵗʰ the Angells, and Archangells, I cry holy, holy Lord God of Sabbath, to thee alone is all praiſe due to perpetuity. Amen.

[75] A Prayer when I was with Child

Great God and Chriſt heare the prayer of me that am thy Servant, I know, Lord, every one's time may suddenly come of departure from this [76] life, and mine now, to my knowledge may be neere, being not far off the time of my delivery; ô Lord preserve me and give me a confidence in thee, yᵗ thou wilt be as ready to helpe me, [77] in my diſtreſse as thou hast beene of all my other Children, thou hast blest me withall, and Lord I beg yᵉ same goodneſse to me in this, that it may be borne without any [78] deformity, so that I and it's Father may not be punish't for our sinnes, in the deformity of our Babe; ô Lord, this I beg, knowing the vncleanes of my Soule, but thou art ever full of kindneſse, [79] therefore I doubt not, but we shall see

---

[31] 2 Cor 5:17.

our Babe with perfect shape, to both vs it's parents comforts; and when that time comes Lord grant me y^t joyfull sight; so may I sing thee [80] prayſes in the gates of Sion, then may I say, if I forgett thee ô Jerusalem, lett my tongue cleave to the roofe of my mouth, if I remember not thee, ô Sion;[32] and now I beseech thee againe, to [81] preſerue my soule, with the knowledge of thy Sonne's death, and reſurrection, and that it is hee that doth wash me from the taint of all my Sinnes: if it please thee y^t I shall not longer [82] continue here, grant that I may rejoyce with thy Saints in glory.

A Prayer when I continued w.th Child, after I thought I should haue fallen in Labour.

My Christ and my Jesus, I beseech thee [83] give me a sure confidence in thee, for I confeſse, Lord, my fault, and my most grievous fault, y^t when I thought I should haue fallen into the great paine of Childbirth, I was fearfull, not of thy [84] mercyes, but of the paine, for when I consider thee, I know thou art full of goodneſse, and lovingkindneſse; giue me, my God a heart full of comfort, y^t when my paine comes, I may goe [85] through it with a knowledge that thou wilt not leave me, nor forsake me, and that Ô may endure this height of torture, without grudging at thy holy will; and Ô Lord, giue me [84a] patience, and that I may beleeve that what I endure is to receive another bleſsing from thee, my God; to beare a nother sweet babe, and to see it with perfect forme and so to add to my [85a] praiſes of thee, in this land of the living: Chriſt strengthen me with the knowledge of thy sufferings, and giue me a Mite of thy patience in the extremitie thou [86] enduredst for me, so may I not doubt, but with thy leave, to endure this paine, with a contented heart, as I haue gon through wth the rest of my deare babes, thou hast bleſsed me, [87] and my deare huſband withall; ô make vs both joyfull with this comfort that thou art pleaſed to send vs, and grant it a long life, and let thy holy spirit be ever with it, [88] and all the rest thou hast given me; and this I beg for thy sonne my Saviour's sake.

A Prayer when I was with Child

O great God Almighty, I come now [89] prostrate before thy divine Maj^{tie}, beseeching thee to heare this my prayer, and praiſes to thee; I give, ô Lord, most humble thanks, that thou hast created in me another sweet babe, [90] ô grant it, I pray thee, a right shape, and perfect, and y^t it may ever have a

---

[32] Ps 137:5.

true vnderstanding in thy holy words and Commandem:ᵗˢ and giue me I
humbly beseech thee, the [91] comfort of it's happy birth, and that it may
be borne with life as all the rest haue, as thou hast blest me withall; and I
humbly beg, from the bottome of my heart, that thou [92] wilt give it a
long life, and not punish me, nor it's Father, for our sinnes, in taking it
away from vs, as thou hast done some others; but ô Lord blesse it, and send
it, and these I have [93] a true knowledge, and faith, and feare of thee, and
of thy Sonne our bleſsed Lord and Saviour, and I beseech thee, ô God, let
his sufferings eaſe me, when I am in the greate paine [94] of Childbirth,
and when thoſe paines come vpon me, ô Lord mittigate them, and giue me
confidence, and hope in thee, and that thou wilt not leave me, nor forsake
me; and what [95] I suffer is to receive a nother comfort from thee, the
great bleſsing of a nother sweet babe, wᶜʰ is to increaſe the number of thy
Elect; and ô Lord, give it thy holy Spirit, and make [96] it partaker of
Baptiſme, that so it may be cleansed from the originall sinne, and that we
may bring it vp to beleeve in thy Sonne, who dyed that it might live for
ever, being washed from [97] originall and actuall sinnes, and ever giue it,
and these I haue, I humbly beg, a long life as thou didst the Children of
Israel, and giue me comfort in it's birth, yᵗ I may magnifie [98] thy name for
thy mercyes, in my safety, and the safe birth of it, & the bleſsing thou hast
given me in a nother deare babe; and so let my mouth, and tongue, ever
sing thy praiſe [99] whilest I haue breath;³³ and that my deare affectionate
Huſbands mouth may praiſe thee wᵗʰ joyfull lipps, for thy great mercyes to
vs both in our safety; ô Lord heare, ô Lord forgiue, and [100] let not my
sinnes, stopp the way betwixt me, and thy mercyes, but, ô Lord, in my great
paine, send me comfort from thy holy hill, and Sanctuary, and let me never
doubt but the [101] Jesus hath a blessing for me, and that he will giue me
patience, and eaſe me in my greatest extremity, and giue me the happy sight
of this my deare babe, and giue me [102] the comfort and joy, of its long
life, and these he hath already blest me wᵗʰall; and I humbly beg for them,
and their Father, long life, to the joy and comfort of me, who am thy
vnworthy [103] servant, not fitt to make these my prayers vnto thee, but to
cry with the Publican, Lord be mercyfull to me a sinner; yet since I come
wᵗʰ a faithfull and submiſsive heart, [104] full of petition and thanksgiving,³⁴
Lord I hope thou wilt heare and forgive: ô thou three persons, and one

---

³³ Ps 71:8.
³⁴ Lk 16:1–13.

God, looke downe with mercy and give vs safety in the great danger, I and my babe are [105] to paſse through, and if it be thy will giue me an eaſy and speedy labour; but not as I will, but as thou wilt, ô Lord God my salvation; but I beg for bleſsings vpon vs both, who am [106] vnworthy to looke vp vnto thee, but beg the Crumes y^t fall from thy Table which is sufficient to feede our soules; and let mine, and me, ever be fedd with the Crumes of thy Bleſsed Table,[35] [107] and then let vs never doubt, or be in diſpaire of comfort, for we are bleſsed for evermore being fedd with thy grace, & so let vs ever praiſe thy holy name both now & ever Amen. Amen.

[108] A Prayer when I was with Child of Stuart

O my God, great Almighty, I beg wth a Sincere heart, first, ô Lord that thou wilt pardon my Sinnes, wch are infinite, and then [109] ô Lord I beseech thee to heare my thanksgiving for that thou hast blest me wth another Child, and infus'd life into it, so infuse thy holy Spirit into it; Ô God thou send'st me it, when thou [110] did'st afflict me, wth taking one away from me, and since it hath beene thy bleſsed will, to bleſse it so long in the wombe, as to goe through the sickneſse of two of my Children with the [111] smale pox, and the death of another, be pleased to goe a long with it still, and give it thy holy Spirit of grace & give me, o Lord patience in the labour, and birth, and make me a Joyfull [112] mother, in beholding my babe with true shape, and forme, after the worke of thy owne hands, and give me comfort in its birth; ô Lord Jesus, be with it, and me, and leave vs not [113] destitute, but give me, if it be thy will a quick and speedy labour, and bleſse the Child, and these I have, I beseech thee, with long life and health, and let me not in extremity run into diſpaire, [114] but ever have my faith in thee, and as thou hast never left me in my extremity, so, ô Lord, leave me not now, nor let me doubt of thy mercyes, for they are many, and let me put my trust in [115] Christ Jesus, who dyed for me, and, through his merits, I haue hope of my redemption, so let me trust in the three perſons, and one God, Father, Son & Holy ghost, that still thy holy spirit [116] may be with me to direct me that I sin not, through my owne Frailty of impatience, but ever in my extremity call vpon thee for mercy and helpe, and be confident that thou ô Lord wilt [117] heare the afflicted in their sorrowes, and bleſse my deare Huſband in this sweet babe, that he may haue the comfort of it, with rest of his deare Children, so that he, and I may praiſe thy holy and [118]

---

[35] Mt 15:27.

bleſsed name, for thy great mercyes in releiving vs both out of our extremityes, in giving the babe life, and bringing vs out of so greate danger; so may we laude and bleſse thy holy name for [119] evermore; and this I humbly beg for thy Sonne Jesus Christ's sake, who liveth & raigneth now and for evermore. Amen.

[120] A Meditation mixt with prayer

Consider and heare me ô Lord my God, lighten my eyes yᵗ I sleepe not in death, but so let thy word be a Lanthorne to my feete and a light vnto my paths, that [121] I be not as the Foole, that said in his heart there is no God, but give me I beseech thee a Spirituall light, neuer to run the way of a miſbeleeving corrupt life, nor to say tush thou God carest not for it: [122] Heare my prayer ô God, and hide not thy selfe from my petition, but give me a heart of zeale to keepe all thy testimonies, and not to beleeve this crooked and vntoward generation, who [123] furiouſly rage together, and so do they imagine a vaine thing; but in thee ô Lord put I my trust, ô Lord, be not farr from me but shew me the light of thy countenance and I shall be holy; I [124] am thine, o save me for thy mercyes sake, for I know I am the worst of all thy Creatures; ô Lord leave me not destitute, but deliver me, or else I stick fast in the deepe mire where no water is:³⁶ The Lord [125] me in the day of trouble, thy name o God of Jacob defend me, send thy helpe from the Sanctuary, and strengthen me out of Sion; thou that hearest yᵉ prayer vnto thee shall all flesh come, [126] and in that number I appeare; though most vnworthy; For thou ô Lord art the King be the people never so impatient, he sitteth among the Cherubims,³⁷ be the earth never so vnquiet, ô give [127] vnto the Lord, and call vpon his name, tell the people what things he hath done, for he is our God, & greatly to be feared, for he giveth knowledge vnto his people, and to his Saints for ever. and all [128] that beleeve and trust in him, and his sonne, shall never be confounded, nor left destitute.

---

³⁶ Ps 69:14.
³⁷ Ps 80:1.

A Prayer and Resolution against Despaire

O Lord I am vile being sinfull but let [129] me not run into despaire, for thou my Christ hast redeemed me, and though my sinnes have blacked my soule with the smoak of vngodlineſs,[38] so that I cannot looke to thy Throne of Justice, [130] but be struck downe with my owne guilt, yet thy mercyes will purifye me with the sweet smelling incenſe of thy loving, kindneſse for thou hast given me this comfort, y.ᵗ those that were heavy laden, if they come [131] vnto thee thou would'st ease them, and those that were sick, thou would'st heale them, so come I to thee, my Lord loden w.ᵗʰ sickneſse, for my dayly infirmities, and wᵗʰ heavy burdens weighing me downe [132] with iniquity; so weighty they are ô God, that without thy mercyes the ballance would turne me into vtter ruine, therefore I stand amazed at my owne vnworthyneſse, not knowing how to appeare before thy [133] holyneſse, but yet I come, with a knowledge of my owne sinnes, to thee, my Saviour, who well may be named my Saviour, who by thy death, & paſsion hast saved me, and by thy bloud spilt I am relieved from the feare of everlasting death, and [134] brought to an aſsured hope of everlasting life, in endleſse Joyes; therefore to thee all Honour, and power be given now and for evermore.

[135] A Prayer before the receiving the Communion at Easter.

O great and glorious Lord God, I haue often come to aske a pardon for my sins, and yet returne to vileneſse a gaine, how now shall I [136] come to beg now more forgiveneſse? Ô t'is the time my bleſsed Saviour suffered for me, to wash me cleane from my Sinnes, and made his reſurrection from the grave, to raiſe me from dead works, so to renew [137] me to good works, in the reall beleife of him, who commands me to repent, and to be in Charity with all, and to forgiue, as we would be forgiven, ô Lord pardon my tranſgreſsions, and renew a right spirit [138] within me, so may I heare of Joy, and gladneſse, that the bones which thou hast broken may rejoyce: Thus do I Joy that I have a Saviour to Fly to, yᵗ if I aske, and pray, I shall be pardoned; [139] So come I to thee, ô my bleſsed Jesus, with faith and repentance, and beg pardon, and so may hope to receive comfort, and a new life, and not a condemnation to destroy me; Ô God, renew my [140] beleife, so as I may not diſpaire of thy mercyes, for I know thy pardon is greater then my offence, but my ingratitude is abominable, ô Lord have

---

[38] Rev 9:2.

mercy, haue mercy vpon me, and giue me [141] a pardon, that so I may receive and take thy ble∫sed body and bloud with a pure heart, ernestly desiring thy pardon, and to resolve of a new life, of amendment; thus do I prepare [142] for thy holy Table who am vnworthy of so great a favour, being so vngratefull a Creature, not acknowledging, so often as I ought thy manyfold ble∫sings to me; so I cry with my whole [143] heart, and Soule, mercy sweet Jesus, mercy to me mi∫serable Sinner.

A Prayer before the receiving of ye Communion.

O God, ô my God, and the only God of all true beleivers, I do [144] earnestly beg a pardon for my dayly offences, wch to me are innumerable, but wth thee, Lord, I know they are all numbred, and one day they will be reckoned to me, y^t when I come to repetition I shall then truly repeate my owne [145] ruine, knowing if Justice takes effect, I am cast into the deepe, being guilty of ye often broken steps I haue made in thy Commandem:^ts but ô Lord let me now aske pardon, & that vnfainedly, y^t y^u wilt be pleased to [146] bury in ye grave, my sinnes, wch was the occa∫ion of thy Son my Saviour's death, and as there was many mourning, whereof Mary Magdalen was one, to see him lye dead in the earth for vs, having our sinnes [147] cleared by his innocent death, so let me mourn and be sorry for my sinnes, y^t not only then was guilty of his death, but of Crucifying him againe by my often transgre∫sions, ô my God I will bewaile my selfe till I can come to [148] receive ye ble∫sing thy Son, thy only Son, did give me, wch is to receive him Spiritually, wch doth shew me y^t he had a resurrection not only for himselfe, but, Lord, for me; y^t if in receiving I truly repent, before I eate of this thy holy Manna, [149] have a resurrection; for my sinnes are buryed, and my spirits are renewed by this holy Sacram^t of Christ's body, and bloud; to wch I desire y^t I may now come, wth a preparation of a lively faith, and wth true Charity to all [150] men, y^t I may not doubt but I have my wedding garm^t:^39 but ô Jesus, I know I am a vile wretch, and must come in my raggs of infirmities, so dare not approach, yet I may say wth the woman, ye Children may eate [151] of the Cru͂es that falls from thy Table of mercyes; but ô Lord Christ, thou hast made me happy, for thou callest sinners,^40 and in that number I come, to receive thee Spiritually, wch to me

---

^39 Mt 22:11.
^40 Mt 9:13.

art the well of living waters,[41] for [152] thou truly washest me from all my sinnes, as Baptiſme did from my originall sins; w.ch gives me the comfort that I shall enjoy everlasting felicity wch God of thy mercy grant me.

[153] A Prayer before the Communion.

My God, and my Lord, of thee I beg compaſsion as to a Sinnfull creature, vnable without thy especiall grace, to receive a pardon of my many Sinnes [154] committed before thee, but thou, ô Lord, gavest vs a testimony of our redemption, in thy Son my Saviours death, that who beleives in him shall have eternall life, and doth truly repent them of their sinnes, Lord [155] I beleeve help thou my vnbeleife, and I confeſse I am full of guilt, not fitt to come to thy Table, but being thou callest the lame, and the Sick, I come as one loden wth. infirmities of Sin, so I come to thee, the Physition of all [156] Soules, to be healed; so, ô Christ, shutt me not out of the land of the living, but make me one of thy Saints in glory, and now I approach to thine Altar, to have the full remiſsion of all my sinnes, and whilest I am in this life, keepe me [157] I beseech thee in the feare and love of thee to the praiſe of thy holy name; this I beg for thy Sonne, my Saviours sake.

[158] A Prayer before the Communion at Easter, being at ye same time wth Child.

This thy reſurrection I intend, wth thy leave, ô Jesus, to receive the moſt bleſsed Sacramt thou gavest vs as a remembrance of the Cruell [159] death thou sufferedst for me and made me happy by thy torments and by thy resurrection made many dead people riſe with thee; and thou wast pleaſed to continue some space on earth, t'was thy great goodneſse, ô [160] Lord, to make vs see thee after so many torments thou sufferedst for vs, to make vs see yt wthout any hatred, thou didst entertaine vs into thy holy presence, and since thou so willingly layd'st downe thy life for vs, should not we [161] as freely lay downe our sinnes, for to come to thee? but, ô Lord, we are as vnwilling to lay downe our sinnes, as if it were our lives, though for our owne Salvation; and, ô Lord though we lay them downe, we are apt to [162] take them vp againe; thus the evill spirit provokes vs to our ruine; but ô Lord give me thy holy Spirit, & then my sins will never bury me in ye grave, not hinder me to wash my hands in Innocency, that [163] I may come to thy Altar, to offer vp a contrite heart for my miſdoings; Lord I

---

[41] Is 12:3.

know not whether this may be the last time I shall come to receive the Commemoration of thy blefsed body and bloud; Deare God, [164] make me truly thine, and give me thy Spirit, and the babe I am now wth all, and let it refresh vs, and make me never to defpaire of thy mercyes to me, in my greatest extremity; and if it pleafe thee that I shall be no [165] more in this life, Grant me sure confidence, & faith y^t I shall enjoy thy Heavenly Kingdome. Amen.

A Prayer after delivery before receiving ye Communion on Chrijtmas day.

Thou, ô Christ, which on this day, wast Borne [166] to suffer death for me, to make me cleane from all impurity, give me a contrite heart, to lament my sinnes, that I may become pure, for there is, ô God, nothing impofsible wth thee, ô take away all evill spirits from me, [167] and let Sathan ye Devill never haue any power to make me difobey thee, or to fall into the Sin of defpair; Lord y^u hast multiplyed thy blefsings innumerable vpon me, and hast preserved me, and brought me out of the [168] late danger of Childbirth, by thy mercyfull hand, and seeing thy great goodnefse is such, why should I doubt of thy mercyes to a penitent sinner, who repents of all my mifdeeds? Lord, I can not prefume to eate at thy Table, but [169] desire the Crumes y^t fall from thy goodnefse; I know, Lord y^u camest to call sinners, and in that number I come, and wth a faithfull heart; I know that thou ô Jesus, art pittifull, and so I call wth the blind man, thou sonne of David [170] haue mercy on me,[42] & take away my sinnes from me; so may I take my Bedd of comfort wth me evermore lauding and praifing thee, my God, my Saviour.

[171] A Prayer before receiving ye blefsed Sacrament.

My God let me not think, by reafon I haue received the blefsed Sacram^t lately, y^t I am so pure as that I need not come to the holy Table now, but, my Chrift, I know I am [172] borne in Sin and dayly, transgrefse therefore give me a penitent heart, humbly to acknowledge my many mifdoings, for, ô Lord they are many; but by thy death, and pafsion, I am cleared, & washed from all my faults: [173] St Paul saith, as often as you eate of this Bread, and drink of this Cupp, you shew the Lords death till he come; & he saith, let vs examine our selves, and so let vs come to this holy Table; ô my Christ, I come wth an humble [174] heart, defiring ye forgivenefse of all my

---

[42] Mt 9:27.

sinnes, & wth a desire to receive thee & to feede on thee in my heart by faith; therefore, ô my God strengthen my faith & all theirs y^t come to so holy a Table, y^t we may receive spirituall food, & not eate & drink our owne [175] damnation; and this I beg of thee my God and only Saviour.

A Meditatiō concerning Fasting before ye receiving of the Holy Communion.

Now y^t I am come to ye time to receive ye blest [176] Sacram^t, I begin to examine my selfe and enquire how I may make my selfe moſt submiſsive for my great & manifold sins & tranſgreſsions, wch. is as I conceive, to obey Gods commandem^{ts}, to have a hearty repentance, & to beg remiſsion of God, [177] for my dayly living in a perverſe way, ever committing & never omitting, any of my sins; Now for a preparation I account Fasting ye best, not y^t: I hold a merit in it, but y^t I esteeme eating so as may fill the stomack drawes vpon vs a sluggishneſse, wch admitts [178] of no hearty devotion, & t'is not Fish, or any other meates, y^t I hold better then Flesh, but not to eate so, as to overfill your selfe, and so to eate y^t wch soone diſgests, & I account it much better to eate, then, if you do not, to wish the day past, y^t you might eate to your [179] owne appetite; this y^t I speak for Fasting, our Saviour speakes of it in many places; watch, & pray, lest you enter into tempation,[43] & againe, you shall fast when ye Bridegroom shall be taken from you,[44] wch he meant by himselfe, then sure we have reaſon to [180] fast, before we receive this Bridgroom spirituall, but yet we are not denyed to eate, but I must say, wth St Paul all things are lawfull for me, but all things are not expedient; all things are lawfull for me, but all things edify not;[45] [181] whatsoever is sold in ye shambles, y^t eate, asking no questions, for Conscience sake, for ye earth is ye Lords, & ye fullneſse thereof, conscience I say, not of thy owne, but of another's, for why is my liberty Judged by a nother mans conscience? for if I by grace [182] be a partaker why am I evill spoken of, for y^t for wch I give thanks? whether therefore you eate, or drink, do all to ye glory of God.[46]

---

[43] Mt 26:41.
[44] Mk 2:20.
[45] 1 Co 10:23.
[46] 1 Co 10: 25–31.

A Prayer after I had received the Ble∫sed Sacramᵗ

I was washed cleane, ô Lord, by thy most [183] ble∫sed Body & bloud, & I cannot say, nor think, but I am turned vile againe, but, ô my God, keepe me from running further astray, & tye me, ô Lord, fast to thee, by yᵉ string of Faith, so may I be obedient to thy commandements, then may I not [184] a theife, to steale away from my godline∫se, wᶜʰ is to linger my time, in not giving thee, my God, true prai∫es for all thy ble∫sings to me, in not reading and meditating of thee and of thy most holy name; but I know wᵗʰ thee there is [185] mercy, so, ô Lord, harden not my heart, as yᵘ dids't Pharao's,⁴⁷ but still give me thy spirit, yᵗ my soule may be thine, & be elevated into thy Kingdome, when my dissolution comes: w.ᶜʰ Lord of thy abundant goodne∫se, Grant me, for thy [186] Son my only Saviour's sake. Amen.

Considerations concerning Marriage

Some account of Marriage as an vnhappy life, by rea∫on there is an obedience mu∫t belong from yᵉ wife to yᵉ Hu∫band;⁴⁸ & 'tis great rea∫on [187] it should so be, since we are commanded, by those yᵗ are aboue our Capacity of rea∫on, by God himselfe, & truly I think yᵗ person vnhappy yᵗ will not esteeme of Matrimony so as to take yᵗ tye into consideration, to inquire with themselves, whether or no they could esteeme of such [188] a person so as to value his judgmᵗ, & in matter of consequence, to yeild to his Councell; not to be in such awe of him, as a Servant of his Master, as not to speak, to contradict yᵉ least word he saith, but to have an affection, & love to him, as to a friend, & so to speak their [189] mind, & opinion freely to him, yet not value him yᵉ le∫se; & if he have a reciprocall affection to his wife, it makes them both blest in one another, where as otherwayes if yᵉ wife be so meeke, & low in Spirit, to be in Subjection for every word, She makes him feare he is troublesome, & yᵗ [190] She had rather be a lone then in his company; this is farr from a Companions way; if hye, & lofty, & willfull, then of the other side he is not himselfe when he is wᵗʰ her, so then rather, though he loves her, then bring himselfe into an vnquiet di∫turbed life, he leaves her to goe into [191] some other company, careing not how little he is wᵗʰ her, & when he sees her in company, doubts she will give him some vndigested words, & if so, then he is di∫contented wᵗʰ yᵉ sight of her, so

---

⁴⁷ Ex 1–14.
⁴⁸ Col 3:18.

must giue her a reprehenſion, at least in private, thus doth this indiſcretion cauſe a miſerable life [192] to them both; & if she be over awed by her owne Fancyes, 'tis a sad life to her selfe, & a trouble to her Husband, who otherwayes would be a friendly companion, wch makes a marriage happy, eſpecially when a woman values her huſband in buſines of weight, not so much [193] minding every petty action, as to think, now he loves me not, but love him sincerely; & if he be hasty, 'tis fitt she should be silent, giving him no cauſe to be angrey, & then his anger cannot last long; if he be fickle & various, not careing much to be wth his wife at home, then thus may ye wife [194] make her owne happineſse, for then she may give her selfe vp to prayer, wch St Paul speakes as if a marryed person could not,^{49} & thus in his absence, she is as much Gods, as a virgin; & if she haue a loving diſcreet huſband, & one y^t feares God, he will doubtleſse not hinder her duty to [195] God, but endevour ye increaſe of her faith, & holyneſse, & there is no doubt, but where both these parties do perfectly agree, wth paſsionate and sincere affection, but 'tis the happyest condition, a friendshipp never to be broke, as ye words of Matrimony say, till death them depart, [196] Now God grant all my friends to enjoy this happy & bleſsed friendshipp.

Of Marriage and of Widdowes

As concerning Marriage; I would never haue married, if I had thought I could not serve God; & obay man, but our God [197] is great & meryfull, & he it was y^t allowed of marriage, & decreed it to be so, for he said to Abraham, goe from thy Fathers houſe, & I will give thee a great portion, & I will make thy name great;^{50} & we are aſsured y^t our God is gratious, & he knew we might serve him, though he [198] commanded vs to obay a huſband,^{51} for God is never vnjust to set vs a taske wch we cannot performe; for though 'tis an action hard to vnderstand, by our blind & dull apprehenſion, yet if he commands it, he enables vs to performe what is his pleasure; so let vs not beleeve god would [199] put an affliction vpon vs, instead of a bleſsing, for in giving Children he makes vs honoured in this world, & happy in ye next, in giving vs the hope of having them of ye Elect in heaven; so bringing of them here vp, to obay his commandem^{ts} & feare him, & in fearing him they will [200] obay him, so we have a comfort on

---

^{49} 1 Cor 7:34.
^{50} Ge 12:1–2.
^{51} 1 Pe 3:1.

earth, to see our posterity likely to out live vs, & to beleeve they shall have
a Crowne of Glory hereafter: & our Saviour, yᵉ first miracle he did was at
a marriage, turning the water into Wine;⁵² & doubtleſs if he had not
allowed it, [201] he would haue shewed some other miracle; but for
Widdowes I am in yᵉ opinion of Sᵗ Paul, not for them to marry, having
been once one mans wife, & having Children, to make themselues, after
they haue served yᵉ Lord, a Nurſe to them & theirs, doing dayly actions of
[202] Charity to yᵉ poore wᶜʰ is yᵉ only service they can do to their departed
friend:⁵³ if they haue no Children, yet then not to marry, but live to obay
God, & to bewaile yᵉ loſse of their deare huſband, taking their leaves of
their friends, haveing lost their friend they ever most loved, & lived wᵗʰall.

[203] Against Sluggishneſse and Lazineſse in Religious duties

The condition wᶜʰ we are in in this world, is not for vs to linger out our
time, & in yᵗ sluggishneſse to put of our devotion, & so to think, now I will
repay it, & then I will performe my duty, this is as if we would make our
selues [204] equall wᵗʰ God, as to think we do him a good, as to pay what
we owe, not considering yᵉ ill we do our selves; Can we lymitt time? alaſse
when we let our time slide from vs, we loose our selues, & in yᵗ are enemies
to our owne soules, for our lives are casuall & who knowes to day [205]
whether we can liue till tomorrow? And if we liue, health is vncertaine, &
when sickneſse comes it reduces vs to a stupifyed dullneſse wᶜʰ brings vs
from what we should render to our God; then let vs in health dayly strive to
serve our Allmighty God, wᵗʰ all true [206] devotion, & wᵗʰ a Sincere heart,
of piety, & to put off all impure thoughts, & fully to resolve not to put off
our time till yᵉ last, & then to thinke yᵗ to repent one Second of an houre,
is sufficient to keep vs from endleſse torment; but grant me, ô God, both in
sickneſse and in health, [207] to studdy to serve thee, & I beseech thee give
me such a proportion of thy grace, yᵗ meditation, & ejaculations be never
wanting from me, to thee, to praiſe thee, ô Jesus, for thy manifold bleſsings
to me, & teach me o Lord, thy statutes yᵗ I may apply my heart to wiſdome,
[208] & not be as a runnagate, to forgett thee & thy Sonne my Saviour, &
when he should think to find a place of holyneſse, to find a den of all
impurity, & see many, many dayes employed to my selfe, & not so much as
one minute to himselfe; ô Lord pardon ô Lord [209] forgiue, & returne me

---

⁵² Jn 2:1–10.
⁵³ 1Tim 5:4.

from my trangreſsions, & since I owne guilty, stop yᵉ ruinous way against me, wᵗʰ thy spirit, then may I say returne, returne vnto thy rest, ô my soule for yᵉ Lord hath dealt gracioußly wᵗʰ thee.

[210] A Perswaſion to the forgiving of Injuries.

Let vs endeavour to follow this holy Doctrine, to forbear one another, & forgive one another, if any man have a quarrell against any, even as Christ forgaue vs, so also ought we so to do;[54] for sure we have great [211] reaſon, since we have so bleſsed an example, as our Lord Jesus, who hath forgiven vs who are so great offenders, yᵗ we still heape sin vpon sin, yet we find him so mercyfull, yᵗ he dayly accepts our weake endeavours of amendmᵗ bringing vs to his Father, whoſe anger through his gracious [212] interceſsion, endures but yᵉ twinkling of an eye, to whom let vs lift vp our hearts, & eyes wᵗʰ sincere repentance, & beg his grace, yᵗ we may truly forgive wᵗʰout murmuring; & let vs not reckon to our selves, how oft any offendeth vs, & so retort to them; for yᵗ in effect doth but returne yᵉ more scorne vpon our selves, [213] & at length brings a torture to our owne; Soules nor let vs enquire of our selves, how oft to forgiue but do it freely wᵗʰout restraint, & if there be such a thing as Injury done vs, let vs thinke no further, then how to returne good for yᵗ evill, for in this world we are as nothing, nor ought we here to value one thing [214] aboue a nother or to remember what hath been done this day, as to returne yᵉ like for it, but totally to apply our minds to gaine yᵉ salvation of our owne Soules; For our Saviour, by saying let to morrow take care for it selfe,[55] shewes yᵗ no injury should be retayned in our thoughts, but yᵗ rather when any smites [215] vs on yᵉ one Cheek, we should turne to him yᵉ other,[56] by wᶜʰ it evidently appeares to vs, yᵗ we should not esteeme of this world more then to account ourselves truly happy, yᵗ it hath pleaſed Allmighty God to send vs hither, to serue & waite vpon him, & yᵗ by obedience to his commands, & through his [216] mercy in Jesus Christ we may at last obtayne yᵉ glorious sight of yᵉ Heaven of Heavens; wᶜʰ yᵗ we may come to, let vs follow our Saviour's Stepps, who when he was reviled, reviled not againe.

---

⁵⁴ Mt 6:14.
⁵⁵ Mt 6:34.
⁵⁶ Lk 6:27–30.

[217] **A Cõmendatiõ of the Socyety of Deare and Neere friends.**

To have yᵉ company of deare & neer friends, is yᵉ greatest felicity this world can afford; & for life if we have nothing to Heighten nature, wᵗʰ some spectacle of pleasure, it soone turnes to a Melancholy wᶜʰ at last makes a Stupefaction, & in this World [218] they are accounted miſserable; & I hold what comfort this Ball of earth can yeild to vs, is nothing if we have not yᵉ health, friendship, & love of dear friends, wᶜʰ happineſse I have, & should I not return my thanks to him that gives althings, wᶜʰ is my only true God, in yᵉ eternall world, w.ᶜʰ is to come, I should not only [219] account my selfe, but be a most miſerable wretch, & I beseech thee, o God, let me not wander so much into folly, as to give any thanks, as due in this life, to any particular object, or Subject, for they can owne no Government here, but to thee ô God all praiſe is due and more then the tongue [220] of me an vnworthy Sinner can expreſse.

A Meditation on yᵉ Confidence of forgiveneſse of Sinnes.

Our sinnes are great, & what Creature can owne they have none? but let vs endeavour to keepe them from vs, by an earnest re= [221] & let vs hold fast yᵗ practice yᵉ whole time of our life, lest we as Chaffe, be fann'd away from yᵉ Allmightie's sight to yᵗ place where is bitterneſse in y.ᵉ end;⁵⁷ but let vs not deſpaire of our true felicity though we have sinnes, if we truly strive not to retaine them, for we have a Saviour who hath made to his Father [222] a reconcilation for vs, through his bloud, & though our Sinnes be as red as scarlet, he can make them as white as snow,⁵⁸ & what comfort is here to a true Christian? let vs ever continue in this comfortable Joy, & keepe such a watch before our eyes, yᵗ we may not see any sight yᵗ should lead vs into yᵉ fetters of sinne, but [223] let vs lift vp our hearts freely to our God, & Saviour, wᵗʰ whom we shall inherit our Salvation.

Against Judging of others; wᵗʰ encouragem:ᵗˢ to beare affliction.

Let vs not value this World as we see it full of varietys, for all yᵗ is but guilded vanities, pollished wᵗʰ deceite, to entrapp vs from [224] our holy thoughts, of our eternall seat of bliſse; nor let vs give our selves to be yᵉ Judge of Gods works, seeing one or many, in this life, to yᵉ outward appearance proſperous, to be opinionated, becauſe I am not so, God hath

---

⁵⁷ Mt 3:12.
⁵⁸ Isa 1:18.

forsaken me, & left me to be punished; shall I compare this world for punniſhmᵗ wᵗʰ our Higher? ô no! 'tis [225] yᵉ life of our Soules wᶜʰ we must answer for, not this worlds earth, for 'tis oblivion not to be remembred; if diſliked, we goe to a deeper place of torment, where there is no water of Grace to coole our tongues, for God hath left vs; but yᵉ afflictions we suffer here, are Gods tryalls, & if we endure wᵗʰ patience, yᵉ more Grace [226] he constantly affords vs, to make vs more his, & suffers vs not to haue a heart like Pharaoh, still to be perverse in our waies, let vs not follow his example; when God is pleased to bring vs out of affliction, to think of worldly triffles, & to forgett him our maker, who hath been mercyfull to vs in sending his Sonne to dye [227] for our sinnes, wᶜʰ aſsurance is our greatest consolation.

To take care rightly to vnderstand our selves.

Let vs not forgett our selves, but Remember wᵗ we are, affliction we have dayly in this world, & no hower of happineſse; but that we haue a mercyfull God, yᵗ hath [228] given vs his Children repentance for our sinnes, yᵗ if we truly beleeve in our most bleſsed Saviour, who endured yᵉ bitter death on yᵉ Croſse (ô yᵉ mirror of patience) to make vs joyfull in yᵉ sweet knowledge of our Celestiall prosperity, to conceive such a bleſsing as to be wᵗʰ him in paradice: 'tis not merit yᵗ can make vs hope for so bleſsed [229] a Habitation, but his holy words, wᶜʰ every true beleiver must build vpon; Aske & yee shall have, seeke & yee shall find, knock & it shall be opened to you[59] & these are yᵉ stepps by wᶜʰ we must goe on to our houſe of hope, to our true eternity.

[230] A Meditation of purity before receiving the Communion.

We all ought to give our obedience to God who made vs according to his owne Image, & gaue vs a heart to acknowledge him,[60] therefore let vs make it our Altar to offer vp our sacrifice of holy thoughts, to him, for no evill should ever place it selfe there; [231] for Moſes & Aaron never would let any thing come neere yᵉ Altar, but yᵗ wᶜʰ should be wᵗʰout staine,[61] so let vs approve our selves Gods Children, to let no impurity come to lodge wᵗʰin Gods Table of our hearts: In yᵉ old law God never suffered any to eate

---

[59] Mt 7:7.
[60] Gen 1:26–27.
[61] Lev 21:21–23.

of bloud,[62] wch sure was to make vs ye purer to come to take his bloud, who doth wash away [232] all our sins; but alaſse we was too too guilty, not only to shed his bloud, but to take his life away, & all this he was patient in, for to heale vs, ought not we much more clenſe our selves for this most holy remembrance of this holy man, & God, then they did their Burnt offering? that was for his remembrance, of [233] him to come, this for his love, & mercy to vs past, therefore let vs come wth true Godlineſse & a sorrowfull soule for our actuall, & full of immerit for our originall tranſgreſsions, & a thankfull heart for our redemption.

[234] An Exhortation to confidence in Gods mercy.

Let vs in affliction never doubt of Gods mercy, for in our greatest extremity he will bring vs out of our distreſse, as he did Joseph out of ye priſon, & gaue him a reward in this world, becauſe he beleived in him,[63] for if we nothing doubt of his goodneſs here, he gives vs a Crowne of Glory in ye world to come, [235] therefore let vs yeild our selves to him as Members of his Church, & sacrifice our selves to his will as Abraham would his sonne vpon ye Altar.[64]

Repent in Dust & Ashes.

That is truly to repent, wthout pride, or wth a forced repentance, & to repent [236] wth a cleare heart, for our selves are but dust & Ashes; for Dust we are & to dust we shall returne;[65] for we are nothing wthout God infuses his grace into vs, & wthout life as wthout fyer, we returne to Ashes; So we can owne nothing wthout his great mercy, wch he was pleased to bestow vpon vs, by sending his Sonne for ye remiſsion of our sins wth was to [237] give vs a testimony of ye miſtery of our salvation.

Vpon occasion of the vnwinding of a skeane of Silke

Vnwinde me ô Lord from my sins, wch my vile life is ever apt to be entangled wth, was it not for thy Son my Jesus, who came to unravell ye skeane of my tranſgreſsions, [238] wth his bloud, & though they be black wth sinfull vnworthyneſse, since I do not wholy think vpon thee, & of thy service,

---

[62] Lev 3:17.
[63] Gen 41:41–57.
[64] Gen 22.
[65] Gen 3:19.

yet yᵘ ô God wast gracious, & sent'st me a Saviour, to wash yᵗ blacknefse
away wᵗʰ his loving kindnefse, wᶜʰ makes yᵗ white wᶜʰ I had soyled wᵗʰ my
vnrighteous life; Lord amend me, & make me become a new Creature, so
to spin yᵉ Thread [239] of purity, as to be one of thy Elect, where I shall be
blefsed for ever.

Vpon recovery out of a sicknefs after Delivery

O Lord God to thee all thanks & praife belongs from me, for all thy infinite
greate & vnspeakable benefitts to me in releiving me in my greatest
extremity, [240] & in my sicknefse, wᶜʰ to bring me out of was a blefsing
farr beyond any desert of mine, but thy mercy is aboue thy Justice, for had
yᵗ taken place, I had not beene releived from my affliction, neither had'st yᵘ
blefsed me in giving my deare Babe life, & giving so many to me; ô Lord,
let me not forgett yᵉ blefsing yᵘ gauest me in giving me [241] my deare
Hufband, ô still blefse him, & his to me wᵗʰ long life, ô Lord, though yᵘ
wast pleafed to affict me in taking a way from me two Babes, yet o Lord
stay thy hand as yᵘ hast & blefse them yᵘ hast given me, & all my neere
friends, & still giue me yᵉ Comfort of their lifes, I humbly beg for thy
Sonne my Saviour [242] Jesus Christ's sake, to whom I give all thanks &
glory now & for ever more.

Vpon occasion of my Husbands Birth day

O my God, yᵉ only & everlasting God, to thee I dedicate a true
acknowledging heart for this happy day, wherein yᵘ hast [243] blest my Deare
Husband to see 27 yeares; my Lord my prayers ought to be to thee
everlastingly, & yᵘ hast kept him from all dangers; thy infinite mercyes to
him, & me in him, is praife aboue what I thy sinfull servant can give, but I
will strive to obay & give thee praifes for yᵘ callest not yᵉ righteous but sinners
to repentance,⁶⁶ Lord I will turne from [244] my evill wayes, therefore I
beseech thee heare this my thanksgiving, & turne thy eare to me, yᵗ begs yᵉ
increafe of this my Joyed day, & blefsed be it long to him, wᵗʰ health &
profperity, & be yᵘ ever wᵗʰ him in his greatest extremity and diftrefse.

A Prayer for my Husband.

O my Christ give me once more leave to Petition thee, to beg of thee [245]
to have mercy on my Deare Hufband, who hath enemies about him seeking

---

⁶⁶ Mt 9:13.

to put some violence vpon him; ô sweet God, father of goodneſse, & full of pure mercy, I beseech thee preserve him out of their hands, & let not the son of man have any power to hurt him, but be yᵘ Jesus Sonne of God, ever wᵗʰ him to protect him from [246] their hands of Cruelty, seeking to arrest him; Lord God keepe him from their ensnaremᵗˢ of impriſsonmᵗ, & make his returne hither safe, wᵗʰout being entrapped by any of their allurem:ᵗˢ God grant these & all other things wᶜʰ are most needfull for him, for thy Sonne my Lord & Saviours sake, in whoſe name yᵘ ever bidd'st me call & yᵘ wilt heare.

[247] **Vpon occaſion of yᵉ death of my Boy Henry.**
If God be pleaſed to give me a Child, & to take it from me, let me not fall to wish I never had borne it, rather then to part wᵗʰ it; Loose it I cannot say, if I be a Chriſtian, though yᵗ word is often pronounced by nature's paſsion in this world, for in these expreſsions nature overflowes [248] it selfe, into a Heathenish thought, thinking no further then our eyes behold; but if Grace dwells in me I must consider who gave me yᵗ Child, is it not God yᵗ gaue it? & then sure he may take it a way, let me not therefore repine, but vnderstand my owne estate, is this a place to live for ever? no I must so live here, as to walk wᵗʰout sin, yᵗ I may live everlastingly; but I [249] cannot owne to be wᵗʰout sinne, but by repentance, & by yᵗ we are made happy, for our Allmighty father sent his Sonne to dye for our sins, & he aſſureth vs, if we truly repent vs of our Sins, & beleive in him, we shall inherit eternall life; if we do not walke vprightly, but still returne to wallow in yᵉ Mire of sin, wᵗʰout repentance, we then shall bring vpon our selves [250] perpetuall puniſhmᵗ in yᵉ deepe of torments, being banish't God's sight; since I see plainly we are not to continue in this world, let me endeavour to prepare my selfe so, yᵗ I may be so happy as to go to yᵉ Heaven of Heavens, where I may see yᵉ Trinity in vinity bleſsed for ever, & if God be pleased to give me grace, sure I cannot desire to live here otherwayes, [251] then to covett to enlarge my selfe in Godlyneſse, to make me yᵉ fitter for him; & in yᵉ knowledge of all this, why should I wish my Babe had not beene, rather then to dye? I must not let paſsion overflowe so much, as not to let religion come into my memory; & let me never goe so farre, ô Lord, as David did, would God I had dyed for thee my Child, as he said of his [252] Sonne Absolon;⁶⁷ but if my Child dye young; let me take it for an affiction from

---

⁶⁷ 2 Sam 18:33.

Gods hands, & acknowledge it is a rod of Chaſtisem:ᵗ· from him, & in what troubles & calamities soever, let me not grudge at his actions, but take them with a grieved heart, knowing he afflicts for my Sinns, & so let me returne from my wickedneſse, yᵗ he may bleſse me wᵗʰ all manner of bleſsings, [253] & give my Children health & long life, wᶜʰ· God of his mercy grant to them yᵗ he hath given me, to his glory & my comfort.

On my Boy Henry.
Here lyes a Boy, yᵉ Finest Child from me,
Which makes my Heart & Soule sighe for to see,
Nor can I think of any thought, but greeve,
For Joy or Pleasure could me not releeve;
[254] It lived dayes as many as my yeares,
No more wᶜʰ cauſed my greeved teares;
Twenty & Nine was yᵉ Number;
And Death hath parted vs a sunder.
But yᵘ art Happy, sweet'st on High,
I mourne not for thy Birth, nor cry.

When I lost my Deare Girle Kate.
My sorrow is great, I confeſse, I am much greived for yᵉ loſse [255] of my deare Girle Keatty, who was as fine a Child as could be, she was but a yeare and Ten Months old, when, by yᵉ Fatall diſease of yᵉ smale pox, it was Gods pleasure to take her from me, who spoke any thing one bid her, & would call for any thing at Dinner, & make her mind knowne at any time, & was kind to all, even to Strangers, & had no Anger in her; [256] all thought she loved them, her Brothers & Sister loved her wᵗʰ a fond love; She was so good, she never slept, nor played, at Sermon, nor Prayers; She had received yᵉ Sacramᵗ of Baptiſme, wᶜʰ washed her from her originall sinne, & she lived Holyly; she tooke delight in nothing but me, if she had seene me; if absent, ever had me in her words, desiring to come to me, neuer [257] was there so Fond a Child of a mother, but she now is not in this world, wᶜʰ greeves my heart; even my Soule, but I must submitt, & give God my thanks, yᵗ he once was pleased to bestow so great a bleſsing as yᵗ sweet Child vpon me.

On yᵉ same occaſion.
It was Gods pleasure to afflicte me, not her, in calling her from me, for [258] he hath made her happy, giving her yᵉ Joyes of Heaven, & to yᵗ end

I know we bring them, to God, not to our selves, if God gives them grace, wch I hope he hath, & will, so are they fitter for him, then me; for all our lives is but to live here y^t we may live wth our Saviour for ever; & he saith of such is ye Kingdom of Heaven, y^t is of sweet Children, so innocent;[68] thus do I not doubt her [259] happine∫se, but yet greeve I for my owne lo∫se, & know it was Gods puni∫hm:^{t} for my sinnes, to separate so soone y^t deare Body & Soule of my sweet Babe, though her Soule is singing Alelujahs, yet is her sweet body here seised on by Wormes, & turned to dust, till ye great day shall come when all appeare vnited, both body & Soule, before ye iudgement seat of God; [260] Ô let me cry vnto God, & let none wonder y^t I should lament for my lo∫se, & know 'tis God w:^{ch} hath afflicted, me, & let me aske pardon, & beg of ye Lord to stay his hand, & to preserve my Deare Hu∫band, & those :5: Deare Babes I haue, & my neere friends, as My Deare Si∫ters, & Brother, w:^{ch} are deare to me; & lett me not think I am abler to beare afflictions then David, who was [261] according to Gods owne heart, who mourned for his young Child, & for Absolon his Sonne, who fought against him, Crying ô Absolon my Son; my Son;[69] & Jacob who mourned for Joseph, when he thought he had been dead;[70] ô lett me beg Gods mercy, & pray w:th David remove thy Stroak away from me: when y^u w:th rebukes dost correct man for iniquity y^u makest his [262] beauty to consume away like smoake, surely every man is vanity:[71] Heare my prayer o Lord give eare vnto my cry, hold not thy peace at my teares, for I am a Stranger wth thee & a Sojourner wth thee, as all my Fathers were; But; ô Lord stay thy hand of affliction, & pardon my sinnes, & make me truly to trust in thee, & lett vs say, ô Lord send vs helpe from trouble, for [263] vaine is ye helpe of man, for 'tis God alone y^t doth all things, he gives, & he takes, & lett us say wth Job ble∫sed be ye name of the Lord;[72] ô lett vs ever looke vp vnto him, for he is our life & salvation, a very present helpe in trouble; so let vs pray vnto him, & beg his ble∫sing to vs & our deare ones, & to ble∫se y^e Child I am now withall infusing his spirit of [264] Grace into it, y^t when our Change is come, he may call vs all to his ble∫sed Kingdome, to live wth him for ever.

---

[68] Mt 19:14.
[69] 2 Sam 18:33.
[70] Gen 37:34–35.
[71] Ecc 1:2.
[72] Job 1:21.

On the same.

In y^e sight of vs y^e vnwi$\int$e, y^e righteous seeme to dye, & their departure is taken for mi$\int$ery, & their going from hence, as vtter destruction, but they are in [265] peace; & my deare Jewell to shew she was going to happine$\int$se, when her eyes were sett (Death having sei$\int$ed vpon her) y^e last word she spoke was to me, when in Passion I asked her, if I should Ki$\int$se her, she said, yeas, Lengthening y^e word as if she was in high Blisse, & lay so sweetly, desiring nothing, but her Lord Jesus. Thus her life & death was nothing but [266] sweetne$\int$se, shewing vs what we should performe at our last day; And God found her worthy of himselfe; So must my sorrow submitt.

Made on a Sight of the Counte$\int$se of Bridgewaters Picture.

On thy true Picture all may looke,
And make of thee a perfect vertuous Booke
For of great Bloud & Birth thou art,
And being gon dost kill each Childe's true heart,
[267] Then thou wert good, & t'was thy Fame,
Thus they do speak, w:th Honour to thy name,
So rest thou happy Soule, 'twas such
Thy Children cannot give thee prai$\int$e too much.

The 4 following pieces were made by JB:

[268] **Spoken Vpon the receiving a Cake of Perfume made vp in the Shape of a Heart.**

My Deare I thank thee, y^t y^u hast so well
Shewed me y^e place wherein thy love doth dwell;
T'is in thy Heart, there let it ever be,
But when y^u putt'st it forth, to shew it me;
I love thee, ever have, & still shall do,
To shew y^t thou & I, are one, not two.

[269] **A Contemplation, vpon the sight of a Cushion.**

Every thing I see minds me of y^e Almighty power of God; be it never so small, ther is nothing but one may remember God's omnipotency by; many things of waight may be called to mind only by y^e sight of so incon$\int$iderable a thing as a Cushion; it makes me [270] think of Gods ordering, & di$\int$po$\int$ing of y^e whole world, how he hath set some above others, & according to y^e degrees he placeth men in, so hath he given them severall conveniences; I cannot see so slight a thing, but I presently think of y^e eaſe w:^ch God hath graciouſly been pleaſed to allow, to thoſe he hath set in high place, w:^ch they ought to improve to his glory, y^t God hauing [271] allowed them eaſe for their bodyes, their hearts & soules may be ye more earnest & industrious to set forth his praiſe; ye poore a gaine y^t want such accoṁodations may (& not w^thout just cauſe) sett forth God's mercy, in y^t they dayly find his aſsiſtance in bearing those hardshipps he is pleaſed to allott them, & y^t (w^thout such tenderneſse as he allowes to men of higher degrees) [272] they are, through his grace, enabled to paſs a cheerefull & a Comfortable life, even in ye want of all earthly conveniences being inwardly full stored wth God's grace; thus it is plaine y^t there is nothing so small, but man may, vpon sight of it, if God afford his aſsiſtance, make a good vse of it, to the exaltation of God's holy name.

[273] A Prayer in ye Sickneſse of my Girle Franck.

O Lord God Almighty, in whoſe hands are ye keyes of life & death, ye opening of ye Wombe, & ye shutting of ye Graue, y^u God of mercy & compaſsion, who above all thy other attributes delight'st in thy mercy, & hast been pleased to declare y^t thy mercy is above all thy workes; y^u Lord y^t dost give eare [274] vnto ye prayers of thy people, & hast Commanded y^t vnto thee all Flesh should come, & put vp their supplications at thy mercy seate, heare y^u in Heaven, and have mercy, lend a favourable eare to ye prayers, & teares w:^ch w:^th a prostrate heart, bended Knees, & hands vp lifted to thy Throne of Grace, I here put vp vnto thy Divine Majesty; I Know oh Lord, thy great power; y:^t y:^u art able, & I acknowledge thy [275] vnmeasurable loving kindneſse, y^t y^u art willing to helpe all those, y^t heartily & faithfully, & wth a true confidence in thy goodneſse, & all sufficiency, do call vpon thee, in what miſery or calamity soever lyes vpon them; trusting therefore in thee, ô Lord & in thy mercy, I make bold to present my humble petitions to thy eternall & all sufficient Majesty in behalfe of my [276] poore afflicted Infant, y^t now feeles ye Rodd of thy diſpleasure, for ye sinnes of her parents, for I fully trust y^u hast beene pleased to do away all sinnes y^t might cleave to her at her Birth, by ye bleſsed Laver of Baptiſme, of w:^ch y^u haſt beene graciouſly pleased to make her partaker; O gracious father, in ye middest of this thy Judgm^t, be pleased to remember mercy, and [277] suffer ye showers of thy loving Favour to diſtill plentifully vpon this my poor weake sicke Babe; Lord think not on ye originall sinne w:^ch she brought into this world w:^th her, nor on ye sinnes of her sad & much afflicted parents, but for thy mercyes sake, ô God be graciouſly pleased, for this weakene∫se she now lyes vnder, to grant her strength, for this sickne∫se, She [278] now feeles, to afford her health, & for this death, w:ᶜʰ I now feare is ready to seaze vpon her, to ble∫se her wᵗʰ life, yᵗ She & I, & all those yᵗ have any relation vnto her, may render prai∫e & thanks, & give glory to thy name, yᵗ yᵘ hast beene pleased to draw her out of yᵉ jawes of Death, & to shutt yᵉ mouth of yᵉ grave yᵗ gaped wide for her; but if yᵘ hast otherwi∫e [279] di∫posed of her, ô loving Father receive her into yᵉ comforts of thy Heavenly Kingdome, & grant vnto me, & all other her friends, yᵗ she shall leave behind her in this world, patience to endure yᵉ affliction of her lo∫se, wᵗʰ a Godly constancy; & all this I desire at thy hands, for Jesus Christ his sake, who dayly mediates for mercy at thy Throne, for all [280] mankind, & in whom yᵘ hast been plea∫ed to declare y:ᵗ y:ᵘ art well pleased;⁷³ ô Lord, say Amen to these my humble petitions, put vp at thy Throne of mercy Amen, ô gracious & loving, Father, Amen, Amen.

A Preparatory Prayer before yᵉ receiving of the ble∫sed Sacrament of yᵉ Lords Supper.

Most mercyfull father, I thy poore Creature, who am but du∫t [281] & Ashes, & by sinne have made my selfe much wor∫e then nothing, here take yᵉ humble boldne∫se to call vpon thee, by thy name of mercy, in w.ᶜʰ yᵘ hast beene pleased to declare y:ᵗ y:ᵘ delightest, having sett thy mercy aboue all thy other great and glorious attributes; in yᵉ Confidence wᶜʰ thy title of mercy affords vnto me, & in perfect a∫surance of yᵉ [282] merits of my Lord & Saviour, thy Sonne, in whom thou art well pleased, Jesus Christ, I addre∫se my selfe to thee to beg, from thy loving kindne∫se, pardon & remi∫sion of all my manifold Sinnes, oh Lord it is thy mercy yᵗ emboldens me, otherwise how should I dare to looke vp to so great a Majesty, so offended as yᵘ hast beene by me? I dare not, alas, I dare [283] not appeare before thy Throne of Justice, for there my owne conscience tells me I can expect no other then a most severe sentence, yea Lord, if yᵘ beest pleased to call me to that barre, I know I must be Sentenced to eternall darkne∫se, & haue Hell & Damnation for my Just reward; But gracious Father, enter not into Judgm.ᵗ [284] wᵗʰ thy poore servant, for in thy sight can no Flesh living be justified; if yᵘ Lord shouldest marke what is done ami∫se, oh Lord none can abide it; even the most righteous of mankind, when yᵘ proceedest to Judgmᵗ, may well wish yᵉ Hills might fall on them, & yᵉ Mountaines Cover them, but

---

⁷³ Mt 3:17.

can by no meanes [285] avoyd thy fierce wrath; Good God, I come to thee
not trusting in any righteousnesse of my owne (no Lord I throw all such
thoughts farr from me, for, alas, they would but breed my vtter confusion)
but, relying vpon the righteousnesse of my blessed Saviour, I put vp my
Petition to thee, humbly imploring thy divine [286] Majesty to be pleased
to accept of me as a worthy receiver of the blessed Sacrament of the Lord's
supper; none, I know, can be worthy to be partaker of so vnspeakable loving
kindnesse, as, by y^t Sacram^t is bequeathed vnto those that truly receive those
blessed Misteries, but only those whom y^u art pleased in [287] mercy to
make worthy; Father look downe in mercy I beseech thee vpon me y^e most
vnworthy of all thy Servants, a worme & noe man,[74] & make me worthy;
give me, I pray thee, a sound knowledge, y^t I may, in such a measure as may
be acceptable to thee, comprehend the ineffable & vnspeakable mis= [288]
mistery of y^e Trinity of persons in y^e vnity of thy glorious Godhead, y^t I may
vnderstand y^t thou diddest create man in a happy condition, & he by his
disobedience to thy commands, made himselfe, and all his posterity most
miserable, by falling into Sinne, wch thy holy Spirit doth abhorre, & [289]
so made Mankind lyable to the Curse & misery due for sin, wch except thy
mercy prevent, is eternall perdition; Man still continues siñing, & incurres
ye danger of thy wrath, & I more then all others, but Christ hath taken
vpon him humane nature, and hath been pleased to suffer [290] for our
sinnes, & hath so made satisfaction for my sinnes, and for the Sinnes of the
whole world, and so hath wrought redemption for vs through faith in his
death, and now sitts at the right hand of God, excercising his office of
Mediator, and making intercession for vs, and hath of his favour left vs this
[291] blessed Sacrament (of which I humbly desire worthyly to partake) as
a memoriall of that great work which he hath wrought for vs; I humbly
beseech thee to keep from me all irreverent and carnall apprehensions of this
divine Mistery, and grant that I may receive this [292] bread and Wine, not
as bare and ineffectuall bread and Wine, nor with such a grosse conceit as that
I should corporally eate thy Flesh, and drink thy blood, but as bread and
Wine which thou by thy holy institution hast set a part to a Sacramentall vse,
and hast left as a Seale of that [293] wonderfull salvation thou hast wrought
for mankind, & hast appointed to be eaten and drunke, in remembrance of
thee, that thy death may thereby be shewed forth till thou come, that so
corporally eating this bread, and drinking this wine, and elevating my heart

---

[74] Ps 22:6.

and [294] thoughts vnto thee which sittest in the Heavens, my soule may by Faith partake of thy most blefsed body & blood, which thou laydest downe to redeeme vile Sinners, of which, Lord, I am one of the most miferable and wicked, but Lord be y^u pleased to strengthen my [295] faith, that I may not only beleive that my blefsed Saviour Jesus Christ took humane nature vpon him, lived vpon the earth, suffered on the Crofse, dyed, was buryed, and rofe a gaine, but that he did all this for me, and that I shall one day rife againe, & through [296] his merits and mercy, live wth him eternally in glory; but Lord, except I truly repent, I can have no right at all to this beleife, therefore I humbly beseech thee to give me the grace, perfectly to examine my selfe, and to repent of all my sinnes, wch are so abominable in thy sight I [297] must needs acknowledge I haue tranfgrefsed against all thy Lawes, but it is from thee that all graces come; from thee wth all the powers of my Soule, do I humbly beg the blefsed grace of true repentance, that I may totally forsake all my sinnes both knowne, and secret, and [298] serve thee in holynefs, & righteoufnefse all ye rest of ye dayes w:^{ch} y^u wilt be pleased to allot me on ye earth, & when those dayes are ended may be made partaker of thy heavenly Kingdome; & Lord I beseech thee to grant me a perfect Charity, y^t I may be in peace wth all my brethren on ye earth & beare malice to no man, if y^u wilt [299] be pleased to blefse me wth thefe graces then may I wth boldnefse approach to thy holy Table, as having on ye wedding garment appointed by thy selfe, & those whom y^u makest worthy, y^u wilt vndoubtedly accept; ô Lord, I haue no righteoufnefse of my owne, my blefsed Saviour hath enough for [300] me, & all the world, I beseech thee to forgive all my Sinnes, & accept of me in his righteoufnefse; I fall downe before thy Throne of mercy, oh Lord, looke vpon me wth ye eye of compafsion, & write my name in thy Book of life; All this I beg of thy most mercyfull hands, for thy Sonne, my Saviour's [301] sake, to whom with the father and the holy Ghost, be all glory, honour, and power, both now and for evermore. Amen.

Record of Variants

174.0 *In BL, the signature* C. Hammond *is inscribed above the signature Jemima Bridges in the upper right-hand corner of the page.*

174.1 Page 1] Page 1:ˢᵗ BL; 1.ˢᵗ Page 76. || 1.ˢᵗ day 1648ᴧ] BL; 1:ˢᵗ day 1648. 76. || Page … 1648] *Printed as four lines in the left margin beside the three-line title* 77; *Printed as four lines ending in the left margin of the first line of the title* BL; *Printed as three lines ending in the left margin of the first line of the title* 76.

174.2 Confeſsion] BL; Confession 76. || w.ᵗʰ Meditationᴧ] w:ᵗʰ Medita=tion BL; wᵗʰ Meditation, 76. || and] 76; & BL.

174.3 Godᴧ] BL; God, 76. || and] 76; & BL.

174.4 Sanc=tifier] Sanctifyer BL; Sanctifier 76.

174.5 impoſ=] impoſsible BL, 76. || wᵗʰ] BL; with 76.

174.6 haue] BL; have 76. || Mustard-seed] 76; Mustardseed BL.

174.8 impoſsible] 76; im=poſsible BL. || nei=ther] neither BL, 76.

174.9 Gods] BL; God's 76. || mercy] BL; *catchword* mercy *omitted in first line* 76. || Sinner] 76; sinner BL.

174.9–10 Sinner, thatᴧ] sinner, thatᴧ; sinner, that, 76.

174.10 without] 76; wᵗʰ·out BL || redemption] 76; redemptiō BL.

174.11 Saviour,] 76; Saviour: BL. || wᶜʰ] BL; which 76. || the Croſs;] 76; yᵉ Croſse; BL.

174.12 sinnes a way,] sinnes a way; BL; Sinnes away 76. || as] 76; a BL.

174.13 Snowe] BL; Snow 76. || without] BL; with=out 76.

174.14 can not] cannot BL, 76. || which] 76; w.ᶜʰ BL.

174.15 save] BL; saue 76. || Predestination] 76; Predesti=nation BL.

174.16 savedᴧ] *interlined* 77; saved, *not interlined* BL, 76. || Crea=ture] Creature BL, 76. || earth,] 76; ~ ; BL.

174.17 Watch] BL; watch 76. || least] BL; lest 76.

174.18 temptation] BL; temp=tation 76. || the flesh] 76; yᵉ Flesh BL. || weakeᴧ] *interlined* 77; weake; *not interlined* BL, 76.

174.19 goodneſse] goodnesse 76; good=nesse BL. || given] BL; giuē 76.

174.20 saithᴧ] BL; saith, 76. || aske,] BL; ask, 76.

174.21 Seeke,] 76; Seekeᴧ BL. || ye] BL; yee 76. || knock] 76; Knock BL.

174.22 asketh,] 76; askethᴧ BL. || &] and BL, 76. || findeth] 76; find=eth BL.

174.23 knocketh] 76; Knocketh BL.

174.24 &] and BL, 76.
174.25 tast] BL; taste 76. || yᵉ] the BL, 76.
174.26 and without] 76; & w.ᵗʰout BL; and w.ᵗʰout 76. || birthₐ] BL; birth, 76.
174.27 deathₐ] BL; death, 76. || haue] have BL, 76. || resur=rection] BL; resurrectiō 76.
|| leaues] leaves BL, 76.
174.28 leſs] less 76; leſse BL. || nothing,] 76; nothing; BL.
174.29 without] 76; wᵗʰout BL.
174.30 fasting;] ~, BL, 76. || that] 76; yᵗ. BL.
174.31 Fast=ing] fasting BL; Fasting 76.
175.2 together.] BL; ~ , 76. || Bride=groome] Bridegroome BL, 76.
175.3 takē away] taken a way BL, 76. || and] 76; & BL. || then] *interlined* 77; then *not*
interlined BL, 76. || Fast] 76; fast BL. || and] 76; & BL.
175.4 Bridegroome] 76; Bride=groome BL. || Saviour?] BL; ~ : 76. || and] 76; & BL. ||
gone] 76; gon BL.
175.5 haue] have BL, 76. || com=manded] BL; Commanded 76.
175.6 especially] 76; espe=cially BL. || re=ceive] receive BL, 76. || which] 76; w.ᶜʰ BL.
|| Seale] 76; seale BL. || salvation,] salva=tionₐ BL; sal=vation, 76.
175.7 communion] Communion BL; Com=munion 76.
175.8 prayer,] prayerₐ BL, 76. || fasting,] 76; fasting; BL. || which] 76; w:ᶜʰ BL.
175.10 haue] BL; have 76. || our] BL; our *interlined* 76. || sinnes] BL; Sinnes 76.
175.11 Sinne] 76; sinne BL. || have] 76; haue BL. || ô] Ô BL, 76.
175.12 wᵗʰ the Prodigall Sonne,] with yᵉ Prodi=gall sonneₐ BL; with the Prodigall sonne,
76. || haue sinned] haue sin=ned BL; have sinned 76.
175.13 Heaven] BL; Heavē 76.
175.13–14 Sonne, &] BL; Sonne; and 76.
175.14 cry] BL; Cry 76. || man] 76; *catchword* man *omitted in first line* BL.
175.15 that] 76; yᵗ BL.
175.16 faith] 76; Faith BL. || and] 76; & BL.
175.17 haue] BL; have 76.
175.18 then] *interlined* 77; then *not interlined* BL, 76. || doubtleſs] doubtleſse BL, 76.
175.19 likewise] likewiſe BL; Likewiſe 76. || heaven] BL; Heaven 76.
175.20 that] 76; yᵗ BL.
175.21 repentance] 76; re=pentance BL. || sinnes] BL; Sinnes 76. || yʳ] BL; that 76. ||
cry] BL; cry *interlined* 76.
175.22 vsₐ] vs, BL, 76. || sinne] BL; Sinne 76. || desperation] BL; Desperation 76.
175.23 vsₐ saithₐ] vsₐ saith, BL; vs, saith, 76. || wᵗʰ] w:ᵗʰ BL; With 76. || impoſsible] 76;
impossible BL.
175.24 with] w:ᵗʰ BL; wᵗʰ 76. || with] 76; w:ᵗʰ BL. || poſ=sible] poſsible BL, 76.
175.25 vnrighteousneſse] BL; vnrighteouſneſse 76. || mercifull] 76; mercyfull BL.
175.26 sinnes] 76; Sinnes BL. || repenting;] BL; ~ , 76.
175.27 shews] 76; shewes BL. || Thousands] 76; thousands BL.
175.28 af=flicts] afflicts BL, 76. || know] 76; knowe BL. || slow] BL; slowe 76.
176.1 be=cauſe] becauſe BL; because 76.
176.2 having salvation] hauing Salva=tion BL; having Sal=vation 76. || be=leeve] beleeve
BL; beleeue 76. || the] 76; yᵉ BL.
176.3 Ghost,] 76; ~ ; BL. || Meſsenger] meſsenger BL; Meſ=senger 76. || the] 76; yᵉ BL.
176.4 first spirit] 76; first Spirit BL. || tyedings] 76; tydings BL.
176.5 virgin Mary: with which] Virgin Mary: w:ᵗʰ w:ᶜʰ BL; virgin Mary, with which 76.
176.6 the] BL; yᵉ 76. || with] w:ᵗʰ BL, 76.
176.7 migh͡tyer] 76; mightier BL. || commeth] BL; cometh 76. || Bap=tize] Baptize BL,

76. || with] 76; w.th BL.

176.8 with] 76; w.th BL. || then] 76; Then BL. || com=manded] command=ed BL; commanded 76.

176.9 and] BL; *catchword & omitted in first line* 76.

176.10 God.] BL; God, 76. || descending.] BL; descending, 76. || Dove.] Dove, BL, 76.

176.11 be=loved Sonne] be=loved sonne BL; beloved Sonne 76.

176.12 pleased: So] pleased; so BL; pleased; So 76. || haue] BL; have 76. || haue] BL; have 76. || spirit, w^{ch}] Spirit, w:^{ch} BL; spirit, which 76.

176.13 know=ledge] ledge *interlined* 77; knowledge *not interlined* BL, 76. || the] BL; y^e 76.

176.14 Sacrament] 76; Sacra=ment BL. || birth.] BL; Birth, 76. || Parents] 76; parents BL. || we] 76; wee BL.

176.15 sinne] BL; Sinne 76.

176.16 redeem] 76; redeeme BL. || sinne,] 76; Sinnes; BL. || rose] BL; roſe 76.

176.17 ascended] BL; aſcended 76.

176.18 heavenly] Heavenly 76; BL. || judge] BL; judg 76. || judge to] *catchword vs omitted in first line* 77; vs *not omitted* BL, 76. || save] BL; Save 76.

176.19 condemne vs;] BL; Condemne vs, 76. || beleeve] 76; be=leeve BL. || Catholick Church,] BL; Catho=lick Church; 76.

176.20 resurrectiō] resurrection BL, 76.

176.21 on earth.] BL; on earth, *interlined* 76. || Example] 76; example BL.

176.21–22 the Grave,] the Grave? BL; y^e grave? 76.

176.22 receive] 76; receiue BL. || the Sentence] BL; y^e sentence 76. || because] be=cause BL; becauſe 76.

176.23 selves,] 76; ~ ᴧ BL.

176.24 de=livered] delivered BL, 76.

176.25 body.] body: BL, 76. || beleeve] 76; beleeue BL. || everlasting] ever=lasting BL; ever=lasting 76.

176.26 sufferings] 76; suffer=ings BL. || with] 76; wth BL. || adorn=ing mercyes] adorning mer=cyes BL; adorning mercyes 76.

176.27 tak=eth] taketh BL, 76. || vs.] BL; ~, 76. || & beautifies] and beautifies BL; and beauty=fyes 76. || vs] *interlined* 77; vs *not interlined* BL, 76. || wth salvation] with Salvation BL; with salvation 76.

176.28 with] 76; w:th BL. || ashamed] BL; aſhamed 76. || confounded.] confounded, BL, 76.

176.29 without] 76; wthout BL. || gives] 76; giues BL. || y^e] the BL, 76.

176.30 be] 76; be *interlined* BL. || blamlesse] BL; blamleſs 76. || appearance] BL; appea=rance 76. || which] 76; w:^{ch} BL.

176.31 Judgment,] Judgement; BL; judg=ment, 76. || read] 76; reade BL.

176.32 againe] 76; a gaine BL. || grave] 76; Graue BL. || matter] BL; mater 76.

177.1 gladneſse, rejoycing.] gladneſse, rejoycing, BL; gladneſs, rejoycing, 76.

177.2 Archangells] 76; Archan=gells BL. || which] 76; w:^{ch} BL. || the] BL; y^e 76. || gladneſs] 76; gladneſse BL.

177.3 in=nocent] innocent BL; o *of innocent interlined* 76.

177.4 sinner,] sinner. BL; Sinner, 76. || therefore.] BL; therefore, 76.

177.4–5 Lord. re=buke] BL; Lord, rebuke 76.

177.5 chast=en] BL; Chasten 76.

177.6 pray=er] prayer BL, 76. || petition] BL; pe=tition 76. || which] 76; w:^{ch} BL. || is, ô] 76; is. o BL.

177.7 lamp] 76; Lampe BL.

177.8 Heavenly com=fort] Heaven=ly comfort BL; Heavenly comfort 76. || be=seech theeₐ] beseech theeₐ BL; beseech thee, 76.

177.9 watch=ful knowledge] BL; watchfull knowledg 76.

177.10 thouₐ] BL; ~ , 76. || theeₐ yᵉ] thee, yᵉ BL; theeₐ the 76.

177.11 salvation] BL; Sal=vation 76. || give meₐ] giue meₐ BL; give me, 76. || con=tinue] continue BL; con=tinue 76. || inₐ] BL; in, 76. || de=votion] devotion BL, 76.

177.12 yʳ] that BL, 76. || led] 76; ledd BL. || yᵉ] 76; the BL.

177.13 sinneₐ and] sinneₐ & BL; sinne, 76.

177.14 a=gainst] a gainst BL; against 76. || Joy] BL; joy 76. || gladneſs] 76; gladneſse BL. || that] BL; yᵗ 76.

177.15 broken] BL; bro=ken 76. || rejoyce,] reioyce, BL; rejoyce; 76.

177.16 me, &] me, and BL; me; and 76.

177.17 thee,] 76; theeₐ BL. || Sonne,] 76; Sonneₐ BL. || Ghost.] 76; Ghost: BL.

177.18 the Sickneſse] the Sicknesse BL; y:ᵉ sickneſse 76. || Franck.] BL; Frank: 76.

177.19 God,] 76; God. BL. || Humble Heart] humble heart BL; humble Heart 76.

177.20 theeₐ] BL; ~ , 76. || thee, ô] 76; thee, Ô BL.

177.21 Sonne] 76; sonne BL.

177.21–22 and sickneſse,] & sickneſse, BL; and sickneſse; 76.

177.22 have] 76; haue BL.

177.23 and compaſsion] 76; & compassion BL. || dear] deare BL; Dear 76.

177.24 child] BL; Childe 76. || look] 76; looke BL.

177.25 afflic=tionₐ] affliction, BL; afflic=tion, 76. || prayerₐ] BL; prayer, 76.

177.26 whatsoever] 76; what=soever BL.

177.27 be=leeve] BL; beleive 76. || without] 76; w=ᵗʰout BL. || wee] BL; we 76. || nothing,] 76; nothing; BL.

177.28 mag=nifie] magnifie BL, 76.

177.29 ô sweet] Ô sweet BL; Ô Sweet 76. || didst] BL; did'st 76.

177.30 faith, be] 76; Faith, and be BL. || and] 76; & BL.

177.31 whole,] 76; whole, BL.

177.32 impoſsible wᵗʰ thee,] impoſsible with thee, BL; im=poſsible with thee, 76. || thou] 76; y.ᵘ BL.

178.1 shee] BL; she 76. || and w.ᵗʰ] and w:ᵗʰ BL; & with 76.

178.2 spirit] BL; Spirit 76. || Damsell Tabbitha] Damsell Tabbi=tha BL; damsell Tabbitha 76.

178.3 ariſe] 76; arise BL. || beseech] be=seech BL, 76. || her, &] her; and BL; her, and 76.

178.5 meₐ] BL; me, 76. || Lordₐ] BL; Lord, 76. || taking] 76; take=ing BL. || knowₐ] BL; ~ , 76.

178.6 beleive] 76; beleeve BL. || Heaven,] 76; Heavenₐ BL.

178.7 thee,] 76; ~ theeₐ BL. || have com=paſsion] haue compaſsion BL; have compaſsion 76. || herₐ] BL; her, 76. || world,] BL; world; 76.

178.8 nor] 76; not BL.

178.9 wᵗʰ] with BL, 76. || have] 76; haue BL. || yᵉ] the BL, 76. || come,] BL; come; 76.

178.10 glo=rious] glorious BL, 76.

178.11 give] 76; giue BL. || loſse] 76; losse BL.

178.12 grudging,] BL; grudgingₐ 76. || will,] will; BL, 76. || wᵗʰ] BL; w:ᵗʰ 76.

178.13 angry,] 76; angryₐ BL. || speake] speak BL, 76. || w.ᶜʰ] BL; w:ᶜʰ 76.

178.14 which] BL; w.ᶜʰ *interlined* 76. || holy] BL; Holy 76.

178.15 prayer, w.ᶜʰ] prayerₐ which BL; prayer, w:ᶜʰ 76. || son] Sonne BL, 76.

178.16 Heavenₐ] ~ . BL; Heaven, 76.

178.17 Childₐ] Child. BL, 76.

178.18 praiſe] BL; prayſe 76.

178.19 bleſse] BL; blesse 76. || have] BL; haue 76. || with] BL; w:ᵗʰ 76. || hastₐ] BL; hast, 76.

178.20 given] BL; givē 76. || Spirit] BL; spirit 76. || in=fuse] infuse BL, 76. || Spirit] spirit BL, 76.

178.21 it,] BL; itₐ 76. || per=fect shapes] perfect shapes BL; perfect Shapes 76. || seeₐ w.ᵗʰ] seeₐ with BL; see, with 76.

178.22 com=fort] comfort BL, 76. || wᵗʰ=all] w:ᵗʰall BL; withall 76.

178.23 ac=knowledge] acknowledge BL, 76.

178.24 thanks=giving;] thanks giving, BL; thankesgiving, 76. || two,] BL; two; 76.

178.24–25 Male, and Female] 76; Maleₐ and a Female BL.

178.25 Joyfully] BL; joyfully 76. || be=hold themₐ] behold them, BL, 76.

178.26 Sacrament] 76; Sacra=ment BL. || Baptisme,] ~ ; BL; Bap=tisme, 76.

178.27 love=ing] loving BL, 76. || deare Babes,] 76; dear Babesₐ BL.

178.28 me] 76; me *interlined* BL. || give] 76; giue BL. || knowledgeₐ and] knowledge, and BL; knowledge, & 76. || vnderstanding] 76; vn=derstanding BL.

178.29 thingsₐ] things, BL, 76.

178.30 vertue,] BL; vertue; 76. || willₐ] will, BL, 76.

178.31 Justiceₐ and afflic=tion] Justice, & affliction BL; Juſtice, and affliction 76. || take=ing away] takeing away BL; taking away 76.

178.32 youth,] 76; youth; BL. || thou] BL; yᵘ 76. || butₐ Ô] butₐ ô BL; but, ô 76.

179.1 God,] 76; ~ ₐ BL. || with] 76; w:ᵗʰ BL. || eye ₐ] BL; eye, 76. || and] 76; *catchword and omitted in first line* BL. || them,] 76; themₐ BL.

179.1–2 didst Abra=ham, and Jacob,] dids't Abraham, & Jacob, BL; didst Abraham, & Jacob 76.

179.2 Sarah, and Rebekah,] Sarahₐ & Rebekah, BL; Sarah, & Re=bekah, 76. || t'is] 76; 'tis BL. || thy] 76; thy *interlined* BL.

179.3 Kingdom] BL; Kingdome 76.

179.4 purifyed] 76; purified BL. || sinnes.] BL; sinnes: 76. || God,] 76; Godₐ BL.

179.5 have] 76; haue BL. || meₐ] BL; ~ , 76.

179.6 feele,] 76; feeleₐ BL.

179.7 me,] 76; meₐ BL. || thou] 76; yᵘ BL. || en=able] enable BL, 76. || and] 76; & BL.

179.8 sonne,] Sonneₐ BL; Sonne, 76. || Sa=viour] Saviour BL, 76.

179.9 sinnes] BL; Sinnes 76. || ô Sweet] Ô sweet BL; Ô Sweet 76. || the] BL; yᵉ 76.

179.10 la=bour] labour BL, 76. || travaileₐ giue] travaile, give BL; travaileₐ give 76.

179.11 con=fidence] confidence BL; Confidence 76.

179.12 come] BL; Come 76. || I will ease] BL; I *interlined* 76.

179.13 ô] Ô BL, 76.

179.14 giue] give BL, 76. || joy] 76; Joy BL.

179.15 Church; My Sinnes ô] Church: my siñs o BL; Church: My Sinnes Ô 76.

179.16 Sonne's] 76; sonne's BL. || judgment] 76; Judgement BL.

179.17 yᵘ] 76; thou BL. || President, resident] *catchword and omitted in first line* 77; President, and resident BL, 76. || with me,] with me; BL; w:ᵗʰ me, 76.

179.19 love] BL; loue 76. || thee,] 76; thee; BL. || turne] BL; turn 76.

179.20 that] 76; y.ᵗ BL. || and cryes] BL; & Cryes 76.

179.21 meₐ] me, BL, 76. || remiſsion] BL; remission 76.

179.22 punished] 76; punish=ed BL. || ô deare] BL; Ô deare 76.

179.23 Redeemer's] 76; Redeemers BL. || &] and BL, 76.

179.24 Labour.] Labour. BL, 76.

179.25 Jesusₐ] Iesusₐ BL; Jesus, 76.

179.26 truth‸] BL; truth, 76.
179.27 obe=dience] obedience BL, 76. || thee‸] BL; thee, 76.
179.28 grudging] 76; grudg=ing BL.
179.29 and] 76; & BL.
179.30 sweet] BL; Sweet 76. || with] 76; w:ᵗʰ BL.
179.31 deare Child‸ wᵗʰout] dear child‸ without BL; deare Child, w:ᵗʰout 76.
179.32 wᶜʰ] w:ᶜʰ BL; which 76. || won=derfull] BL; wonderfull 76. || far] 76; farr BL.
179.33 sinnes] BL; Sinnes 76. || wᵗʰ a Song] w:ᵗʰ a song BL; w:ᵗʰ a Song 76. || magnified] 76; magnifyed BL.
179.34–34 w.ᵗʰ thanksgiving, ô] w:ᵗʰ thanks=giving; ô BL; w:ᵗʰ thanks=giving, Ô 76.
179.34 Lord heare] *interlined* 77; Lord heare *not interlined* BL; Lord hear *not interlined* 76. || forgiue] forgive BL, 76.
180.1 ac=company] accompany BL, 76. || sinnes] BL; Sinnes 76. || deepe] BL; Deepe 76. || and] BL; & *interlined* 76.
180.3 Chriſt] Christ BL, 76. || everlasting‸] BL; everlasting, 76. || beleife] 76; be=leife BL.
180.4 Saviour.] 76; Saviour: BL.
180.6 praiſe, and] prayse‸ & BL; prayſe, and 76. || that] BL; y:ᵗ 76.
180.7 beene pleaſed] been pleased BL, 76. || Childbirth] child=birth BL; Child=birth 76.
180.8 goodneſse] BL; good=neſse 76. || con=tinue] continue BL, 76.
180.9 work] worke BL, 76. || love] BL; loue 76. || obey,] 76; obey‸ BL.
180.10 beleive] 76; believe BL. || Sonne‸] 76; Sonne, BL. || Saviour] BL; r *of Saviour interlined* 76. || Chriſt] Christ BL, 76.
180.11 pleaſed] pleased BL, 76. || life. ô] life: ô BL; life: Ô 76. || know] knowe BL, 76.
180.12 might=est] mightest BL; mightst 76. || have] haue BL; have *interlined* 76. || smothered] BL; Smothered 76. || this] BL; this *interlined* 76. || yᵉ Wombe] the wombe BL, 76.
180.13 great] 76; greate BL.
180.14 great tor=ture] great torture 76; greate torture BL. || Childbirth; in] childbirth; In BL; Child birth; in 76. || dis=treſse] distreſse BL, 76.
180.15 thankfulneſse, &] thankfullneſs, and BL; thankfulneſse; & 76. || Sinner] 76; sinner BL.
180.16 &] and BL, 76.
180.17 pleasure‸] BL; pleasure, 76. || present with] present w:ᵗʰ BL; pre=ſent w:ᵗʰ 76. || extremity, and] extremi=ty, and BL; extremity, & 76.
180.18 Cryes] 76; cryes BL. || me the vnworthy=est] mee the vnworthyest BL; me yᵉ vnworthyest 76. || Servants; and] servants; and BL; Servants; & 76. || thee o] 76; the ô BL.
180.19 give] 76; giue BL. || Bap=tiſme] 76; Baptisme BL.
180.20 sinne] BL; Sin 76. || his] 76; it's BL. || who‸] BL; who, 76.
180.21 kindneſse] 76; kind=neſse BL. || haue sunck] BL; have sunke 76. || beene] BL; been 76. || immediate hand,] immediate hand; BL; im=mediate hand, 76.
180.22 therefore wᵗʰ the] there=fore w:ᵗʰ the BL; therefore with yᵉ 76.
180.23 Sabbath,] 76; Sabbath‸ BL. || alone] a lone BL, 76. || praiſe] BL; prayſe 76.
180.24 with Child‸] with Child. BL; w:ᵗʰ Child. 76.
180.25 Chriſt] BL; Christ 76. || heare] BL; hear 76. || Servant,] servant, BL; Servant; 76.
180.26 Lord] ô Lord BL; lord 76. || one's] BL; ones 76. || sud=denly] suddenly BL, 76. || come] BL; come *interlined* 76. || de=parture] departure BL, 76.
180.27 knowledge‸] knowledge, BL, 76. || far off the] far of the BL; farre off yᵉ 76. || of] BL; off 76.

180.28 Lord‸ preserve me‸] Lord, preserue me, BL; Lord, pre=serve me, 76. ||
con=fidence] confidence BL; Confidence 76. || yᵗ] that BL, 76.

180.29 helpe me,] helpe me‸ BL; help me, 76. || distreſse‸] BL; ~ , 76. || thou] BL; yᵘ
76. || beene] BL; been 76.

180.30 withall,] ~; BL, with-all; 76. || Lord‸] BL; ~ , 76. || yᵉ] the BL, 76.

180.31 borne without] BL; born w:ᵗʰout 76.

180.32 Father] BL; father 76. || sinnes] BL; Sinnes 76.

180.33 ô Lord,] ô Lord‸ BL; Ô Lord, 76. || vn=cleanes] 76; vncleanes BL.

180.34 kindneſse,] 76; kindneſse‸ BL.

181.1 shape,] 76; shape‸ BL. || comforts] 76; com=forts BL. || and] BL; & 76.

181.2 yᵗ joyfull] that joyfull BL; that Joyfull 76. || prayſes] praises BL; prayses 76.

181.3 the] BL, yᵉ 76. || thee‸] *interlined* 77; thee‸ *not interlined* BL; thee, *not interlined*
76. || lett] 76; let BL.

181.4 cleave] BL; cleaue 76. || remem=ber] 76; remember BL. || thee, ô] 76; thee‸ ô, BL.

181.5 preſerue] preserve BL; pre=serve 76. || soule,] Soule‸ BL; ~ ‸ 76. || knowledge]
knowledg BL; know=ledge 76.

181.6 reſurrection] resurrection BL, 76. || hee] BL; he 76.

181.7 Sinnes:] sinnes: BL; Sinnes; 76. || yᵗ] that BL, 76.

181.8 continue] BL; con=tinue 76. || grant] *interlined* 77, 76; grant *not interlined* BL. ||
that] BL; y:ᵗ *interlined* 76. || with] 76; w.ᵗʰ BL.

181.9 w.ᵗʰ Child,] w:ᵗʰ Child, BL; w:ᵗʰ Child‸ 76. || haue fall=en] BL; have fallen 76.

181.11 Christ‸] BL; Christ, 76. || give] 76; giue BL. || con=fidence] confidence BL, 76.

181.12 confeſse,] 76; confeſse‸ BL. || grievous] gree=vous BL; greevious 76. || yᵗ] 76; that
BL.

181.13 the] BL; yᵉ 76.

181.14 consider thee,] consider thee‸ BL; con ider thee, 76.

181.15 good=neſse] goodneſse BL; goodneſs 76. || loving=kindneſse;] BL; loving
kindneſse, 76. || giue] BL; give 76. || God‸] BL; god, 76.

181.16 yᵗ when] that when BL, 76. || it‸] ~, BL, 76.

181.17 that thou] 76; yᵗ thou BL. || that] yᵗ BL, 76.

181.18 grudging] 76; grudg=ing BL. || and‸ Ô] &‸ Ô BL; and, ô 76.

181.19 giue] BL; give 76. || pa=tience,] patience‸ BL; patience, 76. || that] BL; yᵗ 76. ||
that] BL; yᵗ 76. || endure‸] BL; endure, 76.

181.20 another bleſsing] 76; a nother blessing BL. || thee,] 76; thee‸ BL.

181.21 with] BL; w:ᵗʰ 76. || forme‸] BL; forme, 76. || thee,] 76; ~ ‸ BL.

181.22 Chriſt] Christ BL, 76. || with the knowledge] wᵗʰ the knowledge BL; w:ᵗʰ yᵉ
knowledg 76.

181.23 suf=ferings] BL; sufferings 76. || giue] BL; give 76. || Mite] 76; mite BL. ||
patience‸] BL; patience, 76.

181.23–24 thou enduredst] thou en=duredst BL; yᵘ enduredst 76.

181.24 me,] BL; me; 76. || doubt, but‸ with] doubt‸ but‸ with BL; doubt, but, w:ᵗʰ 76.

181.25 with] w:ᵗʰ BL, 76. || haue gon] BL; have gone 76. || wᵗʰ the] w:ᵗʰ yᵉ 76.

181.26 bleſsed me,] 76; blessed me‸ BL. || and] 76; & BL. || huſband withall] husband
w:ᵗʰall BL; huſband wᵗʰall 76.

181.27 joyfull with] joyfull w:ᵗʰ BL; Joyfull w:ᵗʰ 76. || that] yᵗ BL; that *omitted* 76. ||
thou] BL; yᵘ 76. || pleaſed] BL; pleased 76.

181.28 with] 76; w:ᵗʰ BL.

181.29 sonne] Sonne BL, 76. || Saviour's] Saviours BL, 76. || *In 76, "A prayer after I had
received yͤ blessed Sacram:ᵗ," follows here, instead of at 190.1, where it appears in 77 and
BL.*

181.30 Prayer] BL; prayer 76. || with Child₍ₐ₎] with Child. BL; w:ᵗʰ Child. 76.
181.31 great] 76; Great BL. || Al=mighty] Almighty BL, 76.
181.31–32 Majᵗⁱᵉ beseech=ing] Maj.ᵗⁱᵉ beseeching BL; Maj:ᵗⁱᵉ beseeching 76.
181.32 heare] BL; hear 76. || give, ô Lordₐ] giue ô Lordₐ BL; give Ô Lord, 76.
181.33 that thou] BL; yᵗ yᵘ 76. || created] BL; Created 76. || another] a nother BL, 76.
181.34 ô] BL; Ô 76. || thee,] 76; theeₐ BL. || yʳ] that BL, 76. || have] 76; haue BL.
182.1 vnderstand=ing] BL; vnderstanding 76. || and Com=mandem:ᵗˢₐ] & commandements; BL; and Commandem:ᵗˢₐ 76. || giue meₐ] BL; give me, 76.
182.2 hap=py] happy BL, 76.
182.3 with life₍ₐ₎] w:ᵗʰ life, BL, 76. || the] BL; yᵉ 76. || haue] have BL; have *interlined* 76. || thou] yᵘ BL, 76. || and] 76; & BL.
182.4 beg,] 76; begₐ BL. || the] BL; yᵉ 76. || that thou] y.ʳ yᵘ BL; that yᵘ 76. || give] 76; giue BL.
182.5 pun=ish] punish BL; punniſh 76. || Fa=ther] Father BL; father 76. || sinnes] BL; sinns 76.
182.6 thou] BL; yᵘ 76. || and] BL; & 76.
182.7 have₍ₐ₎] haue BL; have, 76. || knowledge] BL; knowledg 76.
182.8 Sonne] 76; sonne BL. || Saviour, and] 76; Savi=our; & BL. || thee,] 76; theeₐ BL.
182.9 the greate] the great BL; yᵉ greate 76.
182.10 thoſe] those BL, 76. || Lordₐ] BL; ~ , 76. || giue] BL; give 76.
182.11 confidence] 76; confi=dence BL. || that thou] BL; y.ʳ yᵘ 76. || for=sake] forsake BL, 76.
182.12 receive] 76; *catchword* receiue *omitted in first line* BL. || thee] BL; thee *interlined* 76.
182.13 bleſsing] 76; blessing BL. || a nother sweet] 76; another sweete BL. || wᶜʰ] w:ᶜʰ BL, 76. || increaſe the] increase the BL; increaſe yᵉ 76.
182.14 and₍ₐ₎] BL; ~ , 76. || give] 76; giue BL. || Spirit,] 76; spirit, BL.
182.15 Bap=tiſme, that] Baptisme, that BL; Baptiſme, yᵗ 76. || the] BL; yᵉ 76. || that] yᵗ BL, 76.
182.16 be=leeve] BL; beleeve 76. || Sonne] 76; sonne BL. || that] BL; yᵗ 76. || live] liue BL, 76.
182.17 from originall₍ₐ₎] *catchword* it's *omitted in first line* 77; from it's originallₐ BL; from it's Originall, 76. || ac=tuall] BL; actuall 76. || giue] BL; give 76.
182.18 haue] BL; have 76. || hum=bly] humbly BL, 76. || life₍ₐ₎] 76; life, BL. || thou] BL; y.ᵘ 76. || the] BL; yᵉ 76.
182.19 giue] BL; give 76. || com=fort] comfort BL, 76. || yᵗ] 76; that ~ BL. || magnifie] BL; mag=nifie 76.
182.20 the] BL; yᵉ 76. || & the] and the BL; and yᵉ 76. || bleſsing thou] blessing y.ᵘ BL; bleſsing yᵘ 76.
182.21 deare] BL; dear 76. || tongue] 76; tounge BL.
182.22 praiſe₍ₐ₎] BL; ~ , 76. || haue] BL; have 76. || and] BL; & 76.
182.22–23 deare affection=ate Huſbands] deare affectionate Husband's BL; dear affectionate Huſband's 76.
182.23 praiſe] 76; praise BL. || wᵗʰ joyfull lipps] w.ᵗʰ joyfull lips BL; w:ᵗʰ Joyfull lipps 76.
182.24 heare] BL; hear 76. || forgiue] for=give BL, 76.
182.25 sinnes,] siñs BL; sinnesₐ 76. || the] BL; yᵉ 76. || be=twixt] betwixt BL, 76.
182.26 hill, and] BL; Hill, & 76.
182.27 the Jesus] *catchword* Lord *omitted in first line* 77; the Lord Jesus BL; yᵉ Lord Jesus 76. || blessing] bleſsinġ BL, 76. || giue] BL; give 76.
182.28 eaſe] 76; ease BL. || and giue me the] BL; & give me yᵉ 76.

182.29 and giue] and give BL; & give 76. || the] BL; y.ᵉ 76. || joy,] joyₐ BL; Joy, 76. || its] 76; it's BL.

182.30 and] BL; & 76. || wᵗʰ=all; and] w.ᵗʰall; & BL; w:ᵗʰall; & 76.

182.31 and] BL; & 76. || the] BL; yᵉ 76. || and] BL; & 76.

182.33 with the] w:ᵗʰ the BL; w:ᵗʰ yᵉ 76. || Lord] 76; *catchword* Lord *omitted in first line* BL. || sinner] BL; Sinner 76.

182.34 wᵗʰ] w:ᵗʰ BL, 76. || faithfull] 76; faith=full BL. || heart] BL; Heart 76. || and thanksgiving,] and thanks=giving; BL; & thanks giving, 76.

182.35 thou] thou BL; yᵘ 76. || heareₐ and] BL; hear, & 76. || ô thou] BL; Ô yᵘ 76. || persons,] ~ ₐ BL; perſons, 76.

183.1 with] BL; w:ᵗʰ 76. || safety,] BL; safety, 76. || the] BL; yᵉ 76. || and] BL; & 76.

183.2 paſse] 76; paſs BL. || and] BL; & 76. || giue] give BL, 76. || eaſy and] easy and BL; eaſy & 76.

183.3 labour] Labour BL, 76. || thou] BL; yᵘ 76. || sal=vation] salvation BL; Salvation 76.

183.4 looke] look BL, 76.

183.5 the Crumes yᵗ] the crumēs that BL; yᵉ Crumēs yᵗ 76. || Tableₐ which] Table, which BL; Table, w:ᶜʰ 76.

183.6 feede] BL; feed 76. || soules; and] Soules, and BL; Soules; & 76. || and] BL; & 76. || be fedd] be fed BL; bee fedd 76. || with the Crumes] wᵗʰ the Crumes BL; w:ᵗʰ yᵉ Crumēs 76.

183.7 Bleſsed] 76; blessed BL. || and] BL; & 76. || diſpaire] BL; deſpaire 76.

183.8 com=fort] comfort BL, 76. || bleſsed] 76; blessed BL. || ever=more,] ever more, BL, 76. || with] w.ᵗʰ BL; w:ᵗʰ 76. || &] 76; and BL.

183.9 name,] BL; name, 76. || & ever] and ever. BL; & ever. 76.

183.10 Prayer] BL; prayer 76. || Stuart,] Stuart. BL, 76.

183.11 God,] 76; God, BL. || Almighty] Almigh=ty BL; almighty 76. || wᵗʰ] with BL; w:ᵗʰ 76. || first] 76; First BL.

183.11–12 Lordₐ that thou] Lordₐ yᵗ yᵘ BL; Lord, y:ᵗ y.ᵘ 76.

183.12 Sinnes, wᶜʰ] BL; sinnes, w:ᶜʰ 76. || infinite, and] BL; infinit, & 76.

183.13 heare] BL; hear 76. || thanksgiving,] thanksgiving, BL; thanks=giving, 76. || that thou] BL; y.ᵗ y.ᵘ 76. || wᵗʰ] BL; w:ᵗʰ 76.

183.14 and infus'd] and infused BL; & infus'd 76. || Spirit] 76; spirit BL. || Godₐ thou send'st] BL; God, yᵘ send'st 76.

183.15 thou did'st] BL; yᵘ did'st 76. || wᵗʰ] with BL; w:ᵗʰ 76. || away] a way BL, 76. || me] BL; me *interlined* 76. || and] BL; & 76.

183.16 beene] BL; been 76. || will,] 76; ~ ₐ BL. || the] BL; yᵉ 76.

183.17 the sick=neſse] the sickneſse BL; yᵉ sickneſs 76. || Childrenₐ] BL; ~ , 76. || with the] BL; w:ᵗʰ yᵉ 76.

183.18 and the] BL; & yᵉ 76. || another] a nother BL, 76. || a long] BL; a=long 76. || with] w.ᵗʰ BL; w:ᵗʰ 76. || and] BL; & 76.

183.19 Spirit] 76; spirit BL. || grace, & give] graceₐ and giue BL; grace, & give 76. || o Lord,] ô Lordₐ BL; o Lord, 76. || the labour,] the Labour, BL; yᵉ Labour, 76. || and] BL; & 76.

183.20 make] *interlined* 77; make *not interlined* BL, 76. || Joyfull mother,] Joyfull motherₐ BL; joyfull mother, 76. || behold=ing] beholding BL, 76. || with] wᵗʰ BL; w:ᵗʰ 76.

183.20–21 shape, and forme,] shapeₐ and form, BL; shape, & forme, 76.

183.21 the worke] the work BL; yᵉ 76. || and give] and giue BL; & give 76.

183.22 birth; ô] birth; o BL; bearth: Ô 76. || with] BL; w:ᵗʰ 76. || and] BL; & 76. || and] BL; & 76.

183.23 give] 76; giue BL. || will͵] will, BL, 76. || quick and speedy] BL; Quick & Speedy 76. || and] BL; & 76. || the] BL; yᵉ 76.

183.23–24 Child, and] child, and BL; Child, & 76.

183.24 have] 76; haue BL. || with] wːᵗʰ BL; wᵗʰ 76. || and health] BL; & health 76.

183.25 extremi=ty͵] extremity, BL; Extremity͵ 76. || have] 76; haue BL. || thee, and] BL; thee; & 76.

183.26 thou] BL; yᵘ 76. || leave] 76; leaue BL.

183.27 and] BL; & 76.

183.28 and] BL; & 76. || haue] BL; have 76.

183.29 redemption,] 76; redemp=tion͵ BL. || the] *interlined* 77; the *not interlined* BL; yᵉ *not interlined* 76. || perſons, and] persons, and BL; persons, & 76.

183.30 Son͵] Sonne, BL; Son, 76. || Holy ghost] BL; Holy=ghost 76. || that] BL; yᵗ 76. || holy spirit] Holy Spirit BL; holy Spirit 76. || with me͵] BL; wːᵗʰ me, 76.

183.31 direct me͵ that] direct mee, that BL; directe me͵ yᵗ 76. || not,] 76; not͵ BL. || impatience] 76; impa=tience BL.

183.32 extremity] 76; ex=tremity BL. || mercy͵] BL; ~ , 76. || and helpe, and] BL; & helpe & 76.

183.32–33 that thou͵] that thou, BL; yːᵗ yᵘ 76.

183.33 the afflicted] the afflict=ed BL; yᵉ afflicted 76. || and] BL; & 76.

183.34 deare] BL; dear 76. || that he] BL; yᵗ hee 76. || haue the] BL; have yᵉ 76.

183.34–35 with rest] with the rest BL; wːᵗʰ yᵉ rest 76.

183.35 that he,] that he͵ BL; yᵗ he, 76. || and I͵] BL; & I, 76. || holy and] BL; Holy & 76.

184.1 mercyes] BL; mer=cyes 76. || releiving] BL; releeving 76.

184.2 extremityes] extremities BL; Ex=tremitys 76. || the] BL; yᵉ 76. || and bringing] and bring=ing BL; & bringing 76. || greate] great BL, 76.

184.3 laude and] laud & BL; laude & 76. || holy] BL; Holy 76. || evermore] BL; ever=more 76. || and] BL; & 76.

184.4 Sonne] BL; Son 76. || & raigneth] 76; and raigneth BL.

184.5 and] BL; & 76.

184.6 with prayer͵] with Prayer. BL; wːᵗʰ prayer. 76.

184.7 and] BL; & 76. || ô] BL; o 76. || my] BL; myne 76. || yᵗ] 76; that BL.

184.8 let] BL; lett 76. || Lanthorne] BL; Lanthorn 76. || and] BL; & 76.

184.9 the Foole, that] the Foole͵ that BL; yᵉ foole, yᵗ 76. || no] 76; noe BL.

184.10 neuer] never BL, 76. || the] BL; yᵉ 76.

184.11 miſbe=leeving] miſbeleeving BL, 76. || say͵ tush͵ thou] say, tush, thou BL; say͵ tush, yᵘ 76.

184.12 Heare] BL; Hear 76. || and] BL; & 76.

184.13 zeale] BL; Zeale 76. || thy] 76; thy *interlined* BL. || tes=timonies, and] testi=monies, and BL; testimonies, & 76. || not] 76; not *interlined* BL.

184.14 crook=ed and vntoward] crooked and vn=toward BL; Crooked & vntoward 76. || fu=riouſly] furiously BL, 76. || together, and] BL; togeather, & 76.

184.15 im̃agine] 76; immagine BL. || ô Lord,] 76; o Lord͵ BL.

184.16 farr] 76; farre BL. || me͵ the] BL; me, yᵉ 76. || countenance͵ and] BL; countenance, & 76.

184.17 o] BL; ô 76. || the] BL; yᵉ 76.

184.18 Crea=tures] Creatures BL, 76.

184.19 the] BL; yᵉ 76. || water] 76; wa=ter BL. || me] *catchword* hear *omitted in first line* 77; hear me BL; heare me 76.

184.20 the] BL; yːᵉ 76. || o] ô BL; Ô 76. || de=fend] BL; defend 76. || me] BL; me *interlined* 76. || helpe] help BL, 76.

184.21 the] BL; yᵉ 76. || Sanc=tuary,] Sanctuaryʌ BL; Sanctuary, 76. || and strength=en] & strengthen BL, 76. || thou that] BL; y:ᵘ y:ᵗ 76. || yᵉ] 76; the BL.

184.22 flesh] Flesh BL, 76. || and] BL; & 76. || that] BL; yᵗ 76. || appeare;] BL; appeare, 76.

184.23 vnworthy;] 76; ~ , BL. || thou] BL; y:ᵘ 76. || the Kingʌ] the King, BL; yᵉ King, 76.

184.24 impatient] 76; im=patient BL. || the earth] BL; yᵉ earth 76.

184.25 vnquiet,] 76; vnquiet; BL. || vnto] *catchword* thanks *omitted in first line* 77; thanks vnto BL, 76. || the] BL; yᵉ 76. || and] & BL, 76. || name,] 76; name; BL. || the] BL; yᵉ 76.

184.26 &] and BL, 76.

184.27 knowledge] 76; know=ledge BL. || and] & BL, 76. || ever. and] ever. & BL; ever; & 76.

184.28 that beleeveʌ and] that beleeve, and BL; yᵗ beleeve & 76. || and] BL; & 76. || sonne] Sonne BL, 76. || confounded] 76; confound=ed BL.

185.1 and] BL; & 76. || Despaireʌ] Despaire. BL; despaire. 76.

185.2 vile,ʌ] 76; vile, BL. || sinfull,ʌ] sinfull, BL, 76. || de=spaire] despaire BL; diſpaire 76.

185.3 thou] BL; yᵘ 76. || redeem=ed] redeemed BL, 76. || and] BL; & 76.

185.4 with the] BL; w:ᵗʰ y:ᵉ 76. || vngodlineſs,] 76; vngod=lineſseʌ BL. || that] BL; yᵗ 76. || cannot looke] cannot look BL; can=not looke 76.

185.5 with] w.ᵗʰ BL; w:ᵗʰ 76.

185.6 meʌ with the] meʌ w.ᵗʰ the BL; me, w:ᵗʰ yᵉ 76. || in=cenſe] incenſe BL, 76. || loving,] lovingʌ BL, 76.

185.7 kindneſseʌ] *interlined* 77; kindneſse, *not interlined* BL, 76. || thou] BL; yᵘ 76. || y.ᵗ those that] that those that BL; yᵗ those yᵗ 76.

185.8 theeʌ thou] thee, thou BL; theeʌ yᵘ 76. || ease] eaſe BL, 76. || and] BL; & 76. || that] BL; yᵗ 76.

185.9 thou] BL; yᵘ 76. || them,] BL; ~; 76.

185.9–10 Lordʌ loden w.ᵗʰ sick=neſse] Lord, loden w.ᵗʰ sickneſse BL; Lord, Loden w:ᵗʰ sickneſse 76.

185.10 infirmities, and wᵗʰ] infirmities, and w.ᵗʰ BL; infir=mities, & w:ᵗʰ 76.

185.11 with iniquity] w.ᵗʰ iniquitie BL; w:ᵗʰ iniquity 76. || areʌ] BL; are, 76. || that without] that w:ᵗʰ=out BL; y:ᵗ w.ᵗʰout 76.

185.12 mer=cyesʌ] mercyesʌ BL; mercyes, 76. || ruine,] BL; ~; 76. || therefore] BL; therfore 76.

185.13 vnworthy=neſse] vnworthyneſse BL; vnworthyneſs 76.

185.14 holyneſse] holy=neſse BL; Hollyneſse 76. || with] w.ᵗʰ BL; w:ᵗʰ 76.|| sinnes] BL; sinns 76.

185.15 thee,] 76; theeʌ BL. || who well may be named my Saviour,] *interlined* 77; who well may be named my Saviour, *not interlined* BL, 76. || death, &] 76; death, and BL.

185.16 and] BL; & 76. || the] BL; yᵉ 76.

185.17 ever=lasting] everlasting BL, 76. || and] BL; & 76. || aſsured] aſſured BL; assured 76.

185.18 endleſse Joyes] BL; Endleſse joyes 76. || Honour, and] honour, and BL; Honour, & 76. || and] BL; & 76.

185.20 before the] BL; before yᵉ 76.

185.21 and glori=ous] and glorious BL; & glorious 76. || God,] 76; Godʌ BL. || haue] BL; have 76. || a] a *interlined* BL, 76.

185.22 sins, and] sinnes, and BL; sins, & 76. || a gaine] againe BL, 76. || now] 76; now *interlined* BL.

185.23 forgiuene∫se] BL; for=giuene∫se 76. || Ô t'is the] ô t'is yᵉ BL, 76. || Sa=viour] 76; Saviour BL.

185.24 Sinnes, and] sinnes, & BL, 76. || made] BL; made *interlined* 76. || re∫urrec=tion] resurrection BL, 76. || the] BL; yᵉ 76.

185.25 dead works] 76; dead workes BL. || works] 76; workes BL.

185.26 the] BL; yᵉ 76. || me] BL; mee 76. || and] BL; & 76.

185.27 with] 76; w.ᵗʰ BL. || and] BL; & 76. || forgiue] for=giue BL; forgive 76. || forgiven,] for=giuen; BL; for=given; 76. || Lord∧] BL; Lord, 76.

185.28 tran∫gre∫sions] transgre∫sions BL; tran∫gre∫=sions 76. || and renew] BL; & renewe 76. || within] wᵗʰin BL; w:ᵗʰin 76. || heare] BL; hear 76.

185.29 Joy, and gladne∫se] Joy∧ and gladne∫se BL; joy, & gladne∫s 76. || that the] BL; y:ᵗ y:ᵉ 76. || which thou] BL; w:ᶜʰ y.ᵘ 76.

185.30 Joy] BL; joy 76. || have] 76; haue BL. || yʳ] that BL; y:ᵗ 76. || and] BL; & 76.

185.31 come] BL; Come 76. || ble∫sed Jesus,] ble∫s=ed Jesus∧ BL; blessed Jesus, 76. || with] BL; w.ᵗʰ 76.

185.31–32 and re=pentance, and] BL; & repentance, & 76.

185.32 and] BL; & 76. || com=fort, and] comfort∧ and BL; comfort, & 76.

185.33 and] BL; & 76. || condem=nation] condemnation BL; Con=demnation 76. || destroy me; Ô God,] de=stroy me; ô God∧ BL; destroy me: Ô God, 76.

185.34 be=leife] beleife BL, 76. || di∫paire] 76; de=spaire BL. || mer=cyes] mercyes BL, 76.

185.35 greater] 76; great=er BL. || have] 76; haue BL.

186.1 haue] BL; have 76. || and giue] BL; & give 76. || pardon, that so] pardon∧ that so BL; pardon, yᵗ so 76.

186.2 and] BL; & 76. || and] BL; & 76. || with] w:ᵗʰ BL, 76. || ernestly] earnestly BL; Er=nestly 76.

186.3 and] BL; & 76. || resolve] BL; resolue 76. || of] *interlined* 77; of *not interlined* BL, 76.

186.4 holy Table∧] holy Table, BL; Holy Table, 76. || vnworthy] BL; vn=worthy 76. || favour,] 76; favour∧ BL.

186.5 Creature,] 76; ~ ∧ BL. || ac=knowledging,] 76; ac=knowledging∧ BL.

186.6 manyfold] manifold BL; manyfould 76. || heart, and Soule] heart, and soule BL; Heart, & Soule 76.

186.7 sweet] 76; sweete BL. || mi∫ser=able Sinner] mi∫serable sinner BL, 76.

186.8 the] BL; yᵉ 76. || yᵉ] the BL, 76.

186.9 and the] BL; & yᵉ 76. || true] 76; true *interlined* BL.

186.10 earnestly] ly *interlined* 77; ly *not interlined* BL, 76. || offences, wᶜʰ] offences∧ w.ᶜʰ BL; offences, w:ᶜʰ 76. || innumer=able] innumerable BL; innu=merable 76.

186.11 wᵗʰ] w.ᵗʰ BL; w:ᵗʰ 76. || num=bred] numbred BL; Numbered 76. || and] BL; & 76.

186.12 yʳ] that BL; y:ᵗ 76. || repetition∧] repetition, BL, 76.

186.13 knowing∧] BL; knowing, *interlined* 76. || Jus=tice] Justice BL, 76.

186.14 yᵉ] 76; the BL. || haue] BL; have 76. || Commandem:ᵗˢ∧] commande=ments; BL; commandem:ᵗˢ 76.

186.15 ô Lord∧] BL; Ô Lord, 76. || that] BL; y:ᵗ 76. || vnfainedly] BL; vn=fainedly 76. || yᵗ yᵘ] that yᵘ BL; y:ᵗ y:ᵘ 76.

186.16 sinnes, w.ᶜʰ] sinnes, w:ᶜʰ BL; Sinns, w:ᶜʰ 76. || the oc=ca∫ion] BL; yᵉ occa∫ion 76. || Son] 76; Sonne BL.

186.17 and] BL; & 76. || Magdalen] BL; Mag=dalen 76.

186.18 the] BL; yᵉ 76.

186.18–19 sinnes clear=ed] sinnes cleared BL; sins cleared 76.

186.19 and] BL; & 76.

186.19–20 sinnes, y^t] BL; sinns, y:^{t} 76.

186.20 Crucifying] crucyfying BL; Crucify=ing 76. || againe$_\wedge$] BL; againe, 76.

186.21 transgreſions,] trans=greſions; BL; tranſgreſ=sions, 76. || God$_\wedge$] BL; ~, 76. || selfe$_\wedge$] selfe, BL, 76. || can] *interlined* 77; can *not interlined* BL, 76.

186.22 re=ceive y^e] receive the BL; receive y^e 76. || give] 76; giue BL. || w^{ch}] w:^{ch} BL, 76.

186.23 receive] BL; re=ceive 76. || Spiritually, w^{ch}] spiritually, wch BL; Spiritually, w:^{ch} 76. || y^t] BL; y:^{t} 76. || resurrec=tion$_\wedge$] resurrection$_\wedge$ BL; resurrection, 76. || only] 76; onely BL.

186.24 him=selfe] 76; himselfe BL. || y^t] that BL; y:^{t} 76. || receiving] 76; re=ceiving BL.

186.25 thy] BL; thy *interlined* 76. || holy] BL; Holy 76. || have] *catchword* I *omitted in first line* 77; I haue BL; I have 76. || for my sinnes] For my sinnes BL; for my sinns 76.

186.26 and] & BL, 76. || spirits] 76; Spirits BL. || holy Sacram^t] holy Sacrament BL; Holy Sacram:^{t} 76. || and] BL; & 76.

186.27 w^{ch}] wch BL; w:^{ch} 76. || y^t] that BL; y:^{t} 76. || wth] w.th BL; w:th 76. || lively] 76; liuely BL. || and wth] BL; & w:th 76.

186.28 Charity] BL; Charitie 76. || y^t] BL; y:^{t} 76. || doubt$_\wedge$] BL; ~ , 76. || have] 76; haue BL.

186.28–29 wed=ding garm^t:] wedding garment BL; wedding garm:^{t} 76.

186.29 but$_\wedge$ ô Jesus,] but$_\wedge$ ô Jesus$_\wedge$ BL; but, ô Jesus, 76. || and] BL; & 76.

186.30 infir=mities] informities BL, 76. || wth the] w:th the BL; w:th y:^{e} 76.

186.30–31 y^e Children] 76; y^e children BL.

186.31 the] BL; y^e 76. || that] y.^{t} BL; y^t 76.

186.32 mer=cyes] mercyes BL, 76. || thou] BL; y^u 76. || thou callest] BL; y^u Callest 76.

186.33 that] y^t BL, 76. || re=ceive] receive BL, 76. || Spiritually, w^{ch}] spiritually, wch BL; Spiritually, w:^{ch} 76.

187.1 the well] y^e Well BL; y^e well 76. || thou] BL; y^u 76.

187.2 as Baptiſme] 76; as Baptisme *interlined* BL. || did from my originall sins;] 76; did from my originall sinnes$_\wedge$ *interlined* BL. || wch gives] w:^{ch} giues BL; w:^{ch} gives 76.

187.2–3 the com=fort that] y^e comfort y^t BL; y^e Comfort y^t 76.

187.3 everlasting] BL; everlasting *interlined* 76. || felicity$_\wedge$] 76; felicity; BL. || wch God$_\wedge$] w:^{ch} God$_\wedge$ BL; w:^{ch} god, 76.

187.4 the Communion.] the Communion$_\wedge$ BL; y.^{e} Communion. 76.

187.5 and] BL; & 76. || compaſsion] BL; com=paſsion 76. || Sinnfull] sinfull BL; sinnfull 76.

187.6 vn=able$_\wedge$ without] vnable$_\wedge$ wthout BL; vn=able, wthout 76. || grace] BL; Grace 76. || re=ceive] receive BL; receiue 76.

187.6–7 Sinnes com=mitted] sinnes committed BL, 76.

187.7 thou] BL; y^u 76. || testimony] BL; teſtimony 76.

187.8 Son] 76; Sonne BL. || Saviours] 76; Ŝaviour's BL. || that] BL; y:^{t} 76.

187.9 have e=ternall] haue eternall BL; have eternall 76. || and] BL; & 76. || sinnes,] BL; ~ ; 76.

187.10 beleeve$_\wedge$] beleeve, BL, 76. || thou] y^u BL, 76. || vnbeleife, and] vnbeleife; and BL; vnbeleife, & 76. || con=feſse] BL; confeſse 76.

187.11 thou] BL; y:^{u} 76. || the lame,] the lame$_\wedge$ BL; y:^{e} lame, 76. || and the Sick] and the sick BL; & y:^{e} sick 76.

187.12 loden wth] loden w:th BL; Loden w:th 76. || Sin] sin BL, 76. || the] BL, y^e 76. || Physition] 76; Physiti=on BL.

187.13 Soules] 76; soules BL. || so] 76; So BL. || the] BL; yᵉ 76.
187.13–14 the living,] the living; BL; yᵉ living, 76.
187.14 glo=ry, and] glory, and BL; glory, & 76.
187.15 Altar] 76; Alter BL. || the] yᵉ BL, 76. || and] BL; & 76.
187.16 life,] 76; life^ BL. || me^] BL; me, 76. || thee^] BL; ~ , 76. || the] yᵉ BL; y:ᵉ 76. || and] BL; & 76. || thee^] thee, BL, 76. || the] BL; y:ᵉ 76.
187.17 this] 76; This BL. || Sonne,] 76; ~ ^ BL. || Saviours] Saviour's BL, 76.
187.18 before the] BL; before yᵉ 76. || Communion^] BL; ~ , 76.
187.18–19 time^ wᵗʰ] time^ w.ᵗʰ BL, time, w.ᵗʰ 76.
187.20 reſurrection^] ~, BL; resurrection^ 76. || wᵗʰ] w.ᵗʰ BL; w:ᵗʰ 76. || the moſt] the most BL; yᵉ most 76.
187.21 bleſſed Sacramᵗ thou] blessed Sacram:ᵗ thou BL; bleſſed Sacram:ᵗ yᵘ 76. || remem=brance] remembrance BL, 76. || the] BL; y:ᵉ 76.
187.22 thou] 76; yᵘ BL. || me^ and] me, and BL; me, & 76. || torments^ and] torments, and BL; torments, & 76.
187.23 resurrec=tion] 76; resurrection BL. || with thee;] w.ᵗʰ thee; BL; w:ᵗʰ thee, 76. || and thou] BL; & yᵘ 76. || pleaſed] pleased BL, 76.
187.25 torments thou] torments yᵘ BL; Torments y:ᵘ 76.
187.26 yᵗ wᵗʰout] y.ᵗ w.ᵗʰout BL; y:ᵗ w:ᵗʰout 76. || thou didst] y.ᵘ didst BL; y:ᵘ did'st 76. || entertaine] 76; enter=taine BL. || presence] 76; pre=ſence BL. || and] BL; & 76.
187.27 thou so willingly] yᵘ so will=ingly BL; y:ᵘ so willingly 76.
187.29 vnwilling] vn=willing BL, 76.
187.30 Salvation; and] salvation; and BL; Sal=vation; & 76. || Lord^] BL; ~ , 76. || downe] BL; e *of* downe *interlined* 76.
187.31 againe] a gaine BL, 76. || the] BL; y:ᵉ 76. || ru=ine] ruine BL, 76.
187.32 give] 76; giue BL. || Spirit] spirit BL, 76. || &] 76; and BL. || sins] sinnes BL, 76. || yᵉ] 76; the BL.
187.33 not] nor BL, 76. || that] BL; y:ᵗ 76.
187.34 Altar] 76; Alter BL. || con=trite] contrite BL, 76. || miſ=doings] miſdoings BL, 76.
188.1 know] 76; knowe BL. || the] BL; y:ᵉ 76. || receive the] 76; reeive the BL; receive y:ᵉ 76.
188.2 and] BL; & 76. || Deare God,] Deare God^ BL; Dear God, 76.
188.3 and give] & giue BL; & give 76. || Spirit] 76; spirit BL. || and the babe] and yᵉ Babe BL; & y:ᵉ babe 76. || wᵗʰall, and] wᵗʰall, and BL; w:ᵗʰall, & 76.
188.4 and] BL; & 76. || deſpaire] 76; despaire BL.
188.5 and] BL; & 76. || pleaſe thee^] 76; please thee, BL. || that] BL; y:ᵗ 76.
188.6 &] 76; and BL. || yᵗ] that BL; y:ᵗ 76. || enjoy] 76; en=joy BL.
188.7 Kingdome.] 76; Kingdome^ BL.
188.8 delivery^] ~ , BL, 76. || yᵉ Communion^] the Communion^ BL; y:ᵉ Communion, 76. || Chriſtmas] 76; Christmas BL.
188.9 Thou,] 76; ~ ^ BL. || which] wᶜʰ BL; w:ᶜʰ 76. || Borne] 76; borne BL.
188.10 heart] BL; t *of* heart *interlined* 76.
188.11–12 impoſſible wᵗʰ thee,] im=poſſible w.ᵗʰ thee; BL; impoſſible w:ᵗʰ thee, 76.
188.12 away] 76; a=way BL. || spirits] BL; Spirits 76. || and] BL; & 76.
188.13 haue] BL; have 76. || the Sin] the sinne BL; y:ᵉ sin 76.
188.14 deſpair] deſpaire BL, 76. || yᵘ] thou BL; y:ᵘ 76. || multiplyed] BL; mul=tiplyed 76. || bleſſings innumer=able] bleſs=ings innumerably BL; bleſſings innumerable 76. || and] BL; & 76.
188.15 and] BL; & 76. || the] BL: y:ᵉ 76.

188.16 Childbirth] Child=birth BL; childbirth 76. || hand, and] hand; and BL; hand, &
76.

188.17 penitent] 76; peni=tent BL.

188.18 Lord,] 76; ~ ᴀ BL. || can not preſume] cannot presume BL; can not presume 76.

188.19 the Cruṁes yᵗ] the Cruṁes that BL; y:ᵉ Cruṁes y:ᵗ 76. || Lordᴀ yᵘ] Lordᴀ thou
BL; Lord, y:ᵘ 76.

188.20 and in that] and in yᵗ BL; & in y:ᵗ 76. || and wᵗʰ] and w.ᵗʰ BL; & w:ᵗʰ 76.

188.20–21 that thou] that yᵘ BL; y:ᵗ y:ᵘ 76.

188.21 pittifull] 76; pittyfull BL. || and] BL; & 76. || wᵗʰ the] with the BL; w:ᵗʰ y:ᵉ 76.
|| sonne] BL; Sonne 76.

188.22 haue] BL; have 76. || &] 76; and BL.

188.23 Bedd] 76; bed BL. || wᵗʰ] with BL; w.ᵗʰ 76. || laud=ing and] lauding and BL;
Lauding & 76.

188.24 God,] 76; Godᴀ BL.

188.25 yᵉ bleſsed] the bleſsed BL; yᵉ Bleſsed 76. || Sacrament.] 76; ~ ᴀ BL.

188.26 reaſon] 76; reason BL. || haue] have BL, 76. || the] BL; yᵉ 76. || Sacramᵗ]
Sacrament BL; Sacram:ᵗ 76.

188.27 yᵗ] that BL; y:ᵗ 76. || that] BL; y:ᵗ 76. || the] BL; yᵉ 76.

188.28 Chriſt] Christ BL, 76. || Sinᴀ and] sinne, and BL; sin, & 76. || day=ly,] ~ ᴀ BL,
76. || transgreſseᴀ] *interlined* 77; transgreſse, *not interlined* BL, 76.

188.29 give] 76; giue BL. || hum=bly] humbly BL, 76. || for,] 76; for; BL.

188.30 Lordᴀ] BL; ~ , 76. || and paſsion] and paſſion BL; & passion 76.

188.31 Sᵗ Paul] S.ᵗ Paul BL; S.ᵗ Paule 76.

188.32 Bread, and] breadᴀ & BL; Bread, & 76. || Cupp,] 76; Cuppᴀ BL. || the] BL; yᵉ
76. || &] 76; and BL.

188.33 exam=ine] examine BL, 76. || and] BL; & 76.

188.34 wᵗʰ] with BL; w:ᵗʰ 76. || deſiring] 76; desiring BL. || yᵉ forgive=neſse] the
forgiue=neſse BL.

189.1 wᵗʰ] w.ᵗʰ BL; w:ᵗʰ 76. || receive theeᴀ &] receive thee, & BL; re=ceive thee, & 76.

189.2 faith;] BL; ~ , 76. || Godᴀ] BL; ~ , 76. || faithᴀ &] faith, and BL; faith, & 76. ||
yᵗ] BL; y:ᵗ 76.

189.3 yᵗ] BL; y:ᵗ 76. || eateᴀ] BL; ~ , 76.

189.4 damna=tion; and] damnation; and BL; daṁation; & 76. || theeᴀ my Godᴀ and]
thee, my God, & BL; theeᴀ my Godᴀ & 76.

189.5 Meditatiō] BL; Meditation 76. || Fasting,] 76; ~ , BL. || yᵉ] the BL; y.ᵉ 76. || the
Holy] the holy BL; y:ᵉ Holy 76.

189.7 yᵗ] that BL; y:ᵗ 76. || yᵉ time,] BL; y:ᵉ time, 76. || yᵉ blest] 76; the bleſt BL. ||
Sacramᵗ,] Sacram:ᵗ BL; Sacrament, 76.

189.8 exam=ine] examine BL, 76. || selfeᴀ and] selfe, and BL; selfe, & 76. || enquire]
BL; enquier 76. || moſt] most BL, 76.

189.9 manifold sinsᴀ] manyfold sinnesᴀ BL; manyfold sinns, 76. || tranſgreſsions, wᶜʰ isᴀ]
trans=greſsions, w.ᶜʰ isᴀ BL; trans=greſsions, w:ᶜʰ is, 76.

189.10 Gods commandemᵗˢ,] God's commandemᵗˢ; BL; Gods commandem:ᵗˢ 76. || have]
76; haue BL. || repentance, &] 76; repen=tance, and BL.

189.11 God,] Godᴀ BL god, 76. || perverſe] perverse BL; perverſse 76. || com=mitting,ᴀ]
committing,ᴀ BL; committing, 76.

189.12 sins] BL; sinnes 76. || yᵉ best,] the best, BL; yᵉ Best, 76.

189.13 y:ᵗ] 76; that BL. || merit] 76; merite BL. || yᵗ] 76; that BL. || the stomack,ᴀ] BL;
y:ᵉ sto=make, 76.

189.14 sluggishneſse] 76; sluggishnesse BL. || wᶜʰ] w:ᶜʰ BL, 76. || devotion,] 76; ~ ; BL.

189.15 Fish] 76; fish BL. || y^t] BL; $y{:}^t$ 76.

189.16 so,] 76; soe$_\wedge$ BL. || overfill] 76; over=fill BL. || and] BL; & 76. || y^t w^{ch}] that $w.^{ch}$ BL; $y{:}^t$ $w{:}^{ch}$ 76. || &] 76; and BL.

189.17 the] BL; y^e 76. || y^t] that BL; $y{:}^t$ 76.

189.18 y^t] that BL; $y{:}^t$ 76.

189.19 Saviour speakes] 76; Sa=viour speaks BL. || & pray] 76; and pray BL.

189.20 tempation, &] temp=tation; and BL; temp=tation, & 76. || fast] 76; Fast BL. || y^e Bridegroom] y^e Bride=groome BL; $y{:}^e$ Bridegroome 76.

189.21 w^{ch}] $w.^{ch}$ BL; $w{:}^{ch}$ 76. || himselfe,] 76; ~ ; BL. || have] 76; haue BL. || rea∫on] 76; reason *omitted* BL.

189.22 Bridgroom spiritu=all,] Bridegroom spirituall, BL, 76.

189.23 say, wth St Paul$_\wedge$] 76; say$_\wedge$ w^{th} $S{:}^t$ Paul, BL; say, $w{:}^{th}$ $S.^t$ Paul, 76. || lawfull] 76; law=full BL.

189.24 ex=pedient;] expedient; BL, 76.

189.25 what=soever] 76; whatsoeuer BL. || y^e sham=bles, y^t] the Shambles, that BL; y^e shambles, $y{:}^t$ 76.

189.26 Conscience] 76; conscience BL. || y^e] BL; $y{:}^e$ 76. || y^e Lords] the Lord's BL; $y{:}^e$ Lords 76. || & y^e fullne∫se thereof,] and the full=ne∫se thereof, BL; & $y{:}^e$ fullne∫se thereof; 76.

189.27 con=science] conscience BL, 76. || another's] BL; an other's 76.

189.27–28 liberty Judged] Liberty Judged BL; liberty judged 76.

189.28 con=science] conscience BL, 76. || a] *interlined* 77; *not interlined* BL, 76. || partaker$_\wedge$] partaker, BL, 76.

189.29 y^t] BL; $y{:}^t$ 76. || wch I give] $w{:}^{ch}$ I giue BL; $w{:}^{ch}$ I give 76.

189.30 drink] BL; drinke 76. || y^e] the BL; $y{:}^e$ 76. || God] BL; god 76.

190.1 *As noted above, in 76 the parallel entry appears at 181.9.* || the Ble∫sed Sacram^t] the Ble∫sed Sacram$:^t$ BL; y^e ble∫sed sacram$:^t$ 76.

190.2 cleane,] 76; cleane$_\wedge$ BL. || Body & bloud, &] body and bloud, and BL, 76.

190.3 can=not] cannot BL; can not 76. || think,] 76; think$_\wedge$ BL. || againe,] a=gaine, BL; againe; 76. || keepe] 76; keep BL.

190.4 further a=stray, &] further astray, and BL; fur=ther a stray, and 76. || y^e] 76; the BL.

190.5 Faith] BL; faith 76. || obe=dient] BL; obedient 76. || commande=ments] BL; Com=mandements 76.

190.5–6 not a] *catchword* be *omitted from first line* 77; not be a BL, 76.

190.6 theife,] 76; ~ $_\wedge$ BL. || godline∫se, w^{ch}] godline∫se, $w.^{ch}$ BL; godline∫s, $w.^{ch}$ 76.

190.7 prai∫es] 76; prayses BL.

190.8 reading$_\wedge$] BL; ~ , 76. || meditating] medi=tating BL; meditating 76. || thee$_\wedge$] thee, BL, 76. || w^{th}] $w{:}^{th}$ BL, 76.

190.9 heart] 76; *catchword* heart *omitted* BL.

190.10 spirit, y^t] spirit, that BL; Spirit, that 76. || soule] BL; Soule 76. || &] and BL, 76.

190.11 ele=vated] elevated BL, 76. || $w.^{ch}$ Lord$_\wedge$] BL; $w{:}^{ch}$ Lord, 76.

190.12 goodne∫se, Grant] goodne∫s, grant BL; goodne∫s, Grant 76. || me] 76; me *interlined* BL. || Saviour's] BL; Saviours 76.

190.14 Considerations] 76; s *of* Considerations *interlined* BL. || Marriage$_\wedge$] ~ . BL, 76.

190.15 of] BL; of *interlined* 76. || Marriage] BL; marriage 76. || vnhappy] BL; vn=happy 76. || rea∫on] 76; rea-son BL.

190.16 mu∫t] must BL, 76. || y^e] the BL; $y{:}^e$ 76. || y^e] the BL; $y{:}^e$ 76. || great rea∫on] greate reason BL; greate rea∫on 76.

190.17 commanded] 76; com=manded BL. || those yᵗ] those that BL; thoſe y:ᵗ 76. || aboue] 76; above BL. || Capacity] 76; capacity BL.

190.18 reaſon] 76; reason BL. || &] 76; and BL. || yᵗ person] that per=son BL; y:ᵗ person 76. || yⁱ] that BL; y:ᵗ 76.

190.19 Matrimony‸] Matrimo=ny, BL; matrimony‸ 76. || yᵗ] 76; that BL. || con=sideration] consideration BL, 76. || inquire with] in=quire with BL; inquire w:ᵗʰ 76.

190.20 whether] BL; whither 76. || person so‸] BL; perſon so, 76.

190.21 judgmᵗ, &] Judgmᵗ; and BL; judgment, & 76. || con=sequence] consequence BL; conſequence 76. || Councell] 76; councell BL.

190.22 Servant] 76; servant BL. || Master] BL; master 76. || speak] speake BL, 76.

190.23 yᵉ least] the least BL; yᵉ leaſt 76. || word] 76; word *interlined* BL. || have] 76; haue BL. || af=fection, & love] affection, and love BL; affection; & loue 76.

190.24 &] 76; and BL. || speak] speake BL, 76. || & opinion] 76; and opinion BL. || him] *interlined* 77; him *not interlined* BL, 76.

190.25 yᵗ] BL; y:ᵉ 76. || have] 76; haue BL.

190.26 another] 76; a=nother BL. || otherwayes] 76; other=wayes BL. || yᵉ] BL; y:ᵉ 76.

190.27 &] 76; and BL. || Spirit] 76; spirit BL. || Subjection‸] Subjection, BL; subjection 76. || She] she BL, 76.

190.28 & yᵗ She] and yᵗ shee BL; & yᵗ she 76.

190.29 company] BL; Company 76. || farr] 76; far BL. || Companions] companions BL; Companion's 76. || & lofty, &] 76; and lofty, and BL.

190.30 the] BL; yᵉ 76. || side‸] side, BL, 76. || wᵗʰ her, so] w.ᵗʰ her; so BL; w:ᵗʰ her, So 76.

190.31 himselfe] 76; him=selfe BL. || diſturbed] diſ=turbed BL, 76.

190.32 company, care=ing] 76; compa=ny careing BL; company, careing 76.

190.33 wᵗʰ] with BL; w:ᵗʰ 76. || &] 76; and BL. || company] BL; Company 76.

190.34 &] 76; and BL. || diſcontented wᵗʰ yᵉ] diſcon=tented w.ᵗʰ the BL; diſcontented w:ᵗʰ yᵉ 76.

191.1 giue] give BL, 76. || reprehenſion] repre=hension BL; reprehen=ſion 76. || pri=vate,] private; BL; private, 76. || indiſ=cretion] indiſcretion BL, 76.

191.2 miſerable] BL; miserable 76. || & if] 76; and if BL.

191.3 Fancyes] BL; Fan=cyes 76. || sad] BL; sadd 76. || &] 76; and BL. || Husband] BL; Huſband 76.

191.4 otherwayes] 76; other=wayes BL. || wᶜʰ] w.ᶜʰ BL; w:ᶜʰ 76. || a] BL; a *interlined* 76.

191.4–5 happy, eſpecially] happy, especially BL; Happy, eſpecialy 76.

191.5 huſband in buſines] husband in busi=nes BL; Huſband in buſines 76.

191.6 mind=ing] minding BL, 76.

191.7 sincerely; &] 76; sin=cerely; and BL. || he] BL; hee 76.

191.8 angrey, &] angry, and BL; angry, & 76. || an=ger] anger BL, 76.

191.9 &] 76; and BL. || care=ing] BL; caring 76. || wᵗʰ] w.ᵗʰ BL; w:ᵗʰ 76. || yᵉ] the BL; y:ᵉ 76.

191.10 happineſse] BL; happyneſse 76. || she] BL; shee 76. || give] 76; giue BL. || her selfe] BL; herselfe 76.

191.11 wᶜʰ] 76; w.ᶜʰ BL. || mar=ryed person] marryed person BL; married perſon 76. || not, & thus‸] not; and thus, BL; not & thus‸ 76.

191.12 Gods] God's BL, 76. || virgin; &] 76; virgine; and BL. || she haue] BL; shee have 76.

191.13 huſband, &] 76; Husband, and BL. || yᵗ] that BL; y:ᵗ 76. || doubt=leſse] BL; doubtleſse 76.

191.14 endevour yᵉ] 76; endeavour the BL. || & holyneſse, & there] and holyneſse, and there BL; & holyneſse; & ther 76.

191.15 these] 76; theſe BL. || wth] w.th BL; w:th 76. || and] BL; & 76.

191.16 the happyest] the happy=est BL; y:^e happyest 76. || friend=shipp] 76; friendship BL.

191.17 depart, Now] depart. Now BL; de=part, now 76.

191.18 &] 76; and BL. || friendshipp] 76; friendship BL.

191.19 Marriage∧ and] Marriage, and BL; Marriage, & 76. || Widdowes∧] BL; ~ . 76.

191.20 Marriage;] Marriage, BL; marriage; 76. || haue] BL; have 76.

191.21 God;] BL; god, 76. || man,] BL; man; 76.

191.21–22 great & meryfull, &] great and mercyfull, and BL; greate & mercyfull, & 76.

191.22 y^r] that BL; y:^t 76. || marriage, &] 76; Marriage, and BL.

191.23 Fa=thers] father's BL; fathers 76. || &] 76; and BL. || give] 76; giue BL. || &] 76; and BL.

191.24 &] 76; and BL. || aſ=sured] aſsured BL, 76. || y^r] that BL; y:^t 76.

191.24–25 gratious, &] 76; gratious∧ and BL.

191.25 command=ed] com=manded BL; commanded 76.

191.26 huſband] 76; Hus=band BL. || vnjust∧] vn=just, BL; vnjust, 76. || set] sett BL, 76. || w^{ch}] w:^{ch} BL, 76.

191.27 vnderstand] BL; vnder=stand 76. || &] 76; and BL.

191.28 appre=henſion,] apprehen=ſion, BL; apprehenſion; 76.

191.29 vs,] 76; vs∧ BL.

191.30 bleſsing,] 76; ~ ; BL. || giving] BL; giv=ing 76.

191.31 &] 76; and BL. || y^e] BL; y:^e 76. || the] BL; y:^e 76. || y^e] BL; y:^e 76.

191.32 heaven;] 76; ~ , BL. || bring=ing] bringing BL, 76. || commandem^{ts} &] commandem:^{ts} and BL; Commandem:^{ts} & 76.

191.33 &] 76; and BL. || him] BL; him *interlined* 76. || him, so] him, So 76; him; so BL. || comfort] BL; Comfort 76.

192.1 see] BL; See 76. || posterity] BL; poſterity 76. || live] BL; liue 76. || &] 76; and BL. || have] 76; haue BL.

192.2 Glory here=after: &] 76; glory hereafter: and BL. || y^e] the BL; y:^e 76.

192.3 the water] the wa=ter BL; y^e water 76. || Wine] BL; wine 76. || & doubtleſs] and doubtleſse BL; & doubtleſse 76. || he] BL; hee 76.

192.4 haue] BL; have 76. || some] BL; ſome 76.

192.5 y^e] the BL; y:^e 76. || St Paul,] St Paul, BL; S:^t Paul∧ 76.

192.6 been] beene BL, 76. || & having] 76; and have=ing BL. || themselues] them=selves BL; themselves 76.

192.7 haue served y^e] haue served the BL; have served y^e 76. || Nurſe] Nurse BL; nurs 76. || them∧ &] them∧ and BL; them, & 76.

192.7–8 of Charity to y^e] of Charity to the BL; of charity to y^e *interlined* 76.

192.8 poore] Poore BL; poore *interlined* 76. || wch is y^e] w:^{ch} is the BL; w:^{ch} is y^e 76. || service] BL; Service 76.

192.9 haue] BL; have 76. || live] liue BL, 76.

191.10 &] and BL, 76. || y^e loſse] the loſse BL; y:^e loſs 76. || deare huſband] deare Husband BL; dear huſband 76.

192.11 have=ing] 76; having BL. || &] 76; and BL. || wthall] w.thall BL; withall 76.

192.12 Sluggish=neſse∧] slugg=ishneſse, BL; slugishneſse 76. || duties∧] ~ . BL, 76.

192.13 condition w^{ch}] Condition wch BL; condition w:^{ch} 76. || in∧ in] 76; in, in BL.

192.14 &] 76; and BL. || y^r] 76; that BL.

192.15 &] 76; and BL. || per=forme] 76; performe BL.

192.16 wth] with BL; w:th 76.

192.17 y^e] the BL; y:^e 76. || lymitt] BL; limitt 76.

192.18 selues, &] selues, and BL; selves & 76. || y^r] that BL; y:^t 76.

192.19 lives] 76; liues BL. || casuall͵ &] casuall͵ and BL; casuall, & 76.

192.20 whe=ther] BL; whether 76. || liue] BL; live 76. || tomor=row?] to=morrow? BL; tomorrow? 76. || And if] and if BL; And if *interlined* 76. || we liue,] we liue͵ BL; We live 76. || &] 76; and BL.

192.21 sick=neſse comes͵] sickneſse comes, BL; sickneſse comes͵ 76. || stupifyed dullneſse͵ wᶜʰ] stupyfied dullneſse͵ w.ᶜʰ BL; Stu=pifyed dullneſse, w:ᶜʰ 76.

192.22 render] 76; ren=der BL. || day=ly] dayly BL, 76.

192.23 All=mighty] 76; Al=mighty BL. || wᵗʰ] w.ᵗʰ BL; w:ᵗʰ 76. || & wᵗʰ] and with BL; & w:ᵗʰ 76. || Sincere heart,] Sin=sere heart, BL; Sincere heart͵ 76.

192.24 &] 76; and BL. || &] 76; and BL. || resolve] 76; re=ſolue BL.

192.25 yᵉ] the BL; y:ᵉ 76. || &] 76; and BL. || thinke yᵗ to repent] think that to re=pent BL; think that to repent 76. || houre] BL; hower 76.

192.26 endleſse] BL; endleſs 76.

192.27 sickneſse͵ and] sickneſse, and BL; sick=neſse & 76. || be=seech thee͵] beseech thee͵ BL; beseech thee, 76.

192.28 yᵗ] that BL, 76. || & ejaculations] and ejaculations BL; & ejacula=tions 76.

192.29 manifold] BL; many=fold 76.

192.30 me, &] 76; me; and BL. || me͵ o] me͵ ô BL; me, ô 76. || statutes yᵗ] statutes that BL; Statutes y:ᵗ 76. || ap=ply] apply BL, 76.

192.30–31 wiſdome, &] wiſe=dome, and BL; wiſ=dome, & 76.

192.31 runnagate] BL; ruñagate 76. || thee͵ &] thee͵ and BL; thee, & 76. || Sonne͵] BL; sonne, 76. || &] 76; and BL.

192.33 &] 76; and BL. || employed] 76; em=ployed BL. || &] 76; and BL.

192.34 himselfe;] 76; ~ , BL. || pardon͵ ô] pardon, ô BL; pardon, Ô 76. || for=giue, & returne] forgive͵ and re=turne BL; forgive, & returne 76.

193.1 transgreſsions, &] 76; tranſſ=greſsions, and BL. || yᵉ ruin=ous] the ruinous BL; y:ᵉ ruinous 76.

193.2 wᵗʰ] w.ᵗʰ BL; w:ᵗʰ 76. || say͵ returne] say͵ re=turne BL; say, returne 76. || soule͵] Soule, BL; soule; 76.

193.3 yᵉ] 76; the BL. || graciouſly wᵗʰ] graciously w.ᵗʰ BL; graciouſly w:ᵗʰ 76.

193.4 Perswaſion] BL; Perswasion 76. || the forgiving] yᵉ Forgiving BL; y:ᵉ forgiving 76. || Injuries.] 76; ~ ͵ BL.

193.5 endeavour] BL; endevour 76. || follow] 76; fol=low BL. || Doctrine] BL; doc=trine 76. || forbear] BL; forbeare 76. || &] 76; and BL.

193.6 have] 76; haue BL.

193.7 forgaue] BL; forgave 76. || so to] BL; ſo to 76. || have] 76; haue BL. || reaſon] reason BL; a *of* reason *interlined* 76.

193.8 have] 76; haue BL.

193.8–9 forgiven vs͵] forgiven vs, BL; forgivē vs, 76.

193.9 yᵗ] that BL, 76.

193.10 yᵗ] that BL, 76. || dayly] 76; day=ly BL. || weake] BL; weak 76. || amendmᵗ bring=ing] amend=ment bringing BL; amendm:ᵗ bringing 76.

193.11 Father, whoſe an=ger] Father, whose anger BL; father, whoſe anger 76. || in=terceſsion] interceſsion BL, 76.

193.12 yᵉ] 76; the BL. || &] 76; and BL.

193.13 wᵗʰ sincere] w:ᵗʰ sin=cere BL; w:ᵗʰ sincere 76. || &] 76; and BL. || yᵗ] that BL; y:ᵗ 76.

193.13–14 wᵗʰout murmuring; &] w:ᵗʰout murmuring, and BL; w:ᵗʰout murmuring, & 76.

193.14 selves,] 76; ~ ͵ BL. || &] 76; and BL.

193.15 yᵗ] that BL; y:ᵗ 76. || returne yᵉ] re=turne the BL; returne y:ᵉ 76. || vpon] BL; vpō 76.

193.16 &] 76; and BL. || Soules] *interlined* 77; soules *not interlined* BL, 76.
193.17 forgiue‸] forgive, BL; forgive‸ 76. || w$^{th}_{\cdot}$out] wthout BL, 76. || &] 76; and BL.
193.18 In=jury] Injury BL, 76. || vs,] 76; vs‸ BL. || thinke] think BL, 76.
193.19 y^t] that BL; y:^{t} 76.
193.20 nother‸] ~ , BL, 76. || what] BL; w:^{t} 76.
193.21 been] 76; beene BL. || y^e] 76; the BL.
193.22 y^e salvation] the Sal=vation BL; y:^{e} salvation 76. || Soules] 76; soules BL. || say=ing] saying BL, 76.
193.23 y^t] 76; that BL. || retayned] 76; retain=ed BL.
193.24 y^t rather‸] that rather‸ BL; y:^{t} rather, 76. || y^e] the BL; y:^{e} 76.
193.25 y^e] the BL; y:^{e} 76. || w^{ch}] w:^{ch} BL, 76. || vs, y^t] vs‸ that BL; vs, y:^{t} 76.
193.26 ourselves] our selves BL, 76.
193.27 y^t] that BL; y:^{t} 76. || pleaſed Allmighty] pleased Almighty BL; pleased Allmighty 76. || hither,] 76; ~ ‸ BL. || serue &] serve and BL; serve & 76.
193.28 & y^t] and that BL; & y:^{t} 76. || commands, &] 76; com=mands, and BL.
193.29 Christ] BL; Chriſt 76. || y^e] the BL; y:^{e} 76. || y^e] 76; the BL.
193.30 wch y^t] wch that BL; w:^{ch} y:^{t} 76. || Saviour's Stepps] Saviours stepps BL; Saviours steps 76.
193.31 reviled,] reviled‸ BL, 76. || againe] 76; a=gaine BL.
194.1 Com̃endatiō] BL; Commendation 76. || the] BL; y.^{e} 76. || and Neere friends] and neere Friends BL; & neere friends 76.
194.2 have y^e company] haue the Company BL; have y:^{e} company 76. || &] 76; and BL. || neer friends] 76; neere Friends BL. || y^e] the BL; y:^{e} 76. || fe=licity] felicity BL, 76.
194.3 &] 76; and BL. || have] 76; haue BL. || Heighten] 76; heighten BL. || wth] BL; w:th 76.
194.4 spec=tacle] spectacle BL, 76. || Melancholy w^{ch}] melan=choly wch BL; melancholy w:^{ch} 76.
194.5 Stupefaction, &] stupefaction; and BL; stupefaction, & 76. || World] world BL, 76. || miſerable; &] miſerable; and BL; miserable; & 76. || hold‸] BL; hold, 76.
194.6 what] 76; *catchword* what *omitted in first line* BL. || comfort] BL; com=fort 76. || have] 76; haue BL. || y^e] the BL; y:^{e} 76.
194.7 &] 76; and BL. || dear] 76; deare BL. || w^{ch}] w:^{ch} BL, 76. || have, &] 76; haue, and BL.
194.8 return] returne BL, 76. || that gives althings,] y:^{t} gives althings, 76; that giues all things‸ BL. || w^{ch}] wch BL; w:^{ch} 76.
194.9 y^e] the BL; y:^{e} 76. || world,] 76; ~ ‸ BL. || wch is to come] *interlined* 77; wch is to come *not interlined* BL; wch is to come *not interlined* 76. || account] BL; ac=count 76.
194.10 miſerable] BL; miserable 76. || wretch, &] 76; wretch; and BL. || thee, o] thee‸ ô BL; thee, ô 76.
194.11 folly] BL; Folly 76. || give] giue BL, 76.
194.12 object] 76; ob=ject BL. || Subject] 76; subject BL. || Government here,] governm:^{t} here; BL; government here, 76.
194.13 due‸ and] due, and BL; due‸ & 76. || the] y^e BL, 76.
194.14 vnworthy Sin=ner] vnwor=thy sinner BL; vnworthy sinner 76.
194.15 y^e] the BL; y:^{e} 76. || for=giveneſse] BL; forgivneſse 76. || Sinnes] BL; Sinne 76.
194.16 great, &] great, and BL; great; & 76. || Creature] BL; creature 76. || have] 76; haue BL. || let] BL; lett 76. || vs] 76; vs *omitted* BL.
194.17 earnest re=] *catchword* sistance *omitted from line 1* 77; earnest resistance, BL, 76.
194.18 y^t practice y^e] that practiſe the BL; y:^{t} practiſe y^e 76. || life,] 76; ~ ; BL. || we‸] ~ , BL, 76.

194.19 y^e Allmightie's sight$_\wedge$] the Almightie's sight, BL; y:^{e} Allmighties sight$_\wedge$ 76. || y^t] y.^{t} BL; y:^{t} 76. || y.^{e}] the BL; y:^{e} 76. || let] BL; lett 76.

194.20 felicity$_\wedge$] BL; ~, 76. || have] 76; haue BL.

194.21 have] 76; haue BL. || Father] BL; father 76.

194.22 reconciliation] BL; reconsiliation 76. || bloud, &] 76; bloud; and BL. || Sinnes] sinnes BL; sins 76.

194.23 scarlet] BL; scarlett 76. || snow, &] Snow, and BL; snow; & 76.

194.24 Christian] Chriſtian BL, 76. || com=fortable] comfortable BL; Comfortable 76. || & keepe] and keep BL; & keep 76.

194.25 y^t] BL; y:^{t} 76. || sight y^t] BL; sight y:^{t} 76.

194.26 y^e fetters] y^e fet=ters BL; y:^{e} fetters 76. || let] BL; lett 76. || &] 76; and BL.

194.27 w^{th}] BL; w:th 76. || inherit] BL; inherrit 76. || Salvation] 76; Sal=vation BL.

194.28 w^{th}] w:th BL, 76. || beare] 76; bear BL.

194.29 World] world BL, 76. || varietys] 76; varieties BL. || y^t] that BL, 76.

194.30 pollish=ed wth deceite] pollished w:th deceit BL; pollished w:th deceite 76.

194.31 eternall] 76; eter=nall BL. || give] 76; giue BL. || selves] selues BL. || y^e] BL; y:^{e} 76.

194.32 works] BL; workes 76. || seeing] BL; ſeeing 76. || y^e] the BL; y:^{e} 76.

194.33 appearance$_\wedge$ proſ=perous] appearance$_\wedge$ proſ=perous BL; ap=pearance, proſperous 76. || to be] BL; to be *interlined* 76.

195.1 &] 76; and BL. || punished] puniſhed BL; punniſhed 76. || world$_\wedge$] BL; ~ , 76.

195.2 punniſhm^t w^{th}] pun=niſhm:^{t} w.th BL; punniſhment w:th 76. || Higher] 76; higher BL. || no] BL; noe 76. || y^e] the BL; y:^{e} 76. || Soules wch we] soules wch wee BL; Soules w:^{ch} we 76.

195.3 answer] answere BL; anſwere 76. || oblivion$_\wedge$] 76; oblivi=on, BL.

195.4 torment] BL; tor=ment 76.

195.5 vs] *interlined* 77; vs *not interlined* BL, 76. || y^e] 76; the BL.

195.6 &] 76; and BL. || en=dure w^{th}] endure w.th BL; endure w:th 76. || y^e] BL; y:^{e} 76. || Grace] BL; grace 76.

195.7 haue] BL; have 76.

195.8 perverse] BL; perverſe 76. || waies] wayes BL, 76. || example;] Example; BL; example, 76.

195.9 God] BL; god 76. || af=fliction] affliction BL, 76.

195.9–10 trif=fles, &] triffles, and BL; triffles, & 76.

195.10 been] beene BL, 76.

195.11 Sonne] 76; sonne BL. || sinnes, w^{ch}] sinnes, w:^{ch} BL; Sins, w:^{ch} 76. || aſsurance] 76; aſ=surance BL. || consolation] 76; con=solation BL.

195.13 forgett] BL; forget 76. || selves] 76; selues BL. || Remember w^t] remember what BL; Re=member what 76. || are,] BL; ~ ; 76. || have] 76; haue BL.

195.14 this] BL; this *interlined* 76. || &] 76; and BL. || that] BL; y:^{t} 76. || haue] BL; have 76.

195.15 God, y^t] God, that BL; god, y:^{t} 76. || y^t] that BL; y:^{t} 76.

195.16 be=leeve] beleeve BL, 76. || bleſsed] BL; blessed 76. || endured y^e] endured the BL; en=dured y:^{e} 76. || y^e] the BL; y:^{e} 76.

195.17 y^e] 76; the BL. || joyfull] BL; Joy=full 76. || y^e] the BL; y:^{e} 76.

195.17–18 of our] BL; of our *interlined* 76.

195.18 prosperity] pros=perity BL; proſperity 76. || conceive] BL; cōceive 76. || w^{th}] with BL, 76.

195.19 paradice] 76; Paradice BL. || merit y^t] merit that BL; merrit y:^{t} 76.

195.20 w^{ch}] wch BL; w:^{ch} 76. || beleiver] 76; beleever BL.

195.21 & yee] and yee BL; & you 76. || have, seeke & yee] haue, seeke and yee BL; have, seek & yee 76. || knock &] 76; Knock and BL.

195.22 you‸] you, BL; you; 76. || wᶜʰ we must goe] w:ᶜʰ we muſt go BL; w:ᶜʰ wee must goe 76.

195.24 Meditation] 76; Meditatiō BL. || purity] BL; Purity 76. || the] BL; yᵉ 76.

195.25 God‸] BL; ~ , 76. || ac=cording] according BL, 76.

195.26 & gaue] and gave BL; & gave 76. || acknowledge] acknowledg BL, 76. || therefore] 76; there=fore BL.

195.27 Altar‸] BL; ~ , 76. || thoughts,] thoughts‸ BL, 76.

195.28 &] 76; and BL. || never] 76; neuer BL.

195.29 yᵗ wᶜʰ] yᵗ w:ᶜʰ BL; y:ᵗ w:ᶜʰ 76. || wᵗʰout] w.ᵗʰout BL, 76.

195.30 Gods Chil=dren] Gods Children BL; God's Chil=dren 76.

195.31 wᵗʰin] w.ᵗʰin BL; w:ᵗʰin 76. || yᵉ] the BL, 76. || suffered] 76; suf=fered BL.

196.1 bloud, wᶜʰ] bloud, w.ᶜʰ BL; blood, w:ᶜʰ 76. || yᵉ] 76; y.ᵉ BL.

196.2 away] a way BL, 76. || sins] sinnes BL; Sins 76. || guilty] BL; Guilty 76.

196.3 &] 76; and BL.

196.5 &] 76; and BL. || Burnt] 76; burnt BL.

196.6 love, &] 76; loue‸ and BL.

196.7 wᵗʰ] BL; w:ᵗʰ 76. || Godlineſse‸] 76; ~ , BL.

196.8 actu=all, &] actuall, and BL; actuall, & 76. || tranſgreſsions, &] trans=greſsions, and BL; tranſgreſsions, and 76. || a] 76; a *omitted* BL.

196.10 confi=dence] confidence BL; Confidence 76.

196.12 yᵉ] the BL; y:ᵉ 76.

196.12–13 & gaue] 76; and gave BL.

196.13 beleived in him,] beleeved in him, BL; beleived in him; 76.

196.14 goodneſs] goodneſse BL, 76. || Glory] BL; glory 76. || yᵉ] y.ᵉ BL; y:ᵉ 76.

196.15 Members] BL; members 76.

196.16 &] 76; and BL. || sonne] 76; Sonne BL.

196.17 yᵉ] y.ᵉ BL; y:ᵉ 76.

196.18 &] 76; and BL.

196.19 wᵗʰout] wᵗʰ=out BL; w.ᵗʰout 76. || wᵗʰ] 76; w.ᵗʰ BL. || repentance, &] 76; re=pentance, and BL.

196.20 wᵗʰ] BL; w:ᵗʰ 76. || selves] 76; selues BL. || & Ashes] BL; & ashes 76. || Dust] BL; dust 76.

196.21 & to dust] 76; and to Dust BL. || wᵗʰout] 76; w.ᵗʰout BL. || infuses] BL; infuſes 76.

196.22 & wᵗʰout life‸] and wᵗʰout life‸ BL; & w:ᵗʰout life, 76. || wᵗʰ=out] wᵗʰout BL, 76. || Ashes; So] Ashes; so BL; ashes; so 76.

196.23 wᵗʰout] 76; wᵗʰ=out BL. || wᶜʰ] BL; w:ᶜʰ 76. || bestow] BL; bestowe 76.

196.24 yᵉ remiſsion] BL; y:ᵉ remiſsion 76. || sins] BL; sinnes 76. || wᵗʰ] w:ᶜʰ BL, 76.

196.25 yᵉ] BL; y:ᵉ 76.

196.26 occasion] BL; occaſion 76. || the] BL; y:ᵉ 76. || skeane] skean BL; Skeane 76. || Silke‸] ~ . BL, 76.

196.27 sins,] sinnes BL; Sins *interlined* 76. || wᶜʰ] w.ᶜʰ BL; w:ᶜʰ 76.

196.28 en=tangled wᵗʰ,] entangled wᵗʰ, BL; entangled w:ᵗʰ 76. || Son] Sonne BL; son 76. || vnravell yᵉ] vn=ravell the BL; vn=ravell yᵉ 76.

196.29 skeane] BL; Skeane 76. || tranſgreſsions,] transgreſsions‸ BL; transgreſsions, 76. || wᵗʰ] 76; w.ᵗʰ BL. || &] 76; and BL. || wᵗʰ] with BL; w:ᵗʰ 76.

196.30 &] 76; and BL.

197.1 yᵘ] thou BL; y:ᵘ 76. || ô] ô BL; ô *interlined* 76. || &] 76; and BL. || yᵗ] 76; that BL.

197.2 wᵗʰ] w.ᵗʰ BL; w:ᵗʰ 76. || kind=neſse, wᶜʰ] kind=neſse, w.ᶜʰ BL; kindneſse, w:ᶜʰ 76. || yʳ] y.ᵗ BL; y:ᵗ 76. || wᶜʰ] w.ᶜʰ BL; w:ᶜʰ 76. || wᵗʰ] w.ᵗʰ BL; w:ᵗʰ 76.

197.3 Lord] BL; lord 76. || &] 76; and BL. || Creature] creature BL, 76.

197.4 yᵉ Thread] the Thread BL; yᵉ thread 76.

197.6 sickneſs] sickneſse BL, 76. || Delivery₍] ~ . BL; delivery. 76.

197.7 Lord] BL; lord 76. || thanks &] 76; thankes and BL. || belongs] BL; be=longs 76.

197.8 greate & vnspeak=able] great and vnspeakable BL; great & vnspeakable 76. || me₍] me, BL, 76.

197.9 extremity, &] 76; extremyty, and BL. || wᶜʰ] BL; w:ᶜʰ 76.

197.10 farr] 76; farre BL. || mercy] 76; mer=cy BL. || aboue] BL; above 76.

197.11 yʳ] that BL; y:ᵗ 76. || beene] BL; been 76. || had'st yᵘ] hadst thou BL; had'st y:ᵘ 76.

197.12 deare Babe] dear Babe BL; dear babe 76. || &] 76; and BL.

197.13 yᵉ bleſſing yᵘ gauest] the bleſsing yᵘ gauest BL; yᵉ bleſsing y:ᵘ gavest 76. || giving] 76; giue=ing BL.

197.13–14 deare Huſband] deare Husband BL; dear Huſband 76.

197.14 &] 76; and BL. || wᵗʰ] w.ᵗʰ BL; w:ᵗʰ 76. || Lord,] Lord₍ BL, 76. || yᵘ] thou BL; y:ᵘ 76.

197.15 pleaſed] pleased BL, 76. || affict] afflict BL, 76.

197.16 hand₍] hand, BL, 76. || yᵘ hast₍ &] yᵘ hast, and BL; y:ᵘ hast₍ & 76. || yᵘ] thou BL; y:ᵘ 76. || & all] 76; and BL.

197.17 &] 76; and BL. || giue] BL; give 76. || yᵉ Comfort] the com=fort BL; y:ᵉ Comfort 76. || lifes,] lifes₍ BL; lives, 76.

197.18 Sonne] 76; sonne BL. || give] 76; giue BL. || &] 76; and BL.

197.19 & for ever more] and for ever more BL; & for evermore 76.

197.20 occasion] BL; occaſion 76. || Husbands] Husband's BL, 76. || day₍] BL; ~ . 76.

197.21 yᵉ] BL; y:ᵉ 76. || everlast=ing God,] ever=lasting God₍ BL; everlasting god, 76. || dedicate] dedi=cate BL; dedicate 76.

197.22 yᵘ] thou BL; y:ᵘ 76. || Deare 76; deare BL.

197.23 Lord₍] BL; Lord, 76. || prayers] BL; prayses 76.

197.23–24 thee₍ everlastingly, & yᵘ] thee, everlast=ingly; and thou BL; thee₍ everlastingly, & y:ᵘ 76.

197.24 in=finite mercyes] infinite mercyes BL; infinit mercys 76.

197.25 &] 76; and BL. || praiſe aboue] prayſe above 76.

197.26 & give] 76; and giue BL. || praiſes₍] 76; praiſes, BL. || yᵘ call=est] thou callest BL; y:ᵘ callest 76. || yᵉ] the BL; y:ᵉ 76.

197.27 repentance,] 76; ~ ; BL.

197.28 heare] 76; hear BL. || thanksgiving] thanks=giving BL; thanks giving BL. || yʳ] that BL, 76. || yᵉ] the BL; y:ᵉ 76.

197.29 Joyed] BL; joyed 76. || &] 76; and BL. || him, wᵗʰ] him₍ w.ᵗʰ BL; him, w:ᵗʰ 76. || &] 76; and BL.

197.30 & be yᵘ] 76; and be y.ᵘ BL. || wᵗʰ] w.ᵗʰ BL; w:ᵗʰ 76. || extremity₍] BL; ~ , 76. || diſtreſse] 76; distreſse BL.

197.31 Husband] BL; Huſband 76.

197.32 give] 76; giue BL. || Petition] BL; petition 76.

197.33 have] 76; haue BL. || Huſband] 76; Husband BL. || him₍] him, BL, 76.

198.1 vio=lence] violence BL, 76. || God,] 76; God₍ BL. || &] 76; and BL.

198.2 mercy,] 76; mercy₍ BL. || preserve] 76; pre=ſerue BL. || &] 76; and BL.

198.3 son] BL; sonne 76. || have] 76; haue BL. || yᵘ] 76; thou BL. || Sonne] Son BL; sonne 76.

198.3–4 ever w^{th}] euer BL; ever w:^{th} 76.
198.5 keepe him_∧] 76; keep him, BL. || ensnarem^{ts}] ensnarem:^{ts} BL; Ensnarem^{ts} 76. || impriſsonm^{t}, &] 76; impriſonment, and BL.
198.6 safe, w^{th}out] safe_∧ wth out BL; safe, w.^{th}out 76. || entrapped] BL; intrapped 76.
198.7 &] 76; and BL. || w^{ch}] wch BL; w:^{ch} 76.
198.8 & Sa=viours] and Saviour's BL; & Sa=viour's 76. || whoſe] 76; whose BL. || me] BL; me *interlined* 76. || call_∧ & y^{u}] call, and thou BL; and y:^{u} 76.
198.10 y^{e} death] BL; y:^{e} Death 76. || Henry.] 76; ~ _∧ BL.
198.11 pleaſed] 76; pleased BL. || &] 76; and BL.
198.12 wish] wiſh BL, 76. || w^{th}] with BL, 76. || Loose] Looſe BL, 76. || it] 76; it *omitted* BL.
198.13 y^{t}] that BL; y:^{t} 76. || often] of=ten BL. || pronounced] BL; pronoun= *catchword* ced *omitted* 76. || na=ture's] BL; nature's 76.
198.14 world,] BL; ~ ; 76.
198.15 Heathenish] BL; heathenish 76. || be=hold] behold BL, 76.
198.16 me_∧] BL; ~ , 76. || gave] 76; gaue BL. || y^{t}] that BL; y:^{t} 76. || y^{t} gaue] that gaue BL; y:^{t} gave 76.
198.17 &] 76; and BL. || a way,] away, BL; a way; 76.
198.18 live] 76; liue BL. || live] 76; luie BL.
198.19 w^{th}out sin, y^{t}] without sin, y^{t} BL; w^{th}out sinne y:^{t} 76. || live everlastingly] 76; liue everlast=ingly BL. || can=not] cannot BL; can not 76.
198.20 w^{th}out] BL; w.^{th}out 76. || &] 76; and BL. || y^{t}] that BL; y:^{t} 76.
198.21 Allmighty father] 76; Almighty Father BL. || Sonne] BL; sonne 76. || sins, &] sins, and BL; sinnes, & 76.
198.21–22 he aſſureth vs, if we truly repent vs of our Sins, &] he aſureth vs, if we truly repent vs of our sins_∧ & *interlined* BL; he aſsureth vs, if we truly repent vs of our sinnes, & *not interlined* 76.
198.22 beleive] beleeve BL; be=leive 76. || inherit eter=nall] inherite eternall BL; inherit eternall 76.
198.23 walke vpright=ly] walk vp=rightly BL; walke vprightly 76. || y^{e}] the BL; y:^{e} 76.
198.24 w^{th}out] w.^{th}out BL, 76. || selves] 76; selues BL.
198.25 puniſhm^{t}] BL; puniſhm:^{t} 76. || y^{e}] the BL; y:^{e} 76. || tor=ments] torments BL, 76.
198.26 let] BL; lett 76.
198.27 y^{t}] BL; y:^{t} 76. || go] goe BL, 76. || y^{e} Heaven] 76; the Hea=ven BL.
198.28 y^{e}] 76; the BL. || vinity] Vnity BL, 76. || &] 76; and BL. || pleased] BL; pleaſed 76. || give] 76; giue BL.
198.29 cannot] BL; can not 76. || live] 76; liue BL. || otherwayes,] 76; otherwayes_∧ BL.
198.30 Godlyneſse] 76; Godlineſse BL. || y^{e}] the BL; y:^{e} 76. || y^{e}] the BL; y:^{e} 76.
198.31 knowledge] BL; ge *of* knowledge *interlined* 76. || this,] BL; ~ _∧ 76. || wish] BL; wiſh 76. || Babe] BL; babe 76. || beene,] BL; ~ _∧ 76.
198.32 let paſsion overflowe] let paſsion over=flowe BL; lett passion overflow 76. || re=ligion] Religion BL; religion 76.
198.33 & let] and let BL; & lett 76. || ô] 76; o BL.
198.34–35 Sonne Absolon;] sonne Absolon; BL; Sonne Absolon, 76.
198.35 young;] BL; ~ , 76. || affic=tion] affliction BL; af=fliction 76.
199.1 Gods] BL; God's 76. || &] 76; and BL. || is] BL; as 76. || rod] BL; rodd 76. || Chaſtisem:^{t}] Chastisem^{t} BL; Chaſticem:^{t} 76. || &] 76; and BL.
199.2 & calamities] and calamities BL; & Calamities 76. || grudge] BL; grudg 76.
199.3 with] BL; w:^{th} 76. || grieved] BL; greeved 76. || Sinns, &] sinnes, and BL; sinnes, & 76. || re=turne] returne BL, 76.

199.4 y^t] that BL; y:^{t} 76. || wth] with BL; w:th 76.
199.5 give] 76; giue BL. || health$_\wedge$] ~ , BL, 76. || life, w$^{ch.}$] BL; life; w:^{ch} 76.
199.6 y^t] BL; y:^{t} 76. || &] 76; and BL.
199.7 Boy Henry.] BL; boy Henry $_\wedge$ 76.
199.8 Boy,] 76; Boy$_\wedge$ BL. || y^e Finest Child] y^e finest child BL; y:^{e} finest Child 76. || me,] 76; me $_\wedge$ BL.
199.9 Soule sighe] 76; soule sigh BL. || see,] 76; ~ $_\wedge$ BL.
199.11 Joy] 76; joy BL. || Pleasure] pleasure BL, 76. || releeve;] 76; ~ , BL.
199.12 yeares] 76; years BL.
199.13 more$_\wedge$ wch cauſed] more, wch caused BL; more, w:^{ch} cauſed 76.
199.14 &] and BL, 76. || y^e Number] the number BL; y:^{e} number 76.
199.15 Death] 76; death BL. || a sunder.] 76; asunder, BL.
199.16 y^u] BL; y:^{u} 76. || Happy] 76; happy BL. || sweet'st$_\wedge$] Sweetst BL; sweet'st, 76.
199.17 cry] 76; Cry BL.
199.18 Deare] BL; deare 76.
199.19 great,] 76; great$_\wedge$ BL. || greived] greeved BL, 76. || y^e loſse] the losse BL; y:^{e} loſse 76.
199.20 deare] BL; dear 76. || Keatty,] 76; ~ $_\wedge$ BL. || fine] BL; fyne 76. || she] 76; She BL.
199.21 and] BL; & 76. || y^e Fatall diſease] the fatall diſease BL; y:^{e} fatall diseaſe 76. || || y^e smale] the smale BL; y:^{e} small 76.
199.22 pleasure] BL; pleaſure 76. || &] 76; and BL.
199.23 Din=ner, &] Dinner, and BL; Dinner, & 76. || & make] 76; and make BL. || &] & 76; and BL.
199.24 all,] BL; all$_\wedge$ 76. || Strangers] strangers BL, 76. || all] 76; All BL.
199.25 Brothers &] Brothers and BL; brothers & 76. || Sister] BL; sister 76. || wth] with BL; w:th 76. || She] BL; she 76.
199.26 she] 76; She BL. || Prayers] prayers BL, 76.
199.27 y^e Sacram^t] y.^{e} Sacram:^{r} BL; y^e Sacram:^{r} 76. || Bap=tiſme, w^{ch}] Baptiſme, wch BL; Baptiſme, w:^{ch} 76. || washed] 76; waſh=ed BL. || & she] 76; and She BL.
199.28 Holyly; she tooke de=light] Holyly; She took delight BL; Holyly, she tooke delight 76. || she] 76; She BL.
199.29 neuer] never BL, 76.
199.30 Fond] 76; fond BL. || she] 76; She BL. || w^{ch}] wch BL; w:^{ch} 76.
199.31 heart;] ~ , BL, 76. || Soule] 76; soule BL.
199.32 thanks, y^t] thankes, that BL; thanks, y^t 76. || pleased] pleaſed BL, 76. || bestow] 76; bestowe BL. || y^t sweet] that sweet BL; y:^{t} sweete 76.
199.33 vp=on] vpon BL, 76.
199.34 y^e] BL; y:^{e} 76. || occaſion.] 76; occasion$_\wedge$ BL.
199.35 Gods] BL; God's 76. || afflicte] afflict BL, 76. || me,] BL; me *interlined* 76. || not her] 76; and not her BL.
199.36 giving] 76; giuing BL. || y^e] the BL; y:^{e} 76. || &] 76; and BL. || y^t] that BL; y:^{t} 76.
200.1 if God] BL; if god 76.
200.2 w^{ch}] wch BL; w:^{ch} 76. || &] 76; and BL.
200.3 live here$_\wedge$ y^t] liue here, that BL; liue here, y:^{t} 76. || wth] BL; w:th 76. || &] 76; and BL.
200.4 y^e Kingdom] 76; the Kingdome BL. || y^t] BL; y:^{t} 76. || sweet] BL; sweete 76. || in=nocent;] inno=cent; BL; iñocent, 76.
200.5 &] 76; and BL.

200.6 Gods pun=iſhm:^{r}] gods punishm:^{r} BL; Gods puniſhment 76. || y^r] y.^{r} BL, 76.

200.7 Body$_\wedge$ & Soule] body$_\wedge$ and soule BL; body, & soule 76. || Soule] 76; soule BL.

200.8 here$_\wedge$ seised] 76; here, seized BL. || Wormes,] wormes, BL; es *of* wormes$_\wedge$ *interlined* 76. || &] 76; and BL. || y^e] the BL; y:^{e} 76.

200.9 &] 76; and BL.

200.9–10 y^e iudgement] the Judgm^t BL; y^e judgment 76.

200.10 Ô] ô BL; Ô 76.

200.10–11 won=der y^t] wonder y^t BL; wonder y:^{t} 76.

200.11 w:^{ch}] wch BL; w:^{ch} 76. || afflicted,] BL; afflicted$_\wedge$ 76.

200.12 y^e] 76; the BL. || preserve] 76; preserue BL.

200.13 Deare Huſband] 76; deare Husband BL. || Deare] BL; deare 76. || haue] BL; have 76. || neere friends] BL; neare Friends 76. || My] my BL, 76.

200.14 Siſters, &] Siſters, and BL; siſters, & 76. || w:^{ch}] 76; wch BL. || lett] 76; let BL.

200.15 af=flictions] afflictions BL, 76. || ac=cording] according BL, 76.

200.16 Child, &] Child, and BL; Childe, & 76.

200.17 a=gainst] against BL, 76. || him] *interlined* 77; him *not interlined* BL, 76. || Crying$_\wedge$ ô Absolon$_\wedge$] crying$_\wedge$ ô Absolon$_\wedge$ BL; Crying, o Absolon 76. || Son; my Son;] BL; sonne, my Sonne, 76. || Jacob$_\wedge$] BL; Jacob, 76.

200.18 been dead;] beene dead: BL, 76. || ô lett] ô let BL; O Lett 76.

200.19 &] 76; and BL. || w:th David$_\wedge$] w.th David, BL; w:th David, 76. || Stroak] stroak BL; stroake 76. || when] When BL, 76.

200.20 y^u w:th] y^u wth BL; y:^{u} w:th 76. || correct] BL; Correct 76. || iniquity$_\wedge$ y^u] iniquity, y^u BL; iniquity$_\wedge$ y:^{u} 76. || beauty] beau=ty BL, 76.

200.21 Heare] BL; Hear 76. || prayer$_\wedge$] BL; prayer, 76.

200.22 Lord$_\wedge$] BL; ~ , 76. || give] 76; giue BL. || cry] BL; Cry 76.

200.23 Stranger wth thee$_\wedge$] stranger w.th thee$_\wedge$ BL; stranger w:th thee, 76. || Sojourner wth] Sojourner w:th BL, 76. || Fathers] BL; fathers 76.

200.23–24 But; ô Lord$_\wedge$] But$_\wedge$ ô Lord$_\wedge$ BL; But, o Lord, 76.

200.24 sinnes, &] sinnes, and BL; siñes, & 76.

200.25 & lett] and let BL; & let 76. || ô] BL; o 76. || helpe] BL; help 76.

200.26 y^e] the BL; y:^{e} 76. || man,] 76; man; BL. || y^t] that BL; y:^{t} 76. || gives] 76; giues BL.

200.27 lett us] let vs BL, 76. || wth Job$_\wedge$] BL; w:th Job, 76. || y^e] the BL; y:^{e} 76. || the] BL; y^e 76. || ô lett] ô let BL; o lett 76.

200.28 looke] look BL, 76. || him,] 76; him$_\wedge$ BL. || salvation] BL; Salvation 76. || helpe] BL; help 76.

200.29 vs$_\wedge$ &] vs, and BL; vs, & 76.

200.30 &] 76; and BL. || y^e] BL; y:^{e} 76. || withall infusing] wthall, infusing BL; w.thall$_\wedge$ infuſing 76. || Grace] grace BL, 76.

200.31 y^t] y^t BL; y:^{t} 76. || Change] BL; change 76. || Kingdome] 76; King=dome BL.

200.32 wth] with BL; w:th 76.

201.2 In y^e] 76; In the BL. || vs y^e] 76; vs the BL. || y^e] the BL, 76. || righteous] BL; righteous *interlined* 76. || dye, &] 76; dy; and BL. || departure$_\wedge$] BL; ~ , 76.

201.3 &] 76; and BL. || destruction,] destruc=tion, BL; destruction; 76.

201.4 Jewell$_\wedge$] BL; Jewell, 76. || happineſse] BL; Happineſse 76.

201.5 sett$_\wedge$ (Death] 76; sett, Death BL. || seiſed] BL; seised 76. || her) y^e] her$_\wedge$ the BL; her) y:^{e} 76.

201.6 Passion] passion BL; paſsion 76. || asked her,] 76; her$_\wedge$ BL.

201.7 said,] 76; sayd$_\wedge$ BL. || Lengthening y^e] Lengthen=ing the BL; Lengthening y:^{e} 76. || Blisse, &] bliſse, and BL; Bliſse, & 76.

201.8 de=siring nothing,] desiring nothing$_\wedge$ BL; desiring nothing$_\wedge$ 76. || her] *interlined* 77; her *not interlined* BL, 76. || &] 76; and BL.

201.11 Sight] BL; sight 76. || the] y^e BL, 76. || Bridgewaters Picture.] Bridgewaters Picture: BL; Bridgewater's Picture. 76.

201.13 Booke$_\wedge$] 76; Booke, BL.

201.14 great] BL; Great 76. || thou] BL; y:^{u} 76.

201.15 gon] BL; gone 76. || Childe's] 76; Child's BL. || heart,] BL; ~ ; 76.

201.16 thou] y^u BL; y:^{u} 76. || &] 76; and BL.

201.17 w:th] 76; w.th BL. || name,] 76; Name; BL.

201.18 thou happy] y^u happy BL; y:^{u} Happy 76. || such$_\wedge$] 76; ~ , BL.

201.19 give] 76; giue BL. || praiſe] BL; prayſe 76.

201.20 *This statement is found only in* 77.

201.21 Spoken$_\wedge$] BL; ~ , 76. || the] BL; y^e 76. || Perfume$_\wedge$] perfume $_\wedge$ BL; Perfume, 76. || the] BL; y^e 76.

201.22 a Heart.] 76; an Heart. BL.

202.23 Deare$_\wedge$] BL; ~ , 76. || y^t y^u] BL; y:^{t} y:^{u} 76.

201.24 y^e place$_\wedge$] y^e place$_\wedge$ BL; y.^{e} place, 76. || wherein] wherin BL; where in *interlined* 76. || love] 76; Love BL.

201.25 Heart] BL; heart 76. || let] BL; lett 76.

201.26 But$_\wedge$] BL; ~ , 76. || forth,] 76; forth$_\wedge$ BL.

201.27 &] 76; and BL. || do] BL; doe 76.

201.28 shew$_\wedge$ y^t thou &] shew$_\wedge$ y^t y^u and BL; shew, y:^{t} y:^{u} & 76.

201.29 Contemplation,] 76; ~ $_\wedge$ BL. || the] BL; y^e 76.

201.30 I see] *interlined* 77; I see *not interlined* BL, 76. || me] BL; me *interlined* 76. || y^e Al=mighty] the Almighty BL; y^e Almighty 76. || God;] BL; ~ , 76.

201.31 ther] there BL, 76. || God's om=nipotency] Gods om=nipotency BL; God's omnipotency 76.

201.32 y^e] the BL; y.^{e} 76. || inconſiderable] BL; inconsiderable 76.

201.34 y^e] the BL; y:^{e} 76. || set] BL; sett 76. || above] 76; aboue BL. || &] 76; and BL.

201.35 y^e] 76; the BL.

202.1 cannot] 76; can=not BL.

202.1–2 eaſe w:^{ch}] 76; ease which BL.

202.2 hath] *interlined* 77; hath *not interlined* BL, 76. || gra=ciouſly been pleaſed] gra=ciously beene pleased BL; gratiouſly beene pleaſed 76. || thoſe] BL; those 76. || set] BL; sett 76.

202.3 w:^{ch}] 76; wch BL. || improve] 76; im=prove BL. || y^t] that BL; y:^{t} 76. || hauing] having BL, 76.

202.4 bodyes] BL; bodies 76. || & soules] and soules BL; & Soules 76. || y^e] the BL; y:^{e} 76.

202.5 earnest] *interlined* 77; earnest *not interlined* BL; e *of* earne t *interlined* 76. || &] 76; and BL. || y^e] The BL; y^e 76. || a gaine$_\wedge$ y^t] a gaine$_\wedge$ that BL; againe, y:^{t} 76.

202.6 ac=coṁodations] accommodations BL, 76. || &] 76; and BL. || wthout] BL; w.thout 76. || sett] 76; set BL. || y^t] that BL; y:^{t} 76.

202.7 find] 76; finde BL. || pleaſed] 76; plea=sed BL.

202.8 & y^t] and y^t BL; & y:^{t} 76. || wthout] 76; wth=out BL.

202.9 degrees] 76; de=grees BL. || are,] 76; are$_\wedge$ BL. || enabled] BL; ēabled 76. || paſs] paſse BL, 76. || cheerefull &] 76; Cheerefull and BL.

202.10 Comfortable] BL; comfortable 76. || y^e] the BL; y:^{e} 76. || con=veniences$_\wedge$] conveniences$_\wedge$ BL; conveniences, 76. || inwardly] BL; inward=ly 76.

202.11 wth] with BL; w:th 76. || y^t] that BL; y:^{t} 76.

202.12 may,] 76; ~ ∧ BL. || aſſiſtance] BL; assistance 76.

202.13 the exaltation] the Exaltation BL; y:^{e} exaltation 76. || God's] BL; Gods 76.

202.14 y^e Sickneſſe] y^e Sick=neſſe BL; y:^{e} sickneſſe 76. || Franck.] BL; Franck: 76.

202.15 whoſe] whose BL, 76. || y^e keyes] the keyes BL; y^e Keyes 76. || &] 76; and BL. || y^e] the BL; y:^{e} 76.

202.16 y^e Wombe, & y^e] the wombe, and the BL; y^e womb, & y:^{e} 76. || ye Graue, y^u] the grave, thou BL; y:^{e} grave, y:^{u} 76.

202.16–17 & compaſſion] and compaſſion BL; & com=paſſion 76.

202.17 above] BL; aboue 76. || delight'st] BL; delightest 76.

202.18 been pleased] beene pleased BL; beene pleaſed 76. || declare y^t] de=clare that BL; declare y:^{t} 76. || above] 76; aboue BL. || workes; y^u] works; Thou BL; workes; y:^{u} 76. || y^t] 76; that BL.

202.19 y^e] 76; the BL. || people, &] 76; peo=ple, and BL. || Com=manded y^t] Commanded that BL; commanded y^t 76.

202.20 Flesh] BL; flesh 76. || &] 76; and BL.

202.21 seate] Seate BL; seat 76. || y^u] y.^{u} BL; y:^{u} 76. || Heaven, and] heaven, and BL; heaven, & 76. || mer=cy] mercy BL, 76.

202.21–22 y^e prayers, &] y^e prayers, and BL; y:^{e} prayers∧ & 76.

202.22 teares∧ w:^{ch} w:th] teares∧ wch w.th BL; teares, w:^{ch} w:th 76. || a] 76; a *interlined* BL. || Knees, &] knees, and BL; knees, & 76.

202.22–23 vp lifted] BL; vp-lifted 76.

202.23 Grace] BL; grace 76. || vp] *interlined* 77; vp *not interlined* BL, 76. || Divine] divine BL, 76.

202.24 Know∧] know∧ BL; know, 76. || Lord,] 76; ~ ; BL. || y:^{t} y:^{u}] that thou BL; y:^{t} y.^{u} 76. || &] 76; and BL.

202.25 vnmeasurable] 76; vn=measurable BL. || kindneſſe] 76; kind=neſſe BL. || y^t y^u] that y^u BL; y:^{t} y:^{u} 76. || those,] 76; those∧ BL.

202.25–26 y^t hearti=ly &] that hearti=ly and BL; y^t heartely & 76.

202.26 & wth] and w.th BL; & w:th 76. || goodneſſe, &] goodneſſe, and BL; good=neſſe, & 76. || all sufficiency] all sufficien=cy BL; allsufficiency 76.

202.27 them; trust=ing] them; trusting BL; them, trusting 76.

202.28 ô Lord∧] BL; o Lord, 76.

202.29 petitions] 76; pe=titions BL. || & all sufficient Majesty] and all sufficient Majesty BL; & allsufficient Majes:^{ty} 76. || behalfe] 76; be=halfe BL.

202.30 Infant, y^t] Infant; that BL; infant, y^t 76. || y^e Rodd] the Rodd BL; y:^{e} rodd 76. || y^t] 76; the BL.

202.31 y^u] 76; thou BL.

202.32 y^t] that BL; y:^{t} 76. || Birth] birth BL, 76. || y^e] 76; the BL.

202.33 w:^{ch} y^u] wch thou BL; w:^{ch} y:^{u} 76. || haſt beene graciouſly] hast beene graciouſly BL; hast been gratiously 76.

202.34 fa=ther] Father BL; father 76. || y^e] BL; y:^{e} 76. || Judgm^t,] Judgment∧ BL; judgment 76. || be pleased to] be pleased to *interlined* BL; be pleaſed to *not interlined* 76. || remember] 76; remem=ber BL. || and] BL; & 76.

202.35 y^e showers] the Showers BL; y:^{e} showers 76. || Favour] BL; favour 76.

202.36 poor] poore BL, 76. || weake sicke] 76; weak sick BL. || y^e] 76; the BL. || w:^{ch} she] 76; wch shee BL.

202.37 w:th] 76; wth BL. || y^e] the BL; y:^{e} 76. || &] 76; and BL.

202.38 mercyes] BL; mercies 76. || ô] BL; Oh 76. || graciouſly pleased] graciously pleased BL; graciouſly pleaſed 76.

203.1 weake=neſſe she] weakeneſſe She BL; weakeneſſe she 76. || grant] BL; grante 76.

203.1–2 sickneſse, She] sick=neſse, She BL; sickneſse, she 76.

203.2 &] 76; and BL.

203.3 wth] BL; w:th 76. || y^{t} She, & I, &] that She$_\wedge$ and I, and BL; y^{t} she, & I, & 76.

203.3–4 y^{t} have] that have BL; y:^{t} haue 76.

203.4 rela=tion] re=lation BL; relation 76. || render] 76; ren=der BL. || & thanks, &] and thanks$_\wedge$ and BL; & thanks, & 76.

203.5 y^{t} y^{u}] BL; y:^{t} y:^{u} 76. || y^{e}] the BL; y:^{e} 76. || Death, &] death, and BL; death, & 76.

203.6 y^{e}] the BL; y:^{e} 76. || y^{e} grave y^{t}] the Grave that BL; y:^{e} grave y:^{t} 76. || y^{u}] thou BL; y.^{u} 76. || otherwiſe] BL; otherwise 76.

203.7 ô loving] BL; O Loving 76. || re=ceive] BL; receive 76. || y^{e} comforts] the comforts BL; y:^{e} Comforts 76.

203.8 Heavenly] 76; heavenly BL. || &] 76; and BL. || &] 76; and BL. || y^{t}] that BL; y^{t} 76.

203.9 endure y^{e}] en=dure the BL; endure y:^{e} 76.

203.9–10 loſse, wth] 76; loſs, w.th BL. ·

203.10 Godly] BL; godly 76. || constancy; &] constancy; and BL; Constancy, & 76. || Christ] BL; Chriſt 76.

203.11 dayly mediates$_\wedge$] day=ly mediates, BL; dayly me=diates$_\wedge$ 76. || man=kind, &] mankind, and BL; mankind, & 76.

203.12 y^{u}] thou BL; y:^{u} 76. || been pleaſed] been pleased BL; beene pleased 76. || y:^{t} y:^{u}] 76; that y^{u} BL. || ô Lord,] ô Lord$_\wedge$ BL; O Lord, 76.

203.14 ô gra=cious] ô gracious BL; O gracious 76. || loving, Father] loving$_\wedge$ Father BL; loving$_\wedge$ father 76.

203.15 Prayer] prayer BL, 76. || Sacrament of y^{e}] Sacram.^{t} of the BL; Sacrament of y:^{e} 76.

203.16 Supper] supper BL, 76.

203.17 father] Father BL, 76. || Creature] BL, Crea=ture 76.

203.17–18 duſt & Ashes] dust and Ashes BL; dust & aſhes 76.

203.18 have] 76; haue BL. || worſe] 76; worse BL.

203.19 y^{e} humble] 76; the hum=ble BL. || of mercy] 76; of mer=cy BL. || wch y^{u}] which thou BL; w:^{ch} y^{u} 76.

203.20 beene pleased] 76; been pleaſed BL. || y:^{t} y:^{u} delightest] that y^{u} delight=est BL; y:^{t} y:^{u} delight=est 76. || sett] 76; set BL. || mer=cy aboue] mercy aboue BL; mercy above 76.

203.21 great and] BL; greate & 76. || attributes] 76; at=tributes BL. || y^{e} Confidence w^{ch}] the confidence wch BL; y:^{e} confidence w:^{ch} 76.

203.22 affords vnto] BL; affordes un=to 76. || &] 76; and BL. || y^{e}] the; y:^{e} 76. || Lord$_\wedge$ &] 76; Lord, and BL.

203.23 Sonne] BL; sonne 76. || whom] interlined 77; whom not interlined BL, 76. || thou] interlined 77; thou not interlined BL; y:^{u} 76.

203.24 thee$_\wedge$] BL; thee, 76. || loving] 76; love=ing BL.

203.25 manifold Sinnes] many=fold sinnes BL; manyfold sinnes 76. || y^{t} em=boldens] that emboldens BL; y:^{t} emboldens 76. || otherwise] 76; otherwiſe BL.

203.26 Majes=ty] Majesty BL, 76. || y^{u}] BL; y:^{u} 76.

203.27 appeare] 76; ap=peare BL.

203.28 con=science] conscience BL; conſcience 76.

203.29 sentence] 76; sen=tence BL. || Lord,] 76; Lord$_\wedge$ BL. || y^{u}] thou BL; y:^{u} 76. || pleased] BL; pleaſed 76. || that barre] that Barr BL; y:^{t} Barre 76.

203.30 know] BL; knowe 76. || Sentenced] 76; sentenced BL. || & haue] 76; and have BL; & have 76.

203.30–31 & Damnation] 76; and Damna=tion BL.

203.31 Just] just BL, 76. || Fa=ther] Father BL; father 76.
203.31–32 Judgm.^{t} wth] judgment with BL; Judg=ment w:th 76.
203.32 Flesh] BL; flesh 76. || justified] 76; justifyed BL.
203.33 y^{u}] thou BL; y:^{u} 76. || shouldest] 76; should'st BL. || what] BL; w:^{t} 76. || amiſse] a=miſse BL; a=miſſe 76.
203.34 the] BL; y:^{e} 76. || mankind] 76; Mankind BL. || y^{u}] thou BL; y:^{u} 76. || Judgm^{t}] Judgement BL; judgment 76.
203.35 y^{e}] the BL; y:^{e} 76. || & y^{e} Mountaines Cover] and the Moun=taines couer BL; & y:^{e} Mountaines cover 76.
204.1 avoyd] a=voyd BL; a voyd 76. || Good] BL; good 76.
204.2 truſting] trusting BL, 76. || righteouſneſse] righteousneſse BL, 76.
204.3 farr] BL; farre 76. || alas] alaſse BL, 76. || confusion] 76; con=fusion BL.
204.4 the righteouſ=neſse] the righteouſneſse BL; y:^{e} righteouſneſse 76.
204.5 Petition] BL; petition 76. || hum=bly imploring] BL; humbly im=ploring 76. || Majesty‸] BL; ~ , 76.
204.6 the] BL; y^{e} 76. || Sacrament] 76; Sacram^{t} BL. || the] BL; y:^{e} 76.
204.7 know] 76; knowe BL. || partaker] 76; par=taker BL.
204.7–8 loving kind=neſse] loving kindneſse BL; Loving kindneſse 76.
204.8 y^{t} Sacram^{t}] that Sacrament BL; y:^{t} Sa=crament 76. || bequeath=ed] be=queathed BL; bequeathed 76. || those that] those y.^{t} BL; thoſe y:^{t} 76.
204.9 bleſsed Miſteries] bleſs=ed Miſteries BL; bleſsed miſteries 76. || y^{u}] thou BL; y:^{u} 76.
204.10 look] BL; looke 76. || mercy] 76; mer=cy BL. || thee‸] ~ , BL, 76. || y^{e}] the BL; y:^{e} 76.
204.11 Servants] servants BL, 76. || noe] no BL, 76. || &] 76; and BL.
204.12 give] 76; giue BL. || y^{t}] 76; that BL. || may,] 76; ~ ‸ BL.
204.13 accept=able] BL; ble *of* acceptable *interlined* 76. || the] BL; y:^{e} 76. || & vnspeakable] and vnspeak=able BL; & vn=speakable 76.
204.13–14 mis=miſtery] miſtery BL, 76.
204.14 y^{e} Trinity] the Trinity BL; y^{e} Trinitie 76. || persons] Persons BL; perſons 76. || y^{e} vnity] the vnity BL; y:^{e} vnitie 76. || God=head] Godhead BL, 76. || y^{t}] BL; y:^{t} 76.
204.15 thou diddest create] thou didst Create BL; y:^{u} diddest create 76. || happy] 76; hap=py BL. || &] 76; and BL.
204.16 diſobedience] 76; disobedience BL. || com=mands] BL; commands 76. || and] & BL, 76.
204.17 miſerable] 76; miser=able BL. || Sinne, w^{ch}] sinne, wch BL; sinne, w:^{ch} 76. || Spirit] spirit BL, 76. || abhorre] 76; ab=horre BL. || &] 76; and BL.
204.18 Mankind] man=kind BL; mankind 76. || the Curse &] the curse and BL; y^{e} curse & 76. || sin] BL; sinne 76. || w^{ch}‸] ~ , 76; w.^{ch}‸ BL.
204.19 pre=vent] prevent BL, 76. || siñing] BL; sinning 76.
204.20 y^{e}] 76; the BL. || &] 76; and BL. || others] BL; rs *of* others *interlined* 76. || Christ] BL; Chriſt 76.
204.21 and] BL; & 76. || been pleased] beene pleased BL; beene pleaſed 76. || for our] *interlined* 77; for our *not interlined* BL, 76.
204.22 sinnes, & hath so made satiſfaction] *interlined* 77; *not interlined* 76; sinnes, and hath so made satiſfaction *not interlined* BL. || and for the Sinnes] and for the sinnes BL; & for y^{e} sinnes 76. || the] BL; y^{e} 76.
204.23 and] BL; & 76. || re=demption] redemption BL, 76.
204.24 and] BL; & 76. || the] y^{e} BL; y:^{e} 76. || God, exercising] God‸ excer=cising BL; God, excersicing 76.

204.25 Mediator, and] Media=tor, and BL; Mediator, & 76. || interceſsion] 76; interceſ=sion BL. || and] BL; & 76.

204.26 bleſsed] 76; bleſs=ed BL. || which] BL; w:ᶜʰ 76. || desire worthyly] desire worthy=ly BL; deſire worthyly 76.

204.27 memoriall] 76; memo=riall BL. || that] BL; y:ᵗ 76. || work which] BL; worke w:ᶜʰ 76.

204.28 keep] keepe BL, 76. || irreverentₐ and carnall apprehensions] irreverentₐ and car=nall apprehenſions BL; irreverent, & carnall apprehenſions 76.

204.29 Miſtery] 76; miſtery BL. || and] BL; & 76. || that] BL; y:ᵗ 76. || and Wine] & wine BL; & Wine 76.

204.30 and] BL; & 76. || and Wine] and wine BL; & Wine 76. || with] BL; w:ᵗʰ 76. || that] BL; y:ᵗ 76.

204.31 cor=porally] corporally BL; Corporally 76. || Flesh, and] BL; flesh, & 76. || blood] 76; Bloud BL.

204.31–32 and Wine which thou] and wine w:ᶜʰ thou BL; & Wine w:ᶜʰ y:ᵘ 76.

204.32 set a part] BL; sett a=part 76.

204.33 and] BL; & 76. || that wonderfull] that wonder=full BL; y:ᵗ wonderfull 76. || thou] BL; yᵘ 76.

204.34 &] and BL; & interlined 76. || eatenₐ] BL; eaten, 76. || drunke] 76; drunk BL.

204.35 that] yᵗ BL; y:ᵗ 76. || thou] yᵘ BL, 76. || that] BL; y:ᵗ 76.

204.36 coror=ally] corporally BL, 76. || bread, and] 76; Bread, and BL; bread, & 76. || and] BL; & 76. || heartₐ] BL; ~ , 76.

205.1 and] BL; & 76. || which] w:ᶜʰ BL; w:ᶜʰ 76. || the] BL; y:ᵉ 76.

205.2 Faith] BL; faith 76. || body & blood] 76; Body and Bloud BL. || which thou] w:ᶜʰ y:ᵘ BL; w:ᶜʰ y:ᵘ 76.

205.3 Sinners] BL; sinners 76. || which] BL; wᶜʰ 76. || the] BL; y:ᵉ 76. || and] BL; & 76.

205.4 yᵘ pleased] thou pleased BL; y:ᵘ pleaſed 76. || faith, that] Faith, that BL; faith, y:ᵗ 76.

205.5 beleive that] BL; beleeve y:ᵗ 76. || Sa=viour] Saviour BL; Saviour 76. || Christ] BL; Chriſt 76. || took hu=mane] took humane BL; tooke humane 76.

205.6 the earth] BL; yᵉ earth 76. || suf=fered] suffered BL, 76. || the] BL; y:ᵉ 76. || and] BL; & 76.

205.7 a gaine,] 76; againe; BL. || that he] BL; y:ᵗ hee 76. || and that] BL; & y:ᵗ 76.

205.7–8 againe, &] 76; againe, and BL.

205.8 and] BL; & 76. || wᵗʰ] BL; w:ᵗʰ 76. || but] 76; But BL.

205.9 repent] 76; re=pent BL. || have] 76; haue BL. || beleife] be=liefe BL; beleefe 76.

205.10 hum=bly] humbly BL, 76. || the] BL; yᵉ 76. || exam=ine] examine BL, 76.

205.11 and] BL; & 76. || wᶜʰ] which BL; w:ᶜʰ 76. || a=bominable] abominable BL, 76. || sightₐ] sight; BL, 76.

205.12 needs acknowledge] needs ac=knowledge BL; needes acknowledge 76. || haue tranſgreſsed] haue tranſ=greſsed BL; have tranſ=greſsed 76.

205.13 is from] 76; From BL. || that] BL; y:ᵗ 76. || thee, wᵗʰ] thee, with BL; thee, wᵗʰ 76. || the] BL; y:ᵉ 76.

205.14 Soule] 76; soule BL. || the bleſsed] the bleſs=ed BL; y:ᵉ bleſsed 76. || that] BL; y:ᵗ 76.

205.15 forsake] 76; catchword forsake omitted on first line BL. || sinnesₐ] BL; ~ , 76. || knowne, and] knowne ₐ and BL knowne, & 76. || and] BL; & 76.

205.16 holyneſs, & righteouſ=neſse] holyneſseₐ and righteouſneſse BL; holy=neſseₐ & righteouſneſse 76. || y:ᵉ] the BL; y:ᵉ 76. || yᵉ] 76; the BL. || w:ᶜʰ yᵘ] w:ᶜʰ thou BL; w:ᶜʰ y:ᵘ 76.

205.17 allot] BL; allott 76. || yᵉ earth, &] 76; the earth, and BL. || ended] BL; end=ed 76.

205.18 heavenly Kingdome; &] heavenly Kingdome; and BL; heaven=ly kingdome; & 76.

205.19 Chari=ty, yᵗ] Charity, that BL; Charity, y:ᵗ 76. || wᵗʰ] with BL; w:ᵗʰ 76. || yᵉ] 76; the BL. || & beare] and bear BL; & beare 76.

205.20 yᵘ] thou BL; y:ᵘ 76. || wᵗʰ theſe graces,] w.ᵗʰ those graces, BL; w:ᵗʰ these graces, 76.

205.21 wᵗʰ] with BL; w:ᵗʰ 76. || approach] 76; ap=proach BL. || yᵉ wedding] the wed=ding BL; y:ᵉ wed=ding 76.

205.22 appointed] 76; ap=pointed BL. || &] 76; and BL. || yᵘ] thou BL; y:ᵘ 76. || yᵘ] thou BL; y:ᵘ 76.

205.23 accept;] ac=cept; BL; accept, 76. || Lord,] 76; Lord, BL. || haue] BL; have 76. || righteouſ=neſse] righteousneſſe BL, 76.

205.24 &] 76; and BL. || the] BL; yᵉ 76.

205.25 forgive] 76; forgiue BL. || Sinnes, & accept] sinnes, and ac=cept BL; sinnes, & accept 76. || righteouſneſſe] 76; righteousneſſe BL.

205.26 oh] 76; ô BL. || looke] look BL, 76. || wᵗʰ yᵉ] with the BL; w:ᵗʰ y:ᵉ 76.

205.27 com=paſsion, &] com=paſion, and BL; Compaſsion, & 76. || Book] BL; Booke 76.

205.28 Sonne] BL; sonne 76. || Saviour's] 76; Saviours BL. || with the] wᵗʰ the BL; w:ᵗʰ y:ᵉ 76.

205.29 father and the] Father and the BL; father & y:ᵉ 76. || honour, and] honour, & BL; honour, & 76. || and] BL; & 76.

205.30 evermore.] BL; ~ , 76.

205.31 Table ,] BL; ~ . 76.

205.32 faith wᵗʰ] BL; Faith w.ᵗʰ 76.

205.33 yᵉ Sickneſse] the sickneſse BL; y:ᵉ sickneſs 76. || Franck,] Franck. BL, 76. || 34] 30 BL; 19 76.

205.34 w.ᵗʰ] wᵗʰ BL; w:ᵗʰ 76. || 46] 38 BL; 25 76.

205.35 62] 49 BL; 32 76.

205.36 Bedd] BL; Bed 76. || 67] 53 BL; 34 76.

206.1 w.ᵗʰ] BL; w:ᵗʰ 76. || 75] 58 BL; 38 76.

206.2 with] BL; wᵗʰ 76.

206.3 haue] have BL, 76. || Labour,] BL; Labour. 76. || 82] 64 BL; 41 76. || *In 76, the listing "A Prayer after I had received yᵉ bleſsed Sacrament" follows here instead of "A Prayer when I was w.ᵗʰ Child," as in 77 and BL. Variant listings continue through 206.19.*

206.4 w.ᵗʰ] BL; w:ᵗʰ 76. || 88] 70 BL; 47 76.

206.5 w:ᵗʰ] wᵗʰ BL; w:ᵗʰ 76. || Stuart.] ~ , BL, 76. || 108] 84 BL; 55 76.

206.6 Meditation] 76; meditatiō BL. || w:ᵗʰ] wᵗʰ BL, 76. || 120] 93 BL; 58 76.

206.7 ag.ᵗ deſpaire] ag.ᵗ deſpair BL; against despaire 76. || 128] 100 BL; 61 76.

206.8 the] BL; yᵉ 76. || 135] 105 BL; 64 76.

206.9 yᵉ] BL; y.ᵉ 76. || the] BL; yᵉ 76. || 143] 112 BL; 67 76.

206.10 153] 120 BL; 71 76.

206.11 yᵉ] BL; y.ᵉ 76. || Easter,] BL; ~ , 76. || the] yᵉ BL; y.ᵉ 76.

206.12 with Child,] with Child. BL; w.ᵗʰ Child. 76. || 158] 124 BL; 73 76.

206.13 delivery,] ~ , BL; Delivery, 76. || the Communion,] yᵉ Communion, BL; y.ᵉ Communion, 76.

206.14 165] 130 BL; 76 76.

206.15 the Blessed] yᵉ Bleſsed BL; the Bleſsed 76. || 171] 135 BL; 78 76.

206.16 Meditation] 76; meditation BL.

206.17 the Holy] yᵉ holy BL; yᵉ Holy 76. || 175] 139 BL; 80 76.

206.18 the Blessed] the Bleſsed BL; yᵉ bleſsed 76. || 182] 146 BL; 45 76. || *As noted above, the listings are parallel from this line on.*

206.19 Marriageₐ] BL; ~ . 76. || 186] 150 BL; 84 76.

206.20 and] & BL, 76. || Widdowesₐ] BL; ~ . 76. || 196] 161 BL; 89 76.

206.21 Sluggishneſse] BL; slugishneſse 76. || and Lazineſse] BL; *interlined* & Lazineſse 76. || Dutiesₐ] dutiesₐ BL; dutyes. 76. || 203] 169 BL; 92 76.

206.22 yᵉ] BL; y.ᵉ 76. || injuries] Injuries BL, 76. || 210] 177 BL; 96 76.

206.23 the] yᵉ BL; y.ᵉ 76. || and Neere friends] and Neere Friends BL; & neare Friends 76. || 217] 185 BL; 99 76.

206.24 Meditation] 76; meditation BL. || yᵉ Confidence] the confidence BL; y.ᵉ Confidence 76. || Forgiveneſse] BL; forgiveneſse 76. || Sinnes] BL; sinne 76. || 220] 189 BL; 101 76.

206.25 of] BL; of *interlined* 76. || others;] ~ ₐ BL, 76. || wᵗʰ Encouragemᵗˢ] wᵗʰ encouragments BL; w:ᵗʰ encouragem:ᵗˢ 76. || Afflictions] afflictions BL; affliction 76. || 223] 193 BL; 103 76.

206.26 vnderstand] 76; vn=derstand BL. || 227] 198 BL; 105 76.

206.27 purity] Purity BL, 76. || the Communionₐ] BL; yᵉ Communion. 76. || 230] 201 BL; 107 76.

206.28 Exhortation] 76; exhortation BL. || Confidence] confidence BL, 76. || 234] 205 BL; 109 76.

206.29 and] BL; & 76. || 235] 207 BL; 110 76.

206.30 the vn=winding] BL; y.ᵉ vnwinding 76. || Skeane] skeane BL; Sceane 76. || silke] 76; Silk BL. || 237] 210 BL; 111 76.

206.31 sick=neſse] sickneſs BL; sickneſse 76. || delivery] BL; Delivery 76. || 239] 212 BL; 112 76.

207.1 occasion] occaſion 76. || Husband's Birth-day] Hus=bands Birth-day BL; Huſband's birth day 76. || 242] 216 BL; 114 76.

207.2 Husband] BL; Huſband 76. || 244] 219 BL; 116 76.

207.3 occasion] BL; occaſion 76. || yᵉ Death] BL; y:ᵉ death 76. || 247] 231 BL; 117 76.

207.4 253] 231 BL; 122 76.

207.5 lost] BL; Lost 76. || Deare] BL; deare 76. || Kateₐ] ~ . BL, 76. || 254] 232 BL; 123 76.

207.6 the] BL; yᵉ 76. || occasion] occaſion BL, 76. || 257] 236 BL; 125 76.

207.7 the] BL; yᵉ 76. || 264] 244 BL; 129 76.

207.8 the] yᵉ BL; y.ᵉ 76. || Bridgewater's] BL; Bridgewaters 76. || 266] 247 BL; 130 76.

207.9 the] BL; y.ᵉ 76. || perfumeₐ] BL; Perfume, 76.

207.10 the] BL; yᵉ 76. || 268] 240 BL; 131 76.

207.11 contemplation on the] BL; Contemplation vpon yᵉ 76. || Cushion] BL; Cussion 76. || 269] 249 BL; 132 76.

207.12 the] BL; y.ᵉ 76. || Franckₐ] Franckeₐ BL; Franck: 76. || 273] 253 BL; 134 76.

207.13 yᵉ] BL; y.ᵉ 76. || yᵉ Bleſsed Sacrament] the Bleſsed Sacrament BL; yᵉ bleſsed Sacram:ᵗ 76.

207.14 the] BL; yᵉ 76. || 280] 264 BL; 139 76.

Appendix I: "Conclusory Meditation"

As Plate 27 (page 143) indicates, the final entry in HN MS EL 35/C/16, the facsimile of Elizabeth Egerton's holograph "Meditations on the generall Chapters of the Holy Bible . . . ," which (as the folio catalogue notes) was "corrected for copying by her husband" (4: 756), is untitled in the original. One of the slips in John Egerton's handwriting, however, provides the entry with the title "A Conclusory Meditation on all the other Meditations," printed here in angled brackets. A sense of the spontaneous nature of the composition is provided by the section on the loss of children, a subject all readers of the "Loose Papers" know was very dear to the countess, almost omitted in the heat of composition, but artlessly inserted towards the end. I have supplied a small number of citations of biblical allusions as footnotes.

<"A Conclusory Meditation on all the other Meditations">

Now I will make my Confession that I write this of the newe testament & the olde, for my better information; that thus making Comments on them <I>[1] might the better vnderstand the Scripture, & ingrafe it in my memmory; & hope I haue done noething amisse in it, not that I haue done < >thing[2] well, but I hope the Lord will pardon mee, & fforgiue mee my

---

[1] A conjectural reading.
[2] Although this possibly reads "any"thing or "every"thing, I am not sure of the reading.

Sins, that are greate & many, & giue mee Comfort to <brede>[3] Up my Childeren in the feare & Loue of him, that so they may keepe his Commandments all the dayes of their Life, & studdy to obay him, for wee See, in both Bookes, that the wicked are to bee Condemnd into EuerLasting punishement, & the Godly God receaues into EuerLasting Happynes; bringing them vnto himselfe to dwell with him forEuer; olet us Euer obserue this Holly Scripture, & giue praise to God ffor his greate mercys, in giueing vs his Holly, & blessed sonne, to die ffor vs, that through his mercys by his shedding his most pretious Blood ffor us, wee may haue redemtion in him; hee it is that cleanses us from all Sinne, if wee truly Call upon him, & put our trust in him; & hee it is that Sits on the right Hand of God, makeing intercession for us,[4] to his father, that by a Harty repentance wee may bee admitted into his Heauenly Kingdome, & wee must striue to Enter in at the straite gate, ffor Broade is the way to destruction, but narrow is the gate to life;[5] so that wee must not bee tempted with this wourld's pleasures, but must be pleased, with the hopes of the Joyes of heauen, & must know 'tis the Lord that rewards vs; & wee must take all our aflicktions patiently, & pray vnto the Lord to Ease vs, & giue vs Comfort, & not to Lay his Heauy Hand upon vs; of Justice, but his kind hand of mercy; & we must Euer dread, & feare his Judgments, & prayse him ffor his mercy, ffor wee see his mercy Is aboue his Judgments, & hee Can pardon moore then wee Can offend, ffor there is mercy with him, & hee saith hee Calls Not the righteous, but Sinners to repentance,[6] & so let us Come vnto him to bee healed, not haueing the least despaire of his will; but yet let vs dreade our owne Sinns, & infynite ingratitudes & pray, & crie vnto him for mercy, ffor with him is plenteous Redemtion:[7] & I will Euer beg a blessing ffrom God to my Husband, Childeren, freinds, & selfe, that hee will grant us a Long Life here, & EuerLasting Happynes in the next wourld, & this I Humbly beg of our Lord Jesus Christ, to blesse vs, & pardon all our misdeedes, that so age, as well as youth, may prayse him ffor his greate mercys; & let vs neuer ffaile to giue thankes vnto him dailly, as well as to beg mercys, & let vs studdy Euer to obay him, & hee will blesse vs, & wee

---

[3] This is a conjectural reading.
[4] Romans 8:34.
[5] Matthew 7:13.
[6] Matthew 9:13.
[7] Ps. 130:7.

shall bee blessed, & this God of his greate goodnes grant vnto vs, for our Lord Jesus Christ's sake, who Liueth, & raigneth now, & ffor Euermoore; Amen, Sweete Jesus Amen, & his Holly name bee Euer Extolled, now & for Euer; the ffather, sonne, & Holly Ghost, bee magnifyed ffor Euer; & let all the wourld Sing praysses to him that sits in the Highest Heauens; & to him be prayse wourld without End, & Lord pardon my Sins, for they are greate, & so let mee End with this, mercy Sweete Jesus, mercy to mee, & all my ffriends; & this I Humbly beg ffor Jesus Christ's Sake, for by & through his mercy shall Wee bee Eternally Happy, now, & for Euer: & ffor what I haue done amisse, good Lord be mercyfull vnto mee, & pardon mee: Amen: Amen./

I fforgot to mention the Loss of childeren, & ffriends, wherein wee haue a greate measure of Griefe, but noe doubt but the Innocent sweete babes are Sweet saincts in heauen, & are with the Angells praysing, & giuing glory to God, Let us aske pardon ffor our Sinnes, & our great Griefe ffor our Loue of them, they beeing Happyer then with us receaueing all the Joyes Imaginnable; which God grant to us when our departure ffrom hence comes, & that wee pine not in the meanetime into despaire, but that wee put our Whole trust in God, who Can Saue us; which God grant vnto us, by his greate goodnes, who Liueth, & raigneth now, & ffor Euermoore Amen./

Appendix II: "The Vision"

Searchers among the voluminous Bridgewater documents owned by the Huntington have apparently overlooked, till now, the slight manuscript poem dated 1699 composed by one Marie Burghope, a dependent of the Bridgewater family. Burghope's country-house poem in heroic couplets is a significant document for both literary and social historians. For literary scholars, this "woman's work" constitutes a important contribution to the development of the genre of the country-house poem, a genre traditionally thought to have been begun in 1611 with Ben Jonson's "To Penshurst," as well as being in the line of ecphrastic poetry describing paintings or sculpture. In recent years, scholars have recovered and have read with growing excitement "To Cooke-ham," a country-house poem and tribute written in the same year as Jonson's by Aemilia Lanyer, a female retainer of the Clifford family. Scholars have drawn particular attention to distinctions between Jonson's concentration on the hierarchical and patriarchal and Lanyer's depiction of a bucolic community of women.[1] Also of interest is the fact that Burghope chose to present her "description of Ashridge" as a dream vision, a genre, as Josephine A. Roberts has shown, that was particularly congenial to seventeenth-century women writers.[2]

---

[1] Earlier writers on Lanyer include Lewalski ("Good Women," "Lady," "Rewriting," "Imagining") and Woods ("Ben Jonson"). More recent writers—like McGrath ("Let us") and Coiro ("Writing")—have, however, drawn attention to Lanyer's awareness of class boundaries.

[2] Josephine A. Roberts, " 'My Inward House': Women's Autobiographical Poetry in

Burghope's poem is unabashedly intended to glorify the Bridgewaters. The title page testifies that the document was "Written by one of the Female Sex in the Year 1699," and that this description of Ashridge is presented "Together with the History & Characters Of the most considerable Members Of that Noble Family." The prefatory letter addressed to "the Lady Mary Egerton," granddaughter of Elizabeth Egerton, is fascinating on several counts. On the specific subject of this study, it confirms other contemporary descriptions of the marriage of Elizabeth and John Egerton. As an expression of a female point of view, it is consciously supportive of contemporary social hierarchies. Yet the epistle combines this conservative position with a critique of the education of women that matches the following, far less docile plaints of Mary Tattlewell and Joanne hit him-home earlier in the century:

> ... when a Father hath a numerous issue of Sonnes and Daughters, the sonnes forsooth they must bee ... trained up in Liberall Arts and Sciences. ... When we, whom they stile by the name of weaker Vessells, ... have not that generous and liberall Educations, [sic] lest we should bee made able to vindicate our owne injuries, we are set onely to the Needle, to pricke our fingers: or else to the Wheele to spinne a faire thread for our owne undoings, or perchance to some more durty and deboyst drudgery: If wee be taught to read, they then confine us within the compasse of our Mothers Tongue, and that limit wee are not suffered to passe; ... and thus if we be weake by Nature, they strive to makes [sic] us more weake by our Nurture. And if in degree of place low, they strive by their policy to keepe us more under.[3]

---

the Early Seventeenth Century," in *"The Muses Female Are": Martha Moulsworth and Other Women Writers of the English Renaissance*, eds. Robert C. Evans and Anne C. Little (West Cornwall, Conn.: Locust Hill Press, 1995), 129–37.

[3] *The womens sharpe revenge* (London, 1640), sigs. C7–C9v.

The Vision.
Or
A Poeticall View of Ashridge in the County of Bucks.
The ancient Seat of the Right Honorable John Earle of Bridgewater.
Together with the History & Characters Of the most
Considerable Members of that Noble Family.
Written by one of the Female Sex
in the Year 1699

To the Right Honorable the Lady Mary Egerton

Madam

It has been the com̄on Imputation of the Tyrants of the other Sex, that Women had neither Learneing, Prudence nor Conduct, & therefore were fitt only to be the Drudges of Mankind; That they were made up of Passion & Ignorance, & so to be govern'd as a higher Sort of unreasonable Creatures. But these Men have seen themselves confuted by the numerous Examples of our Sex in every Age & Science, & in all Endowments of Body, & Mind. And now lest they shou'd be out done every Way, they begin to declaime against Our Acquision of Knowledge as inconvenient; & pretend Policy to keep us in Ignorance. And the Illiterate part of our Sex (because they are proud & loth others Intellectualls shou'd be better dress'd up then their Own) joyne with them in the com̄on cry. These latter are a Sort of Ignorants that I both pitty & Scorne; & (notwithstanding their other Embelishments) are little better then the Brutes. Only they are proud & envious, (Which Beast are not) They know not the use, & value of Learneing; & like brute Beast speak evill of that which they understand not. And as for the former Their Com̄on Allegation is that one Tongue is enough for a woman, & Learneing is good for Nothing but to make them proud, Idle, & ill hous Wiues. Indeed one Tongue wou'd be thought too much, if some might haue their will, who wou'd use us as dumb Creatures, & make Slaues of us. But if these GentleMen haue any understanding left them amongst all their Invectiues against our Education, They may Consider that the cultivation of the Mind doth not hinder, but advance that of the Body; & that knowledge is so far from being a Burthen, that it enables us to carry Cheerfully that which is design'd for us in this World. That it teaches us our whole Duty, & is a Continuall Monitor, not only to Industry & a prudentiall Management of our Stock, but to Consideration, & a true veiw of things. To Humility & Sobriety; moderation in all

Pleasures, & Patience under all Pressures & finally that the Learned Woman must make the best hous Wife, as well as the best Christian, & if any proue otherwise, tis by reason of the mismanagement of their Learneing, or an ill nature which perverts it.

But of all parts of Learneing, that of Poetry heares worse In a Woman; as that which fills their Heads with Fiction & Chimera's. This ^is^ in part true; & those that giue themselues Intirely to the Muses, are fitt for nothing else but to inheritt the barren Hill of Parnassus. But (Madam) I entertaine them but Seldome as a poor Man doth holy Days, or as a virtuous honest young Gentleman (if there are any Such) shou'd doe his Ingenious M^rs^; be glad of her Company now & then, But not to make Her his Wife till all matters are adjusted, & He finds the conveniency & advantage of Matrimony. I loue to recreate my selfe at leasure Hours with their Company. Tis sure as lawfull & laudable, as our ordinary Chatt, Telling of news, & Backbiteing, Dressing up, Patching, Painting, Putting our Selues into a Posture of Talkeing Nonsence in the Mode, & other the admir'd Qualifications of our Sex. It cañot Sure be any hurt or hinderance to our Worldly concerns, to spend the time of ordinary diversion, in walking alone, & thinking sometimes of the Excellency's of the World, & Sometimes of it's Follys. And if we are Capable of entertaineing the Muse upon either Subject, sure it cannot be criminall.—

And Madam that I may let you know how I haue pass'd away some of my Spare Hours, I haue sent you a Specimen, & so make you Judg of the Matter. Tis a Poeticall Description of your Ashridge, Which is (By the Judgment of all that know it) a noble Subject, & deserves the most judicious Pen. Tho I must own, while I wrote, I Swam with the Tide of Fancy, & the Waters under ^me^ were Boyant. I felt an unusuall Power to carry on the Description, & to bring it to that Perfection you see it now before you. Tho after all I haue reason to fear I haue not done the Seat its Selfe, much less your noble Relations, the Justice I ought; Which yet (I hope) will be imputed rather to my want of Skill, then Reverence or Zeal I haue either for the one or the other.

I know (Madam) I may stand excus'd for the new fancifull way of magageing [sic] this Subject, whilst I plead it has been always my darleing Talent; & may now (I hope) be allow'd no Small Ornament & Beauty to the Whole.

The Muse, (Madam) that has pretended to Inspiration, Knowing that you, as well as all others, must admire & delight in Poesie (tho' their Genious Inclines them not to make it their Business) has in the Body of this Work implor'd your Protection; & I that am acquainted with your sweet Disposition & your other extraordinary Qualifications, am encouraged to joyne in $^{the}_\wedge$ Petition; & will rest satisfied y^t you will pardon all the Defects of it, Since tis only for your Noble Families, & your Ladyships private Diversion; & because I am Madam —

Your most Humble and Obedient Servant. Marie Burghope

A Poeticall Description of Ashridge Com. Bucks.

Cool was the western Air, serene the Day,
And Phoebus did his radiant Beames display.
When I ore shaddow'd in an Arbour sate,
Contemplating the wond'rous Turnes of Fate,
My wand'ring Thoughts such Objects brought in veiw
That Poets scarce could feigne, & yet were true.
The Palaces adorn'd with riseing Towers,
Attended round with humble Walks & Bowers,
And Gardens deck'd with the most fragrant Flowers.
Strong & delightfull Mansions, which might proue
The best for War, the best for Peace & Loue.
Man too imploy'd my Thoughts, their Rise & Fall,
What glorious deeds they've done, & what they shall.
Where are the Hero's of the former Age,
And what are those that now are on the Stage.
How these do domineer upon the Ball,
Till Death stops their Tumultuous Breath, & all
Are carried to the com̄on Funerall.
The World's an $^{Island,}_\wedge$ where We act & do
And is surrounded with a Sea of Woe.
A Land of Sorrows, & a Vale of Teares,
And Man a Machine mov'd with hopes & feares.
Short is his time, yet long his Works remaine,
And Monumentally his Name retaine.
And thus (well pleas'd) I past from Things to Men,
And then as pleas'd from Men to Things agen.
— When lo! there did a Sight appear
Which rais'd my wonder equall to my fear.

An open Chariot, fild with radiant Light,
Drawn by two winged Horses snowey White;
Within a Nymph with graue but louely Face
In awefull Posture, & Majestic Grace,
Sate; with one ^{Hand} supporting of her Head,
The other held a Wand; These words She said.

 "Behold thy Muse appeares,—perceiveing well
"Thou might'st in our Celestiall Art excell,
"Had'st thou a Subject great enough; & be
"My Oracle, as I shall be to Thee.
"Then know, an Object Soon thou shalt descry
"Not only with thy Intellect, but Eye;
"An object, & be sure no Aid I'l spare
"Worthy thy song, & my Poetic Care.

 This said, She lift me up whilst all amaz'd
Much on the Earth, much more on Her I gaz'd.
Swifter then Winds, or quicker far then Thought,
We thro the yeilding trackless Air were brought;
And then descending down.—Tis here said She
The promis'd Earthly Paradice You'l See.

†Cald Princes
Rideing before
the House

 T'was in a Walk† where Art & Nature stroue
To shew their vtmost Skill, & truest Loue.
The Prospect did at once please & Surprize,
Delightfull Wonder danc'd before my Eyes.

 The Stately Beech exactly in a Row
On both the Sides in full proportion grow.
Their lofty Tops so ev'n & verdent are,
You'd think 'em Spacious Pastures in the Air.
So thick that even the Suns all peircing Eye
Can Scarce the Beauty of the Walk descry.
Tho' to adorn, & make it please the Sight
He checkers it with Gems of purest Light.
The Winds all thro the Place came whispering forth
To pleasure more, or more to tell its worth

Tis all With Natures Colours fully spread,
The grownd work green, richly enamelled
With natiue Flowers, neither Sown nor sett.
The Dazy & the blew ey'd Violett.
Their notes the little Winged Chorus raise,
And chant with Sweet Melodious Strains its Praise.
And Eccho too is there, & so will be
To make an Everlasting Harmony.
Here sure the Favourites of the Muses came
(Att lest they Sho'd) to Eternize their Name,
And toak (So great Variety it yeilds)
All they haue Said of the Elisium Feilds.

The Object next that cald away my Eye
†The House   Was a Magestic Palace† Standing by.
its Selfe   Tis Seated on a Rise adorned round
With Trees, by Art & Natures favours Crownd.
Erected too with such aspireing hight,
That tho it pleas'd, it dazl'd soon the Sight,
†The Park   From whence the Woods† & Plains are all descry'd,
Where numerous Traines of well feed Deer reside;
So swift, so grown, that one may well declare
Their Liues scarce in their Masters Power are,
And yet they pay them to reward his Care
So that a Monarch's Palace this might proue,
Or else as Poets Sing the Seat of Jove.

†The Lodge   The very Anti-Palace† seem'd to be
Sufficient Subject for my Muse & me
Tis fairly wrought thr'o out & so compact;
And every frosted Stone laid so exact
With Such a Symetry, It may be sworn
All the whole Mass is but made up of One.
Here my Surprize was great, The Blind & Lame
And other Poor o'rejoy'd togather came.
They were not surer of th'approaching Day
Then to be sent with full Supplys away.
It Still increas'd, in this hard Age to See

All other marks of Hospitality.
Here Friends & Strangers too with equall Care
And bounty vnconfin'd, refreshed are.
And had there not been Nobler Objects nigh
To entertain my Sight, even so had I.

A large & Spacious Square then next was seen,
Bigirt about with never fadeing Green.
So high So thick, & so compacted grown,
You'd think it did Supply the Place of Stone.
Apollo here Sure keeps his Sacred Court,
Whether his sons for Lawrels doe resort:
Or rather $_\wedge^{even}$ a Short and transcient veiw
Inspires Poets, & can crown them too.
And it had been Pernassus Top to me,
If the Indulgent Muse had left me free.
But instantly She wav'd Her powerfull Wand,

†The Library   And So we past into the Vatican.†

Here sacred Learneing do's tryumphant Sitt,
Accompaned [sic] with Eloquence & Witt.
Others for knowledge Travell, cutt the Line,
Hazard those Seas that on the Poles co$_\wedge^n$fine.
From hence the greater World we haue in veiw,
And learne to understand the Lesser too.
Rome may her numbers boast; this do's excell
In better Books & being chosen well,
What e're the Ancients or the Moderns write,
The Brittan, or the Athen—Stagerite
Is here recorded. Science do's appear
In full Meridian & Declention here.
"Haile mighty Founder of these Sacred Piles!
"On the great Owner now extend your Smiles.
"'Tis He alone's design'd, He only can
"And will Compleat what you so well began.
"And thou my Muse my willing Soul inspire
"With such Magestic Sense, & such Poetic Fire;
"That I may Something say, worthy to be
"By Him transmitted to Posterity

"Among those numerous all delightfull Store.
"Grant but this Small Request I'l ask no more.

The Goddest [sic] smil'd in Token of consent;
And so into the stately Hall We Went,
Plac'd in the Front, Whose lofty Top do's show
Aboue the other Building all below.
Hung round with Draughts, so well perform'd, you'd call
The very Copys the Originall.
Here Horse & Hound in full Proportion stand,
And Wonder now, as when aliue comand.

†Some new
Alterations

There's adde'd† too what ere suppos'd to be
Worthy this Age, or of Posterity.
The finest Ornaments to let us know
How great it is, & will be ever so.

†The great
Staires

A large† Ascent was next adorn'd all ore
With Loves, & Cupids, or what pleased more.

†The Picture of
the Battle betwixt
the Giants and
the Gods, which
the Muse describes
& passes by the
rest

The ancient† Battle t'wixt the Gods & Men,
Gigantic Warrs, Pelion on Ossa; When
The mighty Typheus Heaven to conquer stroue,
And was transfix'd by Thunder-bolts of Jove.
Painters & Poets too haue both the skill
Truth in the Guise of Fables to instill.
The Warr in Heaven; the Dragons fallen Powers
Hissing thro Air hott Inferus devours.
This Warr continues Still, Sin Heaven wou'd claime,
And right t'Imortall Pleasures doth maintaine.
Rebellious Man! Remember well the Odds,
Th'unequall combate between Men & Gods.
Condemn'd to Flames like Typheus thou must lie,
And dieing Still must liue & never die.

‖The great
dineing Room

Proceed, sweet Muse, into the‖ Room of State
Where other Objects thy Attendance waite.
High was the Place, magnificently great,
Where Kings or Gods might well accept a Treat.
Each part thereof did wonderfull appear,
And Each deserv'd the strictest Notice here.

The Hangings Keep those Storys fresh in veiw,
That scarce the Pen or Presse cou'd ever doe.
The very Windows in this glorious Sphere
Are so prodigious Big, so wond'rous clear,
That by the Touch alone, not by the Eye,
They are distinguish'd from the crystall Skie.

†The Pictures aboue   But aboue all, those full proportion'd† Draughts
both Sides which the   Most pleas'd, & ^most^ employ'd my Serious Thoughts.
Muse describes
& reflects upon   What did I see? My old admir'd Friends
As She goes on   Drawn out to all th'Advantage Art pretends.
Homer's fam'd Hero's One Side doth display,
The other Virgil's full as fam'd as They.

Patroclus here with Teares for License seeks
To bring Assistance to the Sinking Greeks.
Angry Achilles weeps, Briseis Lost,
And leaues in Rage the hated Greecian Host.
O had He nere return'd! Then Troy had stood,
And Xanthus Waves had nere been stain'd with Blood.

Hector was always my dear favorite Care,
And therefore fear'd to see Him pass to War.
But while He's drag'd att fierce Achilles Wheel
A strang remorse I cañot chuse but feel.
This base vnmanly Ation lost Him more,
Then all He got with th' Aid of Gods before.

Aeneas was secure from Deaths allarmes
By Gods, & by impenetrable Armes.
But Turnus had not One to saue his Life,
But a Week Goddesse, & Joues envious Wife.
And these, in vaine, too late did interpose
The very Fates were listed with his Foes.
Lavinia was engraven in His Heart.
Loue & unwearied Courage took his part.
Aided by these, He fires the Trojan Fleet,
Which chang'd to Naides their Mr Meet.
His Prowess next you see young Pallas felt,

Whilest He with joy Seiz'd on the fatall Belt.
When there I saw Him fall before $\stackrel{his}{\wedge}$ Foe.
Methought t'was pitty that it sho'd be so.
That He had done what ever Man cou'd doe
And was the greater Hero of the Two.

†The withdrawing   The †rest (noe doubt) had rais'd some Sweet debate,
Room & Bed   And all the adjacent Sumptious Rooms of State.
Chamber adjoyning   Their Hangings wrought with Skillfull Ladys Hands
                      The stately Bed, which wonder too comands;
                      Whole Walls of Crystall Mirrors, where you'l find
                      New Rooms, & other Company behind.
†The Cedar &   These had been veiw'd with far more curious Eyes,
the other Gallery   Had not my Guid pass'd to both† Galleries.
hang'd full of the
Pictures of their   Scenes most delightfull, fitt for Recreation
Ancesters   And what's more Manly far, for Contemplation.
                      They are thro-out with finest Peices fill'd.
                      Drawn by some Angell, or by One as skill'd.
                      Or else they'd not Such admiration giue,
                      Nor seem (as Artists own) to think & liue.
                      "O Sacred Power of the Painters Art!
                      "That can both Colour Air & Shape impart.
                      "That can raise former Hero's from the Graue;
                      "And their Externall Part from Sickness saue.
                      "Keep & perpetuate their Looks & Meen,
                      "And reproduce Them on this Mortall Scene.
                      "Painters to Poets by the Learn'd are joyn'd.
                      "Those draw the Face of Man, but these his mind.
                      "Each of them doth the Power of Death controul,
                      "Those represent the Body, These the Soul.
                      Thus all their Ancestors in State appear,
                      And seem Imortall when once placed here.
                      Here the fam'd Line their former charmes pertake.
                      And still a glorious Constellation make.
                      And when our Starrs are added to this Sphere,
                      T'will surely then the milkey way appear.

                      Vrg'd on with ardent Zeal I had said more

But that my Eyes, & Feet pursu'd the Door.
Which led me down the Star's, & let me See

†The
Cloysters

†The old remaines of ancient Piety.

A Fountaine do's the middle part containe
And Art it's Rivall ^{Nature} truely feigne
I had the Idea of the Muses Seat,
And of an Academic Sweet retreat.
Of that Religion too, that is profest.
The very Walls themselues will speak the rest
Tho not in letter, yet in equall worth,
Painters as Books can History sett forth.
In apt Ideas never could there be

‖ The Muse
referrs to the
History of our
Saviours Life &
Passion painted
On the Walls of
The Cloysters

‖ A liuelier Draught of Sacred History.

"Divine, Imence Unimitable Loue!
"Thou dost (cry'd I) my Zeal & pitty moue.
"How liuely Art presents thee to my Veiw!
"Thy Life & Suff'rings seem perform'd anew.
"Lo here thy great Humilitys display'd
"And here the God of Nature's Mortall made.
"How Iñocent & charmeing do'st thou rest
"An Infant att thy holy Mothers Breast!
"So liuely by the Skillfull Artist done,
"I'm ready to adore with Simeon.
"Wonder surrounds me still! Here I behold
"Thy Selfe imploy'd with Wonders manifold
"To thee the Poor, To thee the Lame & Blind
"Adoreing come, & quick Assistance find.
"And here againe I cast my Weeping Eye,
"And see thee in thy bitter Agony!
"Oh how thy dear, Thy precious purple Gore
"Falls down like Tears from every ^{weeping} Pore!
"And here my tortur'd Soul is rack'd to see
"The craggy Steep Ascent of Calverye,
"And thou expanded on the Cursed Tree.
"Att this amazeing Prospect I begin
"To dread the fatall dire effects of Sin.
"But here my fears are past, Thou mounts to Bliss;
"Hence Greif is turn'd to Joy, & Sorrow banish'd is.

†The
Chapel

When thus these Sacred Paintings had posses'd
The uttmost Limits of my Thoughtfull Breast;
I heard a† Choire with graue Composure Sing
Celestiall Anthems to our heavenly King.
Att first I thought it Paradice had been,
And instantly its Glorys sho'd haue Seen.
Nor was I much deceiv'd. The Type it prov'd
Of Heaven, & shou'd ^{as Heaven,} be vs'd & Lov'd.
The noble Owner, & his numerous Traine
By Prayers were rendering Tribute back againe
To Him that all bestows; By Prayers too
Such is his Sense of God, & such He thought his due,
The Service ended as I reach'd the Dore
And I my thoughts imployed as before.

The Cloysters leads you to the House of Prayer,
Fills you with Hevenly thoughts, with Loue & Fear,
Fitt Introduction sure, A proper way,
We ought to meditate before we pray.
No gaudy Pagentry of Rome is there,
Pictures to steal our Eyes, & spoile our Prayer.
But all compleatly decent, fitt to be
An House, not made for Pomp, but Piety.
But what my vtmost Admiration rais'd,
Can't be enough by Men or Angells prais'd,
T'was Now—In these Vile times, erected new.
But what won't Greatness joyn'd with Vertue doe.
T'will stem the vicious Torrent of the Age;
And in the Cause of God without restraint engage.
T'will dare be good, & good Example show,
To Kings, If they will Learn, & Subjects too below.
Tis this the Noble Founder here has done
His Acts all shine, but this outshines the Sun.
This seeming Flight & Hyperbolic Strain
I did or was prepareing to maintaine.————

When lo my Guide directed on, whilst I
Suppos'd no other Objects cou'd be nigh
That might deserue a Thought or please my Eye.
But soon the Supposition prov'd vntrue,

†The
Garden

When the delightfull† Garden past my veiw.
Surely it might with Eden's well compare,
And Eve in Iñocence be Mistress There.
She'd want no Walks nor solitary Bowers,
But liue as pleas'd as then, besett with Flowers.
Yes, & more pleas'd by far (If it can be)
No Serpents there, nor yet forbidden Tree.
The very Maze it selfe These Truths might proue,
Since it inspires with Poetry & Loue,
A Bliss not much unlike the Joys aboue.
So much inspires you'd think the Tunefull nine
Had set each Branch, whilst Cupid drew the Line.
T'was there I wish'd to stay, but wish'd in vaine
For instantly the Scene $^{was}_\wedge$ chang'd againe.
T'was chang'd to that delightfull Walk, where We
At first this Glorious Edifice did See.

T'was there the Muse her Long keept Silence broke,
But words so full of Mystery She Spoke,
I cou'd not comprehend; but stood to see
With expectation what th' Event wou'd be.

†The
Genius
of the
Place

When straite appear'd a† venerable Sire,
Who rais'd my thoughts with admiration higher.
Vpon his ancient hoary Head was Sett
A glittering enamell'd Coronett.
A rich imbroder'd velvett Robe He wore,
Imbossed well with Gold, & wrought all ore
With stately Ash, all green, that seem'd to grow
With Beach, & Oak, & humble Shrubs below.
Beneath the horned Herd in numbers Lay
To shun (as (Nature taught) $^{the}_\wedge$ Scorching Day.
Whilst Others fedd $^{void}_\wedge$ of the usuall fears,
Of Dogs pursuits, or of the Hunters Snares.
So nat'rally that as He nearer drew
I thought they were not figur'd out, but true.
But ere my thoughts had ended this dispute
The Reverend Form did thus the Muse Salute.

"Harmonious Goddess, see at thy desire
"I from my Secret dwelling Place retire.
"I heard thee powerfully invoke my Name,
"To know whats thy com̄ands I hither came.

To whom the Muse (after Obeisance made)
In Tunefull Words, & well adapted said.

"Charm'd with the Beautys of thy Louely Seat,
"And all thats rich, Majesticall, & Great,
"I aske the favour fully to relate
"(For long Thou hast within these Mansions sate)
"Who rais'd this famous Structure; First possest,
"And why so often Chang'd? Thou know'st the rest.

Att which He thus began. This House you see
Was rais'd & given for Works of Piety.
When Loue divine run thro the noblest Blood,

A. Dom. 1260.

Nor yet Religion so corrupted stood.
Ambition had not yet possest the Gown,
Nor rais'd, so high as now, the Triple Crown.

: Edmund Earle
of Cornwall Son to
Richard King of
the Romans

Great ׃ Cornwalls Gift—Whose pure transcendent Mind
The viler Part of Greatness still declin'd.
Not for himselfe a Coronett He wore,
But for well plac'd Devotion, & the Poor.

∴ The Bonehomes
of Ashridge—
Brothers of the
Order of St Austin

He made devoted ∴ Brotherhood his Heir;
Thus did he dye & thus to Heaven repair.

These in true Sanctity & holy Loue,
Were one below, as Saints are One aboue.
Long did They Liue to God & vice disown,
And pray'd for others Good, as for their own.
But when corrupted grew the Fountaine Head,
The Poyson its Contagion quickly Spread,
Thro all the Parts of this fam'd Rivolett,
And then its Purity declin'd, & after Sett.
The Great Jehovah to revenge the wrong
These fall'n degenerate Brothers had so long,
And bassely done to Him, & Piety,

Gaue out a just, but ruinous Decree.

†The
dissolution
of Abbys
in King
H. 8 Reigne &c

†Then did their Lands & Houses pass away
To those who'd use Them better far then They.
Tho (Like a Stream when Winds contrary blow,
Which in its Nat'rall Course Serenely flow)
T'was restless, & disturb'd, impatient still
Vnder each Masters various Powerfull will,

†Tho:
Egerton
Lord Chancellor of
England

Till †Egerton arose.—But then became
Calme as before, & as before the Same.

This mighty Man (who quickley rose so high
By Learneing, Goodness, Justice, Equity)
Purchas'd this Seat; nor was it more then due,
And had possession, & just Title too.

∴John Earle of
Bridgwater the
First Earle of
that name

His ∴Son as Heir of his great Fathers worth,
Had Honour added too Illustrious Birth.
Still did He in a Sphere exalted moue,
A Monarchs Dareling, & the Peoples Loue.

†He was Lord
president of
Wales

And as a Signe of both He had a †Trust
Wherein He Shew'd himselfe both great & Just,
But t'was not long ere Clouds did first Arise
Then with thick darkness overspread the Skies.
Schism in Church, & faction in the state
Did ruine bring, & Sorrows cumulate.
The best of Men & Kings Laid down his Sacred Head.
The truest Church on Earth was bleeding left for dead.

†He died 1649
in the 70th' year of
his Age

Englands Rebellion did his joys abate,
He,† old, gaue up his willing life to fate.

†John Earle of
Bridgwater the
2ᵈ Earle of that
name

But not before his† Son so well had known
To raise his Country [sic] Honours, & his own.
For by Paternall Care He first was taught,
Ev'n all that StatesMen knew, or Nobles ought.
He Soon the depth of Learneing did attaine,
And seem'd to haue (nor is't a Poets Strain)
The Vniversall System in his Brain.
He rose all Loyall, & all Loyall Sett.
Both Piety & Prudence in Him mett.

And for's devotion cou'd I but aspire
To sett it forth with such Seraphic Fire
As He perform'd it, I shou'd never fade,
But as Imortall as himselfe be made.
Methinks I see Him, makeing no account

∴To the
Church of
Little Gaddesden
every 14th day of the
month on which
his Lady died

Of Humane Splendour, pass to∴ Horebs Mount,
As Moses did, & garded still by none,
But Iñocence, & by Himselfe alone.
See how with Lift up Hands & Heart, He bows
Confesses all his Sins, renews his Vows.
With Job He pleads for his whole family.
Thus here He did begin Eternity.

‖ Elizabeth his Lady
Late Countess of
Bridgewater

Near in that Church doth His Lov'd ‖ Consort rest,
Her Soul in Heaven, Her Image in his Breast.
In Natures gifts She did all far excell,
And in all Graces had no Parrallell.

∴The Inscription on
her Tombe over
the Vault in
that Church

Tho Her∴ Memorialls great, yet words by far
Too Scanty are to Speak Her Character.
So when the Objects raised out of Sight
We are not able to describe the flight.
So when the Sun Shines bright, we quickly find
That the bold Gazers Eyes are soon Struck blind.
She was His Life, No Joys He had beside.
To live with Her He Liv'd, to follow Her He dy'd.
He dy'd—

—But yet (Sweet Goddess) now forbeare
To Shed for His Retreat one pittieing Tear.
Since He's not gone, but Still Surviueing Here

†John the 3d
Earle of
Bridgwater at
present
aliue

He's still surviueing in his Noble †Son,
Who well sett out ere th' others Race was run.
And now so strictly do's His Steps pursue,
He must oretake, & even surpass Him too.
He knows both Things & Men as well as Books:
And casts the noblest Rays where e're He Looks.
All that the Wise of truest Worth esteem
Without the Lest Alloy, appears in Him.
Nay! Oft I've thought the Vertues of the whole

Transcendent Line, were Centre'd in His Soul.
His former Patience, & submissive Will
(Which rais'd Men's wonder, & do's Angells still)
Under the worst Ecclips that Heaven 'ere knew,
Or Man withstood, this Character makes true.
So doth his noble Deeds, & well plac'd good,
Er'e Since his Sun in its Meridian Stood.
Exactest Justice is his cheifest care;
Each Subjects property in Peace & War,
Divine Astrea, banished from hence,
Recal'd by Him doth Equity dispence.
The public Good employs his thoughtfull Head,
Nor can He be by Bus'ness wearied.

^ He is yᵉ first
Comissionʳ of
yᵉ Admiralty

Integrity has made Him ^ rule the Seas.
Govern the watry Realms as He please
The Ships direct, & Mariners appease
Nay more ——— Integrity has made Him stand

∴ He is
also one of
the Lord Justices
of England dure
his Majesty aboad
beyond Seas &

Amongst∴ the Petty Kings, who now com̄and
And manage Regall Power, in this Land.
Till Conquer'ing William doth in ttriumph come,
Haueing Secur'd the Peace of Christendom.

Indeed tis fitt He thus adorn'd sho'd be,
None less (tho yet more noble born) then He
Cou'd have obtain'd (What Monarchs might admire
And wish in Vaine) The Sacred Nuptiall Fire,

∴ The present
Countess of
BridgeWater
Daughter to the
Late Duke of
Boulton

And wond'rous Loue of that all conquering ∴ Dame
Who from the Loyns of mighty Boulton came.
This noble Pair are so much one in Loue,
And all the Married Graces from aboue,
That for their Union (One may say indeed)
When Heaven made One the other was decreed.
That Time its selfe the Charmes sho'd never end,
That did her Youthfull bloomeing Years attend.
T'was surely so decreed! — for still appears
(The riseing Sun The glory of the Spheres)
Her virgin-matchless Beauty, tho She be
The Mother of a glorious Progenie:
And all for nobler ends then Sight's design'd.

It figures out the Beautys of the Mind.
From whence (If Skill were not extreemly faint)
I cou'd draw out a most accomplish'd Saint,
Shes pious, not precise, no Bigott, yet unfeign'd.
She dayly merits, tho her Faith's unstain'd.
And here I own I sho'd haue Angells Sight
Rightly to view this this [sic] pure transcendent Light.
Then Pardon If too near Approach I shun.
Tis by its Rays we best describe the Sun.

†My Lord
Brackley the
Eldest

∴ probably —
the Muse —
foretells that
he will be
Lord Justice
of the
fforests.

    And among these the auspicious riseing †Peer
Deserues my first Address, & knowledg here.
Tis He, Tis He, that is design'd to Reigne
Ore ev'ry Stately∴ Wood & ev'ry Plain
Within this Spacious Realm; & will become
The Potent Earle in his great Fathers Room.
When He in triumph do's ascend the Skyes,
His Son (as high as Mortall can) will rise.
And ti's but fitt He sho'd; If Merit be
Rewarded as He ought, it must be He.
For this a basis is so firmly Laid,
Ti's even Impossible to be betray'd
By any basse Ignoble Act; The Sun
May sooner from its well fixt Center run;
Then He goe back that has so well begun.
His Modesty (a Gift divinely good,
Now Little known, Less throly understood)
An humble Speech, hereafter will dispence
Discourse most fluent, & profoundest sense.
His sweet ingageing temper do's foretell
He'l conquer, & all Conquests soon excell.
Those may Mens Bodys possibly subdue;
He will their Hearts, & yet preserve them too,
For this with natiue Knowledge 'tis design'd.
And forreigne too, to cultivate his Mind.
For this to farthi'st Countrys He doth roam,
And with their Spoils att last He will come home.
Thus will His highten'd Virtues quickly show
How great He'l be Aboue, as well as here below.

†Mr.
William

The †^{Second} Son deserues the same esteems;
He'l be no otherwise then what He Seems.
Serious as Age, Actiue as Youth we find;
And more to things of Men, then those of Boys inclin'd.
In time He'l be a Patriot, & pursue
What e're true Principles invite Him to.

∴Mr.
Henry

Then for the ∴third; I wou'd have Eaton say
How pregnant are his Parts, how quick & Gay.
What mighty Hopes We may conceiue of Him
Who drinks So Soon of Learneings Sacred Stream.

∴Mr.
John

∴His
Highēsse
the Duke
of
Glocester

The∴ fourth, Tho Young, already is thought fitt
To be Companion (& do's meritt it)
To the ^{Apparent} ∴Heir of Brittans Crown,
A Prince by birth, more by acquir'd renown.
Whose Sense in Humane Things, & Things divine,
Do's even beyond the reach of Manhood Shine.
And is indeed to such Perfections come,
He's fitt to Leade abroad, & rule att Home.
What then to our Young Hero's due, or Shall,
Who Copys from this great Originall.
What will He be e're halfe his Race is run?
Att lest the primar Star to this Resplendent Sun.

∴Mr. Charles
the Youngest
Son

∴The Youngest Last, in Age th'o but a Child,
May yet a perfect Man in Sense be Stil'd.
He knows, & speaks so well, it do's appear
That without Objects his Idea's are.
Nor that his Knowledge comes by slow degrees,
Or just as He reflects, or as He Sees.
But has it all innate, & wants alone
Corporeall Pow'r to make it fully known.
"Haile wonderous Childe! Thou dost att once Confute,

†about
knowledge ~
whether
naturall &

"And Silence too, Our Sages warme† dispute.
"Those Tenents that before seem'd all untrue,
"Att lest disputed were, are clear'd by you.
"It must be so.—You else nere could haue been

inate or by
reflection &c
"So knowing, Yet so Little taught, or seen.
"Go on—& be our English Stagirite,
"Men's false Conceptions change, maintaine the right.
"By Study proue what Nature do's declare,
"And be our Wonder still, as now you are!

†the Lady
Mary the
Eldest
Daughter
& Patronesse
of this Poem
    †A charmeing Nymph is next—At which the Muse
Some unknown words, that Silenc'd Him, did use.
But yet to me such Pow'r They did Impart,
Methought She Shott Herselfe into my Heart.
Whilst I all rapture, & Inspir'd Said—
"This mighty Task be mine.—Haile Louely Maid!
"Haile! You whom Blushes doe as much adorn,
"As Art do's Nature, or the Sun the Morn.
"Whose Carriage Sweet, & Disposition's So;
"And do's Command all Eyes, all Hearts below!
Att which I fail'd, or durst not higher Sore.
The Goddess thus —
"Admir'd Maria, I your Aid Implore,
"Or else this pleasing Visionary Scene
"Will vanish Soon Like some abortiue Dream.
"Your Patronage will animate much more
"Then all the Heliconian Nymphs before.
"Their aid preserves no works from Destinie;
"But this by Yours, Imortall, as Your Selfe wille be.
Flush'd with these Hopes, This kind Auspicious Fate,
I'l try the Mystic Sequell to relate.
After a Soft, but short melodious straine
Of Music heard, the Sage went on againe,

    I well comend your Care, & Zeal to raise
A Trophy to the fam'd Marias Prayse.
And yet my Off'rings due.—Oft haue I seen
How blest the Sight! How ravishing t'has been!
Her pass along Like some triumphing Queen,
Thro these fam'd Woods, as well to Hunt the Deer,
As take her Solitary foot walks Here.
Att whose Approach the Birds in Consort Sing.

And Woods expect an Everlasting Spring.
The horned Beasts orejoy'd forsake their Shade,
And Gaze, as if She was to be obey'd.
Oft haue I heard the Sylvan Goddess prays'd;
How Men admir'd, & Temples to her rais'd,
The Beast admire here, but Men adore,
Diana much deserved, Maria more.

†The Lady
Elizabeth
the youngest
Daughter

    The fair †Eliza last my thoughts employ,
And fills me with unknown Extatic Joy.
It must be so—When e're Such Witt & Sense
Appears, adorn'd with so much Innocence!
Her pretty Modest Looks, & Sweet address,
Is much beyond an Artist's Skill t'express.
In ev'ry Thing She has her Years Surpast.
She's now admir'd, but will b' ador'd att last.
Maria's fam'd Perfections reigne alone,
The world has yet no equall ever known;
Eliza's but in Bloom, yet do's Surprize;
But when She do's to Her Meridian rise,
T'will surely then be Said within one Sphere
Two Suns without a Paradox appear.—

    Thus ends my Taske—But say who can exell,
Say (bright Celestiall Nymph For thou canst tell)
If there be any Such, say who can be
More pleas'd (or has more reason for't) then me!
Indeed if there's a Paradise below,
Tis here, & I it's uttmost Pleasures know.
Long haue I been its true Domestic Gard,
And liv'd in full Content as a Reward;
And wou'd till this Expanded Frame dissolves.
And Nature to its ancient Heap devolves.
Thus Long I'd Liue under this Noble Race;
Others may higher mount, None find so blest a Place.

    Thus ceas'd the Sage — And then my Sacred Guide
Smileing in this Prophetic Strain reply'd.
Yes now I See! Heaven has the mystic State

Of things to come reveal'd, reveal'd the Fate,
The prosperous Fate, of this delightfull Pile!
I see ten thousand Blessings on it Smile,
Ten thousand thousand Years (If time Com̄ands
So long duration to the whole) it stands.
I see from hence a Race of Hero's come,
A numerous Race! Behold how Christendome
Dreads, & admires their braue diffusiue Soul!
How Fame transmitts their Acts from Pole to Pole!
I see great Brittan free from all Alarm's
Its Monarchs Great, Still Conqu'ring by their Armes,
The Church & State in Lasting Vnion Joyne;
Religion by their Care from Ages Shine.

‖ The Muse
takes her
Leaue of the
Genius

‖ Then as for You thrice Happy Reverend Sire,
Alls given to You, You haue, or can desire.
Here Crown'd with Joy, you'l Liue Just as before,
Till Heavenly Blessings cease, & Times no more,
These Secrets are by Inspiration made,
Retire in Peace, retire into thy Shade.
He Laught, & then harmonious Strains W'ere heard,
Just Like to those Aboue, So dissappeard.

Then did, we in the Shineing Chariot mount,
And of the Earth below make no account.
Ascending upwards instanly we were,
Quicker then Thought, hirl'd thro the Yeilding Air,
And Soon in wond'rous Pomp we did orelight,
Where first I had this visionary Sight.
She sett me down—But whilst I did prepare
Some gratefull Speech.—She vanish'd into Air.
Where full of wonder & Content I sate,
And on the Vision thus did ruminate.

What mean the Fates? & why all this to me
A worthless Thing? Tis Strang that Destiny
Sho'd not assigne Some of Apollo's Heirs,
Sublime in Thought, & Vacant too from Cares
To see as I & Sing this glorious Seat?

T'would be in verse, as in it selfe compleat!
And yet the Honours greater Still I own;
I felt the Power to me before Unknown.

†Samuell   So the devoted† Youth by Heaven was chose.
the Prophet   Before the Learn'd, & aged, to disclose
Things past, & Things to come!—And may my Theme,
Dear Ashridge, flowrish Like Jerusalem.
May it like that ascend, Like that be great,
And share in all Things, But its Sinking State.

The End

Sources Cited

Manuscript Collections

Beinecke Rare Book and Manuscript Library, Yale University
Bodleian Library, Oxford University
British Library, London
Hallward Library, University of Nottingham
Hertfordshire Record Office, Hertford
Huntington Library, San Marino
Mertoun, St. Boswell's

Printed Works

Adamson, J.S.A. "Chivalry and Political Culture in Caroline England." In *Culture and Politics in Early Stuart England*. Eds. Kevin Sharpe and Peter Lake. Stanford, 1993. 161–97.

Armytage, Sir George and W. Harry Rylands, eds. *Staffordshire Pedigrees Based on the Visitation of that County Made by William Dugdale Esquire, Norroy King of Arms in the Years 1663–1664*. London, 1912.

Astell, Mary. *Some Reflections upon Marriage*. London, 1700.

Ballard, George. *Memoirs of Severall Ladies of Great Britain*. 1752. Rpt. Detroit, 1985. With Introduction by Ruth Perry.

Ballaster, Ros. "The First Female Dramatists." In Wilcox. 267–89.

Barroll, Leeds. "The Court of the First Stuart Queen." In *The Mental World of the Jacobean Court*. Ed. Linda Levy Peck. Cambridge, 1991. 191–208.

Beilin, Elaine V. *Redeeming Eve: Women Writers of the English Renaissance*. Princeton, 1987.

Belsey, Catherine. *The Subject of Tragedy: Identity and Difference in Renaissance Drama*. London, 1985.

Behn, Aphra. *Dutch Lover*. London, 1673.

———. *The Lucky Chance*. London, 1687.

———. *Sir Patient Fancy*. London, 1678.

Bennett, Judith M. *Women in the Medieval English Countryside*. New York, 1987.

Bentley, Thomas. *Monument of Matrones: conteining seven severall Lamps of Virginitie, or distinct treatises*. London, 1582.

Bickley, Francis. *The Cavendish Family*. Boston, 1914.

Billington, Ray Allen. "The Genesis of the Research Institution." *Huntington Library Quarterly* 32 (August 1969): 351–72.

Bingham, Caroline. "Seventeenth-Century Attitudes Toward Deviant Sex." *Journal of Intellectual History* 1: 3 (Spring 1971): 447–72.

Biographium faemineum. London, 1766.

Birkenhead, Thomas. "An Anniversary on the Nuptials of John Earle of Bridgewater, July 22. 1652." In Lawes, *Ayres and Dialogues*. Bk. 1: 33.

Bond, Maurice and David Beamish. *The Gentleman Usher of the Black Rod*. London, 1976.

Bowers, Fredson. "Multiple Authority: New Problems and Concepts of Copy-Text." *The Library* 5th series 27. 2 (June 1972): 81–115.

———. "Remarks on Eclectic Texts." *Essays in Bibliography, Text, and Editing*. Charlottesville, 1975. 488–528.

Bradstreet, Anne. *The Tenth Muse*. London, 1650.

Bray, William, ed. *Diary of John Evelyn*. 4 vols. London, 1906.

Breasted, Barbara. "*Comus* and the Castlehaven Scandal." *Milton Studies* 3 (1971): 201–24.

Brodski, Bella and Celeste Schenck, eds. *Life/Lines: Theorizing Women's Autobiography*. Ithaca, 1988.

Brome, Richard. *The Sparagus Garden*. London, 1640.

Brydges, Samuel Egerton. "History of Ashridge Abbey, Bucks." *The Topographer* 12 (March, 1790) No. 3 of Vol. 2: 131–54.

———. "Letter, December 21, 1792, to Mr. Urban." *Gentleman's Magazine* 62 (1792): Second Part (Supplement).

Burke's Genealogical and Heraldic History of the Peerage and Baronetage. 105th edition. London, 1975.

Calendar of State Papers Domestic Series of the Reign of Charles I, 1625–1649. 23 vols. London, 1848–1897.

Calendar of State Papers Domestic Series of the Reign of Charles II, 1661–1685. 28 vols. London, 1860–1939.

Calendar of State Papers Domestic Series of the Reigns of Edward VI, Mary, Elizabeth, and James I. 12 vols. London, 1856–1872.

Calendar of State Papers Domestic Series, 1649–1660. 13 vols. London, 1875–1886.

Cary, Elizabeth, trans. *Reply of the Cardinall of Perron to the Answeare of the King of Great Britaine*. Douay, 1630.

Cavendish, Margaret. *The Description of a New Blazing World*. London, 1666.

———. *Life of the Thrice Noble, High and Puissant Prince William Cavendish*. London, 1667.

———. *Natures Picture Drawn by Fancies Pencil To the Life*. London, 1656.

———. *Natures Picture*. 2nd ed. London, 1671.

———. *Observations upon Experimental Philosophy*. London, 1666.

———. *Orations of Divers Sorts*. London, 1662.

———. *Philosophical and Physical Opinions*. London, 1655.

———. *Philosophical Letters*. London, 1664.

———. *Playes Written by the Thrice Noble, Illustrious and Excellent Princess, the Lady Marchioness of Newcastle*. London, 1662.

———. *Plays, Never before Printed*. London, 1668.

———. *Poems and Fancies*. London, 1653.

———. *Poems, and Phancies. The Second Impression, much altered and Corrected*. London, 1664.

———. *True Relation of My Birth, Breeding, and Life* [appended to *Natures Pictures*]. London, 1656.

———. *CCXI Sociable Letters*. London, 1664.

Cavendish, William. *La methode et Invention Nouvelle de dresser les Chevaux*. Antwerp, 1657.

———. *A New Method and Extraordinary Invention to Dress Horses, and Work them*. London, 1677.

Cecil, William. "William Cecil hauing taken much profit." In Bentley. Lamp 2. Hv^v–Hvi.

Cerasano, S. P. and Marion Wynne-Davies, eds. *Renaissance Drama by Women: Texts and Documents*. London, 1996.

Certain Sermons, or homilies. London, 1627.

Chauncy, Henry. *The Historical Antiquities of Hertfordshire*. London, 1700.

Cheney, Donald. "Westonia on the Gardens of Barvitius." *American Notes & Queries* 5: 2–3 [*Renaissance Texts*. Ed. Anne Lake Prescott] (1992): 64–67.

Church of Jesus Christ of Latter-Day Saints. *International Genealogical Index*. Salt Lake City, Utah, 1981– .

Clarke, Elizabeth, Victoria Burke, and Marie-Louise Coolahan. "Margaret Cavendish: Family Context, Literary Contexts." (unpublished).

Clarke, William. *Repertorium Bibliographicum; or, some account of the most celebrated British Libraries*. London, 1819.

Clarksone, Bessie. *Conflict in Conscience*. Edinburgh, 1631.

Clutterbuck, Robert. *History and Antiquities of the County of Hertfordshire*. 3 vols. London, 1815.

Coiro, Ann Baynes. "Writing in Service: Sexual Politics and Class Position in the Poetry of Aemilia Lanyer and Ben Jonson," *Criticism* 35.3 (Summer 1993): 357–76.

Cokayne, G. E. *Complete Peerage*. 13 vols. in 6. Gloucester, 1982.

Collins, Arthur. *Peerage of England*. London, 1709.

———. *Peerage of England*. 3 vols. in 4. London, 1735.

———. *Peerage of England*. 9 vols. London, 1779.

———. *Peerage of England*. 9 vols. London, 1812.

Cope, Esther S. *Handmaid of the Holy Spirit: Dame Eleanor Davies, Never Soe Mad a Ladie*. Ann Arbor, 1992.

Cope, Esther S., ed. *Prophetic Writings of Lady Eleanor Davies*. New York, 1995.

Cotton, Nancy. *Women Playwrights in England, c. 1363–1750*. Newark, Del. and London, 1980.

Culley, Margo. *A Day at a Time*. New York, 1985.

Davenant, William. *Works*. London, 1673.

Davidson, Cathy N. and E. M. Broner, eds. *The Lost Tradition: Mothers and Daughters in Literature*. New York, 1980.

Davis, Natalie Zemon. "Women's History in Transition: The European Case." *Feminist Studies* 3 (1976): 83–103.

Downame, John. *The Christian Warfare*. London, 1608.

Dowriche, Anne. *The French Historie*. London, 1589.

E., T., comp. *The Lawes Resolutions of Womens Rights*. London, 1632.

Egerton, Lady Alix. *Milton's Comus, Being the Bridgewater Manuscript with Notes and a Short Family Memoir*. London, 1910.

Egerton, Bridget. "A Forme of Confession Grounded vpon the Ancient Catholique and Apostolique Faith" (1636). In *Chetham Miscellanies* 4. Manchester, 1871: 9–31. With Introduction by Sir Philip de Malpas Grey Egerton.

Ellis, Henry. *Original Letters Illustrative of English History*. 3 vols. London, 1824.

Espinasse, Francis. "Egerton, John, second Earl of Bridgewater (1622–1686)," *Dictionary of National Biography*. Eds. Leslie Stephen and Sidney Lee. Oxford, 1917– . 6: 574–75.

Ezell, Margaret J. M. *The Patriarch's Wife: Literary Evidence and the History of the Family*. Chapel Hill, 1987.

———. " 'To Be Your Daughter in Your Pen': The Social Functions of Literature in the Writings of Lady Elizabeth Brackley and Lady Jane Cavendish." *Huntington Library Quarterly* 51. 4 (1988): 281–96.

———. *Writing Women's Literary History*. Baltimore, 1993.

Fage, Mary. *Fames Roule*. London, 1637.

Falk, Bernard. *The Bridgewater Millions: A Candid Family History*. London, 1942.

Ferguson, Margaret W. "Renaissance concepts of the 'woman writer.' " In Wilcox. 143–168.

Findlay, Alison. "Playing the 'scene self' in Jane Cavendish and Elizabeth Brackley's *The Concealed Fancies*." In *Enacting Gender on the English Renaissance Stage*. Eds. Anne Russell and Viviana Comensoli. Chicago, 1999. 154–76.

———. " 'She gave you the civility of the house': Household Performance in *The Concealed Fancies*." In *Readings in Renaissance Women's Drama*. Eds. Marion Wynne-Davies and Susan Cerasano. London, 1998. 259–71.

Findlay, Alison, Gweno Williams, and Stephanie Wright. " 'The Play is Ready to be Acted': Women and Dramatic Production 1570–1670," *Women's Writing* 5 (forthcoming).

Firth, Charles Harding. "Cavendish, William, Duke of Newcastle (1592–1676)." *DNB* 3: 1273–78.

Flecknoe, Richard. *Epigrams of all Sorts, Made at Divers Times on Several Occasions*. London, 1670.

Fogle, French R. " 'Such a Rural Queen': The Countess Dowager of Derby as Patron." In *Patronage in Late Renaissance England*. Eds. French R. Fogle and Louis A. Knafla. Los Angeles, 1983. 3–29.

Ford, John. *Perkin Warbeck*. London, 1634.

Foster, Joseph. *Alumni Oxonienses . . . 1500–1714*. 4 vols. Oxford, 1891. Rpt. Liechtenstein, Kraus, 1968.

Gilson, Julius P. Egerton. *Guide to the Exhibition of Some Part of the Egerton Collection of Manuscripts in the British Museum*. London, 1929.

God and the King. London, 1615.

Goulding, Richard William. *Catalogue of the Pictures Belonging to His Grace the Duke of Portland*. Cambridge, 1936.

Goulding, Richard William, ed. *Letters written by Charles Lamb's Princely Woman*. Lincoln, 1909.

Graham, Elspeth. "Women's Writing and the Self." In Wilcox. 209–33.

Grant, Douglas. *Margaret the First, a Biography of Margaret Cavendish, Duchess of Newcastle 1623–1673*. London, 1957.

Grant, Douglas, ed. *The Phanseys of William Cavendish, Marquis of Newcastle addressed to Margaret Lucas and her Letters in reply.* London, 1956.

Grazebrook, H. Sydney Esq., ed. *The Visitacion of Staffordshire, A.D. 1583.* London, 1883.

Greer, Germaine, et al., eds. *Kissing the Rod: An Anthology of Seventeenth-Century Women's Verse.* New York, 1989.

Greetham, D. C. *Textual Scholarship: An Introduction.* New York, 1994.

Gullans, Charles B., ed. *The English and Latin Poems of Sir Robert Ayton.* Edinburgh, 1963.

Hannay, Margaret. *Philip's Phoenix: Mary Sidney, Countess of Pembroke.* New York, 1990.

Hannay, Margaret P., ed. *Silent But for the Word: Tudor Women as Patrons, Translators, and Writers of Religious Works.* Kent, Ohio, 1985.

Harbage, Alfred. *Cavalier Drama, An Historical and Cultural Supplement to the Study of the Elizabethan and Restoration Stage.* New York, 1936.

Helgerson, Richard. *The Elizabethan Prodigals.* Los Angeles, 1976.

Heltzel, Virgil B., ed. "Richard Earl of Carbery's Advice to His Son." *Huntington Library Bulletin* 11 (1937): 59–105.

Herrup, Cynthia. "The Patriarch at Home: The Trial of the 2nd Earl of Castlehaven for Rape and Sodomy." *History Workshop Journal* 41 (1996): 1–18.

Hibbard, Caroline. "The Role of a Queen Consort: The Household and Court of Henrietta Maria, 1625–1642." In *Princes, Patronage, and the Nobility: The Court at the Beginning of the Modern Age.* Eds. Ronald G. Asch and Adolf M. Birke. London, 1991. 393–414.

Historical Manuscript Commission. *Thirteenth Report. Appendix. Part I. The Manuscripts of His Grace the Duke of Portland.* London, 1891.

Hobby, Elaine. *Virtue of Necessity: English Women's Writing 1649–1688.* Ann Arbor, 1988.

Hopkins, Lisa. "Judith Shakespeare's Reading: Teaching 'The Concealed Fancies.'" *Shakespeare Quarterly* 47: 4 (1996): 396–406.

Houlbrooke, Ralph A. *The English Family, 1450–1700.* New York, 1984.

Howell, James. *Dodona's Grove, or the vocall forrest.* London, 1640.

Hughey, Ruth Willard. "Cultural Interests of Women in England, 1524–1640, Indicated in the Writings of the Women." Ph.D. diss., Cornell Univ., 1932.

Hull, Suzanne W. *Chaste, Silent & Obedient: English Books for Women, 1475–1640.* San Marino, Calif., 1982.

Hyde, Edward. *History of the Rebellion.* 6 vols. Oxford, 1827.

Hyrde, Richard. "Unto the moost studyous." In *Devout Treatyse upon the*

Pater Noster. Trans. Margaret Roper. London, 1524.

Ingoldsby, William "Untitled Note." In "Intramuralia: Books and People." Comp. Carey S. Bliss, *Huntington Library Quarterly* 37. 1 (1973): 89–92.

James I. *Basilikon Doron.* London, 1604.

Jonson, Ben. *The King's Entertainment at Welbeck in Nottingham-shire . . . 1633.* In *Workes of Ben Jonson.* London, 1640. 2: 272–80.

———. *Love's Welcome. The King and Queen's Entertainment at Bolsover . . . 1634.* In *Workes of Ben Jonson.* London, 1640. 2: 281–83.

Kelliher, Hilton. "Donne, Jonson, Richard Andrews and the Newcastle Manuscript," *English Manuscript Studies, 1100–1700.* 4 (1993): 134–73.

Kelly, Joan. "The Social Relations of the Sexes: Methodological Implications of Women's History." In *Women, History & Theory: The Essays of Joan Kelly.* Eds. Blanche W. Cook, et. al. Chicago, 1984. 1–18.

Kelso, Ruth. *Doctrine for the Lady of the Renaissance.* Urbana, 1956.

Kohler, Charlotte. "The Elizabethan Woman of Letters, the Extent of her Literary Activities." Ph.D. diss., Univ. of Virginia, 1936.

Lamb, Mary Ellen, ed. *Brief Confessional Writings. The Early Modern Englishwoman: A Facsimile Library of Essential Works.* Series I. Part 2. London, forthcoming.

Langbaine, Gerard. *An Account of the English Dramatick Poets.* Oxford, 1691.

Lawes, Henry. *Select Ayres.* London, 1669.

———. *Ayres and Dialogues, for One, Two, and Three Voyces.* London, 1653.

Lerner, Gerda. *Creation of Feminist Consciousness From the Middle Ages to Eighteen-seventy.* New York, 1993.

Letters and Poems In Honour of the Incomparable Princess, Margaret, Dutchess of Newcastle. London, 1776.

Lewalski, Barbara K. "The Lady of the Country-House Poem." In *The Fashioning and Functioning of the British Country House.* Ed. Gervase Jackson-Stops, et. al. Washington, 1989. 261–74.

———. "Of God and Good Women: The Poems of Aemilia Lanyer." In Hannay, *Silent.* 203–24.

———. *Protestant Poetics and the Seventeenth-Century Religious Lyric.* Princeton, 1979.

———. "Re-writing Patriarchy and Patronage: Margaret Clifford, Anne Clifford, and Aemilia Lanyer." *Yearbook of English Studies* 21 (1991): 87–106.

———. *Writing Women in Jacobean England.* Cambridge, Mass., 1993.

List of Additions to the Manuscripts in the British Museum in the Years MDCCCXXXVI–MDCCCXL. London, 1843.

Livingstone, Eleanor Hay. *Confession and Conversion.* Edinburgh, 1629.

McClure, Norman Egbert, ed. *Letters of John Chamberlain.* 2 vols. Philadelphia: American Philosophical Society, 1939.

MacFarlane, Alan. "*The Family, Sex and Marriage in England 1500–1800*: Review Essay." *History and Theory* 18. 1 (1979): 103–26.

McGrath, Lynette. "'Let Us Have Our Libertie Againe': Amelia Lanier's 17th-Century Feminist Voice." *Women's Studies* 20 (1992): 331–48.

———. "The Other Body: Women's Inscription of their Physical Images in 16th- and 17th-Century England." *Women's Studies* 26 (1997): 27–58.

Maggs Brothers. "Centenary Catalogue No. 812: A Selection of Books Manuscripts and Autograph Letters of Special Interest and Rarity." London, 1953.

———. "Mercurius Britannicus or Mercuries Swift Messenger ... [including] A selection of Association Books from the Great Bridgewater Library." London, 1951.

Maltby, Judith. *Prayer Book and People in Elizabethan and Early Stuart England.* Cambridge, 1998.

Marotti, Arthur F. *Manuscript, Print, and the English Renaissance Lyric.* Ithaca, 1995.

Mason, Mary G. "The Other Voice: Autobiographies of Women Writers." In *Autobiography: Essays Theoretical and Critical.* Ed. James Olney. Princeton, 1980. 207–35.

Mendelson, Sara Heller. *The Mental World of Stuart Women: Three Studies.* Amherst, Mass., 1987.

Milton, John. *Defensio Pro Populo Anglicano.* London, 1651.

More, Sir Thomas. *St. Thomas More: Selected Letters.* Ed. Elizabeth F. Rogers. New Haven, 1961.

Murray, James A. H., Henry Bradley, W. A. Craigie, C. T. Onions, eds. *Oxford English Dictionary.* Oxford, 1961.

Needham, Francis, ed. *Welbeck Miscellany.* No. 2. Bungay, Suffolk, 1933–1934.

Nixon, Howard M. and William A. Jackson. "English Seventeenth-Century Travelling Libraries." *Transactions of the Cambridge Bibliographical Society* 7.3 (1979): 294–321.

Olney, R. J. "The Portland Papers." *Archives* 19. 82 (October 1989): 78–87.

Ong, Walter J. "Latin Language Study as a Renaissance Puberty Rite." *Studies in Philology* 56 (1959): 103–24.

Osborne, Dorothy. *Letters to Sir William Temple.* Ed. Kenneth Parker. 1987.

Pagitt, Ephraim. *Christianographie.* London, 1635.

Parry, Graham. *The Golden Age Restor'd: The Culture of the Stuart Court, 1603–42.* Manchester, 1981.

Pebworth, Ted-Larry. "Scribal Publication and the Countess of Bridge-water." (unpublished).

Peele, James. *Pathewaye to perfectness*. London, 1569.

Pepys, Samuel. *The Diary of Samuel Pepys*. Eds. Robert Latham and William Mathews, et al. 11 vols. Berkeley, 1971.

Percy, C. H. Herford and Evelyn Simpson, eds. *Ben Jonson*. 11 vols. Oxford, 1941.

Perry, Henry Ten Eyck. *The First Duchess of Newcastle and her Husband as Figures in Literary History*. Boston, 1918.

Perry, Ruth. *The Celebrated Mary Astell: An Early English Feminist*. Chicago, 1986.

Randall, Catharine. "Telling Tales: Women, Gossip, and the Revision of Institutions in Early Modern France." (unpublished).

Roberts, Josephine A. " 'My Inward House': Women's Autobiographical Poetry in the Early Seventeenth Century." In *"The Muses Females Are": Martha Moulsworth and Other Women Writers of the English Renaissance*. Eds. Robert C. Evans and Anne C. Little. West Cornwall, Conn., 1995. 129–37.

———. "An Unpublished Literary Quarrel Concerning the Suppression of Mary Wroth's *Urania*." *Notes & Queries* 222 (1977): 532–35.

Roberts, Josephine A., ed. *The Poems of Lady Mary Wroth*. 2nd ed. Baton Rouge, 1983.

Rose, Mary Beth. "Where Are the Mothers in Shakespeare? Options for Gender Representation in the English Renaissance." *Shakespeare Quarterly* 42 (1991): 291–314.

Sampson, William. *Honour Triumphing over Death*. London, 1636.

Sarasohn, Lisa. "A Science Turned Upside Down." *Huntington Library Quarterly* 47 (1984): 289–307.

Schotz, Myra Glatzer. "The Great Unwritten Story: Mothers and Daughters in Shakespeare." In Davidson and Broner. 44–54.

Schwoerer, Lois G. "Seventeenth-Century English Women Engraved in Stone?" *Albion* 16 (1984): 389–403.

Scott, Joan Wallach. *Gender and the Politics of History*. New York, 1988.

Shakespeare, William. *As You Like It*. Ed. Agnes Latham. London, 1975.

Shirley, James. *The Traitor*. London, 1635.

A Short Title Catalogue of Books . . . 1475–1640. 2nd ed. Begun by W. A. Jackson and F. S. Ferguson. Completed by Katharine F. Pantzer. 3 vols. London, 1986–1991.

Smith, G. C. Moore, ed. *Victoria, a Latin Comedy by Abraham Fraunce*.

Louvain, 1906.

Smith, Hilda. *Reason's Disciples: Seventeenth-Century English Feminists.* Urbana, 1982.

Smith, Hilda L. and Susan Cardinale, comps. *Women and the Literature of the Seventeenth Century: An Annotated Bibliography based on Wing's Short-title Catalogue.* Westport, Conn., 1990.

Smith, Sidonie. *A Poetics of Women's Autobiography: Marginality and the Fictions of Self-Representation.* Bloomington, 1987.

Sotheby & Co. "Catalogue of the Remaining Portion of the Bridgewater Library Sold by Order of the Rt. Honble the Earl of Ellesmere." London, 1951.

Southwell, Robert. *S ^{t}. Peters Complaint.* London, 1620.

Speght, Rachel. *Mortalities Memorandum.* London, 1621.

———. *Mouzell for Melastomus.* London, 1617.

Starr, Nathan, ed. "The Concealed Fansyes: A Play by Lady Jane Cavendish and Lady Elizabeth Brackley." *PMLA* 46 (1931): 802–38.

Steen, Sara Jayne. "Behind the Arras: Editing Renaissance Women's Letters." In *Voices of Silence: Editing the Letters of Renaissance Women, 1990 MLA Panel.* Ed. Josephine A. Roberts. Amherst, Mass., 1990. 1–15.

Stone, Lawrence. *The Family, Sex and Marriage in England 1500–1800.* New York, 1977.

Strong, S. Arthur. *A Catalogue of Letters and Other Historical Documents Exhibited in the Library at Welbeck.* London, 1903.

Sutton, Christopher. *Godly Meditations upon the most holy Sacrament of the Lords Supper.* London, 1622.

Tanselle, G. Thomas. "Editing Without a Copy-Text." *Studies in Bibliography* 47 (1994): 1–22.

———. "Editorial Apparatus for Radiating Texts." *Library* 5th Series 29 (1974): 330–37.

———. "The Editorial Problem of Final Authorial Intention." In *Selected Studies in Bibliography.* Charlottesville, 1979. 309–53.

———. "Textual Criticism and Literary Sociology." *Studies in Bibliography* 44 (1991): 83–143.

———. "The Varieties of Scholarly Editing." In *Scholarly Editing: A Guide to Research.* Ed. D. C. Greetham. New York, 1995. 9–32.

Tattlewell, Mary (pseud.) and Joane hit him-home (pseud.). *The womens sharpe revenge.* 1640.

Taylor, Jeremy. *Rule and Exercises of Holy Dying.* London, 1651.

———. *Rule and Exercises of Holy Living.* London, 1650.

Tesauro, Emmanuele. *Reverendi Patris Emanuelis Thesauri e Societate Iesu Caesares*. Oxford, 1637.

Thomas, Keith. "The Double Standard." *Journal of the History of Ideas* 20 (1959): 195–216.

Thackeray, William Makepeace. *Vanity Fair*. New York, 1958.

Thorpe, James. "The Founder and His Library." *Huntington Library Quarterly* 32 (August 1969): 291–308.

Thorpe, Thomas. "Catalogue of Ancient Manuscripts." 1835.

Todd, Henry John. *History of the College of Bonhommes, at Ashridge*. London, 1823.

Todd, Henry John, ed. *Comus, a mask*. London, 1798.

———. *The Poetical Works of John Milton ... in Six Volumes*. London, 1801.

———. *The Poetical Works of John Milton ... in Seven Volumes*. 2nd. ed. London, 1809.

———. *The Poetical Works of John Milton ... in Six Volumes*. 3rd ed. London, 1826.

———. *The Poetical Works of John Milton*. 4th ed. 4 vols. 1842.

———. *The Poetical Works of John Milton*. 5th ed. 4 vols. London, 1852.

Tomlinson, Sophie. "'My Brain the Stage': Cavendish and the Fantasy of Female Performance." In *Women, Texts, & Histories 1575–1760*. Eds. Clare Brant and Diane Purkiss. London, 1992. 134–63.

Travitsky, Betty S. "Down-Home Bacon, or, a Seventeenth-Century Woman's 'Considerations concerning Marriage.'" *American Notes & Queries* 5.1–2. [*Renaissance Texts*. Ed. Anne Lake Prescott] (1992): 134–37.

———. "'His wife's prayers and meditations': MS Egerton 607." In *The Renaissance Englishwoman in Print: Counterbalancing the Canon*. Eds. Anne M. Haselkorn and Betty S. Travitsky. Amherst, Mass., 1987. 241–60.

———. "The New Mother of the English Renaissance." Ph.D. diss., St. John's Univ., 1976.

———. "The New Mother of the English Renaissance: Her Writings on Motherhood." In Davidson and Broner. 33–43.

———. "Reconstructing the Still, Small Voice: The Occasional Journal of Elizabeth Egerton." *Women's Studies* 19 [*Women in the Renaissance: An Interdiscipinary Forum*. Eds. Ann Rosalind Jones and Betty S. Travitsky] (Summer 1991): 193–200.

Travitsky, Betty, ed. *Paradise of Women: Writings by Englishwomen of the Renaissance*. 1981. Rpt. New York, 1989.

Trease, Geoffrey. *Portrait of a Cavalier: William Cavendish, First Duke of Newcastle*. London: Macmillan, 1979.

Turberville, A. S. *A History of Welbeck Abbey and Its Owners*. 2 vols. London: Faber and Faber, 1938/39.

Venn, John. *Alumni Cantabrigienses*. 2 parts in 10 vols. Cambridge: Cambridge Univ. Press, 1922.

Vives, Juan Luis. *Instruction of a Christen Woman*. Trans. Richard Hyrde. London, 1529.

Walker, Kim. *Women Writers of the English Renaissance*. New York, 1996.

Wallas, Ada. *Before the Bluestockings*. London, 1929.

Walpole, Horace. *Catalogue of the Royal and Noble Authors of England, Scotland, and Ireland*. 5 vols. London, 1806.

Warton, Thomas, ed. *Poems upon Several Occasions ... by John Milton, with notes*. 2nd ed. London, 1791.

Wayne, Valerie. "Advice for Women from Mothers and Patriarchs." In Wilcox. 56–79.

White, Helen C. *English Devotional Literature [Prose] 1600–1640*. New York, 1966.

———. *Tudor Books of Private Devotion*. Madison, Wis., 1951.

Whitney, Isabella. *Sweet Nosgay*. London, 1573.

Wilcox, Helen, ed. *Women and Literature in Britain, 1500–1700*. Cambridge, 1996.

Williams, Jane. *Literary Women of England*. London, 1861.

Williams, Robert. "A Moon to Their Sun. . . ." *Fine Print* 11.2 (April 1985): 88–98).

Wing, Donald Goddard. *Short title catalogue ... 1641–1700*. 2nd ed. 3 vols. New York, 1972–1988.

Wiseman, Susan. "Gender and Status in Dramatic Discourse: Margaret Cavendish, Duchess of Newcastle." In *Women, Writing, History 1640–1740*. Eds. Isobel Grundy and Susan Wiseman. Athens, Ga.: Univ. of Georgia Press, 1992. 159–77.

Wolfthal, Diane. "Women's Community and Male Spies: Erhard Schön's How Seven Women Complain about their Worthless Husbands." In *Attending to Early Modern Women*. Eds. Susan D. Amussen and Adele F. Seeff. Newark, Del. and London, 1999. 117–54.

Woods, Susanne. "Aemilia Lanyer and Ben Jonson: Patronage, Authority, and Gender." *Ben Jonson Journal* 1 (1994): 15–30.

Woods, Susanne, ed. *Poems of Aemilia Lanyer*. New York, 1993.

Index

Note: Women are listed under their last married name.